WORK TEAMS:
PAST, PRESENT AND FUTURE

Social Indicators Research Series

Volume 6

This new series aims to provide a public forum for single treatises and collections of papers on social indicators research that are too long to be published in our journal *Social Indicators Research*. Like the journal, the book series deals with statistical assessments of the quality of life from a broad perspective. It welcomes the research on a wide variety of substantive areas, including health, crime, housing, education, family life, leisure activities, transportation, mobility, economics, work, religion and environmental issues. These areas of research will focus on the impact of key issues such as health on the overall quality of life and vice versa. An international review board, consisting of Ruut Veenhoven, Joachim Vogel, Ed Diener, Torbjorn Moum and Wolfgang Glatzer, will ensure the high quality of the series as a whole.

WORK TEAMS:
PAST, PRESENT AND FUTURE

Edited by

MICHAEL M. BEYERLEIN

Center for the Study of Work Teams,
Department of Psychology,
University of North Texas

KLUWER ACADEMIC PUBLISHERS

DORDRECHT / BOSTON / LONDON

A C.I.P. Catalogue record for this book is available from the Library of Congress.

ISBN 0-7923-6699-9

Published by Kluwer Academic Publishers,
P.O. Box 17, 3300 AA Dordrecht, The Netherlands.

Sold and distributed in North, Central and South America
by Kluwer Academic Publishers,
101 Philip Drive, Norwell, MA 02061, U.S.A.

In all other countries, sold and distributed
by Kluwer Academic Publishers,
P.O. Box 322, 3300 AH Dordrecht, The Netherlands.

Printed on acid-free paper

Printed and bound in the Netherlands.

We are all angels with only one wing.
We can only fly while embracing each other.

Luciano de Crescenzo
20th Century Italian Poet

Contents

SECTION IV. FOUNDATION OF 21ST CENTURY TEAMS

Contributors

Yuri Alexandrov, Ivanova State Power University, Russia
Vikas Anand, Arizona State University, United States
Conny Antoni, University of Trier, Germany
Richard Badham, University of Wollongong, Australia
David Baker, University of North Texas, United States
Jos Benders, Catholic University of Nijmegen, The Netherlands
Michael Beyerlein, University of North Texas, United States
Elizabeth Blickensderfer, Naval Air Warfare Center, United States
Janis Cannon-Bowers, Naval Air Warfare Center, United States
John Cordery, University of Western Australia, Australia
Hans Doorewaard, Catholic University of Nijmegen, The Netherlands
Lillian Eby, University of Georgia, United States
Merrelyn Emery, Australian National University, Australia
Takahiro Fujimoto, University of Toyko, Japan
Stanley Gully, Rutgers University, United States
Jon Gulowsen, Bodo College, Norway
David Johnson, University of Minnesota, United States
Karin Jurše, University of Maribor, Republic of Slovenia
Alexander Karyakin, Ivanova State Power University, Russia
Monty Lynn, Abilene Christian University, United States
Charles Manz, University of Massachusetts, United States
Raymond Miles, University of California--Berkeley, United States
Matjaž Mulej, University of Maribor, Republic of Slovenia
Christopher Neck, Virginia Tech, United States
Tommy Nilsson, Swedish National Institute of Working Life, Sweden
Anthony Parisi, University of Georgia, United States
Gayle Porter, Rutgers University, United States
Erik Poutsma, Catholic University of Nijmegen, The Netherlands
Ronald Purser, San Francisco State University, United States
Sabine Remdisch, University of Giessen, Germany
Eduardo Salas, University of Central Florida, United States
Beverly Sinoway, University of Georgia, United States
Sabine Sonnentag, University of Amsterdam, The Netherlands
Karon Tedford, University of North Texas, United States
Dean Tjosvold, Linnang College, China
Andrey Tseshinsky, Ivanova State Power University, Russia

Dedication

This book is dedicated to the pioneers in the field of work teams, thought leaders that opened our eyes and our minds to new possibilities of collaborative work designs and set exemplary standards for applying social science to human problems:

Kurt Lewin, Eric Trist, Fred Emery, and

to the students of these exemplars who have carried on the pioneering work and to their students who will carry it on into the next half century--what exciting developments they will generate on the foundation that has been built during the 20th century.

Acknowledgements

The book started as an idea from Professor Raymond Miles of the University of California at Berkeley. The idea first took the form of panel presentations at the Academy of Management meetings in 1995 and 1996. Professor Miles participated in recruiting panel members and played that role himself. The idea for the book emerged during that time. Again, Professor Miles contributed--both by helping to identify potential contributors and by writing a Foreword for the book. Without his broad perspective from more than 40 years of work with organizations with teams, the need for this book would not have been realized.

Thanks to Dr. Susan Beyerlein for her careful reading and constructive feedback on the preface and first chapter, in particular, and on the chapters in general. Her knowledge and skill in the area of business strategy were particularly valuable in work on the last sections of chapter 1.

Finally, a big thank you goes to Melanie Bullock. The work on the panels and the book span more than five years. During that time, Melanie kept the project organized, on track, and on schedule to the extent that was humanly possible. She corresponded with authors in 10 countries in providing them with information, manuscript feedback from the editor, and support. She managed the relationship with the publisher with skill and patience. And, she prepared the camera-ready copy for the printers. Without her enduring support this book might never have been completed.

Preface

Michael Beyerlein
University of North Texas, Denton, Texas, United States

Those of us in the process of advanced maturation are regularly called upon to the historical development of current practice and understanding of work teams is broad in scope emerging from a complex mix of historical sources. I am not aware of a published source that represents that history comprehensively; full treatment may require multiple publications. There are excellent sources that present useful coverage of some components of that history, such as the three anthologies that Trist and his colleagues edited for the Tavistock Institute between 1992 and 1997 (Trist, Emery, & Murray, 1997; Trist, & Murray, 1990; Trist, Murray, & Trist, 1993), sections of Kleiner's 1996 book on the history of organization development (OD), biographical works on the thought leaders, occasional collections (e.g., Davis & Taylor's *Design of Jobs: Selected Readings*, 1972; Susman's *Autonomy at Work: A Socio-technical analysis of Participative Management*, 1976; Pasmore & Sherwood's *Socio-technical Systems: A Sourcebook*, 1978; Pasmore, Francis, Haldeman, & Shani's Socio-technical systems, 1982: A North American reflection on empirical studies of the seventies; Glaser's *Classic Readings in Self-Managing Teamwork*, 1992; and French, Bell, & Zawacki's *Organization Development and Transformation: Managing Effective Change*, 1994), and occasional chapters and articles scattered throughout the literature on teams and organization design and change.

This book consists of chapters that deliberately focus on key historical developments of work teams. The chapters were all written specifically for this book. The authors represent 10 countries and address developments spanning nearly two centuries. Even with that scope, significant contributions to the history cannot be addressed in a single volume. For example, the history of organization development (OD) is fairly interwoven with the history of work teams (e.g., Kleiner, 1996). Also, there is a wide spread belief that importing the quality movement from Japan to the U.S. contributed to the development of work teams as companies tried to adapt quality circles to U.S. work settings and overcome some of their limitations. However, in the scholarly tome on the history of the quality movement edited by Juran in 1995, work teams, self-directed work teams, and empowerment are only addressed on six of the 688 pages (this is somewhat surprising, since he started work at the Western Electric plant in 1924 as an engineer--see Juran, 1997).

Team work and possibly work teams in various forms have probably been used for thousands of years. But, because they were taken for granted, most of that time must be considered a prehistory of current theory and practice. (The earliest use of the word "team" referred to a team of horses in the 16th century.) The history of work teams covers a shorter time span when scholars began to pay attention to the nature of work, job design, and organizational structure. It is an emergent history based on an interweaving of research and practice. Initially, practitioners experimented with new ways to organize work in coal mines, textile plants, fishing boats, pajama plants, etc. A few researchers had an opportunity to observe those work experiments. Their consulting (often action research) and publication contributed to spreading the ideas to other organizations. That cycle of experiment-observe-publish with its informal partnership between business people and researchers happened many times in spreading ideas about effective design and development of work teams. The cycle continues today, although consultants may have played a larger role in the past decade than researchers in influencing business practices with their numerous books.

The historical roots of work teams reside in a number of sources and disciplines across different points in time, including industrial engineering, organization development, sociology, management, communications, social psychology, National Training Labs, the Tavistock Institute, and the Research Center for Group Dynamics. Many of the sources emerged almost concurrently about fifty years ago, including the founding of the Tavistock Institute in1947, the National Training Labs in 1947, Deming's (e.g., http://www.deming.org) work in Japan in1950, and the first issue of the journal *Human Relations* in1947. Several of these items may have been stimulated by the extensive Hawthorne studies of the 1920's and 1930's (Roethlisberger, & Dickson, 1939; see also Purser's chapter in this volume). Other influences followed. For example, participative decision making emerged in the 1960's; work democracy (especially in Norway and Germany—see chapters by Gulowsen, by Antoni, and by Sonnentag & Remdisch) emerged in the late 1960s and 1970s; lean manufacturing emerged in Japan in the late 1970s (see chapter by Fujimoto); total quality management and business process re-engineering focused on process which was sometimes interwoven with teams after the early 1980. New roots are also emerging which include: (a) application of chaos theory, complex systems theory, and non-linear dynamics to the work place; (b) recognition and development of intellectual capital in employees; (c) virtual and network organization, (d) the learning organization, and (e) empowerment. Changes in the business landscape have driven scholars and practitioners to invent or find new ways of competing--the history of work teams involves many of those inventions.

However, predating those roots of the 20th century, one finds natural work groups in prior centuries that resemble work teams in a number of ways (e.g., Tudor, Trumble, & Gerard, 1996 on 2500 years of influence on Japanese teams; Alexandrov, Karyakin, and Tseshinsky on two centuries of historic roots in Russia in this book). The trade guilds of Europe in the 17th century also had similar characteristics. Yet, the momentum we observe today for using team-based work design, especially in the U.S. (see, e.g., chapters by Porter & Beyerlein and by Gully) and Australia (see chapter by Cordery), results from developments of the 50 or 60 years. A search of Psychological Abstracts back to 1916 (the first year of publication for the *Journal of Applied Psychology*) uncovered articles referring to four types of work teams prior to 1945: medical, military, psychiatric, and research. In 1944, the first production work team reference appears in the journal by Mayo and Lombard.

Teamwork has been recognized as a method for increasing work effectiveness for a long time. However, the modern forms of work teams as a way of organizing work have predominantly 20th century roots. Early attempts at utilizing team-based job designs were rare, because the influence of Frederick Taylor's scientific management and Henry Ford's assembly line pervaded management thought.

The costs of implementing and sustaining work teams as an organizing tool became justifiable to managers only when products and services evolved to levels of complexity that demanded interdependent inputs from multiple contributors. At that point bureaucracy, with top-down control reserving decision making for top managers, could not generate sufficient employee commitment, quality, innovation, and customer service.

As the work of social scientists, such as Lewin and his colleagues in the U.S. (see chapter by Tedford & Baker), Trist and Emery (Emery, 1978; Emery & Trist, 1965; Emery & Trist, 1969; Trist, 1981; Trist & Bamforth, 1951;Trist, Higgin, Murray, & Pollock, 1963) and their colleagues in England and Australia (see chapter by Eby, Sinoway & Parisi), Thorsrud in Norway, de Sitter in Holland (see chapter by Benders, Doorewaard, & Poutsma), and Mogenson in Yugoslavia (see chapter by Mulej), was published, it made managers aware that teams represented an alternate design tool for work. Examples of the success of work teams for dealing with problems such as turnover, absenteeism, safety, commitment, and quality became more available in academic publications and gradually in business publications. A significant increase in such publications occurred in each of the subsequent decades: the 1950's, 1960's, 1970's, 1980's, and 1990's.

Early examples included the coal mines of central England (Trist & Bamforth, 1951), Prudential Life Insurance Company (Waters, 1995); Procter & Gamble (e.g., Klein, 1996) in the U.S.; textile mills in India (Rice, 1958); and several kinds of plants in Norway (Thorsrud, Sorensen, & Gustavsen, 1976) and automobile plants in Sweden (Norstedt & Aguren, 1973). In the 1970's other examples emerged in Western Europe and the U.S., such as the General Foods Plant in Topeka, Kansas (Walton, 1977, 1985).

By the 1980's, several dozen major companies were using work teams to some extent in production settings. One of the best known examples was the Digital Equipment plant in Enfield, Connecticut. Many managers visited the plant over the dozen years of its operation, before a change in corporate leadership decided to close the operation. The Enfield plant was a "greenfield" operation, meaning that teams were introduced when the plant was built, in contrast to an existing operation that undergoes transformation to a team-based structure (called a "brownfield"). The Uddwalla, Sweden Volvo plant was also a greenfield site; it was closed for a few years and re-opened (see chapter in this book by Nilsson). The Boeing plant in Corinth, Texas was a greenfield site, started in 1987 but reverting to traditional management five years later, and now working to become team-based again.

Abandonment of team initiatives has been fairly common. The philosophy, values, structure, and operations differ so radically from those of the traditional, bureaucratic company that the team-based operation may be perceived as alien—difficult to understand, difficult to relate to, and difficult to control. The dominant management paradigm of this century has been one with a locus of decision making at the top, with a belief that front-line employees were not capable of making sound decisions, hence they did not need information, and did not warrant significant reward. There may have been some truth to the paradigm 100 years ago, but education of workers in industrial nations created a major change in the work force that demanded a different approach to management.

Work teams were then gradually adapted by large companies in knowledge work settings, typically in the form of cross-functional teams, to replace matrix structures that had been tested for 20 years but remained flawed. However, many of the new efforts to use teams for knowledge work continued to use the production team or socio-technical system model, so the design of the team did not fit the nature of the work in knowledge settings (e.g., Mohrman, Cohen, & Mohrman, 1995; Purser & Pasmore, 1992; Sitkin, Sutcliffe, & Schroeder, 1994).

In the past 10-20 years, work teams has become an increasingly popular management response to such problems as employee morale, turnover, sabotage, etc. The use of work teams has spread from manufacturing to other industries, to government, non-profit organizations, and from the countries where original work was done to most other parts of the world. Lawler and his associates have done a survey of the pervasiveness of empowerment and teams in Fortune 500 companies every three years since 1987. Their results map the increasing use of teams.

However, the most important aspect of work teams is that it embodies one or more shifts in paradigm for how to think about and organize work. Emery (1978) gave examples of the difficulty of people comprehending that a shift was occurring in the 1950's. He contrasted the bureaucratic model of organizations with the socio-technical systems (STS) paradigm that emerged from work by himself and Eric Trist (e.g., Emery 1978; Emery & Trist,1969; Trist, 1981). The STS paradigm remains an important cornerstone of the redesign of organizations to team-based structures, but new forms of paradigm shift are also occurring (e.g., Purser & Cabana's 1998 book on self-managing organizations). The shift to a knowledge society is forcing a recognition that knowledge and learning are more important than information and routine, and that human and social capitals are at least as important as financial and physical capitals. The shift from a business world dominated by manufacturing to one dominated by service and knowledge work change the nature of work, focusing on relationship and thought, which are much more difficult to manage effectively within a bureaucratic framework.

Ten years ago differentiation of teams by type was in its infancy. Clearly there were different forms even then, but the criteria for selecting a specific form for a specific work environment were not well articulated. Contributions by Macy (1993), Alexander (1992), Sundstrom, DeMeuse, & Futrell (1990), Hitchcock & Willard (1995), Cohen and Bailey (1997), and others have helped in developing useful typologies for teams and identifying the contingencies for when one type is more appropriate than another for structuring work to emphasize collaboration. Sundstrom, McIntyre, Halfhill, and Richards (in press) in their review of 92 empirical studies of work groups and work teams from the literature of the past 20 years continue to call for work to clarify team type and the related contingencies.

Finally, a recent group of books and recent research has suggested that teams and team initiatives often fail. This is not surprising. Jim Underwood of Lucent has suggested that 75% of all process oriented business transformations fail. The literature on TQM suggests that at least 70% of all quality programs fail. So, suggesting that 50-70% of all teams and team-based initiatives fail seems to be in line with other work transformation efforts and with our own research with teams (e.g., Beyerlein, Hall, Harris, & Beyerlein, 1997). Recognition of the predominance of failure has led some writers to focus on causes of failure and both preventive and remedial action that can be instituted to deal with the problem. Mohrman and Tenkasi (1997) suggested that 90% of the failures of teams are due to causes outside the team, in the context or environment. Support systems that a team depends on for input of information, goal clarity, leadership, communication, etc., have been identified by the work of Sundstrom (1998) and Hall (1998) as major sources of failure. So emerging writing by both researchers and practitioners has begun to focus on context issues and the sustainability of teams and team initiatives.

The book consists of five sections and a preface and forward. Raymond Miles contributed the Preface. He planted the seeds for this project in 1994 when he lunched with the team from the Center for the Study of Work Teams. Two panel presentations at the Academy of Management annual conference followed that discussion and provided some groundwork for the book. Ira Kaplan's chapter here resulted from one of the panels, as did some of Mile's Preface.

Section I is titled The Evolving Ideas and Theories. It includes an overview of the history of work teams by Gayle Porter and myself. Then Stan Gully has provided a focused review of developments in recent years. Ira Kaplan's paper integrates many of the developments in open systems theory that have emerged since the classic work by Katz and Kahn (1978). Richard Badham and Jos Benders trace cell-based manufacturing and illuminate both the similarities and differences from other teaming models. Ron Purser takes a novel perspective to re-examine the Hawthorne studies that played a pivotal role in the 1920's and 1930's and beyond. Finally, Merrelyn Emery builds on the work she and her husband Fred Emery did over the past 20 years to articulate what they refer to as the second stage model of organization--a model that utilizes principles of democracy and builds a work environment that stimulates trust and joy. That paper then points toward one way that future developments may happen and are happening (e.g., Purser & Cabana's book on the self-managing organization presents 15 case studies that are based on the Emery principles).

Section II is entitled An Appreciative Look at the Major Thinkers. This section consists of short biographical pieces that provide an appreciative overview of the lives and work of some key thought leaders in the area of team-based organizations. The section begins with a biography of Kurt Lewin by Karon Tedford and David Baker. Lewin contributed a wide range of ideas, methods, and frameworks for improving groups and organizations. Another contributor with worldwide influence was Eric Trist. The chapter by Lillian Eby, Beverly Sinoway and Anthony Parisi provides a glimpse of the extensive contributions Trist made, including the Tavistock Institute, and in conjunction with Fred Emery, socio-technical systems theory. Dean Tjosvold and David Johnson have written a tribute to their mentor Morton Deutsch; their own work has carried on his tradition in constructive controversy and other facets of teamwork. From Holland, Jos Benders, Hans Doorewaard, and Erik Poutsma have described the work of Ulbo de Sitter that generated a unique STS movement in Dutch industry. Finally, Matjaž Mulej has described the contributions of Allen Mogensen to Yugoslavian STS changes.

What we know about the developmental history of teams is available only through surviving publications and memories of surviving contributors. Many writers have contributed significantly to the development of team theory and practice. Multiple volumes could be dedicated to biographies of the group, including Fred Emery, Mary Follett, Chester Bernard, Richard Walton, Frederick Taylor, Richard Hackman, Henry Sims, Jr., Susan Mohrman, Charles Manz, Chris Argyris, Lyman Ketchum, Rensis Likert, A. K. Rice, Einer Thorsrud, Stanley Seashore, Ronald and Gordon Lippitt, Edgar Schein, William Foote Whyte, Andre Delbecq, George Strauss, Richard Hackman, Janice Klein, and Michael Beer and some of the contributors to this volume. Practitioners who have not published, especially the unsung heroes within single work sites that championed the implementation of teams, also deserve attention, but their contributions are only available in the few hundred case studies that have published in edited books, conference proceedings, and on the internet, through magazine and newspaper interviews, through conference presentations, or not at all. They made local impact where they worked.

Section III is entitled Development of Work Teams around the World. Historical roots for work teams are international in origin. This section describes some of the independent discoveries that occurred and some of the cross-fertilization that occurred across national boundaries. The longest perspective represented consists of tracing team utilization in Russia over about 150 years in a chapter by Alexandrov, Karyakin, and Tseshinsky. Western European developments are addressed in chapters on Germany by Sabine Sonnentag and Sabine Remdisch and by Conny Antoni, on Norway by Jon Gulowsen, on Yugoslavia by Monty Lynn, Matjaž

Mulez, and Karen Jurše. Australia may be more active in the expansion of teams and the publication of research on teams than any country besides the U.S.A. John Cordery provides an overview of that rapid expansion in Australia. In the U.S.A., the use of teams in the military has been extensive, and the research base for that use has been significant. The chapter by Elizabeth Blickensderfer, Eduardo Salas, and Janis Cannon-Bowers reviews that history since World War II.

Section IV is Entitled Pivotal Examples of Work Team Implementation. There has been a number of pioneering implementations in companies around the world that stimulated the use of teams in other companies and countries. The list would include the coal mines in England, Western Electric, the non-linear plant in California, the failed attempt at the British Leyland truck plant, the Gaines Pet Food Plant in Topeka, Kansas, the Digital plant in Enfield, Connecticut, and the Saturn plant in Springhill, Tennessee. Several additional pioneering operations are described in chapters in this book. Procter & Gamble tried an experiment in two plants in the 1960's that showed such outstanding results from the use of work teams, that they kept it an industrial secret; the only way we know about it is through the writing of former managers after they left the company (Kleiner, 1996). Other companies have also kept the details of their work with teams confidential, in the tire industry, the banking industry, etc. An early success that has waxed and waned has been Volvo's plants in Sweden. The chapter by Tommy Nilsson describes several of the plants, including the closing and reopening of one. Finally, Takahiro Fujimoto describes the shift toward socio-technical systems in Japan after discovering that lean manufacturing had some limitations by focusing on recent changes at Toyota.

The closing section of the book consists of two chapters. Christopher Neck, Charles Manz, and Vikas Anand build on their extensive research with teams to project into the future and present a plausible scenario of future developments. Then Eduardo Salas and Janis Cannon-Bowers summarize the lessons learned from the chapters in this volume by organizing them into 10 themes and explaining their importance.

The history of team theory and practice is broad. In addition to the material presented above, it could include such ideas, events, people and organizations as: (a) the impact of the Baldrige Award and other prizes for quality and effectiveness; (b) the first teams conference; (c) the National Labor Relations Board ruling in 1937 currently referred to as the Team Act; (d) the 1994 plan of the AFL/CIO; (e) lean manufacturing, agile manufacturing, and factory of the future; (f) the shift in HR paradigms from human relations to human resources to human investment; (g) the activities of the Institute of Work Psychology, the Center for Effective Organizations, the Center for the Study of Work Teams, the A. K. Rice Institute, and the Tavistock Institute; and (h) contributions from writers not covered here. Such exhaustive coverage would require a multi-volume work on the history of teams.

Are we creating new developments with the design and practice of work teams or merely rediscovering the ideas of prior generations of managers and researchers? Fred Emery, a major contributor to democratic work design research for 50 years addressed this same kind of question in 1978 and concluded that, although the basic principles published 25 years before were still valid, new practices had been added to them. In the 20 years since Emery wrote that, we have continued to add to our understanding and practices. As more organizations experimented with work team structures and more researchers published descriptions of the results of those practice experiments, we can see and increasingly differentiated and integrated understanding emerging. There are an increasing number of types of work teams, and increasing number of facets of team design and support have emerged in practice, and our theories of team effectiveness have been more inclusive of key facets of team functioning. However, we should expect this trend of discovery to continue for at least another 25-50 years, as many questions remain and new ones emerge in the first half of the 21st century. For example, although the term "virtual team" has become somewhat common in the past three or four years, almost no research has been published on the topic and practice of virtual teaming has typically been limited to an exchange of information, such as the use of e-mail messages. We have only a few studies of cross-cultural teams, yet there has been a rapid increase in the number of cross-cultural settings that demand effective collaboration. Theory and practice of team measurement and compensation is just beginning to show some signs of publishing strong guidelines for practice. The alignment of support systems, and change initiatives that impact team functioning has received attention only in the past year or two. New forms of leadership have been identified in the past few years that make it the responsibility of everyone in the organization. And such critical psychological factors of team performance as a sense of ownership, personal control over work, efficacy, and personal validation remain key principles that receive little direct attention in practice. So, this collage of history presents a picture of emergence, cross-fertilization, bench-marking, experimentation, and learning that shows that we have made some progress, that we owe a great deal to a few courageous thinkers and practitioners, and that we have a long way to go to develop a sufficient understanding of work teams to enable us to reap the full benefit of their potential synergies and to sustain their development over time in the face of new challenges.

The meaning of the term "team" has been ambiguous, partly because teams come in many forms and are not always differentiated by unique terms and partly because there are multiple names for the same form. If we broaden the meaning of team to refer to any kind of collaborative work structure, the number and variety of organizational units encompassed by the term expands from self-directed team, self-managing team, self-governing team, etc., and may even include such forms as strategic alliances, mini-companies, cellular and network organizations, and virtual organizations. The amount of publishing in research and practitioner literature on work teams has increased exponentially since 1990; surveys suggest that the use of teams in organizations has also increased rapidly. It may be many years before those trends level off. The next 50 years of research and practice with teams will determine how many of the principles of the small work team apply to more complex forms of collaboration. That expansive effort should be interesting and productive.

References

Alexander, J. O., & Mayfield, R. D. (1992). From values to evaluation: How to design, staff, and empower the four team types. *Proceedings of the International Conference on Self-Managed Work Teams*, pp. 160-168.

Beyerlein, M., Hall, C., Harris, C., & Beyerlein, S. (1997). The failure of transformation to teams. *Proceedings of the International Conference on Work Teams*, pp. 57-62.

Cohen, S. G. & Bailey, D. E. (1997). What makes teams work: Group effectiveness research from the shop floor to the executive suite. *Journal of Management, 23*(3), 239-290.

Davis, L. E., & Taylor, J. C. (Eds.) (1972). *Design of jobs: Selected readings*. Harmondsworth: Penguin.

Emery, F. E. (1978). *The emergence of a new paradigm of work*. Australian National University: Centre for Continuing Education.

Emery, F. E., & Trist, E. L. (1965). The causal texture of organizational environments. *Human Relations, 18*, 21-32.

Emery, F. E. & Trist, E. L. (1969). Sociotechnical systems. In F. E. Emery (Ed.) *Systems Thinking*. New York: Penguin.

French, W. L., Bell, C. H., Jr., & Zawacki, R. A. (Eds.) (1994). *Organization development and transformation: Managing effective change*. Boston, MA: Irwin McGraw-Hill.

Glaser, R. (Ed.) (1992). *Classic readings in self-managing teamwork*. King of Prussia, PA: Organization Design and Development, Inc.

Hackman, R. E. (Ed.) (1990). *Groups that work: And those that don't: Creative conditions for effective teamwork*. San Francisco: Jossey-Bass.

Hall, C. (1998). *Organizational support systems for team-based organizations: Employee collaboration through organizational structures*. Dissertation, University of North Texas.

Hitchcock, D., & Willard, M. (1995). *Why teams can fail and what to do about it: Essential tools for anyone implementing self-directed work teams*. Burr Ridge, IL: Irwin Professional Publications.

Juran, J. M. (Ed.) (1995). *A history of management for quality: The evolution, trends, and future directions of managing for quality*. Chicago: American Society for Quality.

Juran, J. M. (1997). Early SQC: A historical supplement. *Quality Progress, 30*(9), 73-81.

Katz, D. & Kahn, R. L. (1978). *The Social Psychology of Organizations*. New York: Wiley & Sons.

Kleiner, A. (1996). *The age of heretics: Heroes, outlaws, and the forerunners of corporate change*. New York: Doubleday.

Macy, B. A. (1993). North American organizational design and work innovation: Bottom-line impacts from 1961-1991. *Proceedings of the International Conference on Self-Managed Work Teams*, pp. 82-101.

Mayo, E., & Lombard, G. F. F. (1944). Teamwork and labor turnover in the aircraft industry of Southern California. *Harvard University Graduate School of Business Publication*, No. 32, vii + 30.

Mohrman, S. A., & Tenkasi, R. (1997). Patterns of cross-functional work: Behaviors and benefits. Paper presented at the University of North Texas Symposium on Work Teams, Dallas, TX.

Norstedt, J. P., & Aguren, S. (1973). *The Saab-Scania report*. Stockholm: Swedish Employers' Confederation.

Pasmore, W., Francis, C., Haldeman, J., & Shani, A. (1982). Sociotechnical systems: A North American reflection on empirical studies of the seventies. *Human Relations, 35*, 1179-1204.

Pasmore, W. A., & Sherwood, J. J. (Eds.) (1978). *Sociotechnical systems: A sourcebook*. La Jolla, CA: University Associates.

Purser, R. E., & Cabana, S. (1998). *The self-managing organization: How leading companies are transforming work of teams for real impact*. New York: Free Press.

Purser, R. E. & Pasmore, W. A. (1992). Organizing for learning. *Research in organizational change and development, 6*, 37-113.

Rice, A. K. (1958). *Productivity and social organization: The Ahmedabad experiment*. London: Tavistock Publications.

Roethlisberger, F. J., & Dickson, W. J. (1939). *Management and the worker*. Cambridge, MA: Harvard University Press.

Sitkin, S. B., Sutcliffe, K. M., Schroeder, R. G. (1994). Distinguishing control from learning in total quality management: A contingency perspective. *Academy of Management Review, 19*, 537-564.

Sundstrom, E., DeMeuse, K.,& Futrell, D. (1990). Work teams: Applications and effectiveness. *American Psychologist, 45*(2), 120-133.

Sundstrom, E., McIntyre, M., Halfhill, T., & Richards, H. (in press). Work groups: From the Hawthorne studies to work teams of the 1990s and beyond. *Group*

Sundstrom, E (Ed.) (1998). *Supporting work team effectiveness: Best management practices for fostering high performance*. San Francisco: Jossey-Bass.

Susman, G. I. (1976). *Autonomy at work: A socio-technical analysis of participative management*. New York: Praeger.

Thorsrud, E., Sorensen, B. S., & Gustavsen, B. (1976). Sociotechnical approach to industrial democracy in Norway. In R. Dubin (Ed.), *Handbook of work, organization, and society*. Chicago: Rand McNally.

Trist, E. L. (1981). The sociotechnical perspective: The evolutions of sociotechnical systems as a conceptual framework and as an action research program. In A. H. Van de Ven & W. F. Joyce (Eds.), *Perspectives on organization design and behavior*, 1975. New York: Wiley.

Trist, E. L., & Bamforth, K. W. (1951). Some social and psychological consequences of the Longwall method of coal getting. *Human Relations 14*, 3-38.

Trist, E. L., Higgin, G. W., Murray, H. Pollock, A. G. (Eds.) (1963). *Organizational Choice: Capabilities of Groups at the Coal Face Under Changing Conditions*. London: Tavistock.

Trist, E., Emery, F., & Murray, H. (Eds.) (1997). *The social engagement of social science: A Tavistock anthology, Vol. 3: The socio-technological perspective*. Philadelphia, PA: University of Pennsylvania Press.

Trist, E., & Murray, H. (Eds.) (1990). *The social engagement of social science: A Tavistock anthology, Vol. 1: The socio-psychological perspective*. Free Association Books.

Trist, E., Murray, H., & Trist, B. (Eds.) (1993). *The social engagement of social science: A Tavistock anthology, Vol. 2: The sociotechnical perspective*. Philadelphia, PA: University of Pennsylvania Press.

Tudor, T.R., Trumble, R. R., George, G. (1997). Significant historic origins that influenced the team concept in major Japanese companies. *Journal of Applied Business Research, 12*(4), 115-128.

Walton, R. (1977). Work innovations at Topeka: After six years. *Journal of Applied Behavioral Science, 13*, 422-433.

Walton, R. (1985). From control to commitment in the workplace. *Harvard Business Review, 63*, 77-84.

Waters, P. (1995). Prudential. Part of panel presentation: A retrospective on work teams: Historical developments in theory and practice. Paper presented at the annual meeting of the Academy of Management, Dallas.

Foreword

Raymond Miles
University of California, Berkeley, California, United States

Those of us in the process of advanced maturation are regularly called upon to provide "historical" perspective on topics of current interest. This book had its beginnings out of several such "perspective" discussions I had with Mike Beyerlein and his colleagues and students at The University of North Texas (UNT) in the early 1990s.

I had become impressed with the team research and development program Mike, Doug Johnson (a Berkeley Ph.D.), and others at the Center for the Study of Work Teams had created and I had taken part in several of their public conferences. In those sessions I frequently traced the beginnings of modern research and development efforts back to earlier works, many of which one of my colleagues or I had had a hand in. On one of my visits to UNT (my undergraduate alma mater), Mike asked me to share some of those earlier experiences with his staff and students. We enjoyed these sessions and soon began wondering why this topic was not more heavily discussed. To encourage such discussion, we put together a panel for the Academy of Management meetings in Vancouver, in 1994 and followed up with a second session at Dallas in 1995. A book as an extension of the papers given at these sessions was a natural and this forward is intended to provide a précis of sorts of my conversations with the "teams" team at UNT.

My historical perspective on teams and team building is highly selective and impressionistic. I tend to view teams as a key aspect of organizational life evolving in pace with evolutions in managerial thinking and organizational forms. What we hope to get from work teams and what we are willing to invest in them is shaped by when and where we are. For example, in the first half of this century, when the term team was invoked, it usually was within a sentence dealing with morals, loyalty or commitment. Team meetings and discussions could be a plus, managers thought, but they weren't crucial to the work process and thus not worth a heavy investment of time or attention.

Most recently, when teams are mentioned, it is usually in connection with such words or phrases as empowerment, customer service, entrepreneurship, etc. Today, in many organizations, managers depend on largely self-managing teams to provide the increasingly customized and innovative products and services the modern market place expects. In these firms, steady streams of returns are anticipated from team building and team empowerment efforts.

How and why we got from the earlier attitudes and behaviors to the latter ones is the subject not only of my conversations at UNT but of several of my recent writings which I will also draw on in the following paragraphs. For the sake of exposition and perhaps to spark a bit of chronological controversy, I have tried to characterize the dominant team associated "theme" and or "innovation" in each of the decades beginning with the 1920s.

The Twenties: Teams "Light"

The twenties (and the decades just before) were pictured in Reinhardt Bendix's splendid history (*Work and Authority in Industry*, 1956), as a period of managerial awakening. The typical manager was just recognizing what Henry Ford had seen much earlier, that the new age factory and office with their narrowly defined and specialized tasks were heavily dependent on a loyal and committed workforce. Supervisory training emphasized humane treatment and the era of company newsletters, picnics, and suggestion systems was born. It is not surprising that near the end of this decade of paternalistic enlightenment, the Western Electric Company would allow experiments with its factory work groups improve the conditions of work. It was perhaps even less surprising that the researchers would attribute most of their results to team member satisfaction with managerial attention and the opportunity to influence their work lives (see, e.g., Rothlisberger & Dickson, 1939). From these and most other work teams in the era, nothing crucial to the work process was expected (or wanted) except that workers remain on the job and reasonably cooperative. If these behaviors could be purchased with a little attention and some limited opportunity to be heard, it was a small price to pay.

The Thirties: Human Relations plus the Scanlon Plan

The good-times supported worker involvement programs of the twenties soon gave way to the hard-times labor battles of the thirties. Nevertheless, some of the enlightenment of the earlier period carried over into the depression era. As evidenced in the steel plants where union leader Joe Scanlon helped create worker-management cost savings/sharing plans that kept a number of companies productive and profitable even in the depths of nation wide economic crisis (Frost, Wakeley, & Ruth, 1974).

While the greatest work related achievement of the thirties was the foundation laid for employee organization and effective collective bargaining, the Scanlon Plan's successes made it clear that multi-level, multi-department participative systems could and did work, even within unionized firms in the midst of a deep depression (and as later research showed, in good times as well). The Scanlon Plan's use of worker and management cost cutting and productivity improving ideas to generate higher profits and pay bonuses throughout the plant made it clear that teams produced money as well as morale -- they were a direct engine of economic success producing efficiency gains based on previously untapped know-how.

Unfortunately, the crisis driven lesson that worker know-how was an important source of increased economic value was learned mainly by those directly involved and did not change the prevailing view that worker involvement was primarily a contributor to increased worker loyalty.

The Forties: Team Based leadership in the Plant and the Plane

For the U.S., WW II began in the resurgent manufacturing plants turning out lend-lease equipment for soon to be wartime allies. In the better managed firms, lessons from the twenties and thirties were pushed by personnel managers and training programs drawing on government supported research and brought major improvements in worker and supervisory skills.

Then, as the U.S. became a full participant in the European and Pacific conflicts, worker training and supervisory development became top priorities across the economy as a third of the prime age workforce went to war. The plants on which the war effort depended were now themselves dependent on a new work force that featured women, minorities, and others who had previously had little opportunity for involvement. The success stories of the era were widely shared (to boost morale) and eye opening. Individuals previously believed to be untrainable not only learned key skills but exceeded all productivity predictions. People with disabilities not only built airplanes, they played major league baseball. Against the backdrop of death and destruction, the nation was taught a lesson it could never again forget – people of all kinds had the potential to be productive participants in the economy. If the investments were made, there were far fewer barriers to skill development and know-how utilization than almost anyone had believed.

Simultaneously, every branch of the military was engaging in research and training experiments as they sought to create a global fighting force virtually overnight. Officer selection and training programs laid the foundation for modern assessment centers and team building programs and research findings confirmed again that the effective military team knew no ethnic or gender bounds and, whether in tank, plane, ship, or on foot, was the most important element that had to be constructed. (Retrospective documentaries and films such as The Tuskegee Airmen and Twelve O'Clock High educational tools.) Not surprisingly, many war time researchers and training program developers returned to academia and provided the post-war push for improved civilian efforts in management training and participative systems.

The Fifties: T-Groups and Management Development

While Peter Drucker was extolling the organizational virtues of decentralization and management by objectives, a broad movement emerged in the late forties aimed at removing underlying barriers to leadership effectiveness – sensitivity training. Using group members to provide feedback on the impact individual behavior had on others and on the group, social experimenters developed a technology that came to be known as the Training Group, or most commonly, the T-group. Under the better leaders, process focused groups provided insightful, frequently mind-opening revelations to managers and leaders from businesses, government agencies, and religious, military, educational, and voluntary organizations.

The core concept was straightforward – if leaders and teams were to be effective, they had to become more aware, more sensitive, to the impact that their behaviors had on others. The obvious virtues of increased insight propelled T-groups into prominence and ultimately, in the following decades, into a social movement with all of the plusses and minuses that accrue to such phenomena.

At the time, however, they were merely one more important element in a post-war ideology that emphasized management development as the key to organizational and national success. They were accompanied by related leadership and organizational research and theorizing that by the end of the fifties had produced some of the most enduring literature in the history of the field, including Bendix's *Work and Authority in Industry*, Whyte's *Money and Motivation*, Maslow's *Motivation and Personality*, Gouldner's *Patterns of Industrial Bureaucracy*, Cartwright and Zander's *Group Dynamics*, Fiedler's *Leader Attitudes and Group Effectiveness*, March and Simon's *Organizations*, and important articles by Levitt, Bennis, Bavelas, and many others.

The Sixties: Organizational Development -- The Early Days

The sixties began with the promise of insight and application contained in McGregor's *Human Side of Enterprise*. While he proclaimed that his effort was not to divide managers with regard to the virtues of Theory X and Theory Y, his intention to show the positive benefits of effective participative management was clear. Similarly, Likert's *New Patterns of Management* a year later argued uncompromisingly for a management system that emphasized leadership combining high expectations and supportiveness with a team based organizational design – a model he developed in greater detail later in the decade in his book, *The Human Organization*. The concept of leader attitude change supporting team based organizations became the focus of implementation focused programs at numerous universities and training centers. All used some variation of member feedback to heighten leader awareness and improve group processes, whether survey feedback as pioneered by the Survey Research Center at Michigan, modified T group approaches used by Beckhard and others at MIT, or the concept-based exercises designed by Black and Mouton as the University of Texas.

By the end of the decade, the focus of the implementation effort had shifted upward and outward beyond the team to include major organizational units and even the firm itself. Some of the broadest efforts, particularly those undertaken through the Center for Research in the Utilization of Scientific Knowledge (under Floyd Mann and others) at Michigan, were attempting survey-based programs featuring rapid, wide ranging roll-outs of development cascading down the organization from top management to bottom line work teams and their supervisors. The sixties was an era of change in every institution, and the merging of research, theory, and practice in the OD movement fit the decade to at T (group).

The Seventies: Organizational Development – The Latter Days

By the seventies, the temperature of the OD movement had dropped a degree or two, but in the more progressive companies, serious, committed, long term team building efforts were underway. It was clear to most practitioners, if not to most academics, that team building know-how had reached the stage that the process was no longer experimental. If you went through the steps with care and dedication, the time and energy invested would pay off with work teams capable of exercising strong self-direction and contributing substantively to organizational performance and profitability.

Despite numerous highly publicized success stories, two problems remained. First, the broader movement had generated many weakly supported efforts to rebuild team efforts in paternalistic systems. These "fad" efforts usually produced positive but unimpressive results which offered critics ample ground for questioning the efficacy of team building programs. Secondly, and more importantly in the intermediate run, highly developed teams ran into real economic barriers to continuous growth. That is, they frequently reached the limits of output that their systems could employ. Their capabilities grew faster than the larger organization could grow and/or accommodate. With little opportunity left to grow, teams settled down into long term superior performance, but with at least some diminishment of excitement and commitment (see Walton, 1980; Miles & Rosenburg, 1982).

Moreover, the emerging "portfolio" strategies of the seventies focused much corporate effort on the quick financial gains available from mergers and acquisitions. While these strategies primarily benefited the earliest movers who acquired assets below their market value, they diverted the attention of many managers from long term gains achievable through investments in human capital (Miles & Miles, 1998).

The Eighties: Competition, Collapse and Rebirth of the Quality Movement

Few things show up poor managerial decisions more effectively than strong competition. The push of European and Japanese products into key US industries in the eighties demonstrated again the veracity of two well-documented lessons. First, unrelated diversification of the sort common in the acquisitions and mergers of the late sixties and seventies has no long term economic justification – organizational know-how is difficult to apply in truly diverse arenas and technical and other synergies may cost more to achieve than they are worth. Second, failure to provide consumers with the high quality well designed goods and services available from competitors is a certain route to lower market share if not to total collapse.

Thus, while Europeans and Japanese were expanding well trained work-forces and the Japanese in particular were using US developed approaches to achieve dramatic quality breakthroughs, many US firms were chasing quicker dollars through capital redirection. The awakening process in the US was dramatic and costly. Several million workers and middle managers were caught in the process of corporate redesign as firms refocused on core areas of expertise, disaggregated under-utilized assets horizontally and vertically and began rebuilding internal capabilities in the areas of quality improvement and product/service customization and innovation.

The rebirth of the quality movement that flourished in the US in the forties and early fifties provided a rich new arena for team development. Borrowing quality circle team concepts back from the Japanese, US firms, such as Motorola, began to lay a new foundation for competitiveness that in the best managed organizations expanded, utilized, and fully rewarded team based know-how. In the less well managed firms, lesser gains were obtained from lower levels of investment and sometimes exploitive cost cutting efforts.

Moreover, information technology and the growing availability of both domestic and foreign partners allowed firms to search for their most profitable niche along the value chain. The emergent global networks promoted further efficiencies along with continuous quality and customization achievements. They also made it possible for less enlightened managers to seek short-term gains at the expense of long term investments in productive relationships. We will return to this point in our next and final section.

The Nineties: A Key Breakthrough – the Entrepreneurially Empowered Team

As noted above in our description of the team building successes of the seventies, a key barrier to further team growth was the ability of the larger system to fully utilize the team's output potential. For example, teams in one plant that we worked with in the seventies did not realize full team-based profitability potential until the plant moved beyond production solely for its parent's use and began contract production for other down stream partners. This example of belated "networking" is occurring across most industries and offers the opportunity for many units to become important centers of profitability. The ability of teams to exercise informed self-direction in the provision of high quality customized goods and service to multiple partners becomes the principle source of added economic value.

Nevertheless, even in these settings, a major barrier to the full utilization of empowered teams remains. Most networks are ultimately bounded by the entrepreneurial competency of their furthest downstream partners – those with direct linkages to the ultimate consumers of new products/services. If innovations in final product/service design can be made more continuous and efficient, less constrained by plan and precedence, the entire network has the potential for higher rates of utilization.

It is my expectation that downstream design firms will move toward the "cellular" configuration that we have seen in several leading edge firms in various parts of the world (see Miles et al.," Anticipating the Cellular Organization," 1997). These cellular organizations are essentially collections of small firms, each responsible for its own entrepreneurship – its own location, development, and service to customers. Cells draw on the know-how of all of the other cells in the system as they provide unique customer solutions and they consciously share the learning that flows from each new design process with the total system. Thus every piece of the organization is constantly learning – acquiring new know-how and adding to the organization's total knowledge assets to which it has total access.

In the smaller cellular organizations the cells are essentially team size. In the larger, cellular structures, the cells (firms) are themselves likely to be heavily team-based in order to diffuse entrepreneurial responsibility. Finally, most cellular firms, as noted, are located at the "head" (downstream end) of a network of partners who provide technical and/or manufacturing support.

Concluding Comment

The chapters you are about to read do not fall neatly into my chronological categories. Each, however, provides a rich opportunity to explore the development and use of teams within a particular location and across a particular period of time, as is thoughtfully captured in Porter and Beyerlein's overview in the next chapter. Moreover, I think as you read these chapters you will feel the forces shaping teams and their organizational context and share some of my impressions of the evolutionary process.

It is clearly my view that we are entering a rich new period for teams – one that we can best appreciate and take advantage of, if we understand how we got here. Indeed, as a professional perspective provider, how could I feel otherwise.

References

Bavelas, A. (1951). Communication patterns in task-oriented groups. In D. Lerner & H. D. Lasswell (Eds.), *The policy sciences*, pp. 193-202. Stanford, CA: Stanford University Press

Bendix, R. (1956). *Work and authority in industry*. New York: John Wiley.

Bennis, W. G. (1959). Leadership theory and administration behavior. *Administration Science Quarterly*, 4, 259-301.

Cartwright, D. & Zander, A. (1951). *Group dynamics: Research and theory*. Evanston: Row Peterson.

Drucker, P. (1964). *The practice of management*. New York: Harper and Brothers.

Feidler, F. E. (1958). *Leader attitudes and group effectiveness*. Urbana, IL: University of Illinois Press

Frost, C. F., Wakeley, J. H., & Ruh, R. A. (1974). *The Scanlon plan for organizational development: Identity, participation, and equity*. Michigan State University Press

Gouldner, A. W. (1954). *Patterns of industrial bureaucracy.* Glencoe, IL: Free Press

Likert, R. (1961). *New patterns of management.* New York: McGraw-Hill.

Likert, R. (1967). *The human organization.* New York: McGraw-Hill.

March, J. G. & Simon, H. A. (1958). *Organizations.* New York: John Wiley

Maslow, A. (1954). *Motivation and personality.* New York: Harper

McGregor, D. (1960). *The human side of enterprise.* New York: McGraw-Hill

Miles, R. E., & Rosenburg, H. R. (1982, Winter). The human resources approach to management: Second-generation issues. *Organizational Dynamics*, pp. 26-41.

Miles, R. E., Creed, W.E. (1995). Organizational forms and managerial philosophies: A descriptive and analytical review. In L. L. Cummings & B. M. Staw (Eds.), *Research in organizational behavior*, Vol 17. Greenwich, CT: JAI Press, Inc.

Miles, R. E., Snow, C. C., Mathews, J. A., Miles, G., & Coleman, H. J. (1997). Organizating in the knowledge age: Anticipating the cellular form. *Academy of Management Executive.*

Miles, R. E., & Miles, G. (1998). Leadership and collaboration. In J. Conger (Ed.), *The leader's change handbook.* San Francisco: Jossey Bass.

Rothlisberger, F. J., & Dickson, W. J. (1939). *Management and the worker.* Cambridge: Harvard University Press

Walton, R. (1980). Establishing and maintaining high commitment work systems. In J. R. Kimberly & R. H. Miles (Eds.), *The organizational life cycle.* San Francisco: Jossey Bass.

Whyte, W. F. (1955). *Money and Motivation: An Analysis of Incentives in Industry.* New York: Harper.

SECTION I.

EVOLVING IDEAS AND THEORIES

Chapter 1

Historic Roots of Team Theory and Practice

Gayle Porter
Rutgers University, Piscataway, New Jersey, United States

Michael Beyerlein
University of North Texas, Denton, Texas, United States

Abstract

Current levels of development in the theory and practice of work teams rest on a complex historical foundation. This chapter provides an overview of that foundation with an emphasis on early laboratory research and practical developments at work sites in Western Europe, the U.S., and Australia. The contributions of major thought leaders are mentioned, including Lewin, Emery, and Trist. And the path of development is traced up to the recent use of virtual teams. The theory continues to be further elaborated by field studies in a wide range of settings and by practice that has spread to new areas of business, to non-profit organizations, and to government. Finally, the business case for use of teams is briefly addressed, emphasizing the point that teams are so widely used now that the quality of their implementation rather than their presence is the key to competitive advantage.

Introduction

Current theories of work teams have broad historical roots, and the practices have become more sophisticated and differentiated over the past few decades. In today's organizations, teams may be either temporary or a permanent feature of the structure. Teams may be specialized by job function, or cross-functional with focus on a particular task, product or development activity. Teams exist in manufacturing, service, or knowledge work organizations, and teams are increasingly appearing at all levels in the organization. Tracing a history is not a simple linear path, when the current status of teams includes such diversity of form and function.

Further complicating the selection of historic markers is writer preference. One writer may be primarily concerned with processes within the team, such as decision-making or conflict resolution. Another may prefer to focus on relationships among teams or between team members and individual managers or support functions. Others may choose to highlight the organizational outcomes that result from successful team implementations. When examining how the use of teams has

M.M. Beyerlein (ed.), Work Teams: Past, Present and Future, 3–24.

evolved historically, we are all likely to agree on a few key turning points, but each author will then fill in the detail as it is relevant to his or her individual choice of focus.

Early research more often occurred outside business organizations, often in laboratories, without any particular emphasis on the workplace in discussion of application. Yet those contributions should not be ignored in considering the total body of knowledge we draw from to enhance team development and implementation, as we know it today. Placed in a time-line, the writings on collaborative work—with or without organizational emphasis—provide a historic view of the evolution of interest in team activity. Here we have chosen to review trends in the printed information about collaborative work. We believe that the amount and type of information readily available at a given time is a reflection of the attention to teams in organizations. This evolving record is a primary base upon which practitioners and researchers draw, to formulate both their current activities and future plans.

Table 1 is an effort to provide a quick reference to selected writings on collaborative work. This is by no means an all-inclusive listing, just a sample of notable contributions. And, of course, it is biased by our chosen perspectives and primarily reflects developments in the U.S., Western Europe, and Australia more than other parts of the world. The following discussion briefly explains each source listed in the table, as well as some surrounding work. On the left-hand side of the table are references to work from psychology or social psychology with a focus on groups. They have important implications for teams in organizations, but were not given that emphasis at the time. On the right-hand side are contributions that did specify application in business organizations. Several listings are positioned in the middle, either because the work effectively bridged disciplines, or has subsequently become a "favorite" among practitioners for application to team concerns. The following narrative is presented in the same order as the Table 1.

Some Initial Thoughts on Work Groups Versus Work by Individuals

In Steiner's (1974) review of social psychology paradigms, he begins with the debate over views of Durkheim (1895) and Allport (1924). Durkheim proposed that a group becomes something different than just the sum of its parts; it has its own identity that cannot be adequately understood by piecemeal examination of its parts. In contrast Allport maintained that actions of the group are ultimately those of individuals within the group; the group is just an illusion. At the time of Steiner's article, he expressed that Allport was still supported by social psychologists. In organizations where teams have been successful in transforming both the approach to work and the output potential, we might find more support for the synergistic possibilities in Durkheim's views. This debate was chosen as a starting point in our history review. In timing, it coincides with the industrialization of the U.S. It also exemplifies that there was not a clear starting philosophy for considering unique aspects of work groups to adapt for organizational application.

One early study of people working together indicated that productivity was hindered by group effort (Moede, 1927, as described in Kravitz & Martin, 1986). Subjects engaged in a rope-pull, in which the first measurement was individual performance. When placed into groups to pull, the performance was less than their potential, with potential measured as the sum of the individuals' performance. Groups of three performed at 85% of their potential; groups of eight reached only 49% of their potential. This decrement in performance came to be known as the Ringelmann rope-pull paradigm (named for the researcher whose earlier work was the basis for Moede's experiment). Forty years later, researchers began making efforts to replicate and explain this phenomenon (Ingham, Levinger, Graves & Peckham, 1974; Steiner, 1972). In the meantime, the result was out there as evidence that promoting group effort was questionable, at best.

In the 1920s, the dominant focus for organizational improvement in the U.S. was Scientific Management, based on the work of Frederick Taylor and others over the prior 30 years. The emphasis on job simplification and efficiency fit well in the authoritarian structure of organizations at that time. An alternate perspective in the 1920s was that of Mary Parker Follett, who spoke of creating greater unity of the enterprise as a means to success. Follett directly referenced the image of a team and suggested three ideas (c.f., Graham, 1995). The first was increased cross-functioning between different departments. This would lead to inter-relational, horizontal authority rather than vertical authority. The second recommendation was a system of committees for integration. She described this integration as preferable to either domination or compromise as a means to settle differences of opinion. When A and B have differences, integration means finding a third solution that incorporates both A's and B's wishes. The third suggestion was to develop a sense of collective responsibility, an awareness of the interdependence she described as an asset for any business. The ideas promoted by Follett are very compatible with current thinking on the use of teams in organizations, but they did not affect large-scale change in business strategy at that time.

The Start of the Human Relations Movement

Aside from Follett, one of the few other voices for consideration of social influences in the work setting of the 1920s and 1930s was Elton Mayo. Due to his work on what came to be known as the Hawthorne Experiments, Mayo has been called the founder of the Human Relations Movement, as well as the founder of organizational sociology (Pugh & Hickson, 1989) (see the chapter by Purser in this book for another perspective). Between the years 1927 and 1932, this series of experiments uncovered the informal organization—group members' shared attitudes and reactions to management, with resulting changes in work output (Mayo, 1933; Roethlisberger & Dickson, 1939). The groups they studied might not be called work teams by today's standards, but it was the first study in a work setting that suggested the importance of the group.

Looking back on the reports of the Hawthorne studies, it's hard to realize that social systems were invisible before that time. The prevailing paradigms of work, management and organizing provided no insight to social and group relations. This body of work cast a new light on the responsibilities of management and the means through which to achieve organizational objectives. For that reason, this work is often the starting point for discussion of the history of teams.

A new stage of readiness developed in the U.S. for considering the dynamics of people interacting on a common task, whether in a business organization or other

Table 1. Selected Writings on Collaborative Work Topics

Study of Groups and Group Dynamics	Emphasis on Work Teams in Business Organizations
Some Initial thoughts on Work Groups versus Work by Individuals	
1895/1982 Durkheim - group is not equal to the sum of its parts	
1924 Allport - group exists only as individuals who are members	1920s Follett - cross functional interaction; non-hierarchical committees; recognition of interdependencies (Graham, 1995)
1927 Moede - Ringelmann effect (Kravitz & Martin, 1986)	
The Start of the Human Relations Movement	
← Late 1920s - 1930s Mayo (1933); Roethlisberger & Dickson (1939/1967); Hawthorne studies of social influence in work setting→	
1930s Lewin (1939) - ability of group to influence individuals	
1935 Sherif - norm formation	
The Focus on Group Dynamics	
← 1940s Lewin (1947) - Group climate experiments, Center for Group Dynamics, National Training Laboratories →	
← 1950s Homans - paradigm for analyzing group behavior in organizations→	
1950s Bales (1950 a & b); Bales & Strodtbeck (1951) - stages of group development and empirical technique for studying groups in action	Early 1950's - Trist & Bamforth, 1951; Emery, 1951; Emery & Trist, 1965, 1969 - Tavistock studies on socio-technical systems
1950s Festinger et al. (1954) - social comparison in small groups and cohesiveness	
1952 Asch - conformity behavior in groups	
1959 Thibaut & Kelley - The Social Psychology of Groups	1963 Trist - Organizational Choice in design using Socio-Technical Systems
1965 Tuckman - stages of group development; forming, storming, norming, performing	
1965 Zajonc- Social Facilitation	
	1966 Katz and Kahn - Systems thinking and role theory applied in organizations
	1967 Thompson - pooled, sequential and reciprocal interdependence
	1967 Likert - Participative Group Management
	1971 Hackman & Lawler - Group Influences on Individuals
1970s Steiner (1972, 1974) - Group Process & Productivity	
← 1972 Janis - Groupthink →	
Reconsidering the Person on the Team - Identity and Self-interest	
Late 1970s & 1980s Tajfel (1978, 1982) - group identification, social categories, intergroup behavior	1975 & 1980 Hackman & Oldham - work re-design and job enrichment
1979 - 1980s Latane et al. (1979), Kerr (1983), Kerr & Bruun (1983) - social loafing, free-riders, & suckers	
	1980s Weisbord (1987) Participative work design & QWL
	1981 Ouchi - Theory Z and organizational "clans"

Table 1. Selected Writings on Collaborative Work Topics (*continued*)

Participation with Quality Emphasis - Benchmarking and Continuous Improvement	
	Early 1980s Thompson (1982); Patchin (1983) - Quality Circles
	Early to mid- 1990s Pierce (1991); Dean & Evans (1994); Pegels (1995) - Teams in Total Quality Management (TQM)
	1987 Shea & Guzzo - Group effectiveness and potency
	1980s Fisher (1993) - Proctor & Gamble
	1988 Bernstein (1992) - use of STS at Volvo
	1990 Orsburn, Moran, Musselwhite & Zenger how-to-book on self -directed work teams; further company examples
	1990 Hackman - conditions for effective work teams
	1992 Lawler, Mohrman, & Ledford - second survey of EI in Fortune 500 companies in a series of four
	1994 Stevens & Campion; Campion et al. (1996) - knowledge, skills, abilities for teamwork
Leadership in Team Organizations	
	1986 Hackman & Walton - leading groups in organizations
	1980s Manz (1986); Manz & Sims (1980; 1987) - Self-management and Self-leadership
	1996 Allred, Snow & Miles - Managerial Careers
Competitive Advantage - Re-Instituting the Link to Organizations Strategy, plus Global Perspectives	
	1993; 1994; 1996 Bartmess & Cerny; Barney & Zajac; Cappelli & Crocker-Hefter - critical capabilities, core competencies
	1994 & 1995 Pfefer - Competitive advantage through people
	1992 Lawler - matching strategy & structure for high involvement and competitive advantage
	1993 Katzenback & Smith - Teams for High-Performance Organization
	1992 Jackson & Associates; 1995 Jackson & Ruderman - diversity on work teams
Technology, Distance, and Time	
1989 Gersick - effects of time limits on group process	
	1996 Mankin et al. - teams and technology
	1997 Lipnack & stamps - virtual teams

associations. In the 1930s, Kurt Lewin popularized the term "group dynamics," as his work on personality expanded to consideration of the ability of the group to influence individuals (Cartwright & Zander, 1953) (see chapter in this book on Lewin by Tedford & Baker). Sherif (1935) further clarified the powerful influence of the group with his research on norms. Based on theories of perception and learning, Sherif described norm formation as the process that transforms individuals into groups. Norms are established through interaction of group members and then become the frame of reference for all subsequent judgements and perceptions on related issues (see also summary by Moscovici, 1985).

The Focus on Group Dynamics

The study of group dynamics advanced more rapidly in the U.S. after the Second World War. Americans held a new concern for understanding how democratic organizations could function more efficiently, and the idea that systematic research and scientific method could advance understanding gained acceptance (Johnson & Johnson, 1994). During the 1940s, Kurt Lewin's work emphasized the importance of applying knowledge of group dynamics in organizations, both for leaders and other organizational members. He established the first organization devoted explicitly to research on group dynamics, the Center for Group Dynamics at M.I.T. (later moved to the Institute for Social Research at University of Michigan).

The work of Lewin—along with other major contributors, such as Kenneth Benne, Leland Bradford, and Ronald Lippitt—was also instrumental toward initiating the National Training Laboratories (NTL) (Hirsch, 1987). In this setting, managers received short-term, intense learning experiences focused on interpersonal relations. This represented an important advancement in team history; NTL led to t-groups, which led to sensitivity groups. There was some backlash against sensitivity training and t-groups in the 1970s that may have created a reactionary attitude toward use of teams as being too "touchy-feely" for business use. NTL activities (along with influences from WWII Special Forces training in the military) might also be considered a basis for much of the experiential learning and outdoor education that many businesses enthusiastically endorse.

Although Lewin is referred to as the father of social psychology, his colleagues Lippitt and White, as well as contributors named above and others, were all part of a large movement to recognize the importance of group activity in organizations. Authors have dated origins of the entire field of organizational behavior to this same time frame and cluster of research activity (Lorsch, 1987), citing the first doctoral degree, the first required M.B.A.-level Course, and the first textbook all in the 1940s. This decade was the foundation of the organization development movement.

Sociologists viewed this increased attention to small groups as a revival of interest rather than something new, but they also recognized it as one of the "chief growing points in the systematic study of the behavior of men in society" (Merton, 1950). Homans (1950) undertook the task of integrating five previous studies of groups in organizations, with the intent of summarizing the work into basic elements for continuing research. His book, *The Human Group*, is considered to have established the paradigm for analyzing group behavior in organizations (Lorsch, 1987).

One factor that seems to have changed from earlier sociological research on small groups was the expanding base of business organizations as a context in which to study group activities. Not all researchers chose to focus their work in the business setting, but for others the industrial application was a new opportunity with increasing relevance. Still, most of the work in the 1930s and 1940s would today be classified as the study of general interaction among work groups—cooperative effort or teamwork but not of true teams. More closely resembling the self-managed work teams of today were the coal mining teams in England in the early 1940s (Trist, E. L., Higgin, G. W., Murray, H. Pollock, A. G., 1963; Trist & Bamforth, 1951). The coal mining teams were responsible for the whole task, they made the decisions for who would work on a particular shift or do a particular job within the team, and they were paid on a group bonus.

We look to the work of Trist, Emery, and others affiliated with the Tavistock Institute for many enduring ideas about teams and organizations. They conceptualized the organization as an "open system," a concept from Von Bertalanffy's (1950) work in the 1930s and 1940s in biology which has now been utilized by organization theorists and organization development practitioners for five decades. The premise is simple: any system (biological or business organization) must continually interact across boundaries with its environment to obtain inputs and to discharge outputs. The Tavistock researchers also developed the concept of working groups as socio-technical systems. The name derives from combining social considerations with technological constraints. The technology places limits on work potential, but the work group is more than that. The social and psychological properties of the team are interdependent with the technology--influenced by the context it is embedded in. Much as Einstein created the concept for a unified space-time, Trist and Emery created a socio-technical unified perspective for viewing the work place. Neither aspect alone is sufficient for optimizing the operations of the total system, the aim is for joint optimization which must also have economic validity.

To some extent, the history of work teams is the history of socio-technical systems theory (STS) and the history of STS is the history of Trist's and Emery's work and influence. Others contributed in important ways to the development of STS in general and within specific geographical regions, such as Thorsrud in Norway, Emery in Australia, de Sitter in Holland, Rice in India, Herbst in Sweden, and Cherns and Davis in the U.S.A. (see anthologies, e.g., Emery, 1978; Trist & Murray, 1990; Trist, Emery, & Murray, 1997; Trist, Murray & Trist, 1993).

In continuing work, Trist found that a number of variations were possible within the same technological and economic constraints. Each resulting system of work organization generated different social and psychological outcomes. The 1963 book, entitled *Organizational Choice* (Trist, Higgin, Murray, & Pollock, 1963), summarized the conclusions from this stream of work. It further addressed such topics as mutual learning, self-regulation, and team/management relations—issues that remain at the forefront in today's organizations attempting to change to a team-based structure. Trist and the Tavistock group "illuminated the dynamic nature of organizations and their functioning, the crucial importance of boundary management, and the need for a new approach to organization design" (Pugh &

Hickson, 1989) and presented a convincing case for the self-management potential of work teams.

Whereas, Trist's work in the 1950s most closely relates to today's organizational teams, other researchers pursued specific topics that added to the cumulative knowledge about groups and group processes. Bales (1950a; 1950b) examined role differentiation in a variety of problem solving groups and developed a method for behavior unit analysis, and with Strodtbeck (Bales & Strodtbeck, 1951), further examined group process in decision making as having identifiable phases. Bales further developed the group behavior system into Symlog, a method currently used by consultants to work with groups in business. Asch (1951) and Festinger (1954; Festinger, Schachter & Back, 1950) continued research on the influence on individuals to conform to group standards and expectations, including the concept of cohesion, the pressure/desire to remain part of the group. In 1959, Thibaut and Kelley's book, *The Social Psychology of Groups*, provided a consolidated resource for information about group member relations, including a chapter on group goal setting.

A major focus of attention on groups and teams in both research and practice has been structure. All writers seem to agree that structure for teams changes over time. Different theoretical perspectives have debated how it changes and why. One of the most enduring references used in organizational team building is Tuckman's (1965) developmental stages, commonly known by the rhyming catch phrase: forming, storming, norming and performing. The appeal of current day teams may be a degree of comfort gained through knowing that a stage of conflict (storming) is considered normal and a necessary part of the process for becoming an effective team. An important consideration is that each of the four stages involves both task and interpersonal activity. Tuckman's theory was originally based on extensive review of therapy group activity, and later applied to training groups and groups observed in natural settings. His terms for the four stages (later he added a fifth stage—Tuckman & Jensen, 1977) dominate discussion and training design in industry to this day.

However, alternative frameworks for team development exist that may have significant value for understanding group functioning, including Bales' identification of 12 categories of interaction (1950b); Bennis and Shepard's (1956) two phase model, Bion's (1961) focus on emotionality (Bion was one of the founders of the Tavistock Institute), and Gersick's (1988, 1989, 1991) more recent punctuated equilibrium model which includes elements of chaos theory. Bales' (1950b) work expanded greatly on the category system that preceded it in 1948 which simply classified group member contributions as "who talks to whom" by adding "about what." A number of other category systems elaborated on Bales' in subsequent years, including Hill's interaction matrix (Hill, 1977). Gersick's approach probably represents the next conceptual stage that developmental frameworks will take, however, its sophistication may slow down adoption in practice.

The decade of the 1960s generated a variety of work specific to the environment of business organizations and had implications at the team level. Katz and Kahn wrote their book, *The Social Psychology of Organizations* (1966), to depart from the text tradition of limiting the focus to individuals with only brief introduction to small group experiments. They felt that dealing with social-structural problems required development of new conceptual tools, and this could be accomplished through better integration with the more macro disciplines. Their book was a unique consolidation of systems thinking—again emphasizing the open systems approach—with role theory. It became a standard on the bookshelves of organizational researchers. The broader perspective on the context in which work groups must operate was a valuable addition to understanding team functioning in organizations.

Thompson (1967) explained interdependence in organizations as taking on one of three forms: pooled, sequential, or reciprocal. In pooled interdependence, the contributors are not directly linked to each other, but the total system relies on outputs from each as integral parts of the final whole. Sequential interdependence exists when each stage of a process depends on successful completion of the one before—a typical assembly line set-up. Reciprocal interdependence exists when each contributor both supplies output to and utilizes input from the other, and this type requires the closest coordination. Discussion of types of interdependence seems like a simple tool, yet it continues to be useful in helping organizations define whether (or what types of) teams will benefit operations in a business (e.g., Saavedra & Kwum, 1993).

One of the espoused benefits of teams, especially self-managed or self-directed teams, is the empowerment of employees to make decisions and apply their knowledge and judgement to day-to-day operations. This saves time, places decisions in the hands of the people who know the work best, and provides a more personally rewarding work situation for the employees. This is an extension of the condition that Likert (1967) described as System 4—Participative Group Management. In Likert's conceptualization, an organization chart based on System 4 would be a series of overlapping decision-making groups, connected by individuals called linking pins who are members of more than one group. This horizontal linking is reminiscent of Follett's non-hierarchical committees and similar to the structure in many of today's team-based organizations.

Contributions to understanding group process continued from social psychology. For example, Steiner (1972, 1974) described the benefit of increasing resources through adding group members. However, process loss occurs when adding members and also increases the need for energy directed toward motivation and coordination, sometimes offsetting any gain through added resources. Steiner also developed a typology of tasks (maximizing versus optimizing, additive, disjunctive, conjunctive, discretionary, etc.), which prescribes the process that must be employed for each type to achieve success.

Team builders today recognize that groups do generate pressures to conform, and this pressure may hinder critical analysis and a healthy exchange of ideas. The awareness of this potential for over-cohesiveness is largely due to the work of Janis (1972; Janis & Mann, 1977), who labeled it "Groupthink." In an effort to maintain the unity of the group, members begin to self-censor and ignore information from outsiders they've come to view as weak, evil, or stupid. The team members know their own intentions are good and they usually agree, so why waste time with unnecessary debate? Janis exemplified this phenomenon through discussion of well-known decision fiascoes, such as the Bay of Pigs invasion, the U.S. failure to be prepared for the attack on Pearl Harbor, the Korean War stalemate and the escalation of the Vietnam War. This perspective supplied a context in which people could appreciate the dangers of Groupthink, and the term continues as a shorthand reference for the lack of healthy conflict in team decision-making.

Reconsidering the Person on the Team: Identity and Self-interest

Significant work by Hackman and Oldham (1975, 1976, 1980; Oldham, Hackman, & Pearce, 1976) proposed a plan for job enrichment based on creation of critical psychological states that stem from core job dimensions (skill variety, task identity, task significance, autonomy, and feedback). These psychological states then lead to personal and work outcomes of higher motivation, performance, quality and satisfaction, as well as reduced absenteeism and turnover. Their model was not presented in a team format; it is primarily applied to individual job analysis and re-design. The core job dimensions for individual job enrichment are accomplished through re-structuring to teams that are responsible for work modules rather than repetitive individual functions. Movement toward self-managing teams further increases these dimensions as decision making, power, information, and rewards are pushed down in the organization to those who do the work (Lawler, 1988).

Establishing teams is not the answer in every setting. Having teams is not the only solution. It is one that supplies certain benefits when it is appropriate to the work situation, and appropriateness is typically determined by a close look at the interdependencies required to get the job done. Many jobs are not that interdependent. In sum, work done in the 1970s on job enrichment—exemplified here by Hackman and Oldham's research—is valuable in explaining why use of teams can be beneficial and in providing a perspective on individual work options for those situations in which teams are not the right answer. Many organizations in the 1990s still struggle with the distinction between employee involvement (EI) and teams. By viewing EI as the larger issue, the use of work teams becomes one option to consider. Yet it is an option that involves crucial structural changes in order to succeed. When those changes cannot be adequately supported, individual job enrichment offers another means of employee empowerment and involvement.

When a person is part of a successful team, he or she may begin to experience strong personal attachment to the group. In fact, group membership can become a very important aspect of personal identity. This also leads to the belief that "everyone in my group is like me and everyone not in my group is not like me" (and therefore suspect). The work by Tajfel (1978, 1982) described the impact this has on intergroup relations. Conflicts may arise due to over-identification with the team, to the detriment of organizational objectives. The concerns raised by Tajfel's research are pertinent to work teams today. Although team building activities often encourage identification with the immediate team, this should be accompanied by interactions that reinforce the super-ordinate goals of the larger organization and the role played by all teams in achieving those goals.

Individual self-perception comes into play within the team, as well. In any work group, there is the concern of whether work is being distributed equitably. The term social loafing (Latane, Williams & Harkins, 1979) refers to the tendency for a person to put forth less effort when working with others than when working alone, similar to the Ringelmann effect discussed earlier. One study suggested that social loafing was due to the belief that individual performance was not visible, so there would be no blame or credit for their effort (Williams, Harkins & Latane, 1981). Subsequent work identified the tendency for less able members to leave certain tasks to others, having a "free-rider" effect (Kerr & Bruun, 1983). More capable members, not wanting to fall prey to the "sucker effect" (Kerr, 1983), may also put forth less effort. These are occurrences that most team members have either seen or taken part in at some time in their work experience. Later research found that, when the work was personally involving—resulted in a definite use of some value to the participants—subjects' output was equally high, whether their performance was individually monitored or not (Brickner, Harkins & Ostrom, 1986). Whereas the initial studies identified and labeled the problem, the more recent articles went farther in addressing how to avoid or remedy it, suggesting the importance of cross-training and providing the opportunity for personal involvement in the work.

The idea of work teams is deeply embedded in the broader terminology of participative work design and work place democracy, which has been linked to quality of working life (QWL) (e.g., Walton, 1977). Weisbord (1987) refocused attention to QWL in the 1980s, by comparing current attempts such as self-managing teams to the management practices 20 years earlier. His conclusions were fairly optimistic on the potential for positive change, depending on a willingness to truly invest oneself. He also comments that use of self-managing work teams is the simplest process for improving QWL, as the teams rely on their own energy and expertise, a freely available resource. For organizations interested in improving QWL, Weisbord viewed self-managed teams is a low cost option with a broad range of potential benefits.

By the early 1980s we had heard quite a bit about Japanese management, including extensive use of teams, and the ongoing debate over how applicable it was in U.S. industry. Ouchi (1981) tried to reconcile the need for collaboration with the U.S. individualist traditions, in what he referred to as Theory Z. Differentiating from either hierarchies or markets as the basis for organization, Ouchi wrote about clans—associations of people engaged in economic activity but tied together through a variety of bonds. The individuals in clans are part of a strong culture, in which they are each, effectively, told to do exactly what they want to do. They work toward common achievement, not as a selfless act but, rather, because it serves selfish ends.

Participation with Quality Emphasis: Benchmarking and Continuous Improvement

The specifics of Ouchi's theory are not as important as the reminder he put forth. Business in one country cannot succeed by simply importing methods that have worked in another culture. Those ideas must be blended with local values and customs. One of the Japanese methods commonly adapted for use in the U.S. was Quality Circles. Some of the earliest experiments occurred in the 1970s, at companies like Smith Kline, Lockheed, and Northrop (Patchin, 1983), but the movement to this method became more pervasive in the early to mid-1980s. Along with efforts to effectively express the originating concept for this type of worker participation, writers gave accompanying attention to the question of how to adapt it for optimal use in the U.S. (Thompson, 1982).

By the early 1990s, many companies were involved in some type of quality initiatives under a variety of names, such as Total Quality Management (TQM) or Continuous Quality Improvement (CQI). A flood of books hit the market explaining the basic premise of quality management (Pegels, 1995) as well as how to integrate this perspective into the organization (Dean & Evans, 1994; Pierce, 1991). Not all organizations were successful with this approach. For example, Daniels (1994) reviews a study by Ernst & Young of 584 companies. Those results—across industries as varied as auto, computer, banking, and health care—revealed a wide range of failures in quality improvement activities. One aspect that is considered vital to success of quality initiatives is commitment by the organization's leadership, a separate focus discussed in the next section.

The idea of benchmarking, comparing to others who are exemplary in the desired activity, grew in popularity during this time frame. Books published in the early 1990s provided a first step in this process by providing descriptions of successful team activity in organizations. Bernstein (1992) outlined the learning process at Volvo, one of the organizations best known for using socio-technical systems and work teams, work which actually began prior to 1970 (see Nilsson's chapter on Volvo in this book). Kimball Fisher (1993) wrote about his experiences working at Proctor & Gamble in the 1970s. Orsburn, Moran, Musselwhite and Zenger (1990), one of the first successful how-to books on team implementation, reviewed a number of companies that began utilizing teams in the 1970s and 1980s. These include such leading-edge organizations as Cummins Engine, Xerox, Texas Instruments, Ford, Tektronix, and GE.

While information on the success of these companies may sometimes serve as inspiration to *start* using teams, it doesn't take long for most organizations to realize that *maintaining* effective work teams is an equally daunting task. The concept of continuous improvement prescribes that even good teams should be looking for ways to get better. Hackman (1990) provided broad-based advice covering task competence, group structure, and the organizational context (including leadership) for team success. Hackman also dealt with the difficult topic of team effectiveness, which is not always found in the form of neat, reliable performance measures. He considers effectiveness as a three dimensional concept including: productive output, the degree to which process enhances future interdependent work by the group, and the contribution of the group experience to growth and personal well-being of team members.

Shea and Guzzo (1987) also considered effectiveness and outlined another approach to how and why teams are successful. According to their model, whether a team achieves their goals is a function of three factors: task interdependence (amount of task-driven interaction among members), outcome interdependence (shared consequences), and potency (the collective belief of a group that it can be effective). These factors are, again, issues at the organization level.

Moving to the individual level, Stevens and Campion (1994; see also Campion, Papper & Medsker, 1996) and Salas and his colleagues (e.g., Brannick, Salas, & Prince, 1997; Guzzo & Salas, 1995;) identified the necessary individual knowledge, skills and abilities (KSAs) that relate to team effectiveness. These KSAs encompass interpersonal skills such as conflict resolution, collaborative problem solving and communication, as well as self-management factors of goal-setting and performance management, and planning and task coordination. Knowing the KSAs related to teamwork (as separate from personality traits and technical skills) enables organizations to add an important dimension to their team member selection and development processes.

Leadership in Team Organizations

In the above discussion of quality and continuous improvement, there were repeated references to the importance of leadership. We return to that topic here, under its own heading, because authors have given it priority as a separate branch of interest. Hackman and Walton (1986) wrote about leadership of groups as a focus needing attention separate from the vast array of existing leadership information. Nearly ten years later, Fortune magazine reiterated that leadership in a team environment places new demands on those individuals, and they have not typically been provided with the tools to respond adequately (Caminiti, 1995).

Some of the leadership responsibilities have been absorbed within the teams, creating a substitute for traditional leadership. This process of SuperLeadership and self-management has been well documented by Manz and Sims (Manz, 1986; Manz & Sims 1980, 1987, 1993). Teams are advised to develop skills in goal setting, self-monitoring, and self-correction (including rewards and re-direction)—functions previously reserved for supervisors and managers. Doing so successfully, however, puts different pressure on organizational leadership to provide guidance. In the past, leaders controlled the work through those activities now handled within the team. Now leaders must focus on communicating a very clear and realistic vision of the organization's direction to ensure everyone is working toward common objectives.

General advice for individuals interested in management careers echoes many of the themes prescribed for teams and team leadership. Although starting with a technical specialty, the managers of the future must also learn to be cross-functional, self-managing and proficient in collaborative skills and to express personal traits of flexibility, integrity, and trustworthiness (Allred, Snow & Miles, 1996). In other words, as more organizations shift from traditional hierarchies toward the currently popular network form, future managers will have to be good team members to be successful.

Competitive Advantage: Re-instituting the Link to Organizational Strategy

Competitive advantage emerges when a company innovates to increase organizational effectiveness; process and product innovations create distinctive competencies or critical capabilities, those things a company can do well and that competitors cannot easily copy. When the means are more widely adopted, they become business requirements for staying in the game, but do not add increments of competitive advantage. "Capabilities like these are resident in the company's people and are supported by its procedures, culture, and infrastructure" (Bartmess & Cerny, 1993, p. 5). In defining critical capabilities, there is as much emphasis on how individuals have learned to work together as on any other particular expertise.

Some authors have similarly written about core competencies (eg., Hamel & Prahalad, 1994). As a result of all the "benchmarking" and identification of "best practices" people gained a certain amount of knowledge about what others were doing. This led to questioning how the firm could go beyond replication and differentiate in ways to create competitive advantage. Organizations began to focus on their core competencies and reached similar conclusions about the importance of the human resources (Cappelli & Crocker-Hefter, 1996). From a resource-based view of the firm, competencies and competition seem inextricably linked, although it may not be clear which is the initial influence on the other (Barney & Zajac, 1994).

Some of the means to improved effectiveness that have spread to the point of becoming commonplace include quality management and low cost activities, including offshore manufacturing and assembly and software design. Those means that continue to provide a distinctive competence include the learning organization, lean manufacturing, customer service, and work teams. "Everybody uses work teams" may be a familiar phrase. Clearly, the use of "teams" has spread across sectors, industries, companies, and levels. However, competitive advantage from teams goes far beyond a mere presence; it demands correct practice.

Cost cutting was a distinctive strategy at one time. Our typical, immediate response to increased competition was a cost-cutting frenzy. No doubt there was fat to be trimmed in many cases, but cost-cutting can only bring the company to an even footing with those who are already efficient; any advantage beyond that is likely to be temporary. The methods to accomplish lower cost are easily replicated by others in a short time, so the efficiencies from this strategy quickly lost their distinctive quality.

Most of this cost-cutting tendency was driven by the attempt to boost stock prices in the short term. Downsizing was a cost cutting strategy driven by the business process reengineering (BPR) movement started in the 1980s by Hammer and his colleagues (e.g., Hammer, 1996; Hammer & Champy, 1993). Unfortunately, much of the pain that came about through down-sizings and reorganizations can also be traced to the fact that BPR did not take the people into account that were required to make organizational change successful (Wickens, 1997).

Discussion of critical capabilities and core competencies typically is not initiated from a team perspective. However, it brings the employees and how they work together to the forefront of the discussion and is very compatible with other readings on effectiveness achieved through work teams. Pfeffer (1994, 1995) elaborates on the potential for competitive advantage through effective people management, including the themes of participation and empowerment, plus additional discussion of self-managed teams. Use of teams is no longer relegated to an operating decision, several steps removed from the strategic decisions of the firm. It is now a structural consideration, with implications for employee involvement and competitive advantage that should be considered throughout strategy formation (e.g., Katzenback & Smith, 1993; Lawler, 1992).

The global business environment means an increasing reliance on work teams that are multicultural, whether through employees of many cultures now working in the same location or creation of teams that span national boundaries. Multiculturalism combines with the increase in the numbers of women and U.S. born minorities in the workforce to create great diversity. The diverse membership of the teams increases the resources needed for innovation. Recent work focusing on diversity in the work place, and specifically in work teams, has offered significant information to help companies deal with increasing globalization (e.g., Jackson &

Associates, 1992; Jackson & Ruderman, 1995; Ruderman, Hughes-James & Jackson, 1996).

Technology, Distance & Time

Quality is no longer the primary driving force in organizations. Its importance has not diminished; it has become a fundamental business requirement without which an organization cannot hope to compete--part of the fabric of every major organization. A more recent emphasis is fast-response capability--the ability to use time as a source of competitive advantage. It is not enough to be responsive to the customer; the response must be faster and better than others. It is not enough to correct problems; the correction must be executed at the point in time when the problem first occurs—even better, before it occurs by anticipating that potential. Workers have an increased awareness of time, as well as the capability to do things faster, primarily due to technological advances, and increasingly by organizational design changes that eliminate barriers to communication and workflow.

Teams of people working together are cognizant of time and its implications for successful task completion. In a classic study, Gersick (1989) found that task teams used time markers (most notably the halfway point) to signal opportunities for change—to adjust their agenda or take a fresh approach to the project. She first observed this in an organization, and, subsequently, conducted lab studies on eight additional groups. The teams' attention to time and pacing was a very different transition than the phases or stages of group development cited in earlier research. This could be due to the difference between a short-term task team and work teams that have prolonged interaction, such as self-managing production teams. No recent studies have looked at the same question in rapid technology-based organizations, to compare whatever difference may exist as deadlines become more and more compressed in time.

Technology has made it possible to generate, store, access, share, and communicate information at higher speeds. This forces time compression and results in many activities being done in "real time." For example, ATM and debit card transactions immediately impact ones bank account; the float that was available when writing checks is not available when using plastic. Technology also allows a shrinking of the world, so distributed team members can work together. Increasingly, geographic teams of experts are formed for projects but they may rarely, if ever, meet face to face even though they are able to interact instantaneously. The intellectual interdependencies of their work can be realized, in spite of geographical dispersion. Mankin, Cohen and Bikson (1996) refer to the "new organization" as being one that is team-based and technology-enabled. In contrast to earlier how-to books that took the reader through steps of team implementation alone, these authors consider the change to teams and technology as one integrated process. Their desired end state is an organization without the traditional "boundaries and constraints limiting on how, where, when and with whom we work" (p. 241).

Teams utilizing an array of interactive technologies to cross time and space boundaries are now commonly referred to as "virtual teams." According to Lipnack and Stamps (1997), face-to-face collaboration only occurs easily among people who are located less than 50 feet apart in their work space. Most of us have experienced the difficulties of having a job outcome depend on the contribution of someone who works a different shift, has an office in a different building, or is located in another city. Technology brings this all together, and recent advances in technology are revolutionizing our options. Many of the same skills are required for working in a virtual team as with any other team. In addition, virtual team members may need to have somewhat higher than usual tolerance for the unexpected. We do not yet have an established body of experience on which to base expectations. Organizations currently working with virtual teams are leading the way in this discovery process.

Other Perspectives

This overview began with the admission that any combination of authors would select slightly different readings as key to tracking a history of teams. In the last 20 years, a number of collected writings have appeared which offer a great resource to researchers and managers (examples include special issues of journals, such as the 1979 *Journal of Applied Behavioral Science* issue on small groups and Bettenhausen's review of group literature in 1991; a number of annual series exist that focus on groups and teams, including, Berkowitz's, *Advances in Experimental Social Psychology*, 1973-present; Beyerlein, Johnson, & Beyerlein, *Advances in the Interdisciplinary Study of Work Teams*, 1994-present; Lawler, *Advances in Group Processes*, 1984-present; and new reviews and special issues are appearing, such as the special issue in *Engineering Management Journal* in the fall of 1999, the review article by Cohen & Bailey, in *Journal of Management*, in 1997, the review by Moldaschl and Weber in 1998, and the review of 20 years of empirical studies of team effectiveness by Sundstrom and others scheduled to appear in a special issue at the beginning of 2000 in *Group & Management Studies*). The annual series listed here are not included in our timeline, because they are not a single focus reference. Yet, they are important to mention as part of the evidence of growing attention to teams in recent time.

When the Center for Study of Work Teams first began holding conferences (1990), we subsumed the entire realm of work teams under the name "self-managed work teams." In a 1992 survey, we found 18 different names for what companies were doing, and knowledge about different types of teams is still growing. Historically, there is a similar tendency to focus on the foundations of socio-technical theory (STS), which evolved from the study of production teams (sometimes called manufacturing teams). The theory became a standard for implementing work teams of all types, but recent researchers (e.g., Mohrman, Cohen, & Mohrman, 1995; Pava, 1984; Purser & Pasmore, 1992) have shown that the production model does not fit teams doing creative knowledge work. This is just one of many examples of another branching out of interest that could be included in our timeline. It will gradually become easier to select the important work of the 1980s and 1990s by what endures over time. For now, the rich selection is difficult to prioritize.

Implementing work teams requires changes in both the structure of the organization and the empowerment of the employees. Both of these topics represent large bodies of literature that we might have also chosen to highlight in this chapter. The work of Miles and Snow (e.g., Miles & Snow, 1992, 1994, 1995) over the years has presented on the evolution of organizational forms from functional to divisional to matrix types and consistently revealed new forms of organizations that rely on collaboration and empowerment, such as network and cellular structures. The empowerment literature has earlier roots in the literature on participative decision making and the literature on employee involvement.

Another approach might have been the progression in examining team effectiveness. One approach to that literature would be to focus on why teams fail (e.g., Hackman, 1990; Hall, 1998; Hitchcock &Willard, 1995; Robbins & Finley, 1995; Sundstrom, 1998). Another approach could focus on performance (e.g., Cohen & Bailey, 1997; Guzzo & Salas, 1995; Sundstrom et al., in press). Katz and Kahn (1966/1978) told us the importance of context but we had to re-discover it in relation to effectiveness of teams.

Our tracking is typical of most in its emphasis on U.S and Western European activity. Fortunately, other contributions in this same volume correct that deficit somewhat by offering views from other parts of the world that are necessary supplements to our information

In this chapter, our intention was to provide a brief overview of the development of work team theory and practice. The overview provides a framework for readers with a limited knowledge of that history in order to aid in their integration of the other, more focused chapters in this book. Those chapters focus on specific eras, people, countries, and work sites. Their in-depth coverage fleshes out the skeleton assembled in the opening chapter. The history of work teams is panoramic--it covers an extensive terrain of ideas and practical experiments. Knowing that history will help us understand current practices more deeply--we can build on the past, rather than reinventing it. A deep understanding and appreciation for the rich and valued groundwork laid by the contributors included in this volume and others will enable practitioners to continue to build collaborative work structures that improve the financial, social, and human outcomes of organizations in the 21st century.

References

Allport, F. H. (1924). *Social Psychology*. Boston: Houghton Mifflin.

Allred, B. B., Snow, C. C. & Miles R. E. (1996). Characteristics of managerial careers in the 21st century. *Academy of Management Executive, 10*(4), 17-27.

Asch, S. (1951). Effects of group pressure upon the modification and distortion of judgements. In. H. Guetzkow (Ed.), *Groups, Leadership, and Men*. Pittsburgh: Carnegie Press.

Bales, R. F. (1950a). A set of categories for the analysis of small group interaction. *American Sociological Review, 15*, 257-263.

Bales, R. F. (1950b). *Interaction Process Analysis: A Method for the study of Small Groups*. Cambridge, MA: Addison-Wesley.

Bales, R. F. & Strodtbeck, F. L. (1951). Phases in Group Problem-Solving. *The Journal of Abnormal and Social Psychology, 46*, 485-495.

Barney, J. B. & Zajac, E. J. (1994). Competitive organizational behavior: Toward an organizationally-based theory of competitive advantage. *Strategic Management Journal, 15*, 5-9.

Bartmess, A. & Cerny, K. (1993). Building competitive advantage through a global network of capabilities. *California Management Review, 35(2)*, 2-27.

Bennis, W. G., & Shepard, H. A. (1956). A theory of group development. *Human Relations, 9*, 415-437.

Berkowitz, L. (1967-present). *Advances in experimental social psychology* (32 volumes). New York: Academic Press.

Bernstein, P. (1992). The learning curve at Volvo. In R. Glaser (Ed.), *Classic Readings in Self-Managing Teamwork*. King of Prussia, PA: Organization Design and Development.

Bettenhausen, K. L. (1991). Five years of group research: What we have learned and what needs to be addressed. *Journal of Management, 17(2)*, 345-381.

Beyerlein, M. M., Johnson, D. A., & Beyerlein, S. T. (1994-present). *Advances in the interdisciplinary study of work teams* (six volumes). Greenwich, CT: JAI Press.

Bion, W. R. (1961). *Experiences in groups*. New York: Basic Books.

Brannick, M. T., Salas, E., & Prince, C. (Eds.) (1997). *Team performance assessment and measurement: Theory, methods, and applications*. Lawrence Erlbaum Associates.

Brickner, M. A., Harkins, S. G. & Ostrom, T. M. (1986). Effects of personal involvement: Thought-provoking implications for social loafing. *Journal of Personality and Social Psychology, 51(4)*, 763-769.

Caminiti, S. (1995, February 20). What Team Leaders Need to Know. *Fortune*, 93-100.

Campion, M. A., Papper, E. M. & Medsker, G. J. (1996). Relations between work team characteristics and effectiveness: A replication and extension. *Personnel Psychology, 49*, 429-452.

Cappelli, P. & Crocker-Hefter, A. (1996, Winter). Distinctive human resources are firms' core competencies. *Organizational Dynamics, 24(3)*, 7-22.

Cartwright, D. & Zander, A. (1953). *Group Dynamics: Research and Theory*. New York: Harper & Row.

Cohen, S. G., & Bailey, D. (1997). What makes teams work: Group effectiveness research from the shop floor to the executive suite. *Journal of Management, 23*, 239-290.

Daniels, A. C. (1994). *Bringing Out the Best in People*. New York: McGraw-Hill.

Dean, J. W. Jr. & Evans, J. R. (1994). *Total Quality Management, Organization, and Strategy*. Minneapolis: West.

Durkheim, E. (1895/1982). *Rules of Sociological Method*. New York: Free Press.

Emery, F. E. (1959/1978). *The emergence of a new paradigm of work*. Canberra, Australia: Center for Continuing Education, Australian National University.

Emery, F. E., & Trist, E. L. (1965). The causal texture of organizational environments. *Human Relations, 18*, 21-32.

Emery, F. E. & Trist, E. L. (1969). Socio-technical systems. In F. E. Emery (Ed.) *Systems Thinking*. New York: Penguin.

Festinger, L. A. (1954). A theory of social comparison. *Human Relations, 7*, 117-140.

Festinger, L. A., Schachter, S. & Back, K. (1950). *Social Pressures in Informal Groups*. New York: Harper.

Fisher, K. (1993). *Leading Self-Directed Work Teams: A Guide to Developing New Team Leadership Skills*. New York: McGraw-Hill.

Gersick, C. J. (1988). Time and transition in work teams: Toward a new model of group development. *Academy of Management Journal, 31*, 9-41.

Gersick, C. J. (1989). Marking time: Predictable transitions in task groups. *Academy of Management Journal, 32(2)*, 274-309.

Gersick, C. J. (1991). Revolutionary change theories: A multilevel exploration of the punctuated equilibrium paradigm. *Academy of Management Review, 16*, 10-36.

Graham, P. (Ed.). (1995). *Mary Parker Follett—Prophet of Management: A Celebration of Writings from the 1920s*. Boston: Harvard Business School Press.

Guzzo, R. A., & Salas, E. (1995). *Team effectiveness and decision making in organizations*. San Francisco: Jossey-Bass.

Hackman, J. R. (Ed.). (1990). *Groups that Work (and Those That Don't): Creating Conditions for Effective Teamwork.* San Francisco: Jossey-Bass.

Hackman, J. R., & Lawler, E. E., III (1971). Employee reactions to job characteristics. *Journal of Applied Psychology Monograph, 55*, 259-286.

Hackman, J. R., & Oldham, G. R. (1975). Development of the Job Diagnostic Survey. *Journal of Applied Psychology, 60*, 159-170.

Hackman, J. R., & Oldham, G. R. (1976). Motivation through the design of work: A test of a theory. *Organizational Behavior and Human Performance. 16*, 250-279.

Hackman, J. R., & Oldham, G. R., (1980). *Work redesign.* Reading, MA: Addison-Wesley.

Hackman, J. R., Oldham, G. R., & Pearce, J. L. (1976). Conditions under which employees respond positively to enriched work. *Journal of Applied Psychology, 61*, 395-403.

Hackman, J. R. & Walton, R. E. (1986). Leading Groups in Organizations. In Goodman & Associates, *Designing Effective Workgroups.* San Francisco: Jossey-Bass.

Hall, C. (1998). *Organizational support systems for team-based organizations: Employee collaboration through organizational structures.* Dissertation, University of North Texas.

Hamel, G., & Prahalad, C. K. (1995). *Competing for the future.* Boston: Harvard Business School.

Hammer, M. (1996). *Beyond reengineering: How the process-centered organization is changing our work and our lives.* New York: Harper Business.

Hammer, M., & Champy, J. (1993). *Reengineering the corporation: A manifesto for business revolution.* New York: Harper Business.

Hill, W. F. (1977). Hill Interaction Matrix (HIM): The conceptual framework, derived rating scales, and an updated bibliography. *Small Group Behavior, 4*, 355-381.

Hirsch, J. I. (1987). *The History of the National Training Laboratories 1947-1986: Social Equality Through Education and Training.* New York: Peter Lang.

Hitchcock, D, & Willard, M. (1995). *Why teams can fail and what to do about it: Essential tools for anyone implementing self-directed work teams.* Burr Ridge, IL: Irwin Professional Publications.

Homans, G. C. (1950). *The Human Group.* New York: Harcourt, Brace & Co.

Ingham, A. G., Levinger, G., Graves, J. & Peckham, V. (1974). The Ringelmann effect: Studies of group size and group performance. *Journal of Experimental Social Psychology, 10*, 371-384.

Jackson, S. E. & Associates (Eds.). (1992). *Diversity in the Workplace: Human Resources Initiatives.* New York: Guilford Press.

Jackson, S. E. & Ruderman, M. N. (Eds.). (1995). *Diversity in Work Teams: Research Paradigms for a Changing Workplace.* Washington, DC: American Psychological Association.

Janis, I. (1972). *Victims of groupthink.* Boston: Houghton Mifflin.

Janis, I. & Mann, I. (1977). *Decision making: A psychological analysis of conflict, choice, and commitment.* New York: Free Press.

Johnson, D. W. & Johnson, F. P. (1994). *Joining Together: Group Theory and Group Skills.* Boston: Allyn and Bacon.

Katz, D. & Kahn, R. L. (1966/1978). *The Social Psychology of Organizations.* New York: Wiley & Sons.

Katzenback, J. R. & Smith, D. K. (1993). *The Wisdom of Teams: Creating the High-Performance Organization.* Boston: Harvard Business School Press.

Kerr, N. (1983). Motivation losses in small groups: A social dilemma analysis. *Journal of Personality and Social Psychology, 45(4)*, 819-828.

Kerr, N. & Bruun, S. (1983). The dispensability of member effort and group motivation losses: Free-rider effects. *Journal of Personality and Social Psychology, 44*, 78-94.
Kravitz, D. A. & Martin, B. (1986). Ringelmann rediscovered: The original article. *Journal of Personality and Social Psychology, 50(5)*, 936-941.
Latane, B., Williams, K. & Harkins, S. (1979). Many hands make light the work: The causes and consequences of social loafing. *Journal of Personality and Social Psychology, 37*, 822-832.
Lawler, E. E., III (1984-present). *Advances in group processes* (16 volumes). Greenwich, CT: JAI Press.
Lawler, E. E., III (1988). *High involvement management*. San Francisco: Jossey-Bass.
Lawler, E. E., III (1992). *The Ultimate Advantage: Creating the High-Involvement Organization*. San Francisco: Jossey-Bass.
Lawler, E. E., III, Mohrman, s. A., & Ledford, G. E. (1992). *Employee involvement and total quality management: Practices and results in Fortune 1000 companies*. San Francisco: Jossey-Bass.
Lewin, K. (1947). Frontiers in group dynamics: Concepts, method and reality in social science, social equilibrium and social change. *Human Relations, 1*, 5-41.
Lewin, K., Lippett, R., & White, R. (1939). Patterns of aggressive behavior in experimentally created social climates. *Journal of Social Psychology, 10*, 271-299.
Likert, R. (1967). *The Human Organization: Its Management and Value*. New York: McGraw-Hill.
Lipnack, J. & Stamps, J. (1997). *Virtual Teams: Reaching across Space, Time, and Organizations with Technology*.
Lorsch, J. W. (Ed). (1987). *Handbook of Organizational Behavior*. Englewood Cliffs, NJ: Prentice-Hall.
Mankin, D., Cohen, S. G., & Bikson, T. K. (1996). *Teams & technology: Fulfilling the promise of the new organization*. Boston: Harvard Business School Press.
Manz, C. C. (1986). Self-Leadership: Toward an expanded theory of self-influence processes in organizations. *Academy of Management Review, 11(3)*, 585-600.
Manz, C. C. & Sims, H. P. (1980). Self-management as a substitute for leadership: A social learning theory perspective. *Academy of Management Review, 5(3)*, 361-367.
Manz, C. C. & Sims, H. P. (1987). Leading workers to lead themselves: The external leadership of self-managing work teams. *Administrative Science Quarterly, 32*, 106-128.
Manz, C. C. & Sims, H. P. (1993). *Business without Bosses: How Self-Managing Teams are Building High-Performing Companies*. New York: Wiley.
Mayo, E. (1933). *The Human Problems of an Industrial Civilization*. New York: Macmillan.
Merton, R. K. (1950). Introduction. In G. C. Homans' *The Human Group*. New York: Harcourt, Brace & Co.
Miles, R. E., & Snow, C. C. (1994). *Fit, failure and the hall of fame*. New York: Free Press.
Mohrman, S. A., Cohen, S. G., & Mohrman, A. M., Jr. (1995). *Designing team-based organizations: New forms for knowledge work*. San Francisco: Jossey-Bass.
Moldaschl, M., & Weber, W. G. (1998). The "three waves" of industrial group work: Historical reflections on current research on group work. *Human Relations, 51*, 347-388.
Moscovici, S. (1985). Social Influence and Conformity. In G. Lindzey & E. Aronson (Eds.) *The Handbook of social Psychology*. New York: Random House.
Orsburn, J. D., Moran, L., Musselwhite, E., & Zenger, J. H. (1990). *Self-directed work teams: The new American challenge*. Homewood, IL: Business One Irwin.
Ouchi, W. G. (1981). *Theory Z: How American business can meet the Japanese challenge*. Reading, MA: Addison-Wesley.

Patchin, R. I. (1983). *The Management and Maintenance of Quality Circles*. Homewood, IL: Dow Jones-Irwin.

Pava, C. H. P. (1984). *Managing new office technology: An organizational strategy*. New York: Free Press.

Pegels, C. C. (1995). *Total Quality Management: A Survey of Its Important Aspects*. Danvers, MA: Boyd & Fraser.

Pfeffer, J. (1994). *Competitive Advantage through People*. Boston: *Harvard Business School Press*.

Pfeffer, J. (1995). Producing sustainable competitive advantage through the effective management of people. *Academy of Management Executive, 9(1),* 55-72.

Pierce, R. J. (Ed.). (1991). *Leadership, Perspective, and Restructuring for Total Quality*. Milwaukee: ASQC Quality Press.

Pugh, D. S. & Hickson, D. J. (1989). *Writers on Organizations*. Newbury Park: Sage.

Purser, R. E., & Pasmore, W. A. (1992). Organizing for learning: *Research in Organizational Change and Development, 6*, 37-113.

Robbins, H., & Finley, M. (1995). *Why teams don't work: What went wrong and how to make it right*. Princeton, NJ: Petersons Guides.

Roethlisberger, F. J. & Dickson, W. J. (1939/1967). *Management and the Worker: An account of research conducted by the Western Electric Company, Hawthorne Works*. Cambridge, MA: Harvard University Press.

Ruderman, M. N., Hughes-James, M. W. & Jackson, S. E. (Eds.). (1996). *Selected Research on Work Team Diversity*. Washing, DC: American Psychological Association; Greensboro, NC: Center for Creative Leadership.

Saavedra, R., & Kwum, S. K. (1993). Peer evaluation in self-managing work groups. *Journal of Applied Psychology, 78*, 450-462.

Shea, F. P. & Guzzo, R. A. (1987). Groups as human resources. *Research in Personnel and Human Resources Management, 5*, 323-356.

Sherif, M. (1935). A study of some social factors in perception. *Archives of Psychology, 27*(187), 321-339.

Steiner, I. (1972). *Group Process and Productivity*. New York: Academic Press.

Steiner, I. (1974). Whatever happened to the group in social psychology? *Journal of Experimental Psychology, 10*, 94-108.

Stevens, M. J. & Campion, M. A. (1994). The knowledge, skill, and ability requirements for teamwork: Implications for human resource management. *Journal of Management, 20(2),* 503-530.

Sundstrom, E., McIntyre, M., Halfhill, R., & Richards, H. (in press). Work groups: From the Hawthorne studies to work teams of the 1990s and beyond. *Group Dynamics: Theory, Research, and Practice*.

Tajfel, H. (1978). The achievement of group differentiation. In H. Tajfel (Ed.), *Differentiation between Social Groups: Studies in Social Psychology of Intergroup Relations*. London: Academic Press.

Tajfel, H. (1982) Instrumentality, identity and social comparison. In H. Tajfel (Ed.), *Social Identity and Intergroup Relations*. Cambridge, England: Cambridge University Press.

Thibaut, J. W. & Kelley, H. H. (1959). *The Social Psychology of Groups*. New York: John Wiley & Sons.

Thompson, J. D. (1967). *Organizations in action: Social science bases of administrative theory*. New York: McGraw-Hill.

Thompson, P. C. (1982). *Quality Circles: How to Make Them Work in America*. New York: Amacom.

Trist, E. L. (1981). The socio-technical perspective: The evolution of socio-technical systems as a conceptual framework and as an action research program. In A. H. Van de Ven & W. F. Joyce (Eds.), *Perspectives on organization design and behavior*, pp. 17-75. New York: John Wiley.

Trist, E. L. & Bamforth, K. W. (1951). Some social and psychological consequences of the Longwall method of coal getting. *Human Relations 14*, 3-38.

Trist, E. L., Higgin, G. W., Murray, H. Pollock, A. G. (1963). *Organizational Choice: Capabilities of Groups at the Coal Face Under Changing Conditions*. London: Tavistock.

Trist, E., Emery, F., & Murray, H. (1997). *The social engagement of social science: A Tavistock anthology, Vol. 3: The socio-ecological perspective*. Philadelphia, PA: University of Pennsylvania Press.

Trist, E., & Murray, H. (1990). *The social engagement of social science: A Tavistock anthology, Vol. 1: The socio-psychological perspective*. Free Association Books.

Trist, E., Murray, H., & Trist, B. (1993). *The social engagement of social science: A Tavistock anthology, Vol. 2: The socio-technical perspective*. Philadelphia, PA: University of Pennsylvania Press.

Tuckman, B. W. (1965) Developmental sequences in small groups. *Psychological Bulletin, 63(6)*, 384-399.

Tuckman, B. W., & Jensen, M. A. C. (1977). Stages in small group development revisited. *Group and Organization Studies, 2*, 419-427.

Von Bertalanffy, L. (1950). The theory of open systems in physics and biology. *Science, 3*, 22-29.

Walton, R. E. (1977). Work innovations at Topeka: After six years. *Journal of Applied Behavioral Science, 13*, 422-433.

Walton, R. E. (1985). From control to commitment in the workplace. *Harvard Business Review, 63(2)*, 76-84.

Weisbord, M.R. (1987). *Productive Workplaces: Organizing and Managing for Dignity, Meaning, and Community*. San Francisco: Jossey-Bass.

Wickens, P. (1997). Hammer's horror story is beyond redemption. *People Management, 3(6)*, 51.

Williams, K., Harkins, S.G. & Latane, B. (1981). Identifiability as a deterrent to social loafing: Two cheering experiments. *Journal of Personality and Social Psychology, 40*, 303-311.

Zajonc, R. B. (1965). Social facilitation. *Science, 149*, 269-274.

Chapter 2

Work Teams Research
Recent Findings and Future Trends

Stanley Gully
Rutgers University, Piscataway, New Jersey, United States

Abstract

Research relevant to work teams conducted since 1985 is reviewed with specific reference to whether or not it has addressed five key boundary conditions. These boundary conditions include sampling strategies, team contextual effects, organizational contextual effects, task and technology, and temporal influences. It is determined that strong progress in several areas of theory and research on work teams is being made but some areas still require increased attention. Directions for future theory and research are suggested.

Introduction

It has frequently been stated that small group or team research has been limited in its usefulness for understanding processes and outcomes relevant to teams in organizations (e.g., Collins, 1977; McGrath, 1986, 1991; Kozlowski, Gully, McHugh, Salas, & Cannon-Bowers, 1996). Criticisms of such research often focus on the artificiality of the lab setting, limitations in the types of variables studied, the abstractness of the concepts and theories used in such research, and the lack of generalizability of findings to the real world (McGrath, 1986, 1991; Driskell & Salas, 1992). Several authors have noted that such criticisms may be true and that some group or team research is indeed characterized by highly controlled and unique environments that are designed to provide tests of specific theories. However, they also note that is exactly the point of such research (Driskell & Salas, 1992). Research done in artificial or concocted settings is useful for building and testing theories and refining what we actually know about the behavior of individuals within social settings or team behavior as a whole; such research is an important part of the process of scientific inquiry (Ilgen, Major, Hollenbeck, & Sego, 1993; Mook, 1983; Driskell & Salas, 1992).

The problem is not that laboratory research isn't useful; it is a question of balance in the research enterprise. A disproportionate amount of research has been done with artificial groups in the laboratory, with little work done involving work teams in natural settings (Ilgen et al., 1993; McGrath, 1984). This is a problem because several limitations and boundary conditions prevent generalization from the research on small groups to work teams in organizations (Goodman, 1986; Ilgen et al., 1993;

M.M. Beyerlein (ed.), Work Teams: Past, Present and Future, 25–44.

McGrath, 1986). For example, organizational contexts, training, reward systems, technology, and other factors are likely to have important impacts on the performance of work teams over time (Sundstrom, De Meuse, & Futrell, 1990), and often these factors cannot be effectively studied in artificial settings.

At this point it is useful to consider what is meant by a "work team". Several researchers have distinguished between the small groups characteristic of early research and work teams in organizations (Brannick & Prince, 1997; Goodman, 1986; Ilgen et al., 1993; McGrath, 1984, 1986; Morgan, Glickman, Woodard, Blaiwes, & Salas, 1986; Salas, Dickinson, Converse, & Tannenbaum, 1992). Work teams can be distinguished from the small groups characteristic of early group research, because they produce, create, or do something that is meaningful to an organization (Argote & McGrath, 1993; Goodman, 1986), and they are not composed of strangers. Work teams can also be characterized as having a past, present, and future that affects their process and interaction in the organizational context (McGrath, 1984, 1991). In addition to the distinction made between small groups found in laboratory research and teams in organizations, researchers have suggested that groups and teams can be distinguished as existing on contrasting ends of a continuum of task interdependence (Kozlowski et al., forthcoming; Morgan et al., 1986; Salas et al., 1992). Groups are typically characterized by low role differentiation and low task interdependence, while teams are characterized by high role differentiation, distributed expertise, and high levels of task interdependence.

It should be noted, however, that many of these distinctions are arbitrary and much overlap exists among the various distinctions that have been made (Ilgen et al., 1993; McGrath, 1986; Salas et al., 1992). For the purpose of discussion, *work teams* are defined here as (1) three or more people; (2) who interact in some way; (3) to produce something, solve problems, or make decisions that are relevant to organizations; and (4) which have a past, present, and future. Additionally, work teams can be distinguished from groups or loose collections of people because they perform tasks requiring high amounts of interdependence, with separate roles and distributed expertise among team members (Kozlowski et al., forthcoming). Unfortunately, the literature has often used the terms "group" and "team" interchangeably, so research bearing both labels will be included in this chapter whenever appropriate, but terminology will be changed to be consistent with the discussion at hand. When the term "work group" is used, it will indicate social units with all the characteristics of a work team, but with an unspecified level of task interdependence.

Boundary Variables

The definition of work teams begins to highlight some of the boundary conditions that limit the applicability of small group research to enhancing our understanding of work teams in organizations. Boundary conditions are "those conditions in any particular research study that restrict or qualify the conclusions that can be drawn from that study" (Ilgen et al., 1993). By definition, boundary conditions are key variables that set limits on the generalizability of research results from one setting to another. For example, findings regarding jury decision making groups in laboratories may not be immediately applicable to coal mining teams. The purpose of this chapter will be to identify key boundary conditions and then use these boundary conditions to examine research since 1985 to determine if progress is being made in our understanding of work teams in organizations. Some general conclusions about the current state of knowledge about work teams will be drawn, and some suggestions for future research directions will be provided. The reader may notice that there is some overlap in the boundary conditions presented. For example, sampling strategy is not unrelated to considerations of group and organizational context, but distinguishing context from sample selection is still useful because natural work teams can come from a variety of organizational contexts, each with a different culture, training system, or reward system. Thus, although there is overlap between some of the boundary conditions, each is useful as a heuristic for evaluating progress in research on work teams.

The first boundary condition is one of *sampling strategy*. As previously noted, much of the small group research has been done with artificial tasks and with a limited sample of groups. Often such research has been done using undergraduates in universities, with few studies including intact teams from organizations. Continued reliance on the use of undergraduates as a sampling strategy runs the risk of developing a "science of the sophomore" such that we will learn a lot about how college students behave in artificial groups but we will have little knowledge applicable to understanding how actual work teams function. McGrath (1986) and Goodman (1986) suggested that not only is more research needed involving natural groups, but more research was needed on a variety of natural groups in organizations, including ad hoc committees, task forces, and standard work teams. Thus, sampling strategy is related to the second boundary condition, team context.

The second boundary condition refers to the *team as a context*. Research involving a wide variety of natural teams is important for learning how different team contexts can affect members. Different teams provide different embedding systems for its members. The team context can be affected by the demographic composition of members, team climate, norms, team size, and familiarity among members. The team context provides a pattern of social and physical stimuli that affect the behavior of members within that context (Hackman, 1992). Additionally, socialization and entrainment processes occur at least partially through the context of the group or team (Levine & Moreland, 1990; Moreland & Levine, 1988, 1992). Research on the team as a context will often focus on the individual within the team as the primary level of analysis (Roberts, Hulin, & Rousseau, 1978; Rousseau, 1985). The team context itself is engendered by the organizational context. The team context provides the stimuli that shape the behaviors of members within that unit, while the organizational context provides the stimuli that shape the way the team, as an aggregate, behaves.

Thus, the third boundary condition is *organizational context*. Sundstrom, De Meuse, and Futrell (1990) note that various aspects of the organization can affect work team process and performance, including organizational culture, clarity of team goals and missions, training and consultation, reward and recognition systems, and the physical environment in general. For this reason, a variety of work teams in different organizational contexts must be studied to determine how organizations affect intergroup relations, and team development, process, and performance. To conduct research on work teams in the organizational context, the team has to be treated as the primary level of analysis (Roberts, Hulin, & Rousseau, 1978;

Rousseau, 1985). Task design and technology can be considered a part of the organizational context for work teams (Sundstrom et al., 1990), but because these issues are so important, they will be treated as a separate boundary condition.

Task and technology, the fourth boundary variable, can have profound effects on work team process and how teams develop and perform (Tesluk, Mathieu, Zaccaro, & Marks, 1997). Technology is a program or set of operating rules, heuristics, and criteria for transforming an object or product from one state to another. Tasks are subcomponents of technology representing the specific programs used to complete the transformation process (Goodman, Ravlin, Schminke, 1987). There are a variety of taxonomies that can be used to categorize different tasks or technologies, although the taxonomies for technology are more limited in nature (see Goodman et al., 1987, for an overview). Regardless of which taxonomy is used, it is clear that understanding how technology and task interact with team process and performance is important for developing our understanding of work teams. Such ideas are not new. For example, the socio-technical view (Passmore, 1988; Trist & Bamforth, 1951) embodies the idea that social relationships, technology, and group process and performance cannot be treated without consideration of how each of these dimensions relate to one another (e.g., Kolodny & Kiggundu, 1980). Unfortunately, much of the earlier research on groups and teams failed to explicitly consider the impact of different dimensions of task or technology on the relationship between process and performance. As Goodman et al. (1987) noted, it was uncommon to find out what groups actually did in research studies. Task or technology was often overlooked or described with a few abstract concepts, with little emphasis for how such variables fit into a theory of work teams.

The fifth and final boundary condition to be discussed involves the *temporal dimension*. Work teams and their members are embedded in a context with a past, present, and future. The past, however short it might be, can be expected to have an impact on what occurs in the present, as can expectations for the future. To fully understand how work teams function, researchers must attend to how teams change over time, and they must consider how entrainment processes can affect team development (McGrath, 1990, 1991). Entrainment refers to the idea that "processes are captured and modified in their phase and periodicity by powerful (internal or external) cycles" (McGrath, 1990). For example, groups that are assigned close deadlines work and act in a rushed manner, even when deadlines are changed to be more distant. Conversely, groups that are assigned distant deadlines continue to work at a more leisurely pace, even when deadlines are changed to be closer (Kelly & McGrath, 1985). It is also important to consider how cyclical or periodic effects can affect work team dynamics and performance. For example, tasks for work teams can cycle from a period of high workload to a period of low workload, and these cycles can strongly affect the pattern of behaviors required by group members to be effective (Kozlowski et al., 1996). Consideration of time as a boundary variable requires longitudinal research on teams, with particular reference to temporal issues of team process and performance.

There are also a variety of other issues that may be classified as boundary variables, but they will not be treated as such in this paper. For example, it is important to investigate a broad range of content domains. It is not enough to study groups using only jury decision-making tasks, or to look only at the outcome performance of work teams. To form a comprehensive understanding of teams, it is important to understand how social processes, motivation, behavior, communication, etc. work together to affect work team productivity, satisfaction, attitudes, and turnover (McGrath, 1986). Additionally, a wide variety of methods must be applied to research on work teams, so that constructs can be fit into a nomological network (Cronbach & Meehl, 1955) to build an integrated theory of work teams.

Given that work teams are an important part of today's work environment (Goodman et al., 1987; Sundstrom et al., 1990), it seems worthy to re-examine the theories, methods, and research that have developed since 1985. To conduct this review, a targeted search was made to identify articles, reviews, or books written on any type of group or team, natural or artificial. A specific focus was taken on determining whether or not progress has been made since 1985 in addressing the five boundary conditions and their impact on work teams. This was a non-random sampling, and the presented studies tend to focus on findings from English language journals. Thus, this selection of articles is not meant to be exhaustive nor representative of the entire population of studies available.

Sampling Strategy

In 1986, McGrath suggested that more research was needed on natural groups performing natural tasks (e.g., families, work teams, sports teams), or natural groups performing imposed tasks (e.g., team training exercises). Since that time, a large number of reviews and theoretical frameworks have been published, including a recent review focused specifically on teams (Guzzo & Dickson, 1996). Bettenhausen (1991) reviewed over 250 articles that were published from 1986 to 1990; this research included samples of groups from laboratory studies, work teams, gangs, families, jazz ensembles and even a Japanese religious order. Cannon-Bowers, Oser, and Flanagan (1992) reviewed a moderate number of research articles published on quality circles (QCs), research and development groups (RDGs), and semi-autonomous work teams. Barrick and Alexander (1987) did a review on 33 articles that evaluated the efficacy of QCs, while Levine and Moreland (1990) reviewed literature that was comprised of samples from laboratory groups, work teams, sports teams, sport spectators, office employees, QCs, RDGs, and even a gay bar. Tannenbaum, Beard, and Salas (1992) conducted a review on team building that included command teams, production crews in coal mines, air crews, city employees, and survey teams. Davis (1992) provided a review of selected examples of articles on group consensus decisions. Not surprisingly, many of these studies were comprised of samples of mock juries or lab studies. These are examples of more general reviews.

Several theoretical frameworks have also been published, many of them with an explicit focus on work teams or work groups in organizations (e.g., Argote & McGrath, 1993; Goodman et al., 1987; Guzzo & Shea, 1992; Hackman, 1987, 1992; Kozlowski et al., forthcoming; Shea & Guzzo, 1987a; Sundstrom et al., 1990). A number of books have been published that are expressly focused on teams and teamwork (e.g., Brannick, Salas, & Prince, 1997; Guzzo & Salas, 1995; Jackson & Ruderman, 1995; Sashkin & Sashkin, 1994; Swezey & Salas, 1992), and an annual series on work teams with an interdisciplinary focus was launched as well (Beyerlein, Johnson, & Beyerlein, 1994). This pattern suggests that a diversity of group types are being included in recent research, including actual work groups and teams.

Individual research articles that have been published since 1985 were also evaluated with respect to sampling strategy. Less than half the studies had been conducted with groups in laboratory settings, while more than half of the studies had been conducted with groups in some type of natural setting (e.g., crews in coal mines, executive teams, military teams, sports teams, etc.). Many of the laboratory studies focused on the effects of electronic communication technology, team goals, team process, and task type. Studies from natural settings covered a wider variety of topics, including the effects of team member exchange, member familiarity, leader behaviors, cohesion, collective efficacy, team affect, goals, feedback, and incentives.

These results also suggest that a large amount of research is being done on a wide variety of groups in natural settings, including various types of work teams. This research is being supplemented by work in laboratory settings, but it is clear that the boundary condition of sampling strategy is being met. There was no shortage of articles on work teams, even when only considering those studies involving social units that met the strict definition of work teams or work groups presented earlier (e.g., Campion, Medsker, & Higgs, 1993; Campion, Papper, & Medsker, 1996; Cohen, Chang, & Ledford, 1997; George, 1990; George & Bettenhausen, 1990; Gersick, 1988; Goodman & Garber, 1988; Goodman & Leyden, 1991; Gregorich, Helmreich, & Wilhelm, 1990; Hyatt & Ruddy, 1997; Keck & Tushman, 1993; O'Reilly, Caldwell, & Barnett, 1989; Pritchard, Jones, Roth, Stuebing, & Ekeberg, 1988; Seers, 1989; Zaccaro, 1991). Thus, it appears that research since 1985 has moved toward balancing the scales of laboratory and field research.

Work Teams as a Context

The second boundary condition is the notion of team context. According to McGrath (1986), future research was needed to understand how the groups acted as an embedding system for its members. This research included variables such as team composition, climate, norms, size, familiarity, and socialization. Bettenhausen (1991) noted that the mere fact of group membership could have an impact on how members see themselves, and that groups or teams could affect member behavior through social influence and expectations for conformity. Several theoretical pieces published since 1985 focused on the effects of group or team socialization and development (Argote & McGrath, 1993; Kozlowski et al., forthcoming; Kozlowski et al., 1996; Moreland & Levine, 1988, 1989). Such work suggests that the developmental sequence of work teams has a strong influence on the role development and role transitions of members, and the developmental sequence can be affected by the tasks the team performs. Early experiences are characterized by a building of commitment leading to role negotiation and a shared understanding between the team as a unit and its members. Research by George and Bettenhausen (1990) and George (1990) supported this work; they found the early socialization experiences of members affected the prosocial behavior of the group as a unit.

Other research has been done on the effect of climate, environment, and norms on member behavior. Hackman (1992) suggested that groups or teams provide stimuli to their members that affect behavior. There are two types of stimuli in his model: ambient and discretionary stimuli. Ambient stimuli refers to stimuli that are received by all members, while discretionary stimuli are stimuli provided to specific members for specific reasons. The impact of these stimuli over time are believed to affect the behavior of members and the subsequent development of norms. Ginnett (1990) found the climate set by leaders early in the formation of aircrews had a long-term effect on how the crew performed its tasks, and Gersick and Hackman (1990) asserted that social units form norms that guide their long-term behavior, often without members explicitly considering the nature or influence of such norms.

A large amount of research suggests that diversity within work teams influences processes and effectiveness. For example, Levine and Moreland (1990) suggested that gender composition of a group creates a context for member gender that significantly shapes what transpires within a social unit. Thus, a male member of a team is expected to behave differently depending on whether or not most of the other members are male or female. O'Reilly, Caldwell, and Barnett (1989) found demographic composition was related to turnover in work teams, while Tziner and Eden (1985) found composition of member ability predicted tank crew performance beyond the mean level of ability. Similarly, Campion et al. (1993, 1996) found that composition, social support, and team size predicted significant amounts of variance in different member outcomes, including satisfaction, managerial ratings, and productivity. Watson, Kumar, and Michaelson (1993) established that cultural diversity had an effect on early performance. A book edited by Jackson and Ruderman (1995) addresses many of these issues and summarizes much of the literature on diversity effects in work teams. All of these results suggest that work teams provide a strong embedding context that influences attitudes and behaviors of individual members through norms, expectations, and behavioral stimuli.

Unit size and member familiarity has also been found to affect work groups or work teams. Generally speaking, the larger the unit is, the less satisfied members will be, and the less participation and cooperation the team will get from each member (Bettenhausen, 1991; Levine & Moreland, 1990). Goodman and Leyden (1991) and Goodman and Garber (1988) found that familiarity of coal mining crews affected productivity and accident rates. More familiar crews had fewer accidents and higher productivity than did less familiar crews.

Research involving the team as a context also begins to highlight levels of analysis issues. Often, the notion of the team as a context implies that research has to be done with consideration of individuals within teams or at the team level of analysis (Roberts, Hulin, & Rousseau, 1978). Increasing attention is being paid to levels issues (George & James, 1993; Klein, Dansereau, & Hall, 1994; Kozlowski et al., forthcoming; Rousseau, 1985). For example, George (1990), and George and James (1993), explicitly considered levels issues in their articles. Gully, Whitney, & Devine (1995) found the level of analysis used in studies of cohesion moderated the relationship between cohesion and performance. Individual level studies showed weaker relationships between cohesion and performance than did group or team level studies. New methods for dealing with the issue of levels are becoming increasingly available. For example, hierarchical linear modeling and repeated measures regression are two methods that can be used to deal with multi-level data on work teams (Bryk & Raudenbush, 1992; Gully, 1994; Hollenbeck, Ilgen, & Sego, 1994).

In sum, it appears that current work has pushed our understanding of the work team as a context to new horizons. Consistent evidence suggests that the team context exerts a strong amount of influence on member development, behavior, and attitudes. Additionally, early team socialization experiences are related to later attitudes, behaviors, and performance of the team as a whole. Finally, new theories and methods are being made available to study the effects of teams on individuals.

Organizations as a Context

Organizational contexts can have a strong influence on the behavior and performance of the work team as an aggregate. Research on organizations as a context requires one to focus on the team within the organization as the appropriate level of analysis. Teams are coupled to one another and to the organization as a whole, but their boundaries are distinct enough to give them a separate identity (Alderfer, 1987; Friedlander, 1987). This is similar to the notion of loose coupling, or partial inclusion (Katz & Kahn, 1978; McGrath, 1991). In this sense, boundaries of teams both separate and link the work done by teams (Sundstrom et al., 1990). The organizational context includes such variables as the organizational culture, clarity of team goals or missions, training and consultation, reward and recognition systems, and the physical environment in general. For example, Goodman and Leyden (1988) found the organizational system for job assignment of workers to coal mining teams had an effect on the familiarity of members in the work team and its subsequent productivity. Campion et al. (1993, 1996) and Hyatt and Ruddy (1997) found organizational context (e.g., recognition and rewards, training, information, etc.) to be an important determinant of work group effectiveness.

The reward system of the organization can also have a strong influence on work teams (Gladstein, 1984; Shea & Guzzo, 1987a). Shea and Guzzo (1987a) wrote a theoretical piece related to the reward systems of organizations. They suggest three variables are important to work group performance. These variables include group potency, task interdependence, and outcome interdependence. Task interdependence is the amount of task driven interaction among members, while outcome interdependence is the degree to which outcomes are contingent on the performance of the unit as a whole. Group potency is the shared belief that the group can meet challenges presented to it. They hypothesize that teams that engage in highly interdependent tasks will perform best under a noncompetitive reward system, while groups that engage in tasks low in interdependence will perform best under a competitive reward system. They also state that group potency will moderate several of these relationships. Shea and Guzzo (1987b) provide an example of how these relationships affect the performance of work groups in organizations. Subsequent work by Campion and colleagues (Campion, Medsker, & Higgs, 1993; Campion, Papper, & Medsker, 1996) provide some support for different components of Shea and Guzzo's model.

Several studies have theorized or found organizational level variance in effects on teams. Gregorich, Helmreich, and Wilhelm (1990) found between organization variance in the cockpit management attitudes of flight crews. Keck and Tushman (1993) showed that organizational timeframes have distinct effects on team inertia and change. The longer and more stable an executive team's environment, the less change observed in the executive members' tenure, and the greater the homogeneity of the team. Reorientation, environmental jolts, technological discontinuity, and CEO succession were associated with increased team change and heterogeneity. These findings demonstrate the impact of organizational level characteristics on the internal functioning of work teams.

Anacona (1987) suggested that work teams may adapt to corporate settings through negotiation (bargaining for resources), scanning, profile management (impression management), and buffering (defense). Special roles develop to help work teams perform these functions, and those teams or groups that engage in these functions effectively perform better than those that do not (Anacona & Caldwell, 1988). Argote and McGrath (1993) postulate that work teams must engage in specific functions, termed external relations, to tie the team to its external environment and allow it to be effective. Thus, it appears that members of effective teams must develop member roles that enable it to continually link itself to the organizational context and keep negotiations, communications, and expectations open between the team and the rest of the organization.

Sundstrom et al. (1990) note that training, mission clarity or goals, performance feedback, and the physical environment are all organizational context variables that can have effects on the performance of teams. Campion et al. (1993, 1996) found training, managerial support, and interdependence of goals, feedback, and rewards had an impact on work team effectiveness. Additionally, a body of research has developed to show group or team goals and feedback can have a strong impact on social processes that determine how well the group or team performs (Crown & Rosse, 1995; Matsui, Kakuyama, & Onglatco, 1987; Mitchell & Silver, 1990, O'Leary-Kelly, Martocchio, & Frink, 1994; Pritchard et al., 1988; Weingart & Weldon, 1991). This pattern of findings suggests that the goals and feedback provided to work teams by the organization can have powerful effects on team processes and outcomes.

In sum, it appears that facets of organizational context can have a strong impact on team process, member behaviors, and team effectiveness. Variables in the organizational context include, but are not limited to, reward systems, training, goals, feedback, and team competitiveness. Research since 1985 has increased our knowledge in many of these areas, but more work is needed, particularly when comparing groups or teams across organizations. An aspect of the organizational context that can have a strong impact on work teams is the task performed by the team or the technology used by the work team. These boundary variables are considered separately.

Task/Technology

Several researchers suggest using taxonomies of technology or tasks is not a useful approach for understanding how such variables affect team process and performance. Instead, it is suggested that to truly understand how work teams function, one must understand the *specific* tasks performed and technology used by the group (e.g., Goodman, 1986; Goodman et al., 1987). This is similar to the idiographic approach to research, in which one tries to understand how individual units behave. Other researchers have provided taxonomies for tasks (e.g., Argote & McGrath, 1993; Herold, 1978; McGrath, 1984; Steiner, 1972; Van de Ven, Delbecq, & Koenig, 1976) and technology (e.g., Comstock & Scott, 1977; Perrow, 1967;

Thompson, 1967) that provide methods for generalizations to be made about the influence of task and technology on team functioning. This is similar to the nomothetic approach to research, which focuses on identifying general laws about group or team behavior.

In both approaches, however, task and technology are considered to be important to team performance and functioning. Unfortunately, prior to 1985 little research focused on the impact of task or technology on work team functioning. For example, Gully, Whitney, and Devine (1995) found that many studies on cohesion did not explicitly consider or describe the nature of the task performed by groups and teams in the studies. Similarly, Goodman et al. (1987) noted that what groups actually do is rarely reported in articles. Since 1985, however, increasing attention has been paid to such issues.

For example, Goodman and Garber (1988) and Goodman and Leyden (1991) provide clear descriptions of the nature of the tasks and technology used by coal mining groups. Keck and Tushman (1993) found technology discontinuity was related to increases in executive team change and heterogeneity, and Keller (1994) found the fit between information processing of the group and nonroutineness of the technology was related to the performance of the group. Tesluk, Mathieu, Zacarro, and Marks (1997) suggest that it is important to understand the nature of the task performed by the team because task understanding is useful for identifying critical levers for intervention. They also identify the task as a crucial component to consider when evaluating or measuring team performance.

A growing body of research has looked at the impact of communication technology on the performance of groups and teams (Dennis & Valacich, 1993; Gallupe, Bastianutti, & Cooper, 1991; Gallupe, Cooper, Grise, & Bastianutti, 1994; Kiesler & Sproull, 1992; Straus & McGrath, 1994). McGrath (1990) provided a classification of different types of electronic communication. Basic findings suggest electronic communication technology can change the nature of communication shared between members (Kiesler & Sproull, 1992) and that in general, computer mediated groups do not perform as well as face to face groups, particularly when consensus is required or when time pressure is an issue (Straus & McGrath, 1994). This effect is reversed for brainstorming tasks. Electronic brainstorming groups were found to generate more ideas than normal verbal brainstorming groups, and this effect was believed to be due to reductions in production blocking, evaluation apprehension, and free riding (Dennis & Valacich, 1993; Gallupe et al., 1991; Gallupe et al., 1994). This research suggests communication technology can have a strong effect on group performance, but the positive or negative effect of communication technology may depend upon characteristics of the tasks performed by a work group. Less work has been done involving work teams embedded in organizations, but the results may have implications for such teams.

Certain task characteristics also appear to have the potential for strong effects on work teams. Campion et al. (1993) found characteristics of job design like self-management, task significance, task variety, and task identity affected different group outcomes. Using meta-analytic techniques, Gully et al. (1995) found task interdependence moderated the relationship between cohesion and performance, although Mullen and Copper (1994) only provide indirect evidence for this effect. Saavedra, Earley, and Van Dyne (1993) demonstrated that task interdependence affected the perceived effectiveness of strategy, and task strategy and conflict partially mediated the effects of task interdependence on performance quality and quantity. Similarly, Weingart (1992) found task component complexity influenced performance of groups through the planning and effort of its members. Thompson, Mannix, and Bazerman (1988) demonstrated that the presence of agendas and or decision rules affected coalition behavior in negotiating groups. Additionally, researchers have recently been more explicit about the nature of the task being studied. For example, Weingart and Weldon (1991) and Zaccaro and Lowe (1988) studied additive tasks, while Zaccaro and McCoy (1988) studied disjunctive tasks.

It appears as though research since 1985 has begun to deal with issues of technology and task characteristics. Theories are being developed to describe how the task behaviors are related to the technology used by the work teams (Argote & McGrath, 1993; McGrath, 1991), and recent work has indicated that task and technology will likely affect team process and performance. Furthermore, task and technology have been shown to moderate the relationship between team process and work team performance in many cases. However, this line of research is underdeveloped and future research should continue to explore the clear link between technology, task characteristics, and their impact on processes and outcomes in work team contexts.

Temporal Issues

A final boundary condition involves the temporal dimension. To fully understand work teams, researchers must investigate how team dynamics develop and change over time. This type of research by definition, should involve more longitudinal studies, and it requires a special focus on patterns (e.g., periodic effects, cyclical, nonlinear patterns) that evolve or affect group or team performance. Recent research has clearly become more sensitive to such issues, often using data sets collected over many years. Some key examples include Goodman and Garber (1988) who researched absenteeism and accident rates over a total of 70,000 miner days, and Keck and Tushman (1993) who used archival data to evaluate the effects of organizational timeframes on teams over a total of 2,241 firm years. Pritchard et al., (1988) spent nine months establishing a baseline of performance, five months evaluating the effects of feedback, five months on the effects of goals, and five months on the effects of adding incentives. Many studies included multi-year data from archival sources (e.g., Campion et al., 1993; O'Reilly et al., 1989), or multiple measures over time (e.g., Keller, 1994; Seers, 1989; Watson et al., 1993). Some studies included detailed descriptions of how group processes and performance changed over time (e.g., Gersick, 1988, 1989). As a whole, these studies indicate the issue of temporal effects is being seriously considered, particularly for certain types of groups. Unfortunately, some areas of research were still found to have a limited number of studies involving a temporal orientation. For example, Gully et al., (1995) and Mullen & Copper (1994) found little work on the development or effects of cohesion over time, particularly for units that could be classified as work teams in organizations.

Studies are also finding that teams have internal timelines, and certain events may have long lasting effects depending on the timing of the event. For example, Gersick (1988, 1989) found a "punctuated equilibrium" effect in groups. Groups with deadlines alternated through periods of inertia and revolution, and the halfway point to the deadline was found to have important effects on how the group went about performing its tasks. In a similar vein, Kelly and McGrath (1985) found the imposition of a deadline affected the rate and quality of performance, even after the deadline changed. Orasanu and Salas (1993) found the timing of certain communication behaviors was related to flight crew effectiveness, and Ginnett (1990) suggested that the early formation of air crews could have long-term effects on its performance. Collectively, these findings suggest the timing of key internal and external events have strong impacts on the team that unfold over longer time periods. In particular, early points and midpoints of team development might be useful leverage points for initiating changes in team process and structure.

Recent work by Kozlowski, Gully, Cannon-Bowers and Salas (1996) suggests leader behaviors must change in response to high and low cycles of work load and the developmental sequence of the team. Morgan et al. (1986) stated that the importance of different types of behavior (teamwork and taskwork) changed over time, eventually converging at a single point in time. Kozlowski et al. (forthcoming) suggested the primary level of focus from member's shift from individuals to dyads to the team over time. Lindsley, Brass, and Thomas (1995) assert that perceptions of efficacy can create spiral patterns of performance that increase or decrease over time, and Moreland and Levine (1988, 1989) note that socialization and role transitions within groups unfold over time. These theories all point to the idea that developmental shifts in teams have strong implications for member behaviors, team process, and team performance. Future research is needed to more completely evaluate and test these models of team development.

As a whole, it appears the temporal dimension of work groups and work team performance and functioning is receiving considerable attention. It is clear from the research cited above that the early formation of teams has an effect on their later function and performance. Additionally, the halfway point of teams appears to be important for later performance, although it is not clear what happens to work teams that do not have a clear deadline. Furthermore, recent theory has included periodic or cyclical effects on team development and performance (Kozlowski et al., 1996; Kozlowski et al., forthcoming; Moreland & Levine, 1988; Lindsley et al., 1995; McGrath, 1991).

Conclusions

Overall, the progress in research applicable to work teams is encouraging. A wide variety of groups and teams, both artificial and natural, are being used to study a variety of content domains. Issues involving the team as a context for individuals have been explored, and it seems clear that the climate, norms, and composition of work teams has important effects on member behavior. The organization as a context has received increased attention, with particular reference to goals, feedback, and reward systems. A limited amount of work exists on the effects of intergroup relations between work teams within organizations, so more work is needed. Researchers are providing clearer descriptions of the tasks and technologies used by groups and teams, and recent work has found moderating effects of task complexity and task interdependence on process and performance. It appears that various attributes of task and technology may differentially impact team process and performance. Additionally, increased attention has been paid to temporal issues in work teams. The timing of events as well as the overall sequence of group or team development has received increased attention, as evidenced by the longitudinal studies involving multiple observations or measurements over time. Given the current improvement of the field in applying research and theory to the understanding of work teams in organizations, it is important to consider future directions for research.

One important task is to begin integrating what we already know. Research on groups and teams can be found in the fields of social psychology, industrial relations, sociology, sports psychology, military psychology, organizational communication, to name but a few of the areas in which such research has been published. Unfortunately, even within any given field, a unified approach to the study of teams is missing. For example, the idiographic approach of focusing on specific groups in specific situations proffered by Goodman and his colleagues (Goodman, 1986; Goodman et al., 1987) is an important part of the scientific enterprise, but it has its limitations. As McGrath (1986) stated, such an approach runs the risk of developing a science of "mine shaft 32." Thus, we must find some way to integrate what is known about groups and teams into a more cohesive framework. To begin this process, we must carefully consider how the group and team taxonomies previously developed relate to research currently being conducted (e.g., McGrath, 1984; Sundstrom et al., 1990). We can then begin to integrate and identify gaps in the research done on specific types of work teams within organizations. We need better definitions of technology and better taxonomies for the types of technology that are important to teams in organizations. In a similar vein, we need to test some of the task taxonomies previously provided (e.g., McGrath, 1984; Steiner, 1972) to determine if they capture the important dimensions or attributes of task performance in work teams. Embedded in the taxonomies is a theory of groups and teams, identifying the dimensions along which they can be integrated or differentiated. These taxonomies can be used to link disparate research together, providing a less "piece-meal" approach to the study of work teams.

As we develop a more coherent understanding of work teams in organizations, we may begin to understand how periodic, cyclical, and nonlinear effects of events in time affect the development and performance of specific types of work teams. Work teams operate within different time frames for different types of tasks (McGrath, 1991). The time frame can unfold at different rates for different types of outcomes, so it is important to develop an understanding of how these processes unfold. For example, events that have long lasting effects on teams may often occur early in team development. It is important then, to define what is meant by "long lasting" and "early." These terms may vary according to the type of team, the technology it uses and the tasks it performs. This knowledge is critical, however, because it can lead to theories of change and intervention in work teams for specific types of outcomes.

Also, organizations are increasingly looking to self-managing teams as a means of organizing the business structure. Although teams may vary in the amount of self-regulation available to them (Sundstrom et al., 1990), self-regulation is likely to be an important component of team effectiveness (Cohen et al., 1997; Hackman, 1987; Manz & Sims, 1987). However, theories and research on how work teams develop self-managing skills is relatively sparse. In teams that are self-regulating, success will depend on both the team and the leader (Kozlowski et al., 1996). It may be possible to borrow from theories of individual self-regulation (Karoly, 1993) to extrapolate how such processes may unfold in the work team environment. This will enable researchers and practitioners to devise interventions that will enable teams to become more effective self-regulators. Such teams will be more able to learn from experience, and will engage in active environmental scanning and interpretation (Gersick & Hackman, 1990; Kozlowski et al., 1996).

Future work should continue to investigate a wide variety of team inputs, processes, and outputs, using a variety of methods. Some examples of innovative or varied methods being applied to research on groups and teams include math modeling and petri nets (Coovert & McNelis, 1992; Kleinman, Luh, Pattipati, & Serfaty, 1992), case studies (Ginnett, 1990), thought experiments (Davis & Kerr, 1986), and meeting maps (Gersick, 1988, 1989). Additionally, Klimoski and Mohammed (1994) suggest multidimensional scaling techniques, verbal protocols, and concept mapping might be useful for understanding shared mental models and team performance.

As we continue to gather research on multiple variables using multiple techniques, we must continue to develop our theories about team dynamics and functioning. Currently, our theories and taxonomies for what constitutes an input or process or output in a team are fragmented. For example, in some cases cohesion is considered as an input to team process, in other cases the process itself, and in other cases, an outcome of team process. Integrative theories need to be developed that help to describe how the different variables important to team functioning interrelate, and these theories need to be tested, sometimes using multi-level models. Current theory is expanding to include levels of analysis issues, and methodology is being imported to conduct multi-level work on teams (e.g., Mathieu & Day, 1997). If we continue to push the boundaries of our field to investigate teams in organizations using a variety of techniques, with different variables, in many different situations and over time, we can continue to develop comprehensive theories that allow us to improve how work teams function and perform in organizations.

References

Alderfer, C.P. (1987). An intergroup perspective on group dynamics. In J.W. Lorsch (Ed.), *Handbook of organizational behavior*. Englewood Cliffs, NJ: Prentice-Hall.

Anacona, D. G. (1987). Groups in organizations: Extending laboratory models. In C. Hendrick (Ed.), *Annual review of personality and social psychology: Group processes and intergroup relations* (pp. 207-230). Newbury Park: Sage.

Anacona, D.G., & Caldwell, D.F. (1988). Beyond task and maintenance: Defining external functions in groups. *Group and Organization Studies*, 13, 468-494. Newbury Park: Sage.

Argote, L., & McGrath, J. E. (1993). Group processes in organizations: Continuity and change. In C. L. Cooper and I. T. Robertson (Eds.), *International review of industrial and organizational psychology* (pp. 333-389). New York: John Wiley & Sons.

Barrick, M. R., & Alexander, R. A. (1987). A review of quality circle efficacy and the existence of positive-findings bias. *Personnel Psychology*, 40, 579-592.

Bettenhausen, K. L. (1991). Five years of group research: What we have learned and what needs to be addressed. *Journal of Management*, 17, 345-381.

Beyerlein, M., Johnson, D. A., & Beyerlein, S. (1994-1998). *Advances in interdisciplinary studies of work teams*. Greenwich, CT: JAI Press.

Brannick, M. T., & Prince, C. (1997). An overview of team performance measurement. In M. T. Brannick, E. Salas, and C. Prince (Eds.), *Team performance assessment and measurement* (pp. 3-16). Mahwah, NJ: Lawrence Erlbaum.

Brannick, M. T., Salas, E., & Prince, C. (Eds.). (1997). *Team performance assessment and measurement*. Mahwah, NJ: Lawrence Erlbaum.

Bryk, A. S., & Raudenbush, S. W. (1992). *Hierarchical linear models: Applications and data analysis methods*. Newbury Park, CA: Sage Publications.

Campion, M. A., Medsker, G. J., & Higgs, A. C. (1993). Relations between work group characteristics and effectiveness: Implications for designing effective work groups. *Personnel Psychology*, 46, 823-850.

Campion, M. A., Papper, E. M., & Medsker, G. J. (1996). Relations between work group characteristics and effectiveness: A replication and extension. *Personnel Psychology*, 49, 429-452.

Cannon-Bowers, J. A., Oser, R., & Flanagan, D. L. (1992). Work teams in industry: A selected review and proposed framework. In R. W. Swezey and E. Salas (Eds.), *Teams: Their training and performance* (pp. 355-378). Norwood, NJ: Ablex.

Cohen, S. G., Chang, L., & Ledford, G. E., Jr. (1997). A hierarchical construct of self-management leadership and its relationship to quality of work life and perceived work group effectiveness. *Personnel Psychology*, 50, 275-308.

Collins, J. J. (1977). *A study of potential contributions of small group behavior research to team training technology*. (Contract No. N0014-76-C-1076). Alexandria, VA: Essex Corporation.

Comstock, D. E., & Scott, W. R. (1977). Technology and the structure of subunits. *Administrative Science Quarterly*, 22, 177-202.

Coovert, M. D., & McNelis, K. (1992). Team decision making and performance: A review and proposed modeling approach employing petri nets. In R. W. Swezey and E. Salas (Eds.), *Teams: Their training and performance* (pp. 247-280). Norwood, NJ: Ablex.

Cronbach, L. J., & Meehl, P. E. (1955). Construct validity in psychological tests. *Psychological Bulletin*, 52, 281-302.

Crown, D. F., & Rosse, J. G. (1995). Yours, mine, and ours: Facilitating group productivity through the integration of individual and group goals. *Organizational Behavior and Human Decision Processes*, 64, 138-150.

Davis, J. H. (1992). Some compelling intuitions about group consensus decisions, theoretical and empirical research, and interpersonal aggregation phenomena: Selected examples, 1950-1990. *Organizational Behavior and Human Decision Processes*, 52, 3-38.

Davis, J. H., & Kerr, N. L. (1986). Thought experiments and the problem of sparse data in small-group research. In P. S. Goodman (Ed.), *Designing effective work groups* (pp. 305-349). San Francisco, CA: Jossey-Bass.

Dennis, A. R., & Valacich, J. S. (1993). Computer brainstorms: More heads are better than one. *Journal of Applied Psychology*, 78, 531-537.

Driskell, J. E., & Salas, E. (1992). Can you study real teams in contrived settings? The value of small group research to understanding teams. In R. W. Swezey and E. Salas (Eds.), *Teams: Their training and performance* (pp. 101-124). Norwood, NJ: Ablex.

Friedlander, F. (1987). The ecology of work groups. In J. Lorsch (Ed.), *Handbook of organizational behavior* (pp. 301-314). Englewood Cliffs: Prentice-Hall.

Gallupe, R. B., Bastianutti, L. M., & Cooper, W. H. (1991). Unblocking brainstorms. *Journal of Applied Psychology*, 76, 137-142.

Gallupe, R. B., Cooper, W. H., Grise, M. L., & Bastianutti, L. M. (1994). Blocking electronic brainstorms. *Journal of Applied Psychology*, 79, 77-86.

George, J. M. (1990). Personality, affect, and behavior in groups. *Journal of Applied Psychology*, 75, 107-116.

George, J. M., & Bettenhausen, K. (1990). Understanding prosocial behavior, sales performance, and turnover: A group-level analysis in a service context. *Journal of Applied Psychology*, 75, 698-709.

George, J. M., & James, L. R. (1993). Personality, affect, and behavior in groups revisited: A comment on aggregation, levels of analysis, and a recent application of within and between analysis. *Journal of Applied Psychology*, 78, 798-804.

Gersick, C. J. G. (1988). Time and transition in work teams: Toward a new model of group development. *Academy of Management Journal*, 31, 9-41.

Gersick, C. J. G. (1989). Marking time: Predictable transitions in task groups. *Academy of Management Journal*, 32, 274-309.

Gersick, C. J. G., & Hackman, J. R. (1990). Habitual routines in task-performing groups. *Organizational Behavior and Human Decision Processes*, 47, 65-97.

Ginnett, R. C. (1990). Airline cockpit crew. In J. R. Hackman (Ed.), *Groups that work (and those that don't)* (pp. 427-448). San Francisco, CA: Jossey-Bass.

Gladstein, D. (1984). Groups in context: A model of task group effectiveness. *Administrative Science Quarterly*, 29, 499-517.

Goodman, P. S. (1986) The impact of task and technology on group performance. In P. Goodman and Associates (Eds.), *Designing effective work groups* (pp. 120-167). San Francisco, CA: Jossey-Bass.

Goodman, P. S., & Garber, S. (1988). Absenteeism and accidents in a dangerous environment: Empirical analysis of underground coal mines. *Journal of Applied Psychology*, 73(1), 81-86.

Goodman, P. S., & Leyden, D. P. (1991). Familiarity and group productivity. *Journal of Applied Psychology*, 76, 578-586.

Goodman, P. S., Ravlin, E., & Schminke, M. (1987). Understanding groups in organizations. In B. M. Staw and L. L. Cummings (Eds.), *Research in organizational behavior* (Vol. 9, pp. 121-173). Greenwich, CT: JAI Press.

Gregorich, S. E., Helmreich, R. L., & Wilhelm, J. A. (1990). The structure of cockpit management attitudes. *Journal of Applied Psychology*, 75, 682-690.

Gully, S. M. (1994, April). *Repeated measures regression analyses: A clarification with illustrative examples*. Paper presented at the Ninth Annual Conference of the Society for Industrial and Organizational Psychology, Nashville, TN.

Gully, S. M., Devine, D. J., & Whitney, D. J. (1995). A meta-analysis of cohesion and performance: Effects of levels of analysis and task interdependence. *Small Group Research*, 26(4), 497-520.

Guzzo, R. A., & Dickson, M. W. (1996). Teams in organizations: Recent research on performance and effectiveness. *Annual Review of Psychology*, 47, 307-338.

Guzzo, R. A., Salas, E., and Associates. Editors. (1995). *Team effectiveness and decision making in organizations*. San Francisco, CA: Jossey-Bass.

Guzzo, R. A., & Shea, G. P. (1992). Group performance and intergroup relations in organizations. In M. D. Dunnette and L. M. Hough (Eds.), *Handbook of industrial and organizational psychology* (Vol. 3, 2nd ed., pp. 269-313). Palo Alto, CA: Consulting Psychologists Press.

Hackman, J. R. (1987). The design of work teams. In J. W. Lorsch (Ed.), *Handbook of organizational behavior* (pp. 315-342). Englewood Cliff, NJ: Prentice-Hall.

Hackman, J. R. (1992). Group influences on individuals in organizations. In M. D. Dunnette and L. M. Hough (Eds.), *Handbook of industrial and organizational psychology* (Vol. 3, 2nd ed., pp. 199-267). Palo Alto, CA: Consulting Psychologists Press.

Herold, D. M. (1978). Improving the performance effectiveness of groups through a task-contingent selection of intervention strategies. *Academy of Management Review*, 3, 315-325.

Hollenbeck, J. R., Ilgen, D. R., & Sego, D. J. (1994). Repeated measures regression and mediational tests: Enhancing the power of leadership research. *Leadership Quarterly*, 5, 3-23.

Hyatt, D. E., & Ruddy, T. M. (1997). An examination of the relationship between work group characteristics and performance: Once more into the breech. *Personnel Psychology*, 50, 553-585.

Ilgen, D. R., Major, D. A., Hollenbeck, J. R., & Sego, D. J. (1993). Team research in the 1990s. In M. M. Chemers and R. Ayman (Eds.), *Leadership theory and research* (pp. 245-270). New York: Academic Press.

Jackson, S. E., & Ruderman, M. N. (Eds.). (1995). *Diversity in work teams: Research paradigms for a changing workplace*. Washington, DC: American Psychological Association.

Karoly, P. (1993). Mechanisms of self-regulation: A systems view. *Annual Review of Psychology*, 44, 23-52.

Katz, D., & Kahn, R. L. (1978). *The social psychology of organizations* (2nd ed.). New York: John Wiley and Sons.

Keck, S. L., & Tushman, M. L. (1993). Environmental and organizational context and executive team structure. *Academy of Management Journal*, 36, 1314-1344.

Keller, R. T. (1994). Technology-information processing fit and the performance of R&D project groups: A test of contingency theory. *Academy of Management Journal*, 37, 167-179.

Kelly, J. R., & McGrath, J. E. (1985). Effects of time limits and task types on task performance and interaction of four-person groups. *Journal of Personality and Social Psychology*, 49, 395-407.

Kiesler, S., & Sproull, L. (1992). Group decision making and communication technology. *Organizational Behavior and Human Decision Processes*, 52, 96-123.

Klein, K. J., Dansereau, F., & Hall, R. J. (1994). Levels issues in theory development, data collection, and analysis. *Academy of Management Review*, 19, 185-380.

Kleinman, D. L., Luh, P. B., Pattipati, K. R., & Serfaty, D. (1992). Mathematical models of team performance: A distributed decision-making approach. In R. W. Swezey and E. Salas (Eds.), *Teams: Their training and performance* (pp. 177-217). Norwood, NJ: Ablex.

Klimoski, R., & Mohammed, S. (1994). Team mental model: Construct or metaphor? *Journal of Management*, 20, 403-437.

Kolodny, H., & Kiggundu, M. N. (1980). Towards the development of a socio-technical systems model in woodland mechanical harvesting. *Human Relations*, 33, 623-645.

Kozlowski, S. W. J., Gully, S. M., McHugh, P., Salas, E., & Cannon-Bowers, J. A. (1996). A dynamic theory of leadership and team effectiveness: Developmental and task contingent leader roles. To appear in G. Ferris (Ed.), *Research in Personnel and Human Resources Management* (Vol. 14, pp. 253-305). Greenwich, CT: JAI Press.

Kozlowski, S. W. J., Gully, S. M., Nason, E. R., & Smith, E. M. (forthcoming). Team compilation: Development, performance, and effectiveness across levels and time. To appear in D. R. Ilgen & E. D. Pulakos (Eds.), *The changing nature of work and performance: Implications for staffing, personnel actions, and development*. San Francisco, CA: Jossey-Bass.

Kozlowski, S. W. J., Gully, S. M., Salas, E., & Cannon-Bowers, J. A. (1996). Team leadership and development: Theory, principles, and guidelines for training leaders and teams. To appear in M. Beyerlein (Ed.), *Advances in interdisciplinary studies of work teams: Team leadership* (Vol. 3, 253-291). Greenwich, CT: JAI Press.

Levine, R. L., & Moreland, R. L. (1990). Progress in small group research. *Annual Review of Psychology*, 41, 585-634.

Lindsley, D. H., Brass, D. J., & Thomas, J. B. (1995). Efficacy-performance spirals: A multilevel perspective. *Academy of Management Review*, 20, 645-678.

Manz, C. C., & Sims, H. P. (1987). Leading workers to lead themselves: The external leadership of self-managing work teams. *Administrative Science Quarterly*, 32, 106-128.
Mathieu, J. E., & Day, D. V. (1997). Assessing processes within and between organizational teams: A nuclear power plant example. In M. T. Brannick, E. Salas, & C. Prince (Eds.), *Team performance assessment and measurement* (pp. 173-195). Mahwah, NJ: Lawrence Erlbaum.
Matsui, T., Kakuyama, T., & Onglatco, M. L. U. (1987). Effects of goals and feedback on performance in groups. *Journal of Applied Psychology*, 72, 407-415.
McGrath, J. E. (1984). *Groups: Interaction and performance*. Englewood Cliffs, NJ; Prentice-Hall.
McGrath, J. E. (1986). Studying groups at work: Ten critical needs for theory and practice. In P. Goodman and Associates (Eds.), *Designing effective work groups* (pp. 362-391). San Francisco, CA: Jossey-Bass.
McGrath, J. E. (1990). Time matters in groups. In J. Galegher, R. E. Kraut, & C. Egido (Eds.), *Intellectual teamwork: Social and technological foundations of cooperative work*. Hillsdale, NJ: Lawrence Erlbaum.
McGrath, J. E. (1991). Time, interaction, and performance (TIP): A theory of groups. *Small Group Research*, 22, 147-174.
Mitchell, T. R., & Silver, W. S. (1990). Individual and group goals when workers are interdependent: Effects on task strategies and performance. *Journal of Applied Psychology*, 75, 185-193.
Mook, D. G. (1983). In defense of external invalidity. *American Psychologist*, 38, 379-387.
Moreland, R. L., & Levine, J. M. (1988). Group dynamics over time: Development and socialization in small groups. In J. E. McGrath (Ed.), *The social psychology of time: New perspectives* (pp. 151-181). Newbury Park, CA: Sage.
Moreland, R. L., & Levine, J. M. (1989). Newcomers and oldtimers in groups. In P. Paulus (Ed.), *Psychology of group influence* (2nd ed., pp. 143-186). Hillsdale, NJ: Erlbaum.
Moreland, R. L., & Levine, J. M. (1992). The composition of small groups. In E. E. Lawler, III., B. Markovsky, C. Ridgeway, & H. Walker (Eds.), *Advances in group processes* (Vol. 9, pp. 237-280). Greenwich, CT: JAI Press.
Morgan, B. B., Jr., Glickman, A. S., Woodard, E. A., Blaiwes, A. S. & Salas, E. (1986). *Measurement of team behaviors in Navy environment* (Technical Report NTSC TR-86-014). Orlando, FL: Naval Training Systems Center.
Mullen, B., & Copper, C. (1994). The relation between group cohesiveness and performance: An integration. *Psychological Bulletin*, 115, 210-227.
O'Leary-Kelly, A. M., Martocchio, J. J., & Frink, D. D. (1994). A review of the influence of group goals on group performance. *Academy of Management Journal*, 37, 1285-1301.
Orasanu, J., & Salas, E. (1993). Team decision making in complex environments. In G. A. Klein, J. Orasanu, R. Calderwood, and C. Zsambok (Eds.), *Decision making in action: Models and methods* (pp. 327-345). Norwood, NJ: Ablex.
O'Reilly, C. A., Caldwell, D. F., & Barnett, W. P. (1989). Work group demography, social integration, and turnover. *Administrative Science Quarterly*, 34, 21-37.
Passmore, W. A. (1988). *Designing effective organizations: The Socio-technical perspective*. New York: Wiley.
Perrow, C. (1967). A framework for the comparative analysis of organizations. *American Sociological Review*, 32, 194-208.
Pritchard, R. D., Jones, S. D., Roth, P. L., Stuebing, K. K., & Ekeberg, S. E. (1988). Effects of group feedback, goal setting, and incentives on organizational productivity. *Journal of Applied Psychology*, 73, 337-358.
Roberts, K. H., Hulin, C. L., & Rousseau, D. M. (1978). *Developing an interdisciplinary science of organizations*. San Francisco, CA: Jossey-Bass.

Rousseau, D. M. (1985). Issues of level in organizational research: Multi-level and cross-level perspectives. In B. M. Staw and L. L. Cummings (Eds.), *Research in organizational behavior* (Vol. 7, pp. 1-37). Greenwich, CT: JAI Press.

Saavedra, R., Earley, P. C., & Van Dyne, L. (1993). Complex interdependence in task-performing groups. *Journal of Applied Psychology*, 78, 61-72.

Salas, E., Dickinson, T. L, Converse, S. A., & Tannenbaum, S. I. (1992). Toward an understanding of team performance and training. In R. W. Swezey and E. Salas (Eds.), *Teams: Their training and performance*. Norwood, NJ: Ablex.

Sashkin, M., & Sashkin, M. G. (1994). *The new teamwork: Developing and using cross-function teams*. New York: AMA Membership Pub.

Seers, A. (1989). Team-member exchange quality: A new construct for role-making research. *Organizational Behavior and Human Decision Processes*, 43, 118-135.

Shea, G. P., & Guzzo, R. A. (1987a). Groups as human resources. In K. M. Rowland and G. R. Ferris (Eds.), *Research in personnel and human resources management* (Vol. 5, pp. 323-356). Greenwich, CT: JAI Press.

Shea, G. P., & Guzzo, R. A. (1987b). Group effectiveness: What really matters? *Sloan Management Review*, 28, 35-31.

Steiner, I. D. (1972). *Group process and productivity*. New York: Academic Press.

Straus, S. G., & McGrath, J. E. (1994). Does the medium matter? The interaction of task type and technology on group performance and member relations. *Journal of Applied Psychology*, 79, 87-97.

Sundstrom, E., De Meuse, K. P., & Futrell, D. (1990). Work teams: Applications and effectiveness. *American Psychologist*, 45, 120-133.

Swezey, R. W., & Salas, E., (Eds.). (1992). *Teams: Their training and performance*. Norwood, NJ: Ablex.

Tannenbaum, S. I., Beard, R. L., & Salas, E. (1992). Team building and its influence on team effectiveness: An examination of conceptual and empirical developments. In K. Kelley (Ed.), *Advances in psychology: Issues, theory, and research in industrial/organizational psychology* (Vol. 82, pp. 117-153). New York: North-Holland.

Thompson, J. D. (1967). Organizations in action. New York: McGraw-Hill.

Thompson, L. L., Mannix, E. A., & Bazerman, M. H. (1988). Group negotiation: Effects of decision rule, agenda, and aspiration. *Journal of Personality and Social Psychology*, 54, 86-95.

Trist, E. L., & Bamforth, K. W. (1951). Some social and psychological consequences of the longwall method of coal-getting. *Human Relations*, 4, 3-38.

Tziner, A., & Eden, D. (1985). Effects of crew composition on crew performance: Does the whole equal the sum of its parts? *Journal of Applied Psychology*, 70, 85-93.

Van de Ven, A. H., Delbecq, A. L., & Koenig, R. (1976). Determinants of coordination modes within organizations. *American Sociological Review*, 41, 322-338.

Watson, W. E., Kumar, K., & Michaelson, L. K. (1993). Cultural diversity's impact on interaction process and performance: Comparing homogenous and diverse task groups. *Academy of Management Journal*, 36, 590-602.

Weingart, L. R. (1992). Impact of group goals, task component complexity, effort, and planning on group performance. *Journal of Applied Psychology*, 77, 682-693.

Weingart, L. R., & Weldon, E. (1991). Processes the mediate the relationship between a group goal and group member performance. *Human Performance*, 4, 33-54.

Zaccaro, S. J. (1991). Nonequivalent associations between forms of cohesiveness and group-related outcomes: Evidence for multidimensionality. *The Journal of Social Psychology*, 131, 387-399.

Zaccaro, S., & Lowe, C. (1988). Cohesiveness and performance on an additive task: Evidence for multidimensionality. *Journal of Social Psychology*, 128(4), 547-558.

Zaccaro, S., & McCoy, M. C. (1988). The effects of task and interpersonal cohesiveness on performance of a disjunctive group task. *Journal of Applied Social Psychology*, 18(10), 837-851.

Chapter 3

History of Cell-Based Manufacturing

Jos Benders
Catholic University of Nijmegen, Nijmegen, The Netherlands

Richard Badham
University of Wollongong, Wollongong, Australia

Abstract

Cell-based manufacturing has a long history, and has been differently interpreted within different engineering traditions and countries. The result is a degree of confusion over the nature of "cells", which can foster disagreement and create ambiguities that are exploited by different vested interests in companies introducing cell-based manufacturing. A greater awareness of how and why this occurs would help our understanding of the choices to be made and the factors involved in the design and implementation of team-based cells. This is the rationale for this chapter's provision of a more detailed history of the complex and shifting nature of cell-based manufacturing.

Introduction

To paraphrase one of Nietzsche's comments, if a concept can be clearly defined, it has no history. Cell-based manufacturing has a long history, and has been differently interpreted within different engineering traditions and countries. The result is a degree of confusion over the nature of cells, which can foster disagreement and create ambiguities that are exploited by different vested interests in companies introducing cell-based manufacturing. For example, in one Australian automobile subsidiary a project to implement team based cells in the assembly of instrument panels foundered on confusion and disagreement over the nature of assembly cells. A number of engineers concerned to keep mechanical pacing of work and to continue to operate within traditional assumptions were committed to viewing Japanese "U" shaped assembly arrangements as cells. The social scientists within the design team were committed to an alternative socio-technical model of cell-based manufacturing that decouples individuals and groups from production or assembly processes, and releases work group members to carry out the indirect activities that are an essential part of self-managing teamwork.

M.M. Beyerlein (ed.), Work Teams: Past, Present and Future, 45–57.

A greater awareness of how and why this occurs would help our understanding of the choices to be made and the factors involved in the design and implementation of team-based cells. This is the rationale for the present paper's provision of a more detailed history of the complex and shifting nature of cell-based manufacturing. It does not attempt to resolve such disputes or provide a final clarification of the nature of cell-based manufacturing, but aims to clarify some of the sources of difference and ambiguity. Specifically, we emphasize that the prevailing unilinear account of the history of cell-based manufacturing is far too simple. This account holds that its origins are to be found in Soviet-Russia where Mitrofanow developed Group Technology, which came to be known in Europe via the activities of the English Professor John Burbidge (Alford, 1994). While not untrue, the Mitrofanow route was by no means the only line through which cell-based manufacturing developed.

Basic Forms of Layout

In its most comprehensive sense, cell-based manufacturing can be defined as `the grouping of machines, processes and people into cells dedicated to the manufacture or assembly of a family of similar parts or products'. It is a system of production that stands between the functional layout traditionally adopted in batch manufacturing and line-based mass production.

In a line layout, all operations are placed in the sequence of the product flow. This can only be profitable if a sufficiently large number of products are made, and the number of different products is low, both within a period (product range) as between periods (product variability). The products flow along the line, ideally without interruption. When product range and variability are high, the functional layout, which groups similar operations, can be expected to be found. Its main problems are that the large number of different products makes it hard to oversee and control production progress and that there tend to be large intermediate stocks.

The group layout is an intermediate form, "bringing together related or similar components in a production process in order to take advantage of their similarities by making use of, for example, the inherent economies of flow-production methods" (Gallagher and Knight, 1973, p. 3). In the group layout, machines are placed into specialised cells according to the family of parts or products that they produce. Like line production, cell-based manufacturing groups together all of the equipment (or as much as possible) necessary to carry out all the required operations to produce a dedicated family of parts or products. Parts or products can be more easily transferred from one operation to another within the cell without travelling long distances or involving lengthy waiting periods between operations. The relative independence of cells makes it possible to schedule work decentrally. Unlike the line the group is able to deal with a limited product range (i.e. the product family it was set-up to make), and it is possible to

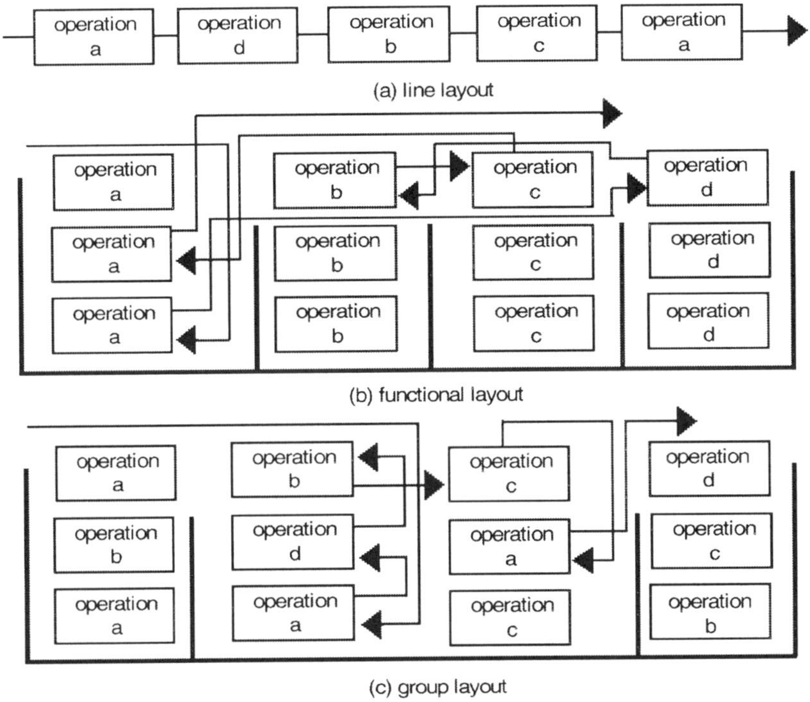

Figure 1. Basic Forms of Layout

customise and adapt a wider variety of products. The level of variation within individual cells determines to what extent a flow can be reached within the cell. One might state that from an engineering point of view the line is the perfect layout, but not always possible as the product range may be too large to set up a line. Ideal typical relationships between layouts and output characteristics are displayed in table 1.

TABLE 1: Output Characteristics and Layout

Lay-out	Product variability	Product range	Production volume
Line	Very low	Small	Large (very)
Cell	Low - intermediate	Small	Intermediate- large
Functional	Intermediate - high	Broad	Varies

Source: Benders (1993, p. 58). Copyright J. Benders. Used with permission.

Forerunners of Group Production

In 1924, R. E. Flanders read to the American Society of Mechanical Engineers. He described how the machine tool manufacturer Jones and Lamson Machine Company applied first product standardisation, and than organized production around these products. Sources in English occasionally refer to Flanders' paper, yet hardly ever to Richard Lang and Willy Hellpach's book *Gruppenfabrikation* (1922). Literally, this means group manufacturing. In the German-speaking world, it is quite well known as an early case of switching from a functional layout to a group layout.

Lang was a manager at the Daimler factory in Untertürkheim (near Stuttgart), and Hellpach a professor of organizational psychology and business economics based at Karlsruhe. Lang wrote only four pages of their joint publication, leaving more than 100 for Hellpach to comment on his description of *Gruppenfabrikation* in the Untertürkheim factory. Its goals are concisely described as `to achieve an enlarged over-see-ability and to save on transport' (p. 1). Producing complete products in groups rather than in a functional layout is seen, amongst other things, to allow engineers, managers and workers to deal with all parts and processes much more deeply; and lead, almost out of necessity, to far-going education and improvement and cheapening of work processes. Despite some acknowledged costs, such as the possible need more machines and a possible larger uniformity for workers, the system was seen as providing the possibility of overseeing the complete production process (Lang and Hellpach, 1922, p. 4).

It remains inconclusive whether Daimler was the first company to apply the group layout. According to Stahlmann, Daimler started the first pilots in its car industry in 1919, but had been applying the principle two years earlier in its aircraft factories (1993, p. 137). From Flanders' article it can derived that Jones and Lamson must have started around 1920. However, a commentator remarked that at "the works of the Brown and Sharpe Manufacturing Company certain lines of manufacturing are carried on in almost identically the same way as described in this paper" (Flanders, 1925, p. 723).

Possibly, the Brown and Sharpe Manufacturing Company had started even before Daimler. It seems reasonable to assume, however, that both the developments in Germany and the United States took place independently of each other, and that the scale at which Daimler implemented the group layout was unprecedented. By 1925, 94 departments in the Untertürkheim factory were structured along these lines and groups operated company-wide (p. 138). Yet further rationalization measures were taken, especially after Daimler and Benz merged in 1926. These measures included the standardization and reduction of the number of components, which on its turn allowed the introduction of production lines. These gradually replaced the groups.

Given the prominent role of Sweden in developing group work in the 1960s, it is interesting to note that truck and bus manufacturer Scania-Vanis had organized much of parts operation in groups in the late 1940s (Giertz, 1991). One of the company's engineers even used the term `group technology' in a lecture delivered in 1949:

> "the principles of group production are an adaptation of line production to machine-shops working on batch production...this implies radical decentralisation into small independent units or groups, each comprising the machines and everything needed for the complete manufacture of a special category of parts" (Gallagher and Knight, 1973, p. 7).

Also shortly after the Second World War, the Italian engineer Patrignani advocated the use of group production. Apparently, he never published his ideas on production management, which included cell manufacturing (*centres de travail*) and set-up time reduction (de Beer, 1987, p. 18-19). Mongon (1957) mentioned Patrignani in his description of changes at Alsthom-Lecourbe.

These examples make clear that the idea of placing those machines in groups, which are required for the production of particular product families, has occurred repeatedly in different countries, and was also put into applied in several instances. Some of the applications have been documented; those at Daimler and Scania-Vabis even quite extensively. Yet these early examples seem to have been lost in the mists of history. At this time, group layout appeared as a number of isolated experiments rather than as a new dominant way of organizing.

Routes of Development

As asserted in the introduction, the history of cell-based manufacturing is considerably more complex than the simple unilinear account of the Mitrofanow route. The latter was certainly important, yet was by no means the only relevant line of development, as demonstrated in this section.

The Mitrofanow Movement

The Russian engineer S. P. Mitrofanow played a vital role in developing classification and coding systems, but was equally important in advocating their use and disseminating knowledge about them. His contributions are well acknowledged, but that does not holds for the work of his predecessors on *tipizatsiya*, which were probably inspired by German *Typisierung*. In 1928, *tipizatsiya* or Type Technology (TT) was defined in an address to the Party central control commission of rationalization as "establishing types for a number of materials, the variety reduction of capital equipment and so on" (Grayson, 1972). The idea probably came from Germany. In Germany, a strong *Rationalisierung*-movement manifested itself in manufacturing and economy, and indeed society at large during the Weimar Republic (1917-1933). Part of this was the call for *Typisierung*: the reduction of the number of forms of final products (Dalhoff, 1928, pp. 54-55). *Typisierung* was the responsibility of individual companies, yet *Normung* (establishing norms) of "frequently occurring' parts was a national issue of which `the necessity is nowadays widely acknowledged" (Dalhoff, 1928, p. 61). The

Normenausschuß der Deutschen Industrie was responsible for this. To the present day, the DIN-norms are widely used in Europe.

The first Soviet classification and coding systems were developed during the five-year plan for 1933-1937. As of about 1936-38 a system for workplace classification developed by Professor A. P. Sokolovsky was first introduced and discussed quite extensively. During the Soviet involvement in second world war (1941-1945) other priorities prevailed, yet in the second half of the 1940s interest in classification and coding systems resumed. By 1953, a student of Sokolovsky, S. P. Mitrofanow had begun to use the principles of setting machines for the manufacture of related components at the Leningrad factory where he worked. The idea was that this allowed improvements in the utilization rate of machines and less time was needed to prepare the machine for making other parts. The use of a single set-up for a family of components also meant that savings could be realized in tooling. Once again, the idea may have come from Germany; Opitz states that *Teilefamilienfertigung* (manufacturing parts' families) was "already used successfully in the first years after 1930 in some mid-German companies" (1964, p. 1269).

A further phase of the development was around 1957 when it was realized that the emphasis on manufacturing families of components, something that came to be commonly termed group technology, made it possible to specialize work places in terms of number and types of operations to be performed required, a phenomenon that came to be more widely termed cellular manufacturing. Extending it to a group of machines for the complete manufacture of families of components made it possible to establish multi-product lines which gave many of the advantages of line production (Grayson, 1972).

In 1959, Mitrofanow published a book *Scientific Principles of Group Technology*, of which a German translation was published in 1960 and an English one in 1966. Much of it is devoted to improving the utilization rates of individual machines for different operations; multi-product lines are discussed yet less extensively. Mitrofanow clearly had a preference for standardization and establishing lines yet realized that this from an engineering point of view ideal situation could not always be achieved (1960, p. 417). Cells appear in Mitrofanow's book as a second-best solution, to be opted for when multi-product lines are infeasible.

Brisch, COPIC and Jeumont

Mitrofanow and his colleagues were by no means the only persons working on coding and classification systems (cf. Stokman, 1969). In the early 1950s London-based E.G. Brisch developed a system to classify items within industrial firms. The Brisch system was meant to be used for various purposes, for instance managing inventory, drawings and work pieces. The part of the Brisch system to classify work pieces was improved by the Parisian technical consulting firm Copic, in full *Compagnie Parisienne d'Ingénieurs-Conseil*, and applied in France at least as early as 1955. Although the system was initially not intended to be used for grouping parts (or machines), it was suitable for such a use.

An early documented case where Brisch-Copic was used to create group layout concerns the French firm *Forges & Ateliers de Construction Electriques de Jeumont*. This company operated six factories. In 1955, COPIC introduced the Brisch system. Classifying the component drawings was a lengthy process, during which it was realized families could be formed of related components and that these could be manufactured by specialized groups of machines. The first production unit (*unité de production*) U.P.1. was formed in 1958. After one experimental year it went into full operation. The experiences were sufficient positive: a second *unité* started in October 1959, the third one in 1960 (Sidders, 1962). Sidders does not discuss how Jeumont's engineers hit upon the idea to form groups. A likely source would be the Italian engineer Patrignani, who had been advocating cell-based production and set-up time reduction at least as early as 1953, and worked as a consultant in France. Patrignani was involved in changing a department of Alsthom-Lecourbe from functional to group production (Mongon, 1957). Another possible source comes from an article on classifications and coding by Gombinski, a managing director of Brisch's consulting firm. In keeping with the original system, he pointed out various possible uses including the possibility of combining similar components into batches. While his formulation implies that he had only individual machines in mind, he also referred to the work of Scania-Vabis' as reported to a congress held in Paris, 1948 (Gombinski, 1964).

The Travel of Ideas

The source of the idea to create cells at Jeumont may not be traceable with certainty given that the company started this work as early as 1958 and that there are at least two plausible sources of inspiration. However, it can be concluded that the history of group technology is far more complex than the unilinear account of what one may call the Mitrofanow route. The relationships between the developments in Continental Europe and the Soviet Union may need additional research, the timing makes clear that the ideas either developed independently, in which case they originate in Europe, or in parallel.

Another matter, however, is their diffusion, or rather the extent to which cells became widely taken up and seen as a real alternative to the functional way of organizing. By 1964, the idea had been published repeatedly in professional journals in different European countries, yet, as one contemporary remarked, "the system is far from being generally known or accepted in the West" (Gombinski, 1964, p. 604). However, the Russian work on group technology did certainly not go unnoticed. Galloway reported to the British Institution of Production Engineers based on a study tour to the Soviet Union and Eastern Europe (1960, p. 94). De Beer (1975) even mentioned a Mitrofanow movement in the Soviet-Union and Eastern Europe, which got attention in journals, newspapers and even television and radio broadcasts. By 1957, there were approximately 270 factories in the Soviet Union that used group technology.

Two years later this had increased to 750, but than the pace of growth declined: in 1965, about 840 factories used group technology. The Soviet's central planning system and standardization policies helped diffusing group technology, yet the reverse was true as well. Reforms in 1965 meant that governmental support largely fell away (Grayson, 1972, pp. 27-29).

John L. Burbidge

In 1962, after a long career in manufacturing and consulting, John L. Burbidge became a Production Expert with the International Labour Organisation. From 1967 to 1976, he was Professor at the International Centre for Advanced Technical and Vocational Training in Turin, Italy. This centre was part of the International Labour Organisation (ILO). Burbidge had a broad interest in the fields of manufacturing and production, and held distinct opinions. Among these was his belief in the inadequacy of a widely used formula to calculate batch sizes. His first book *Standard Batch Control* appeared in 1957.

As a manager, consultant, and author, Burbidge clearly displayed a broad knowledge of production management. However, he appears to have been more concerned with the practical usefulness of his ideas than their exact roots and hence only occasionally used references. It is often difficult to trace where he derived his insights. Yet it is clear that he was acquainted with Patrignani's work before Mitrofanow published his major work in Russian. In one of Burbidge's earliest publications, he referred to the example of Alsthom-Lecourbe as discussed in Mongon's (1957) presentation, although Burbidge did not name Patrignani himself (1959, p. 40). In 1961, he advocated a `new approach' to manufacturing: "It is possible to classify all the components made [..] into 'families', so that all the components made in each family are similar operations, in the same sequence, on the same plant" (1961, p. 783).

In the same paper, he discussed the consequences for such aspects as tooling and setting-up; with respect to the latter he referred to Signor Patrignani as "the leading authority in this field". Hence, it seems likely that Burbidge had acquired his insights on cell-based manufacturing from the traces Patrignani had left in France.

Burbidge clearly became enthused. His major conceptual contribution to the development of cell-based manufacturing lies in developing Production Flow Analysis or PFA (Burbidge, 1963). PFA aims to implement the group layout factory-wide. It involves the following main steps:

1. data collection;
2. finding sub-groups;
3. combining sub-groups into groups\families; and
4. checking the workloads of the groups to be formed.

PFA provided an alternative to classification and coding systems. By investigating how products flow through factories, and grouping the products with similar routings, parts and machine families can be established without using a classification and coding system. The example of *Jeumont* above illustrates well the time and effort needed to put such a system in place. PFA lowered the barrier to introducing cells on a systematic basis. The early examples, however, made clear that neither classification and coding systems not PFA are *per se* needed to implement cell-based manufacturing, yet they are helpful to introduce it on a systematic basis.

Yet Burbidge's contribution to cell-based manufacturing did not stop with developing PFA. Through a large number of publications (1962; 1975; 1979), research projects, lectures and other activities he advocated the use of group production and group technology. In September 1969, he organized a seminar in Turin with participants of Eastern and Western Europe, which was probably the first major international conference on Group Technology. Kay and Suresh state that Burbidge's "drive to publish his ideas [..] led to him becoming known as the Father of Group Technology" (1998, p. xiii). Burbidge's continuous efforts were probably instrumental for putting cell-based manufacturing on the agenda of Western managers. Apparently he well understood the need to market this novel approach persistently. Cell-based manufacturing broke with conventional thinking, and had many organizational and social consequences within firms. Getting managers to see it as legitimate and to adopt it required continuous rehearsal of the message.

Working in Groups

In one of the earliest texts on group technology in English, Edwards notes:

> "Within a cell, or GT unit, men will be required to work as a team. The traditional skill patterns of lathe operator, milling machine operator, and drilling machine operator, involving as they do different degrees and types of skill, present a problem for certain factories which frightens some managers" (1971, p. 68).

This change in the required technical skills means that additional training is required; drillers need to learn how to mill, and millers must learn drilling. The basis for workers' jobs changes from functional specialists to multi-skilled generalists. Craftsmen may perceive this as an erosion of their knowledge, and thus power, basis. As is common in change projects, the persons affected are likely to react based on their perceptions of advantages and disadvantages of the proposed changes. Organizational, social and managerial changes were reported (cf. Stahlmann, 1993):

> "While it is by no means certain that the implementation of group technology demands a radical change in management structure, the actual experience of one large firm, Ferodo was that it did" (Gallagher and Knight, 1973, p. 95).

In two respects, this quote seems typical of early writings on group technology and layout. First, it stresses that the transition from a functional to a group layout does not necessarily require a different type of work organization. Much depends on how the idea is configured in an organization (Badham, 1995). Secondly, the emphasis on changes in work organization seems to have grown out of practical experiences such as at the British firm Ferodo rather than being inspired by conceptual developments.

GT's effects on employees were not investigated systematically until the first half of the 1970s neither was it associated before the mid-1970s with the work on semi-autonomous work groups pioneered by the Tavistock Institute. The emphasis on group work within cell-based manufacturing can be traced back to 1975. In this year, the Geneva-based International Institute for Labour Studies, an ILO research centre, commissioned a project on group production methods and the humanisation of work, which was led by Burbidge (1976). In the course of the project, 477 cases were found in 32 countries, and 54 companies were visited to gather further information. The report was quite positive about the social effects of group production methods. In particular, moves away from the assembly line were seen as direct improvements, directly improving job designs and indirectly increasing participation in decision-making (both for social and economic reasons). The report was probably the first one in the GT-tradition that explicitly mentioned socio-technical work. From then on, the notion of teamwork as a group of persons became associated with cell-based layouts.

The term group production in the ILO-report covered both changes from functional to group layouts and attempts to move away from the assembly line. As Burbidge wrote later, group production within assembly was seen as being introduced mainly for social reasons. From an engineering point of view, creating cells within mass assembly (actually parts or segments within a line that are decoupled via buffers) could not obtain the gains that were obtained from changing from a functional to a group layout in batch production. The line was already seen as a form of flow production (Burbidge, 1979, p. 114). Particularly those emphasising the costs of mass assembly line inflexibility might contest this view. However, the ILO-project was primarily interested in group work from a social point of view, and thus included within group production experiments to break with the traditional assembly line. This move to cell-based assembly from mass assembly on was not included in the original notion of group technology.

Through further research in line with the ILO-report, the benefit of cell-based manufacturing for the quality of working life (QWL) was put on the agenda. Changes to work had been noted before, but QWL became an issue *per se* in the 1970s. This movement advocated teamwork or groupwork as both economically and socially beneficial. Such ideas took root in different countries in different forms. At the end of the 1960s, the Swedish Employers' Confederation SAF set up a national program to stimulate the occurrence of New Factories (Agurén and Edgren, 1980), and Volvo's Kalmar plant became an international example of technology and work redesign. In 1974, the German government launched a large program *Arbeit und Technik* (Work and Technology) that funded a considerable number of research and action project. In the USA, many QWL projects were started in the 1970s. In the Netherlands, similar ideas were incorporated in what was to become Modern Socio-technology (see *Modern Socio-Technology* chapter in this book). Worker and group autonomy became to be seen as key issues, and cell-based manufacturing provides a structure that enhances autonomy. Later other writers pointed to more or less insiduous forms of control that can go hand in hand with teamworking (Badham, McLoughlin and Buchanan, 1998).

While it should be recognized that working in teams has advantages and disadvantages, most authors appear to look favorably upon teams. Economic and social benefits can both be achieved. Yet although this possibility is clearly appealing, it may also give rise to suspicion: perhaps economic effects are only claimed to achieve social benefits? The example in our introduction indicates that such a suspicion still occurs. Again, this dilemma was identified early in history. Hellpach pleaded to consider QWL-benefits as an epiphenomenon (side effect), which could only be realized if economic benefits were achieved (Lang and Hellpach, 1922, p. 49-55).

History Travels On, As Do Ideas...

We started this chapter by paraphrasing Nietzsche: "if a concept can be clearly defined, it has no history." While we have been by no means exhaustive list, we drew on a wide range of literature originating in different countries to sketch the main lines in the history of cell-based manufacturing. Largely due to the persistent activities of staunch advocates and experimenters such as Lang, Hellpach, Patrignani, Mitrofanow and Burbidge, this initially the non-conventional of grouping machines for product families, and assign these to teams of operators managed to become a legitimate alternative for designing production systems. Contemporary textbooks on production and operations management include cell-based manufacturing as an option.

We demonstrated that the history of cell-based manufacturing is more complex than the unilinear version developed by Mitrofanow, popularized by Burbidge. The variety of historical sources is one reason why there are different and sometimes incompatible understandings of what groups, cells and teams constitute. The more popular these ideas become, the greater the number of understandings. The constant moulding of these ideas is likely to endure as long as variation and uncertainty remain within production, producers continue to be committed to technical and economic efficiency and improving workforce flexibility and commitment, and new production concepts are still moulded by the competing interests of employers, employees and their representatives. An understanding of this process can help us to comprehend the expansion and confusion in the meaning of cell-based manufacturing. Terms such as teams, groups, cells, group technology, and cells were and are often used interchangeably. Hopefully, our historical sketch contributes to creating a better understanding of what such terms may mean so that people can make better decisions on how the underlying notions can help in their own situations.

Acknowledgements

The first draft of this paper was written while Jos Benders was a Visiting Senior Fellow at the University of Wollongong. The financial support of the Australian Research Council and the Netherlands Organization for Scientific Research NOW is gratefully acknowledged. Steve Procter provided useful comments on an earlier draft. The enthusiasm and help of Emeritus Professor Carel de Beer greatly increased the joy of doing the research.

References

Agurén, S. and J. Edgren (1980), *New Factories; Job Design through Factory Planning in Sweden*, Stockholm: Swedish Employers' Confederation.

Alford, H. (1994), Cellular manufacturing: the development of the idea and its application, *New Technology, Work and Employment*, 9(1), 3-18.

Badham, R. (1995), Managing Socio-technical Change. A Configuration Approach to Technology Implementation, in: Benders, J., J. de Haan and D. Bennett (eds.), *The Symbiosis of Work and Technology*, London: Taylor and Francis, 63-79.

Badham, R., I.P. McLoughlin and D.A. Buchanan (1998), Human Resource Management and Cellular Manufacturing, in: Suresh, N.C. and J.M. Kay (eds.), *Group Technology and Cellular Manufacturing*, London: Kluwer Academic Publishers, 401-422.

de Beer, C. (1975), de historie van groepentechnologie, *PT-W*, 30(24), 798-800.

de Beer, C. (1987), *Afscheid van de Mechanische Technologie*, Eindhoven: Eindhoven University of Technology.

Benders, J. (1993), *Optional Options: Work Design and Manufacturing Automation*, Aldershot: Avebury.

Burbidge, J.L. (1959), A New Approach to the Batch Quantity Decision, *Productivity Measurement Review*, 17(5), 27-40.

Burbidge, J.L. (1961), The New Approach to Production, *Production Engineer*, 40(12) 769-784, 793.

Burbidge, J.L. (1962), *The Principles of Production Control*, London: McDonalds and Evans.

Burbidge, J.L. (1963), Production Flow Analysis, *Production Engineer*, 42(11), 742-751.

Burbidge, J.L. (1975), *The Introduction of Group Technology*, London: Heinemann.

Burbidge, J.L. (1976), *Group production methods and humanisation of work: the evidence in industrialised countries*, Geneva: International Institute for Labour Studies.

Burbidge, J.L. (1979), *Group Technology in the Engineering Industry*, London: Mechanical Engineering Publications.

Dalhoff, H. (1928), *Die Auswirkung der Rationalisierung auf die Organisation industrieller Betriebe*, Warendorf: J. Schnellsche Buchdruckerei.

Edwards, G.A.B. (1971), *Readings in Group Technology; Cellular Systems*, London: Machinery Publishing.

Flanders, R.E. (1925), Design, manufacture and production control of a standard machine, *Transactions of the ASME*, 46, 691-738.

Gallagher, C.G. and W.A. Knight (1973), *Group Technology*, London: Butterworths.

Galloway, D.F. (1960), Production Engineering Developments in the Soviet Union, *Production Engineer*, 39(2), 79-104.

Giertz, E. (1991), *Människor i Scania under 100 år; Industri, arbetsliv och samhälle i förändring*, Stockholm: Norstedts Juridikförlag.

Gombinski, J. (1964), Classification and Coding, *Engineering, Materials and Design*, 7(September), 600-605.

Grayson, T.J. (1972), *An Assessment of Soviet Technological Performance: Three Case Studies*, discussion paper, Birmingham: Center for Russian and East European Studies, University of Birmingham.

Kay, J.M. and N.C. Suresh (1998), Dedication, in: Suresh, N.C. and J.M. Kay (eds.), *Group Technology and Cellular Manufacturing*, London: Kluwer Academic Publishers, xiii-xiv.

Lang, R. and W. Hellpach (1922), *Gruppenfabrikation*, Berlin: Julius Springer.

Mitrofanow, S.P. (1960), *Wissenschaftliche Grundlagen der Gruppentechnologie* (second printing), Berlin: VEB Verlag Technik.

Mongon, J. (1957), Job regrouping, *CNOF*, 30(12), 150-152.

Opitz, H. (1964), Werkstücksystematik und Teilefamilienfertigung, *VDI-Z*, 106(26), 1268-1278.

Sidders, P.A. (1962), Flow Production of Parts in Small Batches, *Machinery*, 100(April 25), 920-929.

Stahlmann, M. (1993), *Die Erste Revolution in der Automobilindustrie; Management und Arbeitspolitik von 1900 - 1940*, Frankfurt am Main\New York: Campus Verlag.

Stokman, P.G. (1969), *Groepentechnologie en werkstukclassificatie in machinefabrieken*, unpublished Ph.D.-thesis Technical University of Twente.

Chapter 4

The Human Relations Myth Unveiled

Deconstructing the History and Origins of Work Teams

Ronald Purser
San Francisco State University, San Francisco, California, United States

Abstract

This chapter examines the origins of the human relations myth, the effect it has had on the evolution of work teams, and the distortions and misconceptions about self-management that have resulted. While the human relations ideology has had an enormous effect on the management theory and practice for the last seventy years, most popularized accounts fail to show how the famous Hawthorne studies were really a quest for improving managerial control over workers. In this chapter, the famous relay test room experiments are deconstructed, revealing how these early experiments increased managerial control under the façade of humane supervision. Human relations approaches to work teams often inhibit a real transformation to democratic self-management. Many current misconceptions and distortions of self-management, rooted in fallacies and myths propagated by the human relations movement, are also discussed.

Myth is the bubbling lifespring of consciousness...of our highest creativity as well as of our worst delusions, and the secret is all in how it is tended.

Stephen Larsen

Introduction

In many respects, the history of management thought has been marked by the quest for the perfect control mechanism--the Holy Grail of modern organizations. We might even say that this quest for control is the dominant organizational mythology of the twentieth century. Perhaps this explains the proliferation of techniques and methods, all more or less geared toward finding a better mousetrap for increasing *control over* people.

The self-managing organization represents a direct challenge to the control myth that has defined management thinking since the turn of the century. Yet, the only way that we can know with certainty if we are really moving toward a genuinely new paradigm of work is to know something of where we have been. Managers need

M.M. Beyerlein (ed.), Work Teams: Past, Present and Future, 59–83.

to first become aware of the dominant myths that have been guiding their thinking and behavior and then let go of them so that they can lead their organizations to a more viable future. Further, until we understand how modern management myths of control are disguised in current fads, managers will continue to be sold a bill of goods. All too often managers end up carrying the baggage of the control paradigm along with them even as they attempt to embark on the journey toward democratic self-management.

The myths we have inherited from the past structures our thinking and behavior, shaping our choices for organizing the world. We design organizations and manage according to the maps that myths create, yet we are largely unaware that this is happening. Myths are powerful, because they operate outside of our conscious awareness, and we are largely ignorant of their origins. Indeed, we are so thoroughly immersed in our myths that they are invisible to us--like water is to fish. When we are unconscious of the myths we live by, we tend to perceive the world in a distorted way, and act in ways that confirm our myths. However, when the world changes, a myth that once served as our ally may no longer fit the new territory, thus clinging to it can impede our ability to transform and grow. We contend that the guiding myth of managerial control has outlived its usefulness, yet it continues to exert a powerful influence on management thought, because we haven't been able to name it.

Joseph Campbell (1968), perhaps the foremost authority on myths, found that once a tribal culture could clearly describe its myth, it lost much of its power. This is what modern organizations need to do, if they are to release themselves from the stranglehold of outmoded traditions and dysfunctional myths. Just as tribal cultures live according to a mythology they often cannot name, organizations live according to a socially constructed reality--an organizational mythology--that is unbeknownst to them. Turning our conscious attention to these guiding myths is like adding a catalyst to a chemical reaction: suddenly old beliefs and traditions that seemed entrenched and impervious to change begin to fizzle and bubble, sending off bursts of insights and renewed energy. Simply deciphering a dysfunctional myth is a step toward transformative change.

The Human Relations Myth

If there is one myth that still exerts an enormous influence on managerial thought and practice to this day, it is the human relations myth. According to this myth, management could compensate for the loss of dignity, meaning and pride in work by *showing interest* in the worker. The belief was that emotional support systems would mitigate against a bureaucratic organization's tendency to beat up the human psyche. In addition, this myth promises that humane supervision will produce happy and productive workers. It didn't matter if jobs were monotonous, repetitive and degrading. It didn't matter if product defects were passed down the line because workers had no authority to control variances at their source. And it didn't matter if there were seven levels of hierarchy, which slowed decision making. Indeed, nothing needed to be changed in the workplace except for the personality and behavior of the supervisor.

Human relations is a compelling myth that is reflected in a plethora of contemporary management and organization development practices: participative management, survey feedback, teaming, employee counseling, and supervisory social skills training. It is often portrayed as a rebellion against the principles of the classical school that were based primarily upon Taylor's principles of scientific management and Max Weber's writings on the virtues of bureaucracy. What is even more amazing is the genesis of this myth: a series of studies conducted from 1924 to 1933 at Western Electric's Hawthorne Works plant.

The Hawthorne Studies

Several generations of managers, academics and consultants have been influenced by the Hawthorne studies and the human relations movement which it spawned. Knowledge of the Hawthorne studies are based on popular accounts--such as the one found in Peters and Waterman's *In Search of Excellence* (1982), in organizational behavior or industrial psychology textbooks, or other official accounts published by the Harvard and Western Electric researchers that were involved in the studies--such as Roethlisberger and Dickson's *Management and the Worker (1939).*

Most popular accounts (Morgan, 1986; Weisbord, 1987) and descriptions typically inform us that managers at Western Electric's Hawthorne Works plant (a wholly owned subsidiary of the Bell System), in collaboration with Elton Mayo and his team of researchers from the Harvard Business School conducted a series of experiments to measure the effect of industrial illumination and rest periods on productivity. The thinking of the day was that physical conditions of the plant were significantly related to worker morale and productivity. The most popularized account (Roethlisberger & Dickson, 1939) of the Hawthorne studies often describes how researchers introduced different conditions of illumination to an experimental group, while another work group served as a control. Illumination for the experimental group was increased and productivity went up. However, the researchers could not isolate the effects of illumination on productivity. Puzzled by the results, they began to question their theory that illumination was a direct cause of productivity. To test their hypothesis, the researchers decreased the intensity of lighting in the test room and productivity still went up.

Determined to find the answers to what accounted for the productivity improvements, managers at Western Electric sanctioned additional experiments in what is now known as the famous relay assembly test room experiments. This series of experiments began in April 1927 and was terminated February 1933. Popular accounts of this key experiment describe how six women assemblers were selected to work in a special test room where their productivity, social interactions, and attitudes were constantly observed. The research team experimented with altering the number and length of womens' rest periods, offering shorter work days and work weeks (perhaps the first application in flex-time), and providing meals and coffee breaks. For five years, various experimental conditions were introduced and the effect on productivity and morale were recorded. The results were promising: productivity increased by some 34 percent in the first two years and by 46 percent over the entire five years.

After introducing over ten experimental changes, the researchers decided to radically alter the experiment by reverting back to original conditions of the work setting. This period would provide a quasi-experimental control condition. During this crucial twelfth test period, the women worked as they normally had before the experiment began--without rest periods, without midmorning coffee breaks, returning to their regular hours and schedule. The results were similar to the phenomena encountered by the researchers in the illumination experiment: the women broke all previous productivity records on a daily and weekly basis without any drop in output for twelve straight weeks. Their output continued to increase through the following experimental period for thirty one weeks, under the same original work conditions. Researchers concluded that no single experimental factor could explain or be correlated directly to the incremental increases in productivity. Interpreting these findings, Roethlisbeger concluded:

> After Period XII in the Relay Assembly Test Room, the investigators decided to change their ideas radically. What all their experiments had dramatically and conclusively demonstrated was the importance of employee attitudes and sentiments. It was clear that the responses of workers to what was happening about them were dependent upon the significance these events had for them. This was the great *eclaircissement,* the new illumination, that came from the research (1941, p. 84).

Productivity apparently increased in spite of the experimental conditions that the researchers introduced in the study. This apparent discovery is often associated with the studies otherwise known as the "Hawthorne Effect."

Looking back on the relay assembly test room experiments, Mayo interpreted the results in these terms:

> What actually happened was that six individuals became a team and the team gave itself wholeheartedly and spontaneously to cooperation in the experiment. The consequence was that they felt themselves to be participating freely and without afterthought, and were happy in the knowledge that they were working without coercion from above or limitations from below. (1945, p.30)

Textbook accounts attribute the production increases to the fact that the women were treated humanely by their supervisor and the researchers. These accounts claim productivity was influenced more by social factors in the study--the special considerations given by the researchers and supervisors, and workers' attitudes--than by changes in working conditions. The unexpected influences of the researchers on the experiment--the so-called "Hawthorne Effect"-- is a household phrase in the social and behavioral sciences.

The Relay Assembly Test Room Revisited

Popular and textbook descriptions of the Hawthorne studies have relied on official published accounts, not the original experimental records. In his book, *Manufacturing Knowledge* (1991), Richard Gillespie, a curator of the history of science and technology at the Museum of Victoria in Australia, provides a rich narrative account of the Hawthorne experiments based on original archival data. Even Mayo's Harvard research team did not have access to some of the data which Gillespie managed to dig up. His in-depth and detailed historical reanalysis of the Hawthorne experiments--from the point of view of the Western Electric engineers, the Harvard researchers, and the six women themselves who were subjects in the relay test room experiment--tells quite a different story from the popular version that has informed managerial thought and practice for the last seventy years.

Let's begin by taking another look at the relay test room experiments, since they are the most controversial of the experiments. First, it is important to note that the early relay test room experiments, along with the previous illumination studies, were designed and conducted by Western Electric industrial engineers, not the Harvard team. Elton Mayo and his colleagues came on the scene several years after the relay test experiment had begun. We should also be cognizant of how important the relay test room experiments were to Western Electric engineers. The Hawthorne Works plant manufactured and supplied all of the relay switches for the entire Bell System. This plant produced over 6,500 different relays, with a total annual production of 7 million relays. The Relay Department was a major production area within the plant, employing 300 assemblers. The assembly of relays consisted of mounting some thirty five different parts and was highly repetitive work, requiring manual dexterity. Those assigned to relay assembly jobs were unskilled workers. Because the assembly work was labor intensive, speed of production was critical to maintaining output. Western Electric engineers were keen on understanding a variety of questions related to effects of working conditions on productivity.

Humane Supervision or Panoptic Control?

Official accounts of the relay test room experiments fail to describe the extent to which the women in the test room were closely supervised and monitored. The six women that were selected to move to the special test room had previously worked in an area among a hundred or so other women in the Relay Assembly area. Special equipment was built to record the pace and productivity of each individual worker in the test room. Each time a woman completed a relay assembly she placed it in a chute that triggered a paper punching recording mechanism. In addition, a supervisor and an assistant were assigned to the test room. The observer sat directly opposite the workbench where the women were seated. The productivity for each woman was recorded in a logbook every fifteen minutes. The supervisor also methodically filled out a daily history sheet, noting any changes in social interactions or attitudes of the women.

Most of the women assigned to the test room were young immigrants from ethnic communities on the west side of Chicago. Similar to the practices in Ford's sociological department, Western Electric researchers extended their investigations into the personal lives of the women. The researchers questioned the women about their home lives, families, and social activities. Two of the key researchers--Homer Hibarger, the piece rate analyst who was the principal investigator for the illumination experiments, and technical superintendent George Penrock, required the women to have monthly medical check-ups by the company's physicians. Hibarger supplied the physician a list of questions to ask the women, hoping the doctors would gain information that they might otherwise not divulge to supervisors. Even the timing of the women's menstrual periods were known and recorded by the researchers.

Gillespie's (1991) historical reconstruction of Hawthorne shows us that it was a highly controlled and invasive experiment that has little resemblance to popular accounts. Such accounts typically attribute productivity increases among the women in the relay assembly test room to humane supervision, claiming the researchers showed interest in the women by soliciting their preferences and attitudes toward various working conditions introduced during the course of the experiment. Clearly, the women were given more attention, but it was in the form of *closer supervision*. The women were informed each day of their output, and were threatened with reprimands if their output fell below expected levels. Throughout the study, and in the official published accounts, the women were consistently referred to as "girls." Far from having autonomy over their work, the women in the relay assembly test room were under constant surveillance. As Gillespie points out:

> But the supervision in the test room, even if conducted in a less confrontational fashion, was probably more intense and more focused than it was in the department. To be sure, Hibarger was officially the test room observer, and as such he had no supervisory control over the women, nor did he seek it. Disciplinary power remained with the Relay Assembly Department foremen, Mr. Platenka, who could pay only occasional visits to the test room. But the very organization of the test room entailed increased supervision. Each time a worker completed a relay and dropped it down the chute, she was reminded that the time she took to assemble that relay had been measured automatically on the tape. The sound of the falling relays told her how rapidly her fellow workers were proceeding. Each morning Hibarger would announce the previous day's output and translate that into wages. And if output was particularly low, Platenka would visit the room to inform the workers of their poor performance. On at least one occasion the experimental variables were used as a stick; Pennrock directed

Hibarger to hint to the workers that the morning lunches would be discontinued if production and cooperation did not improve." (1991, pp. 60-61).

Supervisory style in the test room was more relaxed in comparison to the traditional autocratic gang boss who typically spared no words in ushering verbal threats and commands. But the supervisory gaze actually intensified in the relay test room. Control remained firmly at the heart of management's agenda. The Relay Assembly Test Room was in many respects a psychic prison, set up to reflect Jeremy Bentham's famous panopticon design for a prison, with its central observation tower allowing inmates to be constantly observed by doctors, workhouse managers, or prison guards. Subtle control mechanisms--reprimands, constant performance monitoring, and entries of unacceptable social behavior in the Daily History Record--clearly demonstrated that the women were under constant surveillance. Two years into the experiment, four additional staff were added to the test room: a junior clerk, a calculator, a typist, and an inspector of the finished relays.

A special payment scheme was also introduced to the six women assemblers that rewarded them for their group output. Prior to the experiment, the women were on a similar group incentive plan except that their earnings were averaged across a group of one hundred. Under their new payment scheme, the six women could easily see the connection between their individual output and the amount of money they could earn. This economic incentive is downplayed in popular and official accounts.

What did the women themselves think of the experiments? Textbooks and publications by the Harvard research team don't provide this perspective. Clearly, the women realized that the experiments were of great interest to Western Electric, and began to take advantage of their informal power. Gillespie reports that one of the women "requested that a screen be placed in front of their workbench to provide them privacy from the male experimenter's gaze" (1991, p.58). The women resented having to be subjected to monthly physical examinations and the personal interrogations by the doctors and nurses. To appease and pacify the women, the experimenters arranged to have parties for the women during their visits to the doctor--providing them cake, ice cream, tea, and music. The women were given all sorts of special privileges that were unheard of in the larger plant.

The women were far from being compliant and submissive. At one point during the experiment, several of the women threatened to go on strike when they learned there had been a miscalculation of their wages. While it was basically an empty threat, it demonstrated how the women had learned how to bargain and negotiate with the researchers in exchange for their cooperation in the experiment. However, not all of the women were so compliant. A year into the experiment, a conflict erupted between two of the women and the Western Electric researchers. The women in the relay assembly test room enjoyed talking while working, but incessant talking often led to slowdowns in production. Hilbager noted the periods when the women talked by marking "19" on the tape. Two of the women objected to this continuous surveillance and threatened to go on strike if he continued to mark "19" on the tape. The researchers warned the women that disruptive talking had to cease, and it did for the most part, except for two women who continued to be defiant. They disregarded the warnings and were removed from the test room, and replaced by two new women who had reputations for being fast assemblers.

Popular accounts also lose sight of the fact that the initial purpose of the Hawthorne experiments was to determine the effects of rest periods on productivity. During the first year, the controlled experiments were designed and conducted by Western Electric's industrial engineers, not social scientists. Careful study was made of the effects of every research variable on productivity. As Gillespie (1991) reports:

> Half of the fourteen conclusions in the relay test report concerned production curves and the effects of rest periods. The slump in production in late morning was found to be due not to fatigue, but to the workers taking time to go to the bathroom. Similarly, the early afternoon slump apparently resulted from the workers feeling tired after having had a heavy lunch--hence the introduction of the midmorning meal to lessen the time between breakfast and lunch and reduce the size of the lunch. The ten-minute rests and morning lunch and afternoon rests periods resulted in the highest production, but the five minute rests brought the most consistent production (p. 66).

What we see here at Hawthorne is not so much humane supervision, but a conscious and deliberate attempt at intensifying managerial control through subtle manipulation of experimental variables. If this is really the case, how did the mythology of Hawthorne get created?

Human Relations Interpretation: Enter Elton Mayo

A year into the experiments, Western Electric engineers still were not confident whether they could attribute productivity increases to the rest periods. There were other factors that offered alternative explanations. Perhaps productivity increased because the women worked together in a small group? Maybe the real cause was simply the introduction of a line-of-sight economic group incentive? Could it be the lunches and free meals? Perhaps a different style of supervision? Determined to find the answers to what accounted for the productivity improvements, managers at Western Electric sanctioned additional experiments and turned to outside advice, inviting Elton Mayo from the Harvard Business School and Clair Turner a statistician from MIT to join the research team.

Mayo first entered Hawthorne in April 1928, where he proceeded to take blood pressure and pulse measurements on each of the women in the test room. It is important to point out that Mayo was a lay Freudian analyst. Going into Hawthorne, Mayo believed that physiological factors related to fatigue were associated with psychiatric disturbances. Having access to the medical records of the two women that had been removed from the experiment, Mayo made a case that one of the women had anemia, indicative of a tendency toward "pessimistic or paranoid preoccupations, fatigue and organic disability." The blood count for the other woman was normal, which Mayo seemed to have ignored. Noting this bias, Gillespie (1991) states, there is "A persistent tendency in Mayo's work to transform any challenge by workers of managerial control into evidence of psychiatric disturbance" (p.73). This practice reminds us of the treatment of dissidents in the former Soviet Union who were exiled to psychiatric hospitals for their protests against the Communist regime.

The inconsistency of the experimental findings coming out of the relay assembly test room allowed for multiple interpretations of the data. At first, the Western Electric industrial engineers were intent on isolating the effects of rest periods on productivity--a tangible change in procedure they could easily introduce into the rest of the plant. When Western Electric researchers began to come under Mayo's influence, and were eventually swayed into thinking that the productivity increases were due to improved "mental attitudes" of the women. However, Mayo's influence on the relay test room didn't really occur until the last two years of the experiments. By this time, a massive interviewing program was already underway in the Hawthorne plant. Over a three-year period, the Harvard team--along with a trained staff of some 300 people--interviewed all 21,000 of the plant's workers in confidence. Mayo surmised that interviews could serve as therapeutic devices that helped the worker to gain insight into his or her "personal situation," and thereby change their "undesirable" attitude or behavior. Interviews helped employees to feel that management cared about their opinions and concerns. Subsequently, employees began to talk about how the conditions in the plant were improving (even if nothing had really changed; in fact, the interviewers had no power or charge to change the problematic conditions identified by employees).

During the fifth year of the experiment, each of the women in the relay assembly test room were required to meet with a woman interviewer, Imogen Rosseau, once a week. The women resented the imposition. In addition to this, an observer, D.D. Davisson, also from the research team, was assigned full-time to the relay assembly test room. The women managed to evade the observer by talking softly enough that he was unable to record their conversations (the noise in the adjacent department drowned out most conversations). The final internal research report issued by the Western Electric managers downplayed changes in working conditions as major reasons for increased production, emphasizing instead the changed "mental attitudes" of the women. But the reports from the woman interviewer and observer questioned this claim. As Gillespie (1991) points out:

> Rosseau and Davidsson were not so sure. After interviewing the women several times and reading the previous reports, Rosseau concluded that "explanation of test group behavior may not lie in as obscure causes as is generally supposed."

> She particularly stressed the importance of increased earnings as a motive, noting that the women had been most concerned that her repeated interviewing would affect their wages. Davisson was equally critical of what he saw as undue emphasis on the supposed lack of supervision in the test room. He claimed that insufficient attention had been paid to such factors as the excellent supply of parts to the test room, the limited number of relay types, and in particular the pay incentive, observing that the women had a keen interest in their daily percentages and a much clearer understanding of the piecework system than other workers. (pp. 87-88)

As we can see, there were competing interpretations for the causes of the productivity increases in the relay assembly test room. Mayo in his writings (1933; 1945) continually discounted the workers' interpretations and perspective. Particularly in the case of the relay test room, Mayo attributed the women's complaints and interpretations as mere "emotional reactions" that shouldn't be taken seriously. His theory of psychopathology reduced workers' complaints about working conditions in industry to their personal problems and social maladjustment--not to any real objective conditions. Mayo theorized the clash between workers and management could be attributed to a fundamental difference in outlooks between the two groups. Attitudinal dispositions of workers followed a "logic of sentiment," whereas management behavior was guided more by a "logic of efficiency." Gillespie (1991) states: "Mayo was now advocating that management take charge of the social relations of production, and he seemed to offer scientific proof that workers could achieve happiness and their full productive potential only if managers recognized that workers were emotional children who needed firm parental guidance" (p.190). For Mayo, the emerging problems in industry could only be solved through the creation of a new "administrative elite" that were trained in proper human relations skills.

Mayo had great interest in using the empirical results of the Hawthorne experiments to further his own social and political theories of industrial organization. In reality, the "Hawthorne effect" and the notion that humane supervision could lead to happier and more productive workers is a socially constructed myth--interpretations and claims that Mayo and his colleagues imposed on the data to further their own disciplinary interests and ideological commitments. The title of Gillespie's historical analysis of Hawthorne, *Manufacturing Knowledge*, underscores the notion that meaning in social science is not discovered, it is imposed. In other words, the cause of productivity increases in the test room was not a scientific fact that simply revealed itself to disinterested and objective researchers. Rather, causal explanations that came to be accepted as "the truth" and "scientific fact" were constructed and legitimized through publications and dissemination of articles that propounded a highly select and stylized account of the Hawthorne studies. Elton Mayo's protégé, Fritz Roethlisberger, along with Western Electric personnel manager William Dickson, put the Harvard stamp on the Hawthorne experiments. Together they published *Management and the Worker*--the official account of the study which gave academic legitimacy to the claim that increased production was due to the development of a "spontaneous type of informal organization," facilitated by the humane supervisory style of the experimenters who paid attention to the needs of the workers.

Enacting the Myth

The human relations myth reinforces the notion that worker satisfaction and higher productivity depends upon enlightened supervisors who are capable of fostering a cooperative, team atmosphere. For nearly half a decade we have been led to believe that workers require a parental guide--that workers are too emotionally immature to be provided the responsibility to assume control over their work. Workers, we have been told, could be made happier by providing them a supportive supervisor--a coach--who could fashion a cohesive group of subordinates into a high performing team.

But what sort of team are we talking about? The human relations myth seems to provide justification that workers should not have any control over their own work, but should take their direction from a nurturing and caring supervisor. However, providing supportive supervision without real autonomy is not authentic care, but manipulation. In reality, the human relations approach is antithetical to the formation of autonomous work groups and self-managing teams. Human relationists have viewed collective action on the part of workers with extreme suspicion. Informal work groups--without close management supervision--"could erupt in irrational behavior," restriction of output, and informal cliques that subvert management's goals[1]. The small informal group represented an anomaly that management was ill prepared to handle. As Baritz (1960) notes:

> Such a group had to be either destroyed or changed. Perhaps management could replace hostile groups with friendly ones of their own creation, or perhaps it could convince the members of a group that hostility to management was pointless. In any case, management, by and large, understandably refused to allow these informal associations to emerge without 'guidance', without control. (p.176)

One of the most significant lessons that Mayo learned from the Hawthorne studies was that informal work groups would follow management's directives, not through coercion or command, but through indirect inducements. The interview program showed that by listening to employees' concerns, their attitudes toward management and their jobs became more positive. The key was to provide work groups psychological inducements so that they would align their interests with management in the pursuit of organizational goals. By using a more indirect approach, the skillful manager could coopt the energies of the small work group by employing various tactics--by winning the informal leader of work groups to his side; by exhibiting a democratic leadership style; by coaching and counseling individual employees; and by keeping a pulse on the group's attitudes and concerns. In short, the skillful human relations manager could induce work group cooperation by becoming a *team leader, coach and counselor.*

Based on a dubious model that effective leadership was a key driver of employee morale and higher productivity, training supervisors in human relations skills became one of the biggest management fads of this century. Effective leadership in the human relations vernacular was lumped together with behaviors that demonstrated a democratic versus authoritarian style of management, being more employee-centered rather than production-centered, and showing a general concern and consideration for the welfare of employees. Daniel Bell characterizes the changing image of "the tough brutal foreman, raucously giving orders, gives way to the mellow voice of the 'human-relations' oriented supervisor." By mastering the new industrial etiquette, a supervisor could effectively soften the blow of his authority.

Documenting the changing norms of social interaction as the absolutist monarchies came into power, Elias (1978) notes how a more refined set of manners and customs--a new social etiquette--emerged that was befitting of appropriate social intercourse in the royal court. According to Elias, "the development of etiquette represented a 'reconfiguration' of the management of human affect within a specific social group in responses to the larger social surround" (cited in Neilsen & Rao, 1990, p.73). Similarly, Neilsen and Rao (1990) argue that the human relations movement served as a vehicle for introducing a new etiquette to the managerial class in response to a series of technical, economic and social changes. With the rise of bureaucracy, this new social etiquette would rationalize "interpersonal relations...by standardizing the expression and articulation of emotions and sentiments." (p83). Bendix (1956) agrees, suggesting:

> ...the changeover from the idealization of the 'strenuous life' to the idealization of 'human relation' may be an adaptation of a similar kind. The manners commended by the personnel experts of modern American industry certainly facilitate the cooperation which management requires, much as the commendation of polite manners facilitated peace at the Royal Court. ...The rules of conduct which are appropriate to teamwork and the ideology which idealizes the values of human relations are attempts to standardize and facilitate the internal operation of bureaucratic enterprises. (pp. 335-336)

Just as knights and nobles had to learn courtly social graces if they were to successfully maneuver within a new political context, supervisors and managers needed to learn new social skills if they were to adapt to the constraints of bureaucratic organization. "Emphasis on leadership and persuasion," Greiner observed, "supplanted the crude demand for discipline and obedience, and the dynamics of supervision relied more on understanding human behavior and ostensibly less on raw power." (Greiner, 1988, p. 173).

From Entrepreneur to Organization Man

After the Great Depression and through the 1950s, the "businessman-as-hero" gave way to the "organization man." Self-employment steadily declined, while the number of people who went to work for large corporations increased. A successful corporate career now required social skills and calculated impression management. The industrial tycoon--with his forceful, outwardly aggressive, and demanding personality--became a bull in the bureaucratic china shop. This brash "management style" was too uncouth for conducting affairs within the modern court of the executive suite. Instead, the new industrial etiquette demanded a high degree of emotional balance, self-control and social competence. The ideal human relations manager in American corporations was polished, soft spoken, well-rounded--not quite an English gentleman, but certainly an agreeable and amiable personality--qualities which were deemed as essential to getting along with others. Dale Carnegie's *How to Win Friends and Influence People* became a best selling guidebook that instructed managers how to play on peoples' emotions through a form of "personality salesmanship." Carnegie wrote that there were essentially four ways we could "win friends and influence people," "by what we do, by how we look, by what we say, and how we say it."

Bureaucratic organizations needed unimaginative "team players," not rugged individualists, visionary entrepreneurs, or aggressive self-starters. "The competitive struggle as a vital force *within* an organization was soft-pedaled." (Scott, 1962, p.52). According to research conducted by Harvard social psychologist David McClelland (1985), the need for achievement dramatically decreased in American society from 1925 to 1950. In fact, by 1950 the organization man had arrived as most Americans were motivated more by a need to form affiliative relationships than by the need to achieve.

David Riesman and his colleagues (1950) were quite concerned with this trend in American society, noting that the average person was shifting from being "inner-directed" to being "other-directed." According to Riesman, inner-directed man was individualistic and an independent product of the Protestant ethic and *laissez-faire* capitalism. In contrast, the "other-directed" man was more concerned about fitting into the crowd, with what others thought of him, and with getting along and being accepted. Other-directed man focused on career advancement and security rather than autonomy. The sense of social isolation and feelings of loneliness inside impersonal bureaucratic organizations opened the doors for "groupism." The lonely individual took refuge in the comforts and security of the small group, and the human relations movement was ideally positioned to exploit the needs of other-directed individuals.

If one closely examines the underpinnings of human relations programs, one will find that much of the burden and locus of control for improvements--whether they be improvements in employee morale, job satisfaction, or productivity--rests on changing the behavior and personality of the supervisor. The human relations movement was ardently intent on reforming the foreman. For human relations theorists, good social skills was the missing ingredient in the industrial equation. By demonstrating effective social skills, supervisors could tame supposedly irrational employee behavior by influencing group members to think constructively, accept management's directives, and identify with the formal goals of the organization. After all, this type of humane leadership behavior and consultative style of supervision was how Hawthorne researchers were able to elicit the cooperation of the women in the Relay Assembly Test room or so it was thought

Douglas McGregor's Theory X and Theory Y Revisited

A seminal figure of the second wave, Douglas McGregor, mounted a challenge to autocracy by questioning management's dominant assumptions regarding human nature. In his often cited and now classic book, *The Human Side of Enterprise* (1960*)*, McGregor criticized the classical principles of bureaucratic organization as being outdated and inappropriate for the management of the modern corporation.

McGregor's main point of leverage for undoing bureaucracy rested on changing managerial assumptions about human nature. As Daniel Wren (1994) points out, for McGregor, "managerial assumptions about human nature and human behavior were all-important in determining the manager's style of operating"(p. 449). McGregor outlined traditional managerialist assumptions as "Theory X," and an alternative set of assumptions as "Theory Y."

Almost every textbook on organizational behavior has presented McGregor's theoretical formulation as polarized opposites. This is also another great myth. McGregor (1960) humbly admitted that Theory Y was merely intended as a thumbnail sketch of a new mode of management which was still yet unknown and emerging. In other words, McGregor had an intuitive sense that a new paradigm of work would be necessary in the future, but he couldn't quite envision nor articulate what the contours of that paradigm were exactly to be. Perhaps if he hadn't had such a premature death he would have gone on to build a firm foundation for the self-management paradigm. Let's also remember that McGregor introduced his formulation of Theory X and Theory Y in 1960 when there were few serious challenges to the traditional command and control structure of management. McGregor's ideas, while tentative and preliminary, were perceived as radical and groundbreaking for their time (and in principle, they still are).

What is clear is that he intended Theory Y to be a starting place for a *new dialogue* on the potentiality of human beings in the workplace. As McGregor stated:

"The purpose of this volume is not to entice management to choose sides over Theory X or Theory Y. It is, rather, to encourage the realization that *theory is important,* to urge management to examine its assumptions and make them explicit" (1960, p. 246, emphasis added).

Even despite his critique of human relation models, McGregor was still very much a human relationist in that he viewed the locus of change for organizational reform was dependent on manager's style of operating. And according to McGregor's theory, a manager's style of operating was a reflection of his or her assumptions of human nature. A manager who held Theory X assumptions would tend toward using traditional command and control practices, coercing, punishing, and directing the work of employees. To the degree that management harbors the assumption that human beings dislike work and are inherently lazy, evil and shiftless, then managers will keep a tight leash on employees.

There is no doubt that a debased view of human nature may run deep in our psyche, but the problem of organizational reform is not primarily a psychological one. Yet, it has become customary to lay the blame for the control paradigm on the "Theory X" assumptions that managers have of people. Many organization development consultants and zealous change agents often use "Theory X" as a convenient label to stigmatize and demonize managers who "resist" their moral exhortations. These consultants still preach the old time, McGregorian "Theory Y" religion. According to them, everything would be just fine if "Theory X" managers would just repent, see the humanistic light, and become "Theory Y" converts. Such superficial guilt-tripping is both misguided and ineffective. This bastardized use of McGregor's theory is far from what he had in mind. Indeed, simply branding and typecasting managers as being either "Theory X" or "Theory Y" is nothing more than stereotyping.

We believe that most managers are decent and intelligent human beings that want to do the right thing within existing organizational constraints. For one, an implicit personal philosophy of management--Theory X--or any other psychological explanation, cannot account for the structural entrenchment of the bureaucratic control paradigm. However high-minded and morally superior Theory Y philosophy may be, such managerial nobility and progressive humanism would be crushed and crippled in organizations where bureaucracy is still retained as the formal structure. It is simply unfair to blame managers for having a "Theory X" orientation, since the values they hold come with the bureaucratic territory. Indeed, bureaucracy is the host institution in which Theory X authoritarian yearnings and control freak behaviors found legitimacy. One can't blame managers for their behavior when they are locked into a structure that sanctions centralized decision making and autocratic control.

McGregor's emphasis on changing managerial assumptions as a means of initiating and sustaining democratic organizational reform depended too much on the idiosycrancies of the individual manager. Even if workers were fortunate to find themselves employed in an organization dominated by genuine Theory Y managers, they would still be under their dominion. The enlightened Theory Y manager was still in control of the supposed transformation toward democracy and self-management. According to McGregor, under Theory Y, it was the essential task of management to unleash man's potential by creating "conditions such that the members of the organization can achieve their own goals best by directing their efforts toward the success of the enterprise."(p. 49). According to this humanistic formula, enlightened management would rise to the occasion, freeing the worker from the shackles of bureaucratic oppression. Not only this, such noble acts of emancipation didn't lose sight of the bottom-line: workers would be freed by redirecting their efforts toward the success of the enterprise.

What is the magical elixir here? Management would accomplish this form of emotional jujitsu by winning over the worker's *commitment.* A consistent theme proffered by the industrial humanists of yesteryear as well as those of recent times is that the responsibility for democratic organizational reform lies in the hands of a few enlightened managers who become "change masters," "liberators," who triumphantly and single-handedly bust up the bureaucracy, emancipating workers from the strictures of domination and authoritarian control.

Industrial humanists are correct in their diagnosis that bureaucratic organization and autocratic management are the culprits, but their prescriptions amount to a weak form of academic medicine: theoretical exhortations urging managers to change their outmoded assumptions by becoming more participative and employee-centered. This was the essential message of the democratic leadership school. But rather than focusing their attention on changing the bureaucratic organization structure and division of labor, academics like Chris Argyris, Douglas McGregor, and Warren Bennis limited their efforts to changing leadership style and managerial philosophy. The locus of change centered on making leadership less autocratic and more "democratic," "participative," and in today's parlance, we might say, more "empowering."

That industrial humanists placed their bets on attempting to change the behavioral and psychological orientation of managers is not surprising given that most of them were educated as social psychologists. We are not questioning or doubting whether industrial humanists, notably Argyris and McGregor, had their hearts in the right place. They did. And there is no argument that their humanistic goals were laudable--that the ends they promoted were unequivocally democratic. But their psychological perspective directed them to focus on such themes as personality development, self-actualization, behavioral change and managerial assumptions. These themes--with their mental health overtones--didn't give them much credibility in the eyes of senior executives. Most industrial humanists were looked upon by top managers at best as "counselors" and "head-shrinks," or at worst, as wild-eyed, left-wing, academic idealists.

While the prescriptions that industrial humanists doled out were not widely embraced by senior management, their ideology of democratic leadership certainly has continued to play to receptive audiences. Nearly forty years have passed since McGregor published his seminal work, and superficial interpretations of his theories still guide practice in training and development circles. Despite their popularity, many contemporary methods--which are simply variants on democratic leadership approaches to change--can be a very expensive and ineffective way of improving organizational performance. The boom in training industry reflects this, as most corporations still run their managers and executives through all sorts of leadership-oriented programs with little return to show for their investment. Many organizations require all their managers to go through training courses in interpersonal skills (what some managers have derogatorily referred to as "charm schools") or to attend workshops where they learn about their Myers-Briggs personality style. Charles Perrow questions the propensity to attribute and reduce organizational problems to human relations issues. Clarifying his concern, he states:

> Of course there are incompetent managers, and workers are sometimes not all that one would like them to be. But the immediate resort to explanations in terms of personality or human relations is not warranted; the first question to be asked is whether the structure of the organization, or unit, or role is an appropriate one for the tasks being demanded (1979, p. 177).

There were other problems related to how managers and consultants interpreted McGregor's work. In essence, Theory Y simply described a new humanistic image of the worker. It lacked theoretical precision and operational specificity. Many consultants who believed in and accepted the "Y image" of human nature began to preach that managers should no longer structure, control, or closely supervise the work of their subordinates. If one was really a Theory Y manager, then he or she should give their subordinates wide latitude, use less external control, and basically take a hands-off approach to managing the work of others. If one really believed people could be trusted, then there was no need to coerce, punish, or issue directives.

But this simplistic interpretation of Theory Y led to a permissive, laissez-faire style of management. Theory Y came to be equated with letting go of control completely, which really missed the whole point of what McGregor really intended. For McGregor, Theory Y implied that people were capable of self-direction and self-control when they were given the proper work conditions. Unfortunately, McGregor was vague on just what those conditions exactly were, but laissez-faire management was certainly not one of them.

Common Misconceptions about Self-Management

The human relations myth has distorted our understanding of democracy at work and the self-managing enterprise. So much emphasis over the years has been directed toward enlightened supervision and improvement of interpersonal group relations that attempts to design self-managing, democratic workplaces are often confused or equated with the human relations approach. Simply changing attitudes, improving interpersonal relations, and even building effective "teams" will not, however, lead to self-management or the democratization of the enterprise. Below we list our top ten list of misconceptions about the self-managing organization:

1. Democracy at work is the same as participative management.

Participative management requires no significant change in the distribution of authority or power between management and work groups. Participative Management programs often talk a good game--espousing such notions that participation is key to fully utilizing the knowledge and skills of employees-- which in turn leads to higher quality decisions. That's true. However, rather than authorizing work groups to make their own decisions (one key aspect of self-management), participation in decision making in such programs is often much more "informal." Many work teams still take their "orders" from an "enlightened supervisor," one that has been trained in a participative style of management. Supervisors are trained to be informal, act friendly, show support, facilitate, and solicit the input from team members, but the final say and authority for decision making still rests firmly with the supervisor. In other words, participation at the level of work groups is not formally sanctioned or codified into the organizational structure. Instead, participation is seen an informal option that the supervisor may elect to enact through his style of leadership. For such teams, participation in decision making is totally dependent on whether the supervisor is willing to share his/her decision making authority with them. Since participation in the organization is informal, supervisors are under no obligation to do so. Participation is cooptive in nature.

2. Democracy at work means people are empowered and have the freedom to do whatever they want.

This misconception is embodied in what is now popularly referred to as "empowerment,'" another contemporary variant of lasseiz-faire management. It is a conceptual disease that has reached epidemic proportions, infecting thousands of organizations in both the private and public sectors. This ill-conceived notion of democracy at work is equated to the existence of self-managing teams that have complete autonomy to make decisions, without any sense of limits or boundaries. Ridden with this mistaken conception of empowerment, management deludes itself into thinking that it has to treat such teams with kid gloves, and backs away from influencing these headstrong teams. The human relations myth has brainwashed managers to forgo efforts to lead change by adopting a "process orientation" that relies more on "facilitation" than on decisive and directive leadership. However, this whole approach is wrongheaded. When management abdicates its role to provide direction and set clear boundaries, teams end up either floundering in ambiguity, or they become involved in matters and decisions that exceed their realm of competence. In either case, failure and disappointment is inevitable. Teams don't need facilitation from above so much as they need a democratic structure that defines their decision rights, allowing them to operate semi-autonomously in collaboration with management. Goal-setting is the nexus for such collaboration between management and teams, and through a process of negotiation, clear performance expectations for teams can be provided that define the scope and limits of their authority.

3. Democracy at work will lead to uncontrollable and fatal errors.

What is often unnerving to managers about democracy at work is its emergent nature and open-endedness. There is no magical blueprint that can be imposed in a top-down fashion. Democracy at work is the result of learning, development and growth from the ground up. It's a grass-roots process that looks messy and chaotic to authoritarian managers who have a low tolerance for ambiguity and prefer to contain human activity in neat boxes. Any hint of disorder or unpredictability sends chills up the spine of these managers who tend to see the world in binary terms--either organizations are designed for control (traditional hierarchy) or they are designed for autonomy (self-management). To make the latter choice, they think, means giving up all control and allowing employees to run amok. It is hard for them to fathom that a group can share responsibility for collective outcomes. For the authoritarian manager, control can only be had by making *someone* accountable, and naturally, accountability can only exist in one person. Authoritarian managers simply shudder at the thought of shifting responsibility for control and coordination to a group--because for them it looks like a sure recipe for chaos. But all this striving for order and stability is the Achilles' heel of bureaucracy. Bureaucratic organizations are designed to function with few degrees of freedom, relying on a fixed repertoire of responses--such systems are *variety-reducing*. Rules, policies, and standard operating procedures are used to buffer bureaucratic organizations from uncertainty. Communication is selectively passed down to subordinates on a "need to know" basis, and flows upward only after people have filtered out anything that could get them in hot water. By design, bureaucratic structures limit the responsiveness and creativity of those closest to the work process or customer. Because bureaucracy is a constellation of tightly specified job descriptions employee's hands are basically tied when a customer makes a special request or a major problem arises (it's not my job). Customers are given the classic run-around. And when errors do occur, employees closest to the problem don't have the authority or responsibility to correct them. Errors either get passed on to the next department, passed up the hierarchy for a manager to deal with, or they get *covered up*. Since authority for making decisions is located several levels above where errors occur, managers are constantly barraged by information from below. They get sucked into a firefighting role. And because employees are afraid of being punished for their mistakes, information and communication is usually distorted or inaccurate. In other words, bureaucratic organizations dominated by authoritarian managers are inherently *error-amplifying systems.* In contrast, democratic organizations are designed so people can learn from their mistakes and correct problems in real-time, they are flexible, error-reducing systems. They are designed to allow people to operate in an optimal zone of performance, within a dynamic equilibrium: not chained to a rigid order at one extreme, nor falling into a black hole of chaos and anarchy at the other, but at a higher order of complexity, which is what democracy is all about.

4. Democracy at work is for the shop floor only.

The emasculated and cooptive form of participation propagated by the human relations myth has reduced democracy at work to something that is good for lower level and front-line employees, not as a systemic approach for redesigning the entire enterprise. This misconception is fed by the proliferation of human relations oriented programs, reengineering, TQM and the STS method which focus primarily on lower level employees and their supervisors. In contrast, Participative Design (Purser & Cabana, 1998) is a method for redesigning work that is not limited to those on the shop floor or the service counter, but includes middle management and senior executive work too, resulting in a fully self-managing organization.

5. Democracy at work means making people happier by letting them work in teams.

This misconception is a direct outgrowth of the human relations myth, derived from the fallacious axiom that happy workers are more productive, and the way to make workers happy is to have them join a team. Human relations advocates use techniques and interventions geared toward enhancing "team feelings" and training team members in group process skills. Because of this emphasis, organization development (OD) facilitators are often viewed as "touchy-feely" types. Organization development consultants often forget that self-management started in the coal mines with workers who never had the luxury of learning about their Myers-Briggs (MBTI) scores, and never required any formal team-building or team development training.

6. Democracy at work means designing self-managing teams that are multi-skilled.

This is partially true, in that self-managing organizations do frequently result in the formation of multi-skilled work teams. But it is only one half of the equation. It is a common misconception today to equate multi-skilled work teams with self-management. Many organizations that have gone through reengineering and socio-technical systems design have made this assumption that multi-skilling around core business processes is the only way to go. It's a step in the right direction, since it allows employees to learn new skills and to take on more responsibility for an entire work process. Self-management encompasses multi-skilling, but operates at a higher level of participation. In fully self-managing organizations, the responsibility for the control and coordination of work is located at the team level, where as many decisions as possible are devolved to team members who can exercise complete control over their team affairs. In addition, every level within the organization is designed to be self-managing--the work of operational employees, middle managers, and senior executives--are all included and integrated into participative decision making.

7. Democracy at work is nothing new, most organizations have implemented teams.

It's a misconception to think that genuine self-managing organizations already exist and are commonplace (just look at all the organizations that have implemented self-directed teams), when in fact the overwhelming majority of organizations that have gone through a redesign or reengineering effort have produced "managed teams," with supervisory team leaders, facilitators and coaches. Their conception of a self-managing organization is by definition made up of teams at the bottom, coaches in the middle, and administrators at the top. They tend to believe that teams cannot manage themselves without the nurturing help of an outside coach who is responsible for the effective interaction of team members. This misconception feeds resistance to change. When we first try to explain self-management to clients, they often tell us, been there, done that, we got teams. However, when we dig deeper and probe the client, we typically find that responsibility for control and coordination is still in the hands of ex-supervisors, and managers haven't formed any kind of self-managing team structure for their own work. This approach is still bureaucracy with a human face. Responsibility for team human relations has simply shifted to a reformed supervisor-turned-coach. The supervisor/coach maintains top-down helping relationships with each person on the team, and if any conflicts come up, they funnel the issues through him for resolution. So-called "team facilitation" is used to calm down potential conflicts and minimize differences, so things don't get out of hand. Heaven forbid a good argument that might lead to an outbreak of creativity in a group.

8. An organization cannot become self-managing without tons of human relations training.

This misconception is popular among organization development consultants and training specialists. According to this view, the way to evolve to a self-managing organization is by improving the human relations inside the organization. The barrier to self-management is seen as purely a lack of interpersonal competence--that employees cannot get along and work together unless they are trained to do so. This leads to an avalanche of top-down training programs that are force-fed to teams. Again, this misconception is a derivative of the human relations myth that friendly supervision and cooperative, happy workers leads to higher productivity. Corporations then require all of their supervisors and employees to be trained in team facilitation, group development, communications, and conflict management skills. Unfortunately, forty years worth of research studies have yielded little empirical support for such a theory (Baritz, 1960; Bendix, 1949; Bramel & Friend, 1981; Carey, 1967; Perrow, 1979).

9. Democracy is a form of public government that has no relevance to private enterprise.

When people think of democracy at work, they usually associate it with a form of government. Democracy, with all its inefficiencies, may work in the public sphere, but it's ill suited to the dog-eat-dog world of private economic enterprises. Our existing notion of democracy is based on what political scientists refer to as "liberal democratic theory," which posits that there are two very separate spheres--the political and the private--and never should the twain meet, except when private individuals put their citizen caps on and go out to cast their perfunctory vote. Liberal democracy, the democracy of representative government, creates a structural division of political labor between the governors and the governed. Every couple of years we elect representatives to do the governing for us, and then we forget about them and go on with more important matters in our social and economic lives. This is what we usually conceive democracy to be all about. Consequently, proposals for bringing democracy to work don't seem relevant or workable. We immediately think such proposals would call for electing representatives, procedural mechanisms for passing legislation, and voting on bills for protecting individual civil liberties. But this is not the form of democracy that we are proposing or talking about. Rather, we are proposing a direct form of democracy, where employees (citizens) are directly responsible for decision making. This notion of direct democracy runs counter to liberal conceptions that require citizens to give up their decision making responsibilities on political matters to elected representatives. This latter formulation of democracy doesn't consider organizations to be political systems too, what Jefferson called "private governments." But organizations are political systems, since decisions are constantly being made about the allocation of resources--who gets what (and who doesn't), when, where, and why. Liberal conceptions of democracy, however, place organizations in the private sphere, where democratic governance has no legitimate role to play. Our existing conception of liberal representative democracy necessarily excludes private enterprises from seriously considering democracy at work as a viable option. In other words, when we look through the lens of liberal democracy, we end up with a rather distorted view of democracy at work--its prospects and possibilities look grim. Only a more radical, participatory form of democracy will allow employees to exercise their inalienable rights of democratic citizenship within private enterprise.

10. Democracy can never be applied in the workplace because it is too impractical and inefficient.

This misconception is a derivative of the above, the stereotypical notion that democracy is an inefficient, representative mechanism for public governance. Democracy at work will never catch on if it is equated with the gridlock of representative government and procedural bickering among competing interest groups. Ethereal and ambiguous conceptions of democracy--such as those offered by the neo-human relations theorists (Argyris, 1957; McGregor, 1960; Likert, 1961; Herzberg, 1959)--only fuel the misconception that democracy is an impractical ideal that simply won't work in systems that are held accountable for economic results. Consider the description proffered by Bennis and Slater (1964, p. xx): "democracy seeks no stability, no end point, it is purposeless, save that it purports to ensure perpetual transition, constant alternation, ceaseless instability." Purposeless? Ceaseless instability? If this is what democracy at work is all about, most senior managers would politely dismiss it outright, and rightly so. Perhaps this conception of democracy might work for universities with large endowments where professors can argue endlessly over the details of what should be included in a capstone course. But for private enterprises, products have to be produced, customers have to be served, and shareholders have to be satisfied. In the real world of private enterprise, purposeful behavior is required to achieve very definite end points.

When this distorted and wishy-washy image of democracy is stacked up against the machine-like efficiency of a traditional autocratic hierarchy, autocracy always wins hands down. Indeed, autocratic command and control organizations have gained a notorious reputation for running tight ships. Military organizations are the epitome of efficiency, obedience and conformity to centralized directives. Consider the efficiency of the Third Reich. Democracy has no place in the military.

Democratic organization may actually be inefficient--a form of overkill--when the task is relatively simple, the environment is relatively stable, when all actions can be planned in advance. Under these conditions (which are rare today), organizations designed along traditional hierarchical lines are indeed more efficient, with the side effect of low morale for those on the frontlines.

Alex Bavelas (1962), a social scientist at MIT, performed a crucial laboratory experiment that sheds considerable light on this misconception. Bavelas was interested in determining how the structure of communication networks influenced task performance. He designed the experiment by creating two different forms of organization. Subjects in the first group were organized in a star-like pattern, where members could communicate with each other only by going through a centralized focal person. He called this the autocratic group. Subjects in the other group were organized in a circular pattern, which allowed them complete equality of communication access, like a network. He called this the democratic group. During the first experimental condition, both groups were instructed to perform a very simple mechanical task under stable conditions. His findings: autocratic groups perform the task more efficiently. The only downside is, with the exception of the focal leader, morale was low among group members. During the second round, Bavelas changed the experimental conditions, making the tasks more complex and changing rules of the game midstream. This time the autocratic group performed quite poorly in comparison to their democratic counterparts. Faced with more challenging tasks and changing requirements, democratic groups solved problems more rapidly and with fewer mistakes. Not only this, democratic group members reported having higher morale than their peers in the autocratic groups. At least under laboratory conditions, Bavelas' experiments show that under conditions of high task and environmental uncertainty, democratic organizations are not only more efficient, but more effective as well.

Contrary to negative stereotypes, democratic organizations display a capacity for active adaptation that is far superior to autocracy. Democracy is perhaps the most practical solution to dealing with complexity and uncertainty. Democratic organizations are by definition learning systems, which are designed to increase the capability of every employee to learn and adapt to on-going change. Under conditions of turbulence, the ability to explore the unknown, exchange ideas freely, and develop novel solutions rapidly is of greater importance than following rules and obeying centralized directives.

Notes

1. Mayo and his colleagues learned just how influential social and informal group factors were upon individual behavior during the Bank Wiring Room experiment. Informal relationships between individuals had an enormous impact on an individual's behavior in the group. Workers had formed their own norms of acceptable behavior and deviance with respect to production rates and their interactions with management. Through their solidarity and group enforced codes of behavior, the workers were able to oppose and resist management's directives.

References

Argyris, C. (1957). *Personality and organization.* New York: Harper & Row.

Baritz, L. (1960). *The servants of power: A history of the use of social science in American industry.* Middletown, CT: Wesleyan University Press.

Bavelas, A. (1962). Toward a truly scientific management: The concept of organizational health. In W. Bennis (Eds.), *General systems yearbook.*

Bendix, R. (1949). The perspectives of Elton Mayo. *Review of Economics and Statistics*, 31, 312-319.

Bendix, R. (1956). *Work and authority in industry.* New York: John Wiley.

Bennis, W., & Slater, P. (1964). Democracy is inevitable. *Harvard Business Review.*

Bramel, D., & Friend, R., (1981). Hawthorne: The myth of the docile worker and class bias in psychology. *American Psychologist*, 36, 867-878.

Campbell, J. (1968). Creative mythology: Vol. 4. *The masks of God.* New York: Viking.

Carey, A., (1967). The Hawthorne studies: A radical criticism. *American Sociological Review*, 32, 403-416.

Elias, N. (1978). *The history of manners: A study of civilizing processes.* New York: Pantheon.

Gillespie, R. (1991). *Manufacturing knowledge: A history of the Hawthorne experiments.* Cambridge: Cambridge University Press.

Greiner, G. (1988*) Inhuman relations: Quality circles and anti-unionism in American industry.* Philadelphia: Temple University Press.

Herzberg, F. (1959). *The motivation to work.* New York: John Wiley & Sons.

Mayo, E. (1945). *The social problems of an industrial civilization.* Boston: Harvard Business School.

McClelland, D. (1985). *Human motivation.* Glenview, IL: Scott, Foresman.

McGregor, D. (1960). *The human side of enterprise.* New York: McGraw Hill.

Neilsen, E. & Rao, H. (1990). Strangers and the social order: The institutional genesis of organization development. In W.A. Pasmore & R.W. Woodman (Eds.) *Research in organizational change and development, Vol. 4.* Greenwich, CT: JAI Press.

Peters, T. & Waterman, R. (1982). *In search of excellence.* New York: Harper & Row.

Perrow, C. (1979). *Complex organizations: A critical essay.* Glenview, IL: Scott Foresman.

Purser, R., & Cabana, S. (1998). *The self-managing organization: How leading companies are transforming the work of teams for real impact.* New York: The Free Press.

Riesman, D., Glazer, N., & Denney, R. (1950). *The lonely crowd: A study of the changing American character.* New York: Doubleday Anchor Book.

Roethlisberger, F. (1941). *Management and morale.* Cambridge, Mass.: Harvard University Press.

Roethlisberger, F. & Dickson, W. J. (1939). *Management and the worker.* Cambridge: Harvard University Press.

Scott, W.G. (1962). *Human relations in management: A behavioral science approach.* Homewood, IL: Richard Irwin.

Weisbord, M. (1987). *Productive workplaces.* San Francisco: Jossey-Bass.

Whyte, W.H. (1957). *The organization man.* New York: Anchor Books.

Wren, D. (1994). *The evolution of management thought* (4th ed.*).* New York: John Wiley & Sons.

Chapter 5

The Evolution of Open Systems to the 2 Stage Model

Merrelyn Emery
Australian National University, Canberra, Australia

Abstract

The current state of the art in open systems goes by the name of the 2 Stage Model. This paper describes it and traces its origins back through history as far as *the group climate* experiments conducted by the team led by Kurt Lewin in the late 1930s. There appears to be a general lack of knowledge and/or much misunderstanding about this history today. Other current methods often share these origins although many also include assumptions and components of the Human Relations movement. An example is the Future Search with which the Search Conference is often confused. Open systems and human relations are two major traditions in today's organizational field and in their modern forms, they both draw from the work of Lewin, albeit different parts of it.

Brief History of the Evolution of Open Systems

Figure 1 contains the overall road map of the evolution of open systems from its more recent origins to the 2-stage model. It is clearly not exhaustive, as the three volume Tavistock Anthology (Trist & Murray, 1997) shows, but includes the critical conceptual and practical breakthroughs. It begins on the left-hand side in the late 1930's with one of the great classics in the history of social science. However, the work of Kurt Lewin was of two quite different types. The first is illustrated by the series of experiments and publications known as the *group climate* experiments which would be called today structural experiments. They established that there are only two genotypical structures and an absence of structure that is known as laissez faire. This was the stream that explored systems, and systemic phenomena concentrating on task mediated relationships. His work provided a foundation for part of the development of open systems.

The second and much smaller body of Lewin's work is exemplified by the paper *The Solution of a Chronic Conflict in Industry*. This did not emphasize structural considerations and has allowed serious misinterpretation of much of his work as fitting within the Human Relations school. Lewin was open to all the influences of the time but as his work and his biographer Marrow make clear, he was a systems man although open systems thinking was yet to come. Lewin was obviously searching for a concept of social environment with the development of the *life space*

M.M. Beyerlein (ed.), Work Teams: Past, Present and Future, 85–103.

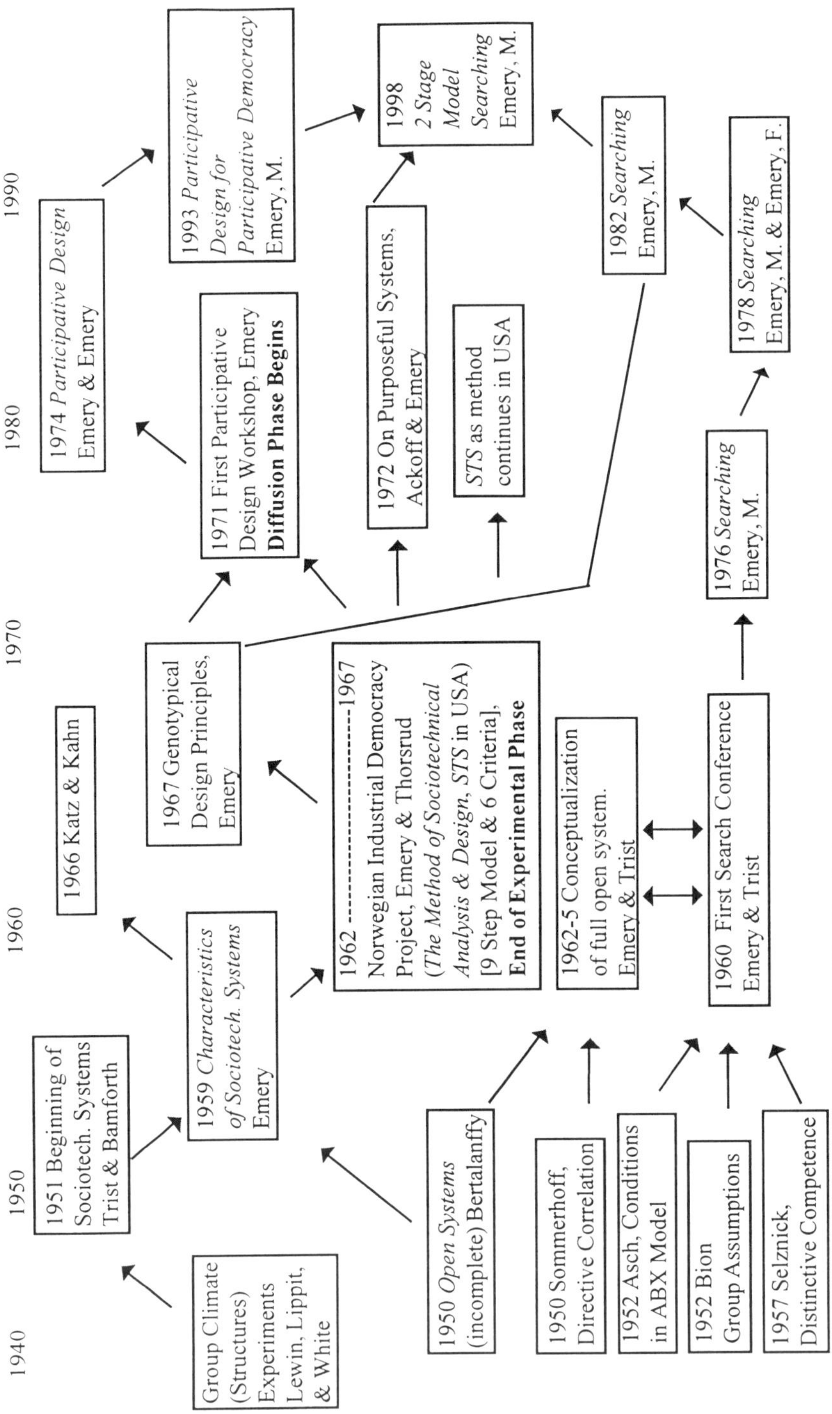

Figure 1. The Evolution of Open Systems Theory to the 2 Stage Model

but his topology remained a closed system. One of the significant antecedents to Lewin's work was of course, the Gestalt school that gave us the formative concepts of *figure/ground, pragnanz* and many other fundamental concepts relating to systems. The split between the open systems and human relations camps took place shortly after Lewin's death as discussed many times by Eric Trist, as for example in his introduction to the Orillia conference in 1985. "We were moving into the society and they were moving away from it" (Trist, 1997, pp. 676-677). The open systems groups were concerned to find the concepts and principles that explain and predict human behaviour in the real life settings in which people purposefully live and work, not artificially constructed or simulated ones. Post Lewinian social science in the USA has been dominated by the human relations school.

The beginning of the socio-technical systems stream is acknowledged to lie in the work and famous paper by Trist and Bamforth (1951) which explored a natural experiment with long wall coal mining. This work pioneered the first break with both human relations methods which centres on improving such matters as personal growth, inter-personal relations and communications. It also provided an alternative to the conventional approach of the time that concentrated on the technical and economic dimensions of work and workplaces. Trist and Bamforth showed that there were gains to be made for both productivity and people when the social and technical systems could be jointly optimized.

At almost the same time, Von Bertalanffy (1950) was working on the concept of an open system and is generally conceeded to be "the father" of this concept. His concept however was incomplete as there was no conceptualization of the environment(s) within which these open systems existed. However, it was a major step forward and was picked up by Fred Emery before he went to work with Trist at the Tavistock Institute in London. Building on Trist and Bamforth and further work and also including the concept of the open system, Emery wrote the other classic in 1959 that changed the concept to that of open socio-technical systems. Open and closed systems were stated as alternative concepts in the development of theory but the intrinsic nature of enterprises dictated that only open systems thinking had the power to comprehensively explain the relations between an enterprise and its external environment.

> "If it is to achieve its ends, an enterprise must reckon upon the constraints implicit in its means and resources, both human and material. Beyond this, the people within an enterprise, particularly those concerned with leadership must come to see that (a) they must organize themselves in ways appropriate to the nature and order of the tasks required by their environment; and (b) their institutional ideologies and self-perception must in some way reflect their real relations with their environment." (Emery, F., 1959, pp. 39-40)

From virtually the very beginnings, therefore, the socio-technical stream was but a subset of open systems. The matter of open versus closed is, however, more serious in its implications than the note about enterprises would indicate, as there is no such thing as a closed system in reality, nor have we even been able to create one. What does it mean that we have many theories based on the notion of a closed system when such a thing does not exist and to the best of our knowledge cannot exist?

Katz and Kahn's book *The Social Psychology of Organizations* (1966) became a major USA source but it was based on *Characteristics of Socio-technical Systems*. The development of open socio-technical systems continued with the Norwegian Industrial Democracy Program that began in 1962 (Emery & Thorsrud, 1969, 1976). It was during this program that the method known as *STS* in the USA was fully developed and exported around the world. In 1967, many international social scientists, including Lou Davis from UCLA attended the Lincoln Conference where what is now called the *Nine Step Model* and the *Six Criteria*, the basic six psychological requirements of productive activity, were presented in a paper by Fred Emery. The *Six Criteria* were first published in Norwegian in 1964 and in English as Appendix V of Emery and Thorsrud (1969). From this point onwards in the USA, use of *STS* continued until it became obvious to many practitioners that it wasn't meeting its purposes very well. It's more recent evolution into participative and fast tracked forms is outside the scope of this paper as it is outside the major line of open systems development.

The *Six Criteria* appear not to have been used as part of STS in the USA but they have proven powerful and are built into the process of the *Participative Design Workshop* (below) as a part of the analysis of what the organization has been doing to its people. They are the intrinsic motivators. No amount of external rewards can substitute for them. The six criteria also balance the tension between autonomy and homonomy, the term which expresses our requirement for belongingess, interdependence with others (Angyal, 1941). The *Six Criteria* are:

1. Elbow Room, autonomy in decision making
2. Continual Learning for which there must be
   a. ability to set goals
   b. accurate and timely feedback
3. Variety
4. Mutual Support and Respect
5. Meaningfulness which consists of
   a. doing something with social value
   b. seeing the whole product or service
6. Desirable Future

The first three criteria must be optimal for each individual. The second three exist within the climate of the system itself and are things you can never have too much of. But the end of the Norwegian project was significant in more ways than one. In 1967, Emery published his first appreciation of the two genotypical organizational design principles. These were to revolutionize the concept of open systems, his method for performing open socio-technical systems redesign and as Figure 1 shows, much else.

The first design principle (DP1) is called redundancy of parts, because there are more parts (people) than are required at any one given time. Its critical feature is that responsibility for coordination and control is located at least one level above where the work or planning is being done. DP1 yields a supervizory or dominant hierarchy. The second organizational design principle (DP2) is called redundancy of functions, because as many skills and functions as possible are built into every person. Its critical feature is that responsibility for coordination and control is located where the work or planning is being done (Emery, F., 1967; Emery & Emery, 1974).

When the design principle of a whole system is changed, the resulting flat *non-dominant hierarchy of functions* operates as a coherent whole with negotiations between peers replacing the former system of instructions. Each self-managing group at each level of the functional hierarchy does productive work that is governed by a comprehensive set of measurable goals covering every major aspect of the work. DP2 structures can operate equitably and safely only when there is a pay for skills and/or knowledge held system in place and all essential training for multi-skilling has been done before the new design goes into operation. DP2 structures evolve and provide the essential flexibility for dealing with changes in either the external environment or the organization itself. Designing on DP2 conveys the capacity to be internally active adaptive.

The results from the four field sites in Norway was accepted by industry, government, unions and academia as proof that democratic structure based on DP2 was a more human and productive alternative than bureaucratic or autocratic structure, based on DP1. So conclusive was this project that no further proof was required. This marked the end of the *experimental phase* of open, jointly optimized, socio-technical systems. As part of the project, Emery and Thorsrud also showed that representative democracy (from DP1) cannot produce the same results as those produced within a participative democracy, that organizational form produced by DP2.

Emery returned to Australia in 1969 and immediately began devising a method for the diffusion of jointly optimized socio-technical or DP2 structures. This method is called the *Participative Design Workshop* (PDW), and he piloted it for the first time in 1971. This marked the beginning of the *diffusion phase* of genotypical change for societal change which had been long discussed (Emery, 1969). Emery and others at the Centre for Continuing Education at the Australian National University (ANU) poured considerable work into testing and developing this method and by 1973, we were sufficiently sure of its efficacy and reliability to write it up (Emery & Emery, 1974). Emery and Thorsrud (1976) included a republication of *Participative Design* as Appendix 1 of their final report of the Norwegian ID Project to reinforce the message that a new method specifically designed for diffusion was available to replace the old STS analysis and design required for scientific validation.

Since that time, we have learnt much more about the whole process of producing participative democracies in many different areas and systems, including education and governance (Emery, M., 1993). This is where we will leave this stream temporarily while we return to look at another part of the work of developing open systems which was occurring simultaneously. And to do that, we return to the 1950s.

As well as the innovations of Trist and Bamforth and Von Bertalanffy in the 1950s, groundbreaking work was also being done by Asch (1952), Bion (1952, 1961) and Selznick (1957). Asch researched the parameters for effective or influential communication and Emery realized that Asch's work amounted to the conditions required to maximize the probability of success of task oriented work within an ABX situation (Newcomb, 1953) where A and B are people or groups and X is an object or purpose of mutual concern. Bion discovered the basic assumptions that groups can make under certain conditions. These basic assumptions interfere with creative task oriented work and learning and are commonly what people refer to as negative group dynamics. Selznick explored some of the dimensions of organizational leadership and devised the concept of the distinctive competence of an organization, what that organization is uniquely good at. These sources are vitally important in the development of open systems theory and practice, as they were the major dimensions Emery built into the design of the first Search Conference held in 1960.

The first Search Conference also departed from the methods available at the time in other ways. It was specifically designed to produce learning and creative work in the pursuit of the task of planning a merger of two existing organizations, without the interruption of Bion's group assumptions, and it almost succeeded in this. The most significant way in which it deviated from conventional methods was that it included as a major part of the work, the task of exploring the extended social field of directive correlations (Emery, F., 1977, 1998) or social environment, called the L_{22} for short (Emery & Trist, 1965). Before we can understand this ground breaking innovation we must also look at the work Emery was doing concomitantly with the development of the social field or environment.

Emery realized that Von Bertalanffy's concept of the open system was incomplete and began researching its completion. He presented the first draft of this work to a meeting of the Informal European Group in 1963. The first publication of the concept of the extended social field of directive correlations (environment) and its causal texture was Emery (1963), *Second Progress Report on Conceptualization*. Doc. T125, TIHR. This was later published as the citation classic *The Causal Texture of Organizational Environments* (Emery & Trist, 1965). Essentially this paper conceptualized the nature of the social environment within which human open systems exist and presented its changing nature over time. Because the systems are open to their environment, this extended social field is a major influence on what a system can and cannot do in the present and in the future. (See Figure 2.) Hence, for an organization to establish active adaptive relationships with its social field, it must be able to explore this field and determine its most probable character in the future time of relevance to the system's strategic plan. It drew upon the formative work of Sommerhoff (1950, 1969) in defining a directive correlation for active adaptation.

The model of directive correlation expresses the idea that for both system and environment to be in an active adaptive relationship, they must be heading for the same direction or goals from the same starting point. That is they are correlated in terms of direction. For directive correlation (Figure 2B), the original, starting condition at t_0 consists of both system and environment. Both system and environment then make changes at the next point in time (t_1). These result in a new set of conditions consisting of a changed system and a changed environment at the next point in time (t_2). In this case, the changes are directively correlated and, therefore, adaptive. There are of course, an infinite number of cases in which system and environment are not directively correlated and, therefore, stand in a maladaptive relationship.

Figure 2 (A) expresses the now well known conceptualization of the open system where L stands for the laws governing the system, the environment and relationships between them, laws which are able to be known (Emery, F., 1967). The function of a system (designated 1) acts upon the environment (designated 2) This is the planning function (L_{12}), putting the actor first. Environment acts upon the system and is known to us through the function of learning (L_{21}). L_{11} and L_{22} express the intrinsic nature of the system and environment respectively. The laws that govern them are implicitly used and learnt about in the Search Conference.

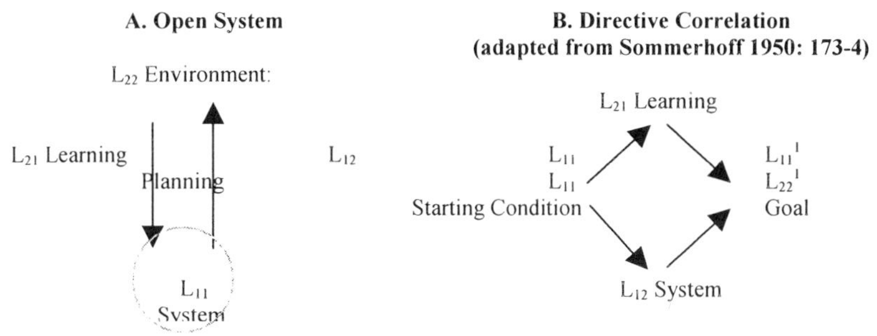

Figure 2. The Basic Models of Open System and Directive Correlation

Both parts of Figure 2 show that system and environment are co-implicated in any current state of affairs and act jointly to produce a new one. The open systems and directive correlation models express the same phenomenon. The critical differences between them are that:

1. the open system is a picture of a point in time with change expressed through learning and planning while the directive correlation is a picture over time,
2. the open system is a *general* model that includes adaptive and maladaptive possibilities while the directive correlation expresses precisely when adaptation is or is not occurring.

The 1960 Search, therefore, explored this social field (L_{22}) for the first time and extrapolated both its novel and predominant characteristics into the relevant future for the strategic plan of the merged organization. The minimal design of the Search Conference, therefore, is the open system, thoroughly exploring the L_{22}, the L_{11} and simultaneously learning how to achieve active adaptation through action planning. Its major task is to clearly establish an active adaptive system principle, that which expresses the unique relationship between that particular system and its environment. In practice, this system principle is a set of strategic goals that are called the *Most Desirable System* set at an appropriate and relevant point in the future.

This innovation has been refined through the continued development of the Search Conference to its current state of the art and set the precedent for many of the methods that are with us today. Without this major phase of work, a method cannot be legitimately called a Search. But the Search as a method is far more complex and comprehensive in its theoretical underpinnings than implied above. Similarly to the development of the PDW, the Search Conference was subjected to a massive testing and development phase by the ANU team through the 1970s and beyond. As Figure

1 shows, there was a continuous stream of publications about it, each showing a quantum leap in our knowledge. The first USA publication about the Search was in Sutherland's 1978 *Management Handbook for Public Administrators*.

During this early development phase I realized that basing the Search firmly within a DP2 structure could overcome many problems in process and dynamics. Up until this time, it had been quite common practice to include small presentations within the Search Conference and this had proven disruptive of task and creative work. We often experienced two of Bion's group assumptions, particularly fight/flight and dependency. More detailed research of Bion's work showed that while his appreciation of the role of structure was minimal, it was present. Further observations of the group assumptions within Searches showed that they are indeed the results of DP1 structure (Emery, M., 1982). From here it was easy to redesign the parameters of the Search Conference so that it encompassed a DP2 structure from the very beginning of the process. Our experience with it from this point has proven conclusively that the so called stages of group formation (forming, storming, norming, and performing) are not inevitable but are structure dependent. When people start task oriented work within a DP2 structure, the group assumptions or negative dynamics do not appear (Emery, M., 1998).

While it is quite clear from the above that there was only one stream of open systems, and the conceptual intertwining and coherence of open systems and structural design is best illustrated in the development of the Search Conference, there was a differentiation of methods for planning and structural redesign. This is for the very simple reasons that the functions themselves are vastly different, require different event designs and the participation of different people. The Search Conference was developed specifically for planning and the PDW for redesign. But by 1982, the intensive conceptual work put into the Search Conference had drawn much more closely together the various components of the theory behind the methods. This integrative work has now been taken further to its current form as the 2 stage model. The 2 stage model is a more comprehensive and practical linking of the methods of the Search Conference and Participative Design Workshop for large scale system change (Emery, M., 1998). It has been in the testing and development phase since 1991 and an earlier discussion of it can be found in Diemer and Alvarez (1995, where the 2 stage model was incorrectly attributed to Fred Emery by the Editor).

The 2 Stage Model

The impetus for initiating the 2 Stage Model came from practice, but its development involved returning to theory. On the practical side, there was the disturbing and continuing failure rate of implementation of Search Conference plans. From the beginning of the seventies, it became clear that there were two classes of Search Conference (SC) failure, those that failed because of inadequate preparation, design and management and those that failed during implementation. The former attracted by far the most attention and much conceptual and practical effort was put into developing the method and various forms of education.

The latter class, failures of implementation, received far less attention. The early SCs in Australia were predominantly community and issue based Searches. Pretty soon, however, after the first few had been tried and news of them diffused, organizational Searches began to be held. A consistently different pattern emerged with a much greater success rate during implementation for these organizationally based events than for the geographical community, industry and issue Searches. Organization was clearly involved.

But not all are as honest as Alan Davies when he noted (1992, p. 281) that many of the Searches he designed and managed "failed to meet their primary organizational objectives." A well designed and managed Search usually only runs into problems in the third phase of implementation. When participants are asked why the Search worked so well, they often say it was because everybody worked so well together as equals, regardless of status and other differences. This observation is accurate because the SC has a DP2 structure. Implementation however, particularly for organizational Searches, proceeds through the current organizational structure that is usually DP1. People, therefore, do not work together as equals, nor do they communicate accurately or when they should. The DP1 structure overcomes the positive experience of the SC. What is missing is the conceptualization of the design principles and their effects. Without it, there is no clearly articulated and understood alternative to DP1 and no barrier to reverting to it. Implementation can then just fade away. While the Search Conference is designed to produce adaptive relations between system and environment, it is insufficient on its own to maintain the adaptation in the long term.

Some SC managers faced with imminent failures of implementation of their community Searches, but without a clear theoretical answer, reverted to the older consultancy practice of holding the client's hand during implementation and working to create the results on the ground. While this almost certainly increased the success rate on the ground, it in no way solved the dilemma and just as certainly slowed the growth of confident self-managing communities.

Even when there was understanding of the cause of the failure, the cases were dealt with in isolation. For example, after the Search for the Future of the Canning Peach Industry in an irrigation area of New South Wales in 1977, the SC community set up a committee to coordinate the implementation of the action plans. Six months later, the Agriculture Extension Officer who was codesigner and manager, was asked to attend a meeting of this committee to help them get the process back on track. Attendance at meetings and subsequent action had steadily declined. Energy for implementation had dribbled away to virtually nothing.

The structure and dynamics of a committee (DP1) as opposed to those of a group (DP2) were already known and so we worked in these cases to restore a group structure in order to put energy and motivation back into the system. While the Search Conference is designed to produce active adaptive relations between system and environment, it was clearly insufficient on its own to maintain the adaptation in the long term. The diagnosis was clear and the remedy was obvious and put into effect. But nobody made the leap to prevention.

On thinking about this, it became clear that a major plank of the theory had been effectively left out of the practice. This was the concept of people as purposeful systems (Ackoff & Emery, 1972) and conscious conceptual knowledge of the organizational design principles was the key to the solution. If people do not know what is causing the problem, they cannot work out the conclusion. As the cause of the problem was lack of knowledge of the design principles and how to design a

DP2 structure, then the solution was obviously to add these components to the Search Conference. Then the purposeful people can make their own most desirable future happen with a much higher probability of success. The solution involved, therefore, a loop back into the evolution of open systems in order to move forward.

Adding Purposeful People to the Open System

The above picture of adaptation between system and environment can be elaborated. What is a system in one context is an environment in another depending on the focus of the inquiry. Let us redraw the open system diagram with purposeful people at the centre. (See Figure 3A) Purposeful people have been recognized as being at the heart of the system for a long time (Ackoff & Emery, 1972; Emery, F., 1959). People are open systems in their own right. Figure 3 shows people as purposeful systems living and working within larger systems which function as task and learning environments. There are, therefore, three sets of adaptive relations, between people and their organizations, i.e., their immediate environments, between people and the extended social field or environment and between the organizations and the field. All must be congruent if there is to be adaptation.

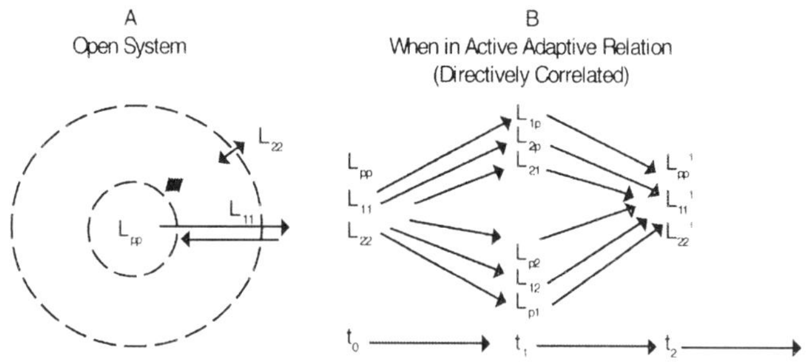

Figure 3. Individuals within Systems within the Extended Social Field

The third set of arrows (L_{2p}, L_{1p} & L_{p2}, L_{p1}) representing the relation between individuals and the extended field is often forgotten, but it is required to completely explain the dynamic nature of the set. It is obvious that people bring to any system or organization values and expectations derived from the whole of their life and their immersion in the broad social field. When these expectations and values are not met an intensifying spiral of discontent is generated. While the system or organization may be aiming for outcomes that are adaptive in terms of the environment, they are producing behaviours in individual people that are maladaptive in terms of these desired outcomes.

The organizational system (L_{11}) acts as an environment for the individual systems within it. Rather than have the simple model of open system in environment which yields the one set of transport equations (L_{21} and L_{12}), the more complex model yields 3 sets of cross boundary relations, the original plus two sets involving the individual purposeful people themselves. If staying with the original notation (1 for system, 2 for environment) and adding a p for individual people, the diagram looks as in Figure 3. The L_{pp} then is the lawful nature and internal dynamics of people themselves. The relations L_{1p} and L_{p1} then define the system acting on the people or the people learning about the system and the people acting on the system, beating the system or otherwise working with it. This model also shows that when people are living and/or working in a system, they also have a continuing set of relationships with the environment or field, learning from it and acting upon it as individuals regardless of the behaviour of the system itself.

In Figure 3B, adaptation can be seen as a constant state of change appropriate to both the nature of people and a continuously changing environment. Learning and dynamism are inherent to active adaptation.

Note however that these sets of relations with the environment ($L_{12/21}$ and $L_{p2/2p}$) cannot be totally independent if the system is a human system as it consists of these people in some type of structured relationships. There is, therefore, constant interdependence between the people and the system but the implications of the model for active adaptation are quite clear. There must be congruence between *all* sets of relations if there is to be genuine continuing active adaptation.

The system itself must be meeting the needs of the people as per the six psychological requirements referenced above. Both the Norwegian Program and subsequently the Participative Design Workshop had proved that open jointly optimized socio-technical (DP2) systems had far superior ability (than non jointly optimized socio-technical, DP1 systems) to achieve directive correlation with their people. Putting together the conceptualizations of the SC and the open socio-technical system and redrawing it in the form of the open system, it is easy to see the implications for implementing the action plans of a Search Conference. (Figure 4 shows the complete model for active adaptation). The relations L_{21} and L_{12} as part of the set required for active adaptation define the process of the SC and are necessary but insufficient on their own. The other necessary and sufficient part is given by the internal active adaptive structure of the L_{11} such that all relations of person, organization and environment (i.e., L_{1p}/L_{p1}, L_{2p}/L_{p2} and L_{21}/L_{12} above) are directively correlated. Therefore, the Search Conference cannot achieve active adaptation unless the organizational structure of the system which implements the action plans is also either designed or redesigned as a DP2 structure.

For continuing long term active adaptation, the system itself must be organized as an environment for learning, in other words, a learning organization. But there is no implication here that organizations learn - they can't, because they don't have nervous systems. The only sensible definition of a learning organization is "an organization that is structured in such a way that its members can learn and continue to learn within it" (Emery, M., 1993, p. 2). Only then do people have the opportunity to continuously learn from and about their changing environment and to continuously and actively adapt their systems to it. It is now necessary to see the focus of active adaptation as purposeful people in environments.

We can now explain failures of SC implementation quite precisely. Because the SC is designed and managed as a DP2 system, at the end of it, one of two things may happen, depending on whether there is an already existing system or not. For an existing system, as in an organizational SC, the system begins to implement the action plans, still with the existing DP1 structure. The people walk out of a democratic system within which they have determined their new future straight back into a bureaucratic one within which they are supposed to implement it.

Immediately, there is a conflicting or maladaptive relationship instituted between the system and environment on the one hand, and the system and the people on the other.

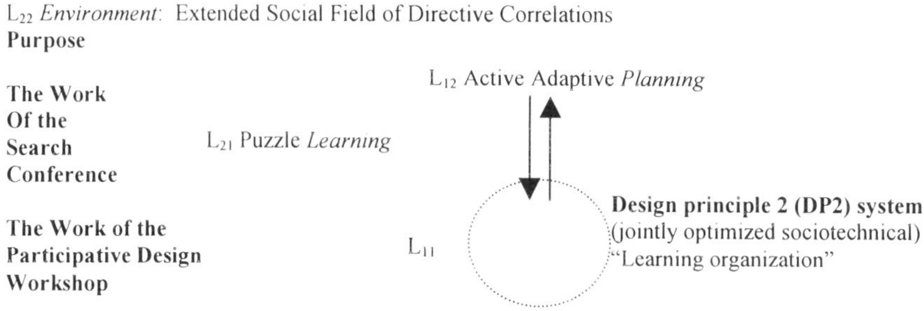

Figure 4. The 2 Stage Model for Active Socioecological Adaptation

In the cases of a geographical community, new networks or issue "Searches" where there is no pre-existing organizational structure, one must be designed to implement the action plans. The hope had been that the experience of the Search as a DP2 structure will be sufficient to inculcate knowledge of the design principles, that is, people will recognize the difference and therefore choose to continue working as they did during the Search. In many cases they do. However, the number of cases in which they haven't shows that the experience of a DP2 structure on its own is often insufficient to overcome the conventional and implicit assumption that there must be a DP1 structure. Despite their experience of something entirely different, there is no *conscious conceptual* knowledge of an alternative. Therefore, they set up what they know, usually a committee structure, with the normal disappointing results.

Practical Outcome

The model is clear. Adaptation must inhere in all sets of relations of people, system and environment. But at the end of a community SC, a geographical community, industry or issue based Search, there is no organization (system) to redesign. One must, therefore, be designed. Note that whether or not this is consciously conceptualized, an organizational structure will be brought into being. And as above, this is precisely where so many failures of implementation have arisen. The very act of people coming together to implement a set of action plans means that an organizational structure has been decided. And when people know of no alternative to bureaucratic (DP1) structures such as committees, this is what they design. They then experience the disillusionment of watching the inevitable results - attendance at meetings fade, energy rapidly drains away and implementation stalls.

If there is an organizational "Search," e.g. the Future of Existing Organization X, best results over the long term will be realized only if the existing structure is redesigned on the second design principle. As stated in the introduction, Searches for existing organizations have a better track record of implementation than do community Searches. And that is simply because there is a known structure regardless of its design principle. Any reasonably well run organization, and most that initiate SCs are amongst the better run, will use the most appropriate parts of the organization to carry the implementation. And for the short term, this is sufficient. The problem for existing DP1 organizations begins later in that the people who live and work within them are not motivated to maintain the adaptive relation between organization and environment. Without a change of design principle and the creation of a learning environment, the entire implicit individual learning of environmental change and its implications is lost to the organization. Worse, when the people realize that the new relation between system and environment has little relevance to their daily work and lives, they will come to regard it with the same cynicism as any other non-fundamental change. Non-fundamental means, of course, no change to the principle of hierarchical dominance (DP1). When people are denied the opportunity to use their capacity to learn, think, make decisions and plan, no amount of money, profit or new technology is going to impress them.

To prevent these failures, all that is required is to tack a modified PDW onto the end of the Search. It is modified because it is to design an organization rather than to redesign an existing structure, which is the purpose of the original PDW. Before we look at PDWs to design organizations, let us look at the original PDW for redesigning organizational structures so that differences are made clear.

The Participative Design Workshop

This workshop is for redesigning organisational structures from DP1 (bureaucratic) to DP2 (democratic), designing back in the human dimension of work which is summarised by the six criteria (Emery & Emery, 1974). Its design is as follows.

1. Phase 1. Analysis
   Briefing 1 - Design Principle 1
   Groups complete matrix for 6 psychological requirements of productive activity.
   Groups complete matrix of skills available.
   Reports and diagnostics.

2. Phase 2. Change
   Briefing 2 - Design Principle 2
   Groups draw up workflow.
   Groups draw up organizational structure and redesign it.
   Reports.

3. Phase 3. Practicalities
   Briefing 3 - What Is Required to Make the Redesign Work
   Groups spell out:
   a. a comprehensive set of measurable goals.
   b. training requirements (from skills matrix).
   c. other requirements, e. g., mechanisms for coordination, changes in technology
   d. the basis for designing career paths.
   e. how the redesign improves scores on the 6 criteria.

The first phase is an analysis of what currently exists, phase two makes the change and phase three designs in all of the practical matters that accompany the systemic change and ensures its effectiveness in practice.

Modified Participative Design Workshops to Create an Organization

The following is the basic model that has emerged for a PDW for organization creation rather than redesign. Using this model after the SC means that the SC community effectively answers the question of "How do we best organise ourselves to make sure we implement our plans?"

Let us deal with the case of the community SC first. The major differences in workshop design between those for redesign and SC follow up (design) are:

1. These people may never have worked together before, and as there is no existing organization, the six criteria must be done on a previous, similar experience. Most people will have been involved in some community or voluntary activity that involved trying to get some plan achieved.

2. Goals have already been set in the Search as the Most Desirable System and action plans have been devised for these.

3. If particular resources such as skills do not reside within the implementing group, they must be brought in. Communities usually will not have the resources to start training up people in specific skills or knowledge. Instead, the community must do some further action planning to acquire the required skills or other resources, either directly or through the process of diffusion. There may be some considerable work done matching and then readjusting immediate steps in implementation with the needs of effective organization for implementation.

The Most Simple Follow-up Design

1. Phase 1. Analysis
   Briefing 1 - Design Principle 1
   Task forces complete the matrix for the six criteria using a previous experience similar to the implementation now facing them.
   Reports and diagnostics
   The community lists the major essential skills required to implement the action plans, then completes the matrix in terms of who holds what skills on the list

2. Phase 2. Change
   Briefing 2 - Design Principle 2
   Design organizational structure for implementation
   Reports and negotiation of final design if necessary

3. Phase 3. Practicalities
   Briefing 3 - What Is Required to Make the Redesign Work
   What other resources do we need, if any? (from the skills matrix)

What else needs to be done? (This may involve more work on action plans or an additional set of action plans.)

For already existing organizations, the members can of course complete the matrix for the six criteria for their own work. Using the PDW in these settings serves as an easy introduction to the design principles and opens the way for further discussion of full-scale organizational change. Other modifications have been used for industrial greenfield designs.

Test to Date (From 1991)

The following initiatives provided opportunities for testing this more comprehensive design for a totally successful process and implementation.

1. Experimenting in short training courses on participative methods for active adaptation at the Centre for Continuing Education (CCE) of the Australian National University (ANU).
2. Designing an introduction to ANU's new Internship program.
3. Community planning in Torres Strait.
4. A participative event to rescue a community from conflicts exacerbated by a Weisbord *Future Search* (Weisbord, 1992; Weisbord & Janoff, 1995).
5. SC for the Future of Participative Democracy in the Americas.
6. Whole system change in Region 9 of the US Forest Service.

During the short training courses at CCE, it became obvious that several participants were taking the course because of an immediate need for holistic organizational change projects which would necessarily involve both SCs and PDWs. They wanted to learn methods for structural change as well as participative planning. They were a sign of the times. Increasingly, organizations were looking for something that actually worked, because everything else hadn't. And there were enough well educated people around who understood the lessons of time to know that long term solutions could not result from short-term fixes. They provided a space to experiment with a range of sessions designed to meet these expectations. A modified PDW to follow the SC was one of these experiments.

I was asked to design an introduction to ANU's new Internship program. It required a modification of the *Participative Design Workshop* such that the Interns could design their own organization for mutual support and learning while working individually in sometimes hostile environments. Interns had no problem conceptualizing their own democratic organization to provide genuine mutual learning and support. Time after time, they decided upon self-managing groups based on common sense practicalities such as research interests, geographical location, etc. Coordination and sharing across the groups has been remarkably easy and productive. It has been handled by informal meetings after scheduled lectures, through events arranged over phones, etc. Nothing further from bureaucratic "meetings could be imagined." Each of the six intakes resulted in a tight knit community.

Successful community planning in Torres Strait required a conceptual understanding, translated and built into a practical organizational infrastructure, sufficiently robust to overcome years of entrenched dependency. This resulted in a two-phase project consisting of individual community SCs followed by two multicommunity integrated training, planning and design workshops. During these workshops, all basic concepts in both the SC and the PDW were briefed and were used to do further joint community action planning and organization for such critical matters as educating their people for customary (indigenous) law and designing effective community meetings. This was to provide the reality of self-management that was so strong in the rhetoric but so weak on the ground. The results have been evaluated in part and built into further planning at the regional level (Emery, M., et al., 1996; Paton & Emery, M., 1996).

The *rescue event* was complex and needed a unique design to bridge the gap between the failed Weisbord *Future Search* and a new more promising start. The original conference followed no logic. Different components of the open system were muddled together and there was some immature action planning (shopping lists) in the middle[1]. This was left hanging and time ran out to return to it at the end. There was no effort to integrate small group reports. The participants (there is no evidence that they became a learning, planning community) were left with an undifferentiated array of data, confusion. There were serious conflicts underlying this confusion that were rapidly exacerbated by the setting up of committees with their predominant dynamic of fight/flight. They needed a clear set of goals and a new effective organizational structure to replace the failed committees. Elements of both the SC and the PDW were woven together in order to begin the necessary reconstruction of goals, action plans and community (Diemer & Alvarez, 1995).

The SC for the *Future of Participative Democracy in the Americas* was a large complex Search to create a network of people committed to improving the chances of a more adaptive and participative democratic Western Hemisphere. It entailed a unique design, the last part of which was a PDW to design the organizational structure to carry the implementation.

Region 9 of the US Forest Service has long been aiming for active adaptive change. Many members of the Forest Service had been trained in the methods discussed here and in December 1995 work began on a holistic system change in Region 9. Of the 16 individual forests within the region, 14 participated in Search Conferences with PDWs attached and one followed up with a full-scale forest organization redesign. The consolidation event to produce a coherent direction for the region was held 14-16 May 1996.

The Future

Most failures of implementation of SC action plans have involved lack of knowledge of the organizational design principles when setting up an organization to implement. The necessary congruence between system, environment and organisational structure had been neglected. This deficiency has now been recognised and addressed. Each of the testings so far for the two-stage model has been successful. People can design a DP2 organization from scratch.

Why has it taken so long for the solution, the preventative method to implementation failures to emerge? The first and foremost answer appears to be that the two methods of the Search Conference and the Participative Design Workshop were conceptualized and, therefore practised, as separate and discrete methods doing two quite separate jobs, the SC for participative strategic planning and the PDW for redesigning existing organizations. They had not been seen as complementary parts of a whole change towards active adaptation and therefore, continuous change.

The second answer is that only specific, conscious, conceptual knowledge of the design principles can overcome our culture's wholescale rush into mechanistic thinking, and therefore bureaucratic structures, from the beginning of the industrial revolution. The active adaptive planning done within the SC to establish a directive correlation between system and environment was necessary but insufficient to fully achieve active adaptation. Active adaptation has to include both an active adaptive relation between the system and the environment, and active adaptive relations within the system itself.

The 2 Stage Model not only raises the probability of successful planning and design, it also speeds up diffusion as more people gain conscious conceptual knowledge of the design principles. It has been successfully tested in the higher education system and here there is a low level of awareness of both the need for fundamental change and the possibility of it (Emery, M., 1998b). As the breeding ground for most of our professionals and managers, this fundamental change is required to encourage creativity and innovation. Large-scale change projects in the education systems will demand new and different designs and we can expect that these will generate substantial new knowledge.

Notes

1. There is much confusion between the Search Conference and the Future Search but they are very different methods. Weisbord's method is often placed within the systems stream but it owes more in its concept and practice to the Human Relations (NTL) tradition through Schindler-Rainman and Lippitt than it does to the method whose name he has appropriated. I have documented the main dimensions of this confusion (Emery, M., 1994). In Weisbord's method, the importance of the external social field and learning about it is trivialized and turned into an element of the human encounter. In 1987, Weisbord used the terms *Search Conference* and *Future Search* synonymously as they were used in Australia. In 1992, he used the term *Future Search* to cover virtually any participative event. With great irony, Weisbord and Janoff (1995, p. 51) reserve the term *Future Search* for their own model and urge others not to use the name for other models. The name *Search Conference* can now be reclaimed for the original and distinct concept.

References

Ackoff, R. L., & Emery, F. E. (1972). *On purposeful systems.* Seaside CA: Intersystems.

Angyal, A. (1941). *Foundations for a science of personality.* Harvard University Press.

Bion, W. R. (1952). Group dynamics: A review. *International Journal of Psychoanalysis, 33,* 235-247.

Bion, W. R. (1961). *Experiences in groups.* Tavistock.

Diemer, J., & Alvarez, R. A. (1995). Sustainable community, sustainable forestry: A participatory model. *Journal of Forestry 93,* 10-14.

Emery, F. E. (1959). Characteristics of socio-technical systems. *The Emergence of a New Paradigm of Work* (TIHR Doc. 527) pp. 38-86. Canberra: Centre for Continuing Education, Australian National University.

Emery, F. E. (1967). The next thirty years: Concept, methods and anticipations. *Human Relations, 20,* 199-237.
Emery, F. (1969). The historical validity of the Norwegian Industrial Democracy Project. Tavistock Document HRC 210.
Emery, F. (1977). *Futures we are in.* Martinus Nijhoff Social Sciences Division, Leiden. (Out of print) Updated and edited version, *Futures we're in,* Southern Cross University Press, http:/www.nor.com.au/business/scupress/web-store.cgi
Emery, F. (1980). Educational paradigms: An epistemological revolution. In M. Emery (Ed.), *Participative Design for Participative Democracy* (pp. 40-85). Canberra: Centre for Continuing Education, Australian National University.
Emery, F., & Emery, M. (1974) Participative design: Work and community life. In M. Emery (Ed.), *Participative Design for Participative Democracy* (pp. 100-122). Canberra: Centre for Continuing Education, Australian National University.
Emery, F. E., & Thorsrud, E. (1969). *Form and content in industrial democracy.* Tavistock.
Emery, F. E., & Thorsrud, E. (1976). *Democracy at work.* Martinus Nijhoff Social Science Division, Leiden.
Emery, F. E., & Trist, E. L. (1965). The causal texture of organisational environments. *Human Relations, 18,* 21-32.
Emery, M. (Ed.). (1976). *Searching: for new directions, in new ways, for new times.* Canberra: Centre for Continuing Education, Australian National University.
Emery, M. (1982). *Searching: for new directions, in new ways, for new times.* Canberra: Centre for Continuing Education, Australian National University.
Emery, M. (Ed.). (1993). *Participative design for participative democracy.* Canberra: Centre for Continuing Education, Australian National University.
Emery, M. (1994). *The search conference in the USA today: Clarifying some confusions.* Canberra: Centre for Continuing Education, Australian National University.
Emery, M. (1996). The influence of culture in search conferences. *Concepts and Tranformation: International Journal of Action Research and Organizational Renewal, 1,.* 143-164.
Emery, M. (1998). *Searching: The theory and practice of making cultural change.* John Benjamins Publisher.
Emery, M., & Emery, F. (1978). Searching: For new direction, in new ways for new times. In J. W. Sutherland (Ed.), *Management handbook for public administrators* (pp. 257-301). Van Nostrand Reinhold Co.
Emery, M., & Purser, R. (1996). *The search conference: A powerful method for planning organizational change and community action.* San Francisco: Jossey Bass.
Katz, D., & Kahn, R. L. (1966). *The social psychology of organizations.* New York: Wiley.
Lewin, K. (1944). The solution of a chronic conflict in industry. In K. Lewin (Ed.), *Resolving social conflicts,* (pp. 125-141).
Lewin, K., Lippitt, R., & White, R. (1960). *Autocracy and democracy: An experimental inquiry.* New York: Harper & Row.
Newcomb, T. M. (1953). An approach to the study of communicative acts. *Psychological Review, 60,* 393-404.
Paton, J., & Emery, M. (1996). From dependency to development. *Journal of Quality and Participation.*
Schindler-Rainman, E., & Lippitt, R. (1980). *Building the collaborative community: Mobilizing citizens for action.* Riverside, CA: University of California.
Selznick, P. (1957). *Leadership in administration.* New York: Harper & Row.
Sommerhoff, G. (1969). The abstract characteristics of living systems.
Sutherland, J. W. (Ed.). (1978). *Management handbook for public administrators.* Van Nostrand Reinhold.
Trist, E. L., Emery, & Murray, (1997). *The social engagement of social science: The socio-ecological perspective.* Philadelphia: University of Pennsylvania Press.

Trist, E. L., & Bamforth, K. W. (1951). Some social and psychological consequences of the Longwall method of coal-getting. *Human Relations, 4,* 3-38.

Von Bertalanffy, L. (1950). The theory of open systems in physics and biology. *Science, 3,* 22-29.

Weisbord, M. R. (1987). *Productive workplaces: Organizing and managing for dignity, meaning and community.* San Francisco: Jossey Bass.

Weisbord, M. R. (Ed.). (1992). *Discovering common ground.* San Francisco: Berrett-Kohler. .

Weisbord, M. R., & Janoff, S. (1995). *Future search: An action guide to finding common ground in organizations and communities.* San Francisco: Berrett-Kohler.

SECTION II.

AN APPRECIATIVE LOOK AT SOME MAJOR THINKERS

Chapter 6

Kurt Lewin

Contributions to Organizational Development

Karon Tedford

University of North Texas, Denton, Texas, United States

David Baker

University of North Texas, Denton, Texas, United States

Abstract

Kurt Lewin (1890 –1947) had a profound impact on the development of work teams. His concepts of field theory and action research created new avenues for social and organizational psychology. Claimed as a progenitor of many areas in applied psychology, Lewin's studies of group dynamics laid the groundwork for many of today's principles concerning work teams. This paper traces his seminal work that earned him a respected place in the history of organizational development.

Introduction

Kurt Lewin's life and work earned him the distinction as a leader and visionary in many areas of psychology. Many think of him as one of the greatest social psychologists of the 20th century. Less well known, but equally impressive, is Lewin's leadership, innovation and contribution to organizational development. Organizational development represents the "O" side of industrial and organizational Psychology (I/O). While the "I" side focuses on personnel issues like measurement, assessment, selection, test construction, and legal concerns, the "O" side focuses more on system issues such as organizational development, team development, change, reorganization, training, and coaching.

The "I" side of I/O was well represented in the early decades of the 20th century by such people such as Hugo Munsterberg at Harvard, Walter Dill Scott at Northwestern, James McKeen Cattell of Columbia University, and Walter Bingham of Carnegie Tech. (For an extended discussion see Landy, 1997). These psychologists sought to apply psychological principles to a variety of issues in labor, industry, and government that resulted in a proliferation of testing methods and tools as well as personnel and job classification practices and procedures. The "O" side did not really get its start until the 1940's. The foundations of organizational development emerged from two sources: (a) the laboratory training movement and (b) the survey research and feedback methodology. Lewin's field theory of social

M.M. Beyerlein (ed.), Work Teams: Past, Present and Future, 107–114.

psychology and his interest in applied behavioral science laid the groundwork for both.

Background

Kurt Lewin was born in the village of Mogilno (now part of Poland) on September 9, 1890. He was the second of four children in a family that owned a small general store. As Jews, the Lewin family was subject to the prejudice and discrimination that was characteristic of Prussia at that time. The Lewin family moved to Berlin when Kurt was 15. After a semester at the University of Fribourg and Munich, Lewin enrolled at the University of Berlin, eventually earning his Ph.D. under Carl Stumpf in 1916. As a student and later as a lecturer at the University of Berlin, Lewin became associated with the new movement, Gestalt Psychology, and with its originators, Max Wertheimer, Wolfgang Kohler, and Kurt Koffka. The rise of Adolf Hitler and the Nazi party made life increasingly difficult and dangerous for Jews in Germany. In 1933, Lewin, his wife, and two children would leave Berlin for the United States. Once in the United States, Lewin obtained faculty appointments at Cornell, Iowa, and finally at M.I.T. (Cernius, 1986).

Early Ideas

Lewin's early choice of studies showed an interest in industrial management and job satisfaction. As a student at Berlin in 1920, Lewin wrote a paper on Taylorism. Frederick Taylor was known for his concept of scientific management that emphasized time and motion studies. Scientific management stressed efficiency and considered the worker, as a person, as unimportant. Followers of scientific management believed that jobs should be divided into small tasks that could be taught to anyone. They also believed that planning a task should be separated from doing the task.

In his paper about Taylorism, Lewin presented new ideas about the worker and the values the worker placed on what the worker was doing. Lewin felt that the satisfaction derived from the work determined how well the employee performed. These ideas would later play a part in current job satisfaction theories and become important in self-managed work teams (Marrow, 1969).

As a young professor at Berlin, Lewin developed a reputation for seeing questions in everyday life that developed into experiments and theories for his students. These were always posited in terms of Gestalt theory as well as the ongoing development of Lewin's own brand of Gestalt psychology. He and his students participated in weekly Saturday morning coffees. Ideas for experiments actually developed during some of these meetings. One of his students, Anita Karsten, found that simple tasks which were repeated until tired would be easy to remember later, but only if they were part of a meaningful whole. Another student, Bluma Ziegarnik noted that waiters had better recall for customer bills that were unpaid than for those that were paid. Known as the "Zeigarnik effect," it reflects Lewin's concept of dynamic equilibrium and goal formation in the functioning of the individual (Zeigarnik, 1984).

Indeed, Lewin's concerns for the individual were evident from an early age and were impacted by his life experiences. He served in the trenches during WW I, was wounded, and received the Iron Cross. During a furlough, he wrote an article about the landscape of war that emphasized the perception of the individual soldier facing the front. In the article, he articulated many aspects of what would become his "field theory" (Marrow, 1969).

Field Theory

Before 1920, most lab experiments were unrelated to each other and involved collecting facts and then analyzing them. Lewin felt that research should be based on a theory and was fond of saying, "There is nothing so practical as a good theory" (Marrow, 1969). He felt theory had two functions: (a) it should account for what is known, and (b) it should lead to new knowledge. The purpose of an experiment should be to test theories instead of just collecting and analyzing or classifying facts (Lewin, 1940).

Gestalt psychology, which was developing at Berlin, proposed that the way an object is perceived depends on its surroundings and its relationship in the perceptual field rather than on the fixed characteristics of the object. Lewin extended the notion of field theory to emotions and behavior. He felt that the past and the future were both part of the dimension, but that behavior depended mostly on the psychological present, the here and now of a person's "life space" (Lewin, 1939). According to Lewin, "behavior is a function of the person and his environment" (p. 43). He believed that a human's life space could be understood as shared fields with forces that could be measured and influenced. He used the formula: $B = f(p,e)$, where B represents behavior which is a function (f) of the interaction between the person (p), and the environment (e). Such theorizing led to the development of force field analysis. Force field analysis is used to analyze problems that can't be measured in ordinary ways, such as why a team is not behaving as expected. Lewin also applied field theory and life space to topics of conflict and conflict resolution. In his 1935 book, *Dynamic Theory of Personality*, he defined conflict as the opposition of equally strong field forces. The three basic conflicts were between two positive valances, between a positive and a negative valance, and between two negative valances (Lewin, 1935). Terms like approach-avoidance conflict and leaving the field are now widely used in psychology and in the management of work teams.

Group Decision Making

Lewin settled in the United States in1933. In America, Lewin first went to Cornell's School of Home Economics and then to the University of Iowa's Child Welfare Research Station. While at Iowa, he became interested in what was to become one of his most important contributions, using the social sciences to solve social problems. Many feel this interest was a direct result of his experiences in Hitler's Germany (Lewin, 1992).

During WW II, at the request of the United States government, Lewin worked with Margaret Mead to find a way to get people to eat less of the food that was rationed and more of the non-rationed food (Lewin, 1943). The experiment involved working with groups of people. Some groups were given facts about patriotism, economy, and nutrition in a logical presentation and then told what they should do. Other groups were presented the same lecture, but they were asked to meet and discuss the facts as well as discuss what they should do. They were not told what they should do. Both groups had initial resistance because they were unaccustomed to buying, cooking, or eating the non-rationed items (tongue, heart, and lung).

A follow-up study found that the groups that used discussion and reached consensus were much more likely to have changed their eating habits than the groups that had only received the lecture. Their involvement in the decision overcame their initial resistance. Involvement "unfroze" their perceptions, broadened their thinking, and allowed them to consider the alternatives. Two cornerstones of dealing with work teams developed from this: (1) people are more likely to carry out decisions they have helped make, and (2) when people are involved in a problem, they are more committed to implementing the solutions.

Lewin's theory of change involved three steps: unfreezing, moving, and refreezing (Lewin, 1947). In the unfreezing stage, new or contradictory information is given. People need to be prepared for change by seeing the need to relinquish old behaviors or thoughts. In the moving stage, people discuss and develop new actions. This involves changes in attitudes, values, and feelings. In the moving stage, prior behaviors or thoughts must be altered. The refreezing stage uses support to maintain the desired change. The new behaviors or thoughts must become new habits. Today's trend from hierarchical management styles to work teams requires a great deal of change. Lewin's change concepts have been incorporated into many of today's change management initiatives.

The Harwood study is considered the first experiment of group decision making and self-management in industry and the first example of applied organizational psychology (Marrow, 1969). The Harwood Experiment was part of Lewin's continuing exploration of participative research. The Harwood company had pajama factories in the northern and the southern part of the United States, but the southern workers only produced half as much as the northern workers. Meetings that involved high and low producers were held and production methods were discussed. This helped the less efficient workers learn about better methods but they were not told they had to change their methods. Rather, the workers were then allowed to set their own output goals. Because they were making the output decisions themselves, they were less resistant to change and were able to increase production on their own (Lewin, 1947). Lewin's belief that shared experiences not only provide material for diagnostic study and evaluation, but are vitally important for changing behavior are used by many consultants charged with the responsibility of developing a work team atmosphere.

Leadership

While working with Ronald Lippitt at the University of Iowa, Lewin coined the term group dynamics" and laid the foundation for today's leadership theories. Lippitt was experimenting with members of the Boys Club to test democratic leaders versus autocratic leaders (Lewin, Lippitt, & White, 1939; Lippitt, 1939). It was found that the groups with democratic leaders stuck to task and had more group spirit and cooperation. Lewin took home movies of the groups and while watching the movies, he realized that there existed a third type of leader that had not been part of the original design.

The third type of leader was neglectful, offering no guidance or structure. Further study found that the individuals in the group with the neglectful leader felt inadequate and blamed their unhappiness on other group members. Another one of his films showed what happened when the leaders of each group left the room. In the autocratic group, weaker members were picked on. In the neglected group, there was a lot of boredom and wandering aimlessly around the room. The democratic group kept on working. This study made national news and an article appeared in the New York Times in September of 1938. The study contributed to the knowledge about groups and made the work and relevance of psychologists more visible to the public.

The democratic versus autocratic study laid the foundation for later work on how management styles impact productivity in work groups. The studies introduced social climate and group atmosphere and began the research in group dynamics, group structure, group decision, and group cohesion. These areas are the backbone of much of the work with organizations and team development.

In developing leaders, Lewin felt that social science techniques would be more effective than traditional academic psychology. In 1946, Douglas McGregor and Lewin started the Research Center for Group Dynamics at the Massachusetts Institute of Technology (MIT). This new center was established to study something that had never been studied scientifically --- group dynamics and group processes. The research center began a revolution in industrial organizational science and management methods that is continuing today. The Center investigated topics such as group productivity, communication, dissemination of influences, social perception, interrelations between groups, group membership, adapting individuals to groups, and training group leaders. Lewin's experiments with groups led to his being recognized as the founder of experimental social psychology (Ash, 1992).

Action Research

Lewin's social conscious formed his theories and laid the groundwork for his research on human behavior. He extended his theories and research into the domains of social action. In 1936, he was a charter member of the Society for the Psychological Study of Social Issues and served as president in 1942-43. The group united the liberals in the American Psychological Association that wanted to expand psychological research beyond academic borders into more applied areas, especially those dealing with the great social problems of the times. Lewin shared their attitude and believed lab experiments were not enough to provide relief from problems such as poverty, racism, war, etc. He felt that all the variables concerning people couldn't always be controlled so easily in real life as they were in a lab. He felt an answer to this problem was to involve the experiment's participants and researcher in the experiment. This became known as "Lewin's Action Research." Action research was unique because the people involved helped define the problem and helped solve it. Action research involved data collection, diagnosis, action, evaluation, and iteration as long as needed. Lewin's method involved doing by learning and learning by experience. He turned research into action and action into research (Weisbord, 1987).

At the same time that the Research Center for Group Dynamics was being established at MIT, Lewin was also establishing the Commission for Community Interrelations (CCI). Lewin envisioned the two organizations working together to combine scientific study and action research to study prejudice. MIT was to be the research lab and CCI was to provide action research based in the community. The last years of Lewin's life were spent with these two organizations in an attempt to bring to life his vision of the interdependence of theory and practice (Marrow, 1969

In 1946, while serving as director of MIT's Research Center for Group Dynamics, Lewin was asked to organize a training session to assist leaders that would deal with intergroup tensions in their home communities. Lewin asked Ronald Lippitt to lead one of the three groups and Lippitt then recruited Kenneth Benne and Leland Bradford to lead the other two groups. Lippitt, Benne, and Bradford would become the founders of the NTL Institute, which is active today in the field of group training, leadership training, and developing change agents.

Action research was often considered a renegade technique outside mainstream psychology. In industrial settings, action research involved case studies where researchers and participants studied the organization at close range, evaluating and modifying along the way (Lewin, 1947). Lewin's concept used the scientific method to explore while continually developing and modifying the hypothesis as well as continually learning from the experiment. He used a working hypothesis that led to a prediction, but he tested the predictions in the organization instead of in the lab. He evaluated the outcomes, modified the hypothesis and the prediction, and then tested further. This was seen as a continuous process. In action research, members of the research teamwork together to solve a problem by critically reflecting upon their actions and assumptions. Data is also collected about behaviors, actions, and outcomes (Desarrollo, 1998).

Contemporary Applications

In the 1960's, social scientists used Lewin's methods to develop a model for diagnosing industrial problems. The Lewinian Consulting Model required that all people involved looked at the data together and that all accepted the action plan (Weisbord, 1987). This model brought the people experiencing the problem into the diagnosis, into the solution, and into the implementation. Today's search conference methods and self-managing teams employ some of these concepts.

Douglas McGregor's book, *The Human Side of Enterprise* (1960) detailed Theory Y type of management. It was based on Maslow's Hierarchy of Needs and had its roots in McGregor's work with Lewin at the Research Center for Group Dynamics. Theory Y's principles stated that people were capable of self direction and self control, could be committed, could accept responsibility and solve problems; all principles that are important to today's successful self-managed teams. Action science is a contemporary development of action research and the action scientist is a practitioner (Argyris, Schein, Putnam, & Smith, 1985). Lewin's influence is evident in the curriculum of many university business programs and courses in organizational behavior, organizational development, and group dynamics.

The Society of the Advancement of Field Theory (SAFT) was formed to revitalize Lewin's Field Theory approach in the social sciences. SAFT organizes a BI-annual International Kurt Lewin Conference to bring diverse researchers together. In 1995, the Royal Netherlands Academy of the Arts and Science formally recognized the Kurt Lewin Institute as a graduate school. The Institute is a joint venture of senior social psychology researchers that are affiliated with five Dutch Universities. Lewin's daughter, Dr. Miriam Lewin, and the American Psychological Association have reissued two of Kurt Lewin's books, "Resolving Social Conflicts" and "Field Theory in Social Science".

Conclusion

Lewin was only 57 when he unexpectedly died of a heart attack in 1947. Many feel that study of group dynamics and work teams would have been greatly accelerated if he had lived. The New York Times (1947) obituary made note of his studies regarding democratic and authoritarian group atmospheres and his analysis of the forces of change in social groups. Lewin is remembered for his use of experimental methodology in social psychology, for the development of theory, and for making theory and research relevant to social practice. One of his most important contributions was his legacy of students that have influenced all areas of psychology.

According to Marrow (1969), Lewin did not publish great volumes of work, and he never held a tenured position, yet his students changed the face of psychology. Lewin's work lived and developed through his students. There are more references to research performed by Lewin's primary students than to any comparable group in child personality and social psychology. The psychologists who were with Lewin at the Research Center at MIT went on to greatly influence social psychology and train the next generation. Eight of the ten most cited social psychologists are direct descendants from this group (Patnoe, 1988). Lewin, or his students, initiated many of the concepts that have influenced today's studies of teams. They include levels of aspiration, anger, frustration, autocracy and democracy in groups, styles of group leadership, effects of group decisions on individual behavior, and conditions favorable to cooperation. Edgar Schein, Professor of Management Emeritus at MIT's Sloan School of Management said, "few people have had as profound an impact on the theory and practice of social and organizational psychology as Kurt Lewin." (Schein, 1998).

Lewin's influence extends past psychology. Lewin and his students' theories have played an important role in organizational behavior, sociology, management and business courses. Business schools are becoming a leading force in the advancement and continuation of Lewin's theories. Modern management owes much to Kurt Lewin. Before 1933, Lewis preferred studying dyads in his experiments. In Iowa, he began experiments with larger groups. He transferred the models he had developed for studying children's playgroups to studying leadership and conflict resolution in adults at work. During his years in America, Lewin shifted from the study of intrapersonal actions to the study of interpersonal actions. His emphasis was on group standards, leadership, group atmosphere, and group decision making. His contributions have influenced the methods of conducting meetings, work design, training, system change, cultural change, leadership styles, participative methods, minority-majority relationships, survey feedback methods, and consultation skills. Kurt Lewin has well earned a place in the history of I/O psychology and his work continues to hold the promise of discovery and innovation in the century ahead.

References

Argyris, C., Schein, R., & Smith, D. M. (1985). *Action science*. San Francisco: Jossey-Bass.

Ash, M. (1992). Cultural contexts and scientific change in Psychology: Kurt Lewin in Iowa. *American Psychologist*, 47, 198-207.

Cernius, V. (1986). The man in transition: Kurt Lewin and his times. In E. Stivers and S. Wheelan (Eds.), *The Lewin legacy: Field theory in current practice* (pp. 21-29). New York: Springer-Verlag,

Desarrollo, (1998). History and definition of action research. http://excelencia.uat.mx/desarrollo/content2.htm

Director of research center for group dynamics at school is dead. (1947, February 13). *The New York Times*.

Landy, F. J. (1997). Early influences on the development of industrial and organizational psychology. *Journal of Applied Psychology*, 82, 467-477.

Lewin, K. (1935). *A dynamic theory of personality*. NY: McGraw-Hill Book Company, Inc.

Lewin, K. (1936). *Principles of topological psychology*. NY: McGraw-Hill Inc.

Lewin, K. (1939). Field theory and experiment in social psychology: Concepts and methods. *American Journal of Sociology*, 44, 868-897.

Lewin, K. (1940). Formalization and progress in psychology. *University of Iowa Studies in Child Welfare*, 16, 9-42.

Lewin, K. (1943). Forces behind food habits and methods of change. *Bulletin of the National Research Council*, 108, 35-65.

Lewin, K. (1947). Frontiers in group dynamics. *Human Relations*, 1, 143-153.

Lewin, M. (1992). The impact of Kurt Lewin's life on the place of social issues in his work. *Journal of Social Issues*, 48(2), 15-29.

Lewin, K., Lippitt, R., & White, R. K. (1939). Patterns of aggressive behavior in experimentally created "social climates." *Journal of Social Psychology*, 10,271-299.

Lippitt, R. (1939). An experimental study of authoritarian and democratic group atmospheres. *University of Iowa Studies in Child Welfare*, 16(3),43-195.

Marrow, A. J. (1969). *The practical theorist: The life and work of Kurt Lewin*. New York, NY: Basic Books, Inc.

McGregor, D. (1960). *The human side of enterprise*. New York: McGraw-Hill.

Patnoe, S. (1988). *A narrative history of experimental social psychology: The Lewin tradition*. New York, NY: Springer-Verlag.

Schein, E. (1998). *Kurt Lewin's change theory in the field and in the classroom: Notes toward a model of managed learning*. http://learning.mit.edu/res/wp/10006.html

Weisbord, M. (1987). *Productive workplaces*. San Francisco, CA: Jossey-Bass Publishers.

Zeigarnik, B. V. (1984). Kurt Lewin and soviet psychology. *Journal of Social Issues*, 40, 181-192.

Chapter 7

Socio-Technical Systems Approach to Work Team Design

The Contributions of Eric L. Trist

Lillian Eby, Beverly Sinoway, and Anthony Parisi

The University of Georgia, Athens, Georgia, United States

Abstract

Eric Landstown Trist focused primarily on real world applied problems through the idiographic research perspective. The following chapter reviews Trist's scholarly work on socio-technical systems and work teams. An analysis of how Trist's research has contributed to theory and research on work teams as well as his impact on practice is also provided.

Introduction

Few scholars have made such remarkable and lasting contributions to the field of social psychology and organizational behavior as Eric Landsdown Trist (1909-1993). As founder and chairman of the Tavistock Institute, Trist committed over 60 years to examining the complex relationships among individuals, groups, organizations, and the external environment. While the level of analysis Trist focused on shifted throughout his career -- from the individual, to the group, to the organization, to society as a whole -- the underlying theme was that individuals are social beings (Emery, 1993). Trist believed that the social aspects of human interaction serve a central purpose in determining individuals' personal fulfillment and productivity in society. Moreover, characteristics of the environment in which individuals operate can facilitate or hinder these human interactions, and in so doing greatly influence psychological well being and performance (Trist, 1981b).

One of the most remarkable features of Trist's career was his dual emphasis on scholarship and practice. Following the tradition of Kurt Lewin's action research, Trist's work focused almost exclusively on real-world applied problems. Trist relied primarily on an idiographic research perspective, consisting of naturalistic observation and qualitative case studies, rather than the dominant experimental paradigm of the time (McGrath, 1984). The response from the prevailing academic community to these methods was scathing (Pasmore & Khalsa, 1993). As Trist himself recounts "Universities would have nothing to do with us (the Tavistock

M.M. Beyerlein (ed.), Work Teams: Past, Present and Future, 115–129.

Institute). There was great hostility...how we survived was a miracle" (Trist, 1993, p. 205). What Trist gained through his unconventional research methodology, however, was a level of contextual and theoretical richness not possible through purely nomothetic research characterized by standardized conditions, controlled environmental contexts, and quantitative analyses.

Formally educated in both England and the United States, Trist studied clinical psychology and social anthropology at Yale prior to the outbreak of World War II (Krantz, 1990). As part of the war effort, Trist was involved in several applied research projects that shaped his later career trajectory (Pasmore & Khalsa, 1993). This included the first use of leaderless group discussions as selection methods for military officers, the use of group therapy for soldiers dealing with the trauma of war, and the design of resettlement communities for former prisoners of war (Bion, 1946; Murray, 1990; Wilson, Trist, & Curle, 1952). These experiences influenced Trist's ideas about group behavior, particularly the role of psychological resistance to change in adapting to new situations, how group self-regulation can emerge from empowering conditions, and the potent role of group processes in understanding human behavior (Pasmore & Khalsa, 1993). After the war, Trist focused his efforts on developing his ideas about self-directed work teams and socio-technical systems.

Synopsis of the Current Chapter and Search Procedure

Trist was truly a Renaissance man, working in a wide range of areas throughout his prolific career. This includes, but is not limited to, socio-technical systems and work teams (the focus of this chapter), quality of worklife (QWL) interventions, work-nonwork balance, counseling and clinical psychology, testing and assessment, and broad-scale community change efforts. Due to space constraints we restricted our coverage to Trist's scholarly work to socio-technical systems and work teams. The interested reader is referred to Pasmore and Khalsa (1993) for a broad overview of Trist's life work or to Trist and Murray (1990, 1993, 1997) for a historical perspective on the development of the Tavistock Institute. In the pages that follow we provide a chronological account of Trist's research on work teams and socio-technical systems. In so doing the current chapter contributions to the scholarly literature by condensing and analyzing decades of Trist's research on work teams and socio-technical systems and has contributed to theory and research on teams.[1] Identifying studies for inclusion in the present chapter proceeded in a three step manner. The first step was an on-line computer search using the key words "Trist," "Teams," "Work teams," "Tavistock," and "Socio-technical." These key words were searched in the following databases: Psychological Abstracts (PsychINFO), Sociological Abstracts (SOCA), a comprehensive bibliography search (WorldCat or OCLC Online Union Catalog), a worldwide business and management database (ABI/INFORM), the Biography Index, and a search of books in the Georgia Academic Library Information Network (GALIN). Step two consisted of cross-referencing works authored and co-authored by Trist based on the sources identified in step one. Finally, an exhaustive listing of 482 citations of Eric Trist's work provided by the Citation Database of the Institute for Scientific Information was cross-referenced to identify studies by Trist in the area of work teams and socio-technical systems.

A Brief Overview of the Socio-Technical Systems Approach

Socio-technical systems theory proposes that an organization's technology and the social aspects of work are independent of each other yet must be complementary in order to maximize both quality of worklife and productivity. In other words, there must be a fit or match between the technical configuration of work and the social arrangement of employees (Trist & Bamforth, 1951; Trist, 1981a, 1981b). This does not mean that technology should dictate the social aspects of work, but rather that the joint optimization of technology and people are the key to effectiveness. An underlying assumption of socio-technical systems theory is that employee participation and interdependent work (i.e., work teams) can positively impact outcomes at the individual, team, and organizational level. In fact, the use of work teams and other forms of cooperative work arrangements (e.g., worker participation in decision-making) are a defining feature of much of Trist's applied and scholarly work. Furthermore, the socio-technical systems approach stresses that organizations are embedded within a larger environment that influences the organization (Trist, 1981a, 1981b). This focus on how the external environment impacts organizations is evident in many of Trist's accounts of socio-technical research projects (Trist, Higgin, Murray, & Pollock, 1963; Trist, Susman, & Brown, 1977).

A Review of Trist's Research on Socio-Technical Systems and Work Teams

The Tavistock Institute of Human Relations was the conduit for much of Trist's early work. The institute had an applied emphasis and was funded by grants (e.g., Rockerfeller Foundation, Ford Foundation) as well as government (e.g., military, Medical Research Council) and industry contracts (Trist, 1981b, 1993). With its dual emphasis on scholarship and applied practice, the institute provided an excellent outlet for Trist to use action-research methods to study real-world problems. In fact, several of Trist's better known research projects, such as the seminal work on the coal mining industry in Great Britain (Trist & Bamforth, 1951), were funded through one of the first grants awarded to the Tavistock Institute (Trist & Murray, 1990).

In the early 1950s, the Tavistock Institute was contracted by the National Coal Mining Board to study problems in the British coal-mining industry (Trist, 1981b). This recently nationalized and newly mechanized industry was experiencing decreased productivity as well as increased turnover and absenteeism. Further, there were on-going labor disputes despite management's attempts to enhance working conditions (Trist, 1981b). Given these conditions, Trist and colleagues set out to compare a high-producing, high-morale mine with a low-producing, low morale mine in order to isolate the factors differentiating the two. Trist and his research team met with resistance at the mines and were unable to conduct the original study. However, one of the research team members (Kenneth Bamforth) was a former miner himself of 18 years and was able to eventually gain access to the mines.

While visiting one of the mines, Bamforth was exposed to an innovative work practice. The mining crews were operating as relatively autonomous groups with minimal supervision from management. Crewmembers were cooperating with one another, sharing responsibilities, and monitoring their own performance. In addition, absenteeism and accident rates were low in this mine and productivity was high. Equally important, "impressive changes" in the miners quality of worklife and group cohesion were reported (Trist & Bamforth, 1951, p. 3). Of particular importance was the *reason* that mining crews were adopting such work practices -- they were adapting to a unique technical condition in the coal seam (Trist & Bamforth, 1951). This ability of the miners to spontaneously adapt their social arrangement to meet the technical demands of the task became the impetus for Trist's theorizing on socio-technical systems.

About this same time a work practice called continuous mining emerged which appeared to be based on socio-technical principles (Sheppard, 1949). This technique took two forms, semi-mechanized (Wilson & Trist, 1951) and fully mechanized (Trist, 1953). Both techniques used autonomous groups of 20 to 25 individuals who were responsible for all the activities on an entire shift, were multi-skilled, and paid the same wage. Qualitative accounts indicated that productivity and job satisfaction were exceptionally high in these mines, lending further support to the idea that a fit or match between the social and technical aspects of work could optimize work outcomes (Trist, 1981b). Based on these observations, a socio-technical development center was created which delivered training to supervisors and crew members in the mines. Drawing from this model, several of Trist's colleagues initiated projects based on socio-technical principles in new and established plants including a fertilizer plant in Norway (Emery & Thorsrud, 1976) a refinery in Great Britain (Hill, 1971), and a textile mill in India (Rice, 1958), among others.

Word of the British coal mining study spread to the United States where the National Union of Mineworkers expressed interest in socio-technical systems principles. A series of research studies by the Tavistock Institute and headed by Trist found the spontaneous use of socio-technical principles in a number of mines in Durham, North Carolina (1955-1958) (Trist, Higgin, Murray, & Pollock, 1963). Like the miners in Great Britain, some (but not all) of the miners formed into autonomous work groups in response to the task and technological conditions they faced. In these autonomous "composites," crewmembers rotated among jobs, alternated shifts, and designed an equitable, innovative pay plan. The technical system in these composite crews was conducive to these changes in the group's social system (e.g., task interdependence, single place working, uncertainty and hazardous working conditions). Similar to the innovative mines studied in Great Britain, output was higher (25%), cost was lower, and both accidents and absenteeism were 50% lower than comparable mines not organized around socio-technical systems principles (Trist et al., 1963). Taken together, these early mining studies led to additional studies of socio-technical systems in the United States and Europe by researchers affiliated with the Tavistock Institute (see Trist, 1981b for a review).

Observing these success stories in the mining industry, Trist became involved in another coal-mining project in Rushton Pennsylvania (Trist, Susman, & Brown, 1977). At this point in his career (1969) Trist was living in United States due to personal reasons and was teaching at Pennsylvania State University (prior to his appointment at Pennsylvania State, Trist was affiliated with the University of California at Los Angeles, 1966-1969). In fact, the Rushton coal mining study was the first funded socio-technical research study in the United States. This was a field experiment designed to examine the impact of implementing socio-technical systems principles in the U.S. coal mining industry. A two year longitudinal experimental-control group design was used and both objective (e.g., tons of coal produced, accident rates) and subjective (e.g., attitudes) indicators of effectiveness were tracked over time. The findings supported the tenets of socio-technical theory. Compared to two different non-autonomous groups (control groups), the experimental group, which was designed around socio-technical principles (e.g., increased autonomy, cross-trained team members, group-level performance management, equitable pay) experienced decreased accident rates and safety violations, decreased operating costs, more favorable employee attitudes, and increased productivity after the system had been in place for one year. This pattern of findings provided strong evidence that the socio-technical design to work teams had applicability in the U.S. coal mining industry.

Trist's interests shifted slightly, as he became increasingly interested in applying socio-technical systems principles at higher levels of analysis (e.g., the organization, the community). In 1973 Trist conducted an anthropological study of a small manufacturing town in northwest New York which was experimenting with several innovative industrial cooperatives. Referred to as the "Jamestown Project", it consisted of several studies of socio-technical systems at the community level (Trist, 1986, 1993). The area was in an economic downturn with several businesses leaving for more prosperous areas that were, perhaps, not so highly unionized. A labor-management committee, the Jamestown Area Labor-Management Committee (JALMC), was organized and the task they were charged with was rebuilding the economic foundation in the immediate region through training, improved labor relations, and improved productivity. Trist was charged with initiating quality of work life (QWL) programs throughout the community.

For the next several years, these specialized committees functioned as multi-level, multi-functional task groups which came to be known as "entrepreneurial work teams" (Trist, 1986). Their main task was not to enhance their own performance, but rather to enhance the performance of community organizations. This included reducing manufacturing costs, increasing new product development, implementing training, and redesigning organizational layouts. The results of these initiatives led to the resurgence of economic growth in Jamestown. Several businesses relocated to the area, unemployment in the area declined, and a new community spirit emerged. The JALMC continues the tradition of involving and empowering the local people through their annual conference and their influence has spread such that other industries in the area (e.g., hospitals) have formed their own specialized committees.

A similar set of initiatives was put in place for the Canadian Federal Public Service (Westley & Trist, 1993). This action research project involved the formation of interdepartmental and intradepartmental QWL committees within a public utility. The goal was to analyze their work setting and to redesign their jobs. Again, positive effects were realized. Changes initiated by the QWL programs resulted in a reduced need for supervision, as well as reduced waste, turnover, and absenteeism.

While much of his applied work continued to be in the area of QWL issues, Trist was also eager to explore whether the socio-technical systems approach to work teams could be successfully implemented in industries other than coal mining. Science and technology-based organizations that were opening new facilities were targeted for study, and several organizations agreed to explore the use of alternative work designs based on socio-technical principles. Participating organizations included Norskhydro, Shell, Alcan, Proctor and Gamble, and General Foods. These plants were designed to have fewer organizational levels, fewer employees, and very few supervisors whose roles were those of facilitator, planner, and trainer (Trist, 1981b). In addition, the new plants implemented a pay-for-knowledge system and adopted a highly participative climate (e.g., shared information, joint problem-solving). Compared to conventional plants, these socio-technically-designed plants had, in general, higher productivity and more favorable employee attitudes (cf. Trist, 1981b). These studies were particularly important, because they extended socio-technical principles beyond the coal mining industry.

Trist's Impact on Theory, Research, and Practice

Trist's work on socio-technical systems and work teams undoubtedly represents a major contribution to scholars' thinking about the role of social and technological factors in organizational behavior. Of particular importance is the recognition that the social and technical aspects of work must be complementary in order to maximize effectiveness. In fact, Trist's approach to self-managed work teams and socio-technical work systems contributed to the major shift in emphasis from individually-oriented work to team-based work. Trist's socio-technical systems approach to work teams has been implemented in several industries, including: hospitals, (e.g., Presbyterian Hospital in Texas, Alliant Health System in Kentucky, the Mayo Clinic, and Hartford Memorial Hospital in Wisconsin); prominent businesses (e.g., Levi's, General Mills, GTE, Hallmark, Hill's, Texas Instruments, NYNEX, and Eastman Kodak Co.); automobile manufacturers (e.g., Saturn, GM, and Ford); and government agencies (e.g., IRS, Palm Beach County, Dade County Schools). On a broader level, Trist's emphasis on empowering work conditions and quality of worklife set the stage for modern day employee involvement programs and a variety of QWL initiatives (cf. Cummings & Huse, 1989).

Trist's ideas about the importance of congruence or fit between social and technical aspects of teams has a prominent place in current research on work teams. However, a closer examination of Trist's work reveals other less-often cited contributions to the field of work teams and organizational behavior. This includes the idea of conceptualizing organizations and teams as self-regulating systems, incorporating observational and qualitative methods into the study of work teams in their natural context, consideration of levels of analysis when studying teams, and the influence of external contextual factors on teams. In the section that follows we examine these ideas in more detail, integrating current research and theory in the area of work teams.

Congruence Between Social and Technical Systems

The social system of the work group refers to roles of the members (e.g., skill heterogeneity, lines of authority), incentives, supervisory relationships, and work culture (Emery, 1959). While secondary, other aspects of the group's social system include interpersonal relations and the social climate within the group (e.g., cooperation, communication, norms, cohesion) (McGrath, 1984; Trist, 1981b). In contrast, a team's technical system includes task configurations, such as the level of mechanization, complexity, automation, unit operations, centralization, and characteristics of the production process (Emery, 1959). This includes the type of task (production and service, project and development), task interdependence, complexity, uncertainty, and the dominant technology (Goodman, 1986; Sundstrom, DeMeuse, & Futrell, 1990).

Recent work examining the relationship between task design characteristics and social processes illustrate how both systems need to be optimized to enhance team effectiveness. One potent example of this relates to the concern that in a team-based setting, individuals will "free-ride" off the efforts of others (Kerr, 1983) -- in short, that social loafing will occur. Interestingly, consistent with Trist's idea that the social and technical aspects of work mutually reinforce each other to influence effectiveness, social loafing appears to be less prevalent under certain task and social conditions (Karau & Williams, 1993). For instance, social loafing is greatly minimized (and in some cases the effects are reversed) when the task is meaningful, important or personally involving, the potential for individual or group evaluation is high, individual inputs can be easily identified, the task is complex, and interpersonal cohesion is high. These are the very work conditions that Trist espoused in his seminal work on socio-technical systems (cf. Trist, 1981b).

Other researchers have stressed the role of technology and uncertainty in placing boundaries on the group's social system and ultimately influencing team effectiveness. Goodman (1986) makes a convincing case that the technological characteristics of work teams are often overlooked as predictors of team effectiveness, yet often technology is more important than the social processes in teams. Likewise, Sundstrom and colleagues (Sundstrom & Altman, 1989; Sundstrom et al., 1990) emphasize that how differentiated a team is from other teams in the organization, as well as how integrated it is with other parts of the organization, can impact the social dynamics that emerge in the team. Consistent with Trist's ideas, the expectation is that a fit or match between the task and technological aspects of work and the social interaction patterns among members is necessary to optimize team effectiveness. Argote (1982) reached a similar conclusion in her study of hospital emergency rooms. Specifically, Argote found that as uncertainty in day-to-day operations increased (i.e., there was more variability in patient symptoms), the staff modified their internal group coordination patterns to accommodate this uncertainty, which in turn influenced group effectiveness. Finally, some recent research suggests that technology and task interdependence may have an interactive effect on team performance. For example, a recent study comparing face-to-face and computer-mediated communication found that as the requirements for task interdependence increased, computer-mediated communication led to lower effectiveness, productivity, and communication understanding, in addition to less favorable member reactions, compared to face-to-face communication (Strauss & McGrath, 1994).

In summary, as predicted by socio-technical theory, one of the most well-established findings in the work teams literature is that the task impacts the social dynamics that develop among members (cf. Hackman & Morris, 1975; McGrath, 1984). Not only does the technical system place limits on the likelihood that certain social processes will develop, it can also contribute significantly to team effectiveness, particularly in highly uncertain and mechanized environments (Goodman, 1986).

Organizations and Teams as Self-Regulating Systems

Throughout his career, Trist and his colleagues discussed the importance of viewing teams, as well as entire organizations, as self-regulating systems (cf., Pasmore & Khalsa, 1993). In fact, one of the tenets of socio-technical theory is that if teams lack social unity and technical ability, they will not be able to effectively self-regulate, and this self-regulation is important in optimizing effectiveness (Trist, 1981b). Organizational environments are also constantly changing and becoming increasingly complex (Emery & Trist, 1965; Trist, 1981b). As such, organizational success is dependent upon the extent to which the organization can successfully adapt to changing internal and external demands. Likewise, teams must constantly and spontaneously adapt to meet changing environmental demands. As discussed previously, this spontaneous adaptation is what Trist and colleagues discovered in their early coal mining studies (Trist & Bamforth, 1951; Trist et al., 1963).

The broader influence of Trist and colleagues' thinking about how organizations and teams are adaptive, turbulent, and ever-changing is evident in many areas of research. Open systems theory (Kast & Rosenzweig, 1972) views organizations as complex, dynamic, interdependent entities that are heavily influenced by their environment. Like socio-technical systems thinking, open systems theory stresses the importance of the social aspects of the organization as drivers of organizational effectiveness. One key aspect of this social system are small groups who are themselves constantly adapting to their environment. The organizational development literature also discusses open systems planning as an intervention to assist firms in the systematic assessment of their environment and develop strategic responses to this environment. Again, the notion is that organizations are complex systems that are influenced by a host of constantly changing and interacting internal and external conditions (Cummings & Huse, 1989).

Trist and colleagues' ideas about self-regulation and adaptability are mirrored in recent work integrating chaos theory (Kauffman, 1993), and its spin-off complexity theory (Waldrop, 1992), with organizational change and adaptation -- whether it be large scale interventions or the transition to team-based work (e.g., Eby, Adams, Russell, & Gaby, in press; Tetenbaum, 1998; Wheatley, 1992). Like Trist's theorizing, chaos and complexity theory suggest that the environment is made up of many different systems which interact in complex ways and are constantly adapting. The paradox is that there is order in this seeming chaos -- the system self-organizes and self-regulates to adapt to its environment (Kauffman, 1993). This bears a striking resemblance to what Trist observed in the coal mines in Great Britain and the United States as miners adjusted to changing technological conditions. Again, Trist's observations of how groups can spontaneously form in response to environmental contingencies has clearly influenced scholars' thinking in a variety of areas, including organizational theory, organizational development, and managing the change to work teams.

Research Methods for Studying Teams

Another contribution of Trist's action research program was the methodology he utilized to study teams and organizations. Trist relied almost exclusively on qualitative research methods, particularly participant observation, to draw insightful theoretical conclusions from his data. In this way his approach was often deductive: observing real world phenomenon then drawing conclusions from these rich descriptive accounts. By using a descriptive, idiographic approach to study real world practical problems, Trist played a major role in the legitimization of field research in the psychological sciences. The focus on practical problems was a philosophical issue for Trist, "...it allows the problems studied to be determined to a greater extent by the needs of the individuals, groups, or communities concerned rather than by the social scientist" (p. 47). Further, Trist strongly felt that research could not be carried out in a pre-planned sequence. Rather, the research team had to respond to existing organizational issues and be adaptable in its approach to the study of organizations (Trist, 1981a).

In reading Trist's work in the coal mining industry (e.g., Trist & Bamforth, 1951; Trist et al., 1963), one is struck with the meticulous attention to detail in describing the nature of the work, the machinery, and the contextual conditions in which the miners operated. More recently scholars have implored researchers to heed Trist's advice and study teams in their natural context, to describe the team's work in detail, and to incorporate rich qualitative accounts of the team's experience rather than rely solely on cross-sectional, survey based methodologies (Goodman, 1986; Ilgen, Major, Hollenbeck, & Sego, 1993). Unfortunately, much of the current research on teams fails to carefully describe the work that team members engage in.

Nonetheless, there are some signs that this trend may be changing. For example, Ancona and Caldwell (1992) provided rich qualitative (and quantitative) analysis of project development teams in organizations, describing in detail the team projects, as well as the specific events that occurred within the teams that contributed to their eventual success or failure. Wageman (1995) also used a combination of qualitative and quantitative methods to examine interdependence among work team members at Xerox, paying careful attention to describing the roles and responsibilities of the teams. Likewise, Doerr, Mitchell, Klasorin, and Brown (1996) conducted a longitudinal field experiment at a fish processing plant, again providing a very detailed description of the work design, technology, and task characteristics. While relatively few in number, these recent studies may signal a shift in attitude among scholars and gatekeepers that in-depth, qualitative research on work teams can yield important insight into the complexities of team life. Like Trist, we strongly encourage future research to adopt descriptive, qualitative methods to the study of teams.

Levels of Analysis in Work Teams Research

While Trist suggests that the work team is the primary building block of socio-technical systems thinking, he clearly acknowledges the importance of influences at higher (e.g., unit, organizational, societal) and lower (i.e., individual) levels of analysis (Trist, 1981a, 1981b; Trist et al., 1963). In fact, a major component of the socio-technical systems approach is that there are several levels of analysis operating simultaneously in organizations which have reciprocal effects on one another (Trist, 1981b). Trist (1981b) goes so far as to suggests that organizations have "micro-societies" which consist of intragroup, intergroup, and aggregate relationships, which together influence organizational effectiveness. Linking back to Trist's ideas about the importance of QWL, he proposes that within these micro-societies workers should be provided with discretion, autonomy, and freedom of movement within the organization. Trist also discusses the critical importance of the organization as a whole being supportive of the socio-technical system in order to effect positive change (Trist, 1981b).

Taking the lead from Trist, current work teams research recognizes the importance of considering multiple levels of analysis when studying teams (Ilgen, 1999; Ilgen et al., 1993). In fact, recent studies in the area of individual differences in teams (e.g., Barry & Stewart, 1997; Eby & Dobbins, 1997), group processes (Kidwell, Mossholder, & Bennett, 1997), and team mental models (e.g., Eby, Meade, Parisi, & Douthitt, in press) explicitly deals with levels of analysis issues in understanding team phenomena. Current interest in levels of analysis issues is also evident in the increased emphasis on conceptual and statistical issues associated with aggregating individual-level phenomenon to the team level.

External, Contextual Influences on Teams

Another major contribution that Trist made to current thinking about work teams is the importance of taking the context into account when trying to understand team effectiveness. Trist describes many contextual factors that influenced his own research. These includes uncertain and dangerous working conditions, union politics, management resistance to change, top management turnover, changes in legislation and company policies, technological advances, and rivalry among groups in the organization, among others (e.g., Trist et al., 1977; Trist, 1981b). Trist summarizes how the context can play a major role in the success of a socio-technical intervention noting that "...unanticipated and uncontrollable events in the broader, as well as immediate, context can influence outcomes in the later stages of an action research undertaking" (Trist et al., 1977, p. 31). In discussing the various external forces which may impact the success of socio-technical systems, Trist notes the particularly powerful role of resistance to change by those outside the immediate work group (Trist et al., 1963). Even with evidence of success, Trist often found resistance to his ideas due to concerns that such initiatives would strip decision-makers of their power and lead to the deterioration of powerful unions (Trist et al., 1963; Trist et al., 1977).

Current research on factors related to resistance to change (e.g., Armenakis, Harris, Mossholder, 1993; Eby et al., in press) continues to examine individual, group, and organizational sources of resistance. Similarly, there is growing recognition that the context and environment in which an organization operates can influence team effectiveness. In Sundstrom et al. (1990) widely cited ecological model of team effectiveness, organizational context has a central role. This includes the organizational culture, task design and technology, mission clarity, the physical environment, and existing human resource management systems. Several empirical studies further support the importance of organizational context as a predictor of team effectiveness. For instance, Kolodny and Kiggundu's (1980) study of a wood harvesting operation demonstrated that organizational arrangements and task conditions jointly influence both group interaction and outcomes. Similarly, Gladstein's (1984) study of 100 sales teams found that the external marketplace was the strongest predictor of objective team performance. Finally, Ancona and Caldwell's (1992) study of new product development teams suggests that interactions *across teams* and how the team manages its boundaries are important contextual variables. Thus, it appears as if some researchers are systematically assessing how a variety of contextual factors may influence team outcomes.

Summary and Concluding Thoughts

Socio-technical systems became an important factor, if not a major one in Trist's lifework on teams. He felt that neither individuals nor groups exist in a vacuum and they are subject to many factors, including the available technology and external contextual factors. To his own surprise, he found that the empowerment associated with team membership was a result of those members taking responsibility in their organization, having the power to initiate change, and seeing the positive results of this empowerment. In fact, Trist was the first to document the potent role that organizational groups can play in understanding human behavior, self-directed work teams, and socio-technical systems.

Trist's contributions to the study of teams are innumerable, as evidenced by the many citations of his work in various studies of teams. In fact, Pasmore & Mlot (1994) state that "Today's team concept grew out of the work of Eric Trist." He has clearly made a significant and lasting contribution to the study of teams within the context of socio-technical systems. Although Emery began work on the social and technical systems of groups, it was Trist who proposed a reframing of these constructs conceptually in terms of the work environment (Van de Ven & Joyce, 1981). The contributions that Trist made to the literature, both as an author and in an advisor/editor role has earned him the title of "Father of Socio-technical Systems" (Fox, 1990, p. 259). However, it must be noted that Trist not only espoused participative work arrangements such as teams and joint labor-management initiatives in organizations, but adopted these principles in his own approach to research collaboration. He led by example, evidenced by the numerous research projects he collaborated on with Emery and others (cf. Pasmore, & Khalsa, 1993). Additionally, Trist contributed to many other studies as an informal consultant rather than author, and many papers he worked on that were never published. In summary, Trist's many contributions reveal that he was clearly ahead of his time. Trist was an extraordinary visionary scholar who was a scientist, practitioner, theoretician, and social change agent.

Notes

1. It is important to note that while Trist pioneered the theory of socio-technical systems other scholars were conducting action research on socio-technical systems

contemporaneously. Their work is beyond the scope of the current chapter, which focuses solely on Trist's research. However, due to Trist's emphasis on collaborative research, it is quite likely that he contributed significant insight into some of these omitted studies, particularly those associated with the Tavistock Institute (see Trist & Murray, 1990, 1993, 1997, for a review).

References

Ancona, D. G., & Caldwell, D. F. (1992). Bridging the boundary: External activity and performance in organizational teams. *Administrative Science Quarterly*, 37, 634-665.

Argote, L. (1982) Input uncertainty and organizational coordination in hospital emergency units. *Administrative Science Quarterly*, 27, 420-434.

Armenakis, A. A., Harris, S. G., & Mossholder, K. W. (1993). Creating readiness for organizational change. *Human relations*, 46(6), 681-703.

Barry, B., & Stewart, G. L. (1997). Composition, process, and performance in self-managed groups: The role of personality. *Journal of Applied Psychology*, 82, 62-78.

Bion, W. R. (1946). The leaderless group project. *Bulletin of the Menninger Clinic*, 10, 77-81.

Cummings, T. G., & Huse. E. F. (1989). *Organization development and change* (4th ed. pp. 253-280). St. Paul, MN: West Publishing.

Doerr, K. H., Mitchell, T. R., Klastorin, T. D., & Brown, K. A. (1996). Impact of material flow policies and goals on job outcomes. *Journal of Applied Psychology*, 81, 142-152.

Eby, L. T., Adams, D. M., Russell, J. E. A., Gaby, S. H. (in press). Perceptions of organizational readiness for change: Factors related to employees' reactions to the implementation of team-based selling. *Human Relations*.

Eby, L. T., & Dobbins, G. H. (1997). Collectivistic orientation in teams: An individual and group-level analysis. *Journal of Organizational Behavior*, 18, 275-295.

Eby, L. T., Meade, A., Parisi, A., & Douthitt, S. (In press). The development of an individual-level teamwork expectations measure and the application of a within-group agreement statistic to assess shared expectations for teamwork. *Organizational Research Methods*.

Emery, F. (1959). *Characteristics of socio-technical systems*. London: Tavistock Institute Document 527.

Emery, F. (1993). An appreciation: Eric Landsdown Trist (1909-1993). *Human Relations*, 46, 1171-1176.

Emery, F. & Thorsrud, E. (1976). *Democracy at work*. Leiden: Martinus Nijhoff.

Emery, F. & Trist, E. L. (1965). The causal texture of organizational environments. *Human Relations*, 18, 21-32.

Fox, W. M. (1990). An interview with Eric Trist: Father of the socio-technical systems approach. *The Journal of Applied Behavioral Science*, 26(2), 259-279.

Gladstein, D. L. (1984). Groups in context: A model of task group effectiveness. *Administrative Science Quarterly*, 29, 499-517.

Goodman, P. S. (1986). Impact of task and technology on group performance. In P. S. Goodman & Associates (Eds.). *Designing effective work groups* (pp. 120-167). San Francisco, CA: Jossey-Bass.

Hackman, J. R., & Morris, C. G. (1975). Group tasks, group interaction process, and group performance effectiveness: A review and proposed integration. In L. Berkowitz (Ed.), *Advances in experimental social psychology*, 8, 45-99.

Hill, P. (1971). *Towards a new philosophy of management: The company development programme of Shell U. K.* London: Gower Press.

Ilgen, D. R. (1999). Teams embedded in organizations: Some implications. *American Psychologist*, 54, 129-139.

Ilgen, D. R., Major, D. A., Hollenbeck, J. R., & Sego, D. J. (1993). Team research in the 1990s. *Leadership theory and research: perspectives and directions*, 245-270.

Karau, S. J. & Williams, K .D. (1993). Social loafing: A meta-analytic review and theoretical integration. *Journal of Personality and Social Psychology*, 65, 681-706.

Kast, F. E., & Rosenzweig, J. E. (1972). General systems theory: Applications for organization and management. *Academy of Management Journal*, 15, 444-465.

Kauffman, S. A. (1993). *The origins of order: Self organization and selection in evolution.* New York: Oxford University Press.

Kerr, N. L. (1983). Motivation losses in small groups: A social dilemma analysis. *Journal of Personality and Social Psychology*, 45, 819-828.

Kidwell, R. E., Jr., Mossholder, K. W., & Bennett, N. (1997). Cohesiveness and organizational citizenship behavior: A multilevel analysis using work groups and individuals. *Journal of Management*, 23(6), 775-793.

Kolodny, H. F., & Kiggundu, M. N. (1980). Toward the development of a socio-technical systems model in Woodlands Mechanical Harvesting. *Human Relations*, 33(9), 623-645.

Krantz, J. (1990). A biography of Eric Trist. *The Journal of Applied Behavioral Science*, 26(2), viii).

McGrath, J. E. (1984). *Groups: Interaction and performance*. Englewood Cliffs, NJ: Prentice Hall.

Murray, H. (1990). The transformation of selection procedures: The War Office Selection Boards. In E. L. Trist and H. Murray (Eds.). *The social engagement of social science: A Tavistock anthology* (Vol. I) (pp. 45-67). Philadelphia: University of Pennsylvania Press.

Pasmore, W. A., & Khalsa, G. S. (1993). The contributions of Eric Trist to the social engagement of social science. *Academy of Management Review*, 18, 546-569.

Pasmore, W. A., & Mlot, S. (1994). Developing self-managing work teams: An approach to successful integration. *Compensation & Benefits Review*, 26(4), 15-23.

Rice, A. K. (1958). *Productivity and social organization: The Ahmedabad experiment.* Liverpool, London: Tavistock Publications.

Sheppard, V. W. (1949). Continuous Longwall Mining. *Colliery Guardian*, 178.

Sheppard, V. W. (1951). Continuous Longwall Mining: Experiments at Bolsover Colliery. *Colliery Guardian*, 182.

Strauss, S. G. & McGrath, J. E. (1994). Does the medium matter? The interaction of task type and technology on group performance and member reactions. *Journal of Applied Psychology*, 79, 87-97.

Sundstrom, E. S., & Altman, I. (1989). Physical environments and work group effectiveness. In L. L. Cummings & B. Staw (Eds.), *Research in organizational behavior*. Greenwich, CT: JAI Press.

Sundstrom, E. S., DeMeuse, K. P. & Futrell, D. (1990). Work teams: Application and effectiveness. *American Psychologist*, 45, 120-133.

Tetenbaum, T. J. (1998). Shifting paradigms: From Newton to chaos. *Organizational Dynamics*, 26(4), 21-32.

Trist, E. L. (1953). *Some observations on the machine face as a socio-technical system.* London: Tavistock Document Series.

Trist, E. L. (1981a). The evolution of socio-technical systems: A conceptual framework and an action research program. *Issues in the quality of working life: A series of occasional papers*, 2.

Trist, E. L. (1981b). The evolution of socio-technical systems as a conceptual framework and as an action research program. In A. H. Van de Ven and W. F. Joyce (Eds.). *Perspectives on organization design and behavior* (pp. 19-75). New York: John Wiley & Sons.

Trist, E. L. (1986). Quality of working life and community development: Some reflections on the Jamestown Experience. *The Journal of Applied Behavioral Science*, 22(3), 223-237.

Trist, E. L. (1993). Guilty of Enthusiasm. In H. I. Ansoff and A. G. Bedeian (Eds.). *Management laureates: A collection of autobiographical essays* (pp. 193-221). Greenwich, CT: JAI Press, Inc.

Trist, E. L. & Bamforth, K. W. (1951). Some social and psychological consequences of the longwall method of coal-getting. *Human Relations*, 4, 3-38.

Trist, E. L., Higgin, G. W., Murray, H., & Pollock, A. B. (1963). *Organizational choice*. London: Tavistock Publications.

Trist, E. L., & Murray, H. (1990). Historical overview: The foundation and development of the Tavistock Institute to 1989. In E. Trist and H. Murray (Eds.). *The social engagement of social science: The Tavistock anthology* (Vol 1. pp. 1-35). Philadelphia: The University of Pennsylvania Press.

Trist, E. L., & Murray, H. (1993). Historical overview: The foundation and development of the Tavistock Institute to 1989. In E. Trist and H. Murray (Eds.). *The social engagement of social science: The Tavistock anthology* (Vol II). Philadelphia: The University of Pennsylvania Press.

Trist, E. L., & Murray, H. (1997). Historical overview: The foundation and development of the Tavistock Institute to 1989. In E. Trist and H. Murray (Eds.). *The social engagement of social science: The Tavistock anthology* (Vol III). Philadelphia: The University of Pennsylvania Press.

Trist, E. L., Susman, G. I., & Brown, G. R. (1977). An experiment in autonomous working in an American underground coal mine. *Human Relations*, 30(3), 201-236.

Van de Ven, A. H., & Joyce, W. F. (1981). Perspectives on organization design and behavior. New York: Wiley & Sons.

Wageman, R. (1995). Interdependence and group effectiveness. *Administrative Science Quarterly*, 40, 145-180.

Waldrop, M. M. (1992). Complexity: *The emerging science at the edge or order and chaos*. New York: Simon & Schuster.

Westley, W. & Trist, E. L. (1993). Socio-technical projects in the Canadian Federal Public Service. In E. L. Trist & H. Murray (Eds.). *The social engagement of social science: A Tavistock anthology* (Vol. II). Pennsylvania: University of Pennsylvania Press.

Wheatley, M. (1992). *Leadership and the new science: Learning about organizations from an orderly universe*. San Francisco, CA: Berrett-Koehler Publishers.

Wilson, A. T., & Trist, E. L. (1951). *The bolsover system of continuous mining*. London: Tavistock Documents, 290.

Wilson, A. T., Trist, E. L., & Curle, A. (1952). Transitional communities and social reconnection: A study of the civil resettlement of British prisoners of war. In G. E. Swanson, T. M. Newcomb, & E. L. Hartley (Eds.). *Readings in social psychology* (pp. 561-579). New York: Holt.

Chapter 8

Deutsch's Theory of Cooperation and Competition

An Enduring Contribution to Teams

Dean Tjosvold
Lingnan College, Tuen Mun, Hong Kong, China

David Johnson
University of Minnesota, Minneapolis, Minnesota, United States

Abstract

Based on social interdependence theorizing and the ideas of Lewin's Center for the Study of Group Dynamics, Morton Deutsch proposed in 1949 that how group members believe their goals are related very much impacts their dynamics and success. Hundreds of studies summarized in meta-analyses document that cooperative goals promote communication and exchange and, more recently, the open-minded discussion of opposing views, dynamics in turn that result in group productivity, individual learning, psychological health, and relationships. Recent research has used the theory to understand such organizational issues as power and to test the theory's universalistic aspirations. Validated procedures are being used around the world to promote educational goals. Leaders and members can use cooperation knowledge to make their increasingly diverse and dispersed teams work.

Introduction

It's easy to get the players. Getting them to play together, that's the hard part.
Casey Stengel

Morton Deutsch's theory and research on cooperation and competition is a profound example of his mentor's, Kurt Lewin, admonition "Nothing is as practical as a good theory." Hundreds of studies conducted by various social scientists have developed and extended the theory. Findings on the effects of cooperation and competition are among the most consistent and strongest in the social sciences. Thousands of educators and other practitioners are applying the theory in their professional work and transforming their organizations. Much has been done, much more needs to be done.

Cooperative, synergistic teamwork has driven the theory's development. Stimulated by scholars at Lewin's Center for Group Dynamics and elsewhere, Deutsch formulated his theory in his dissertation research published in 1949. As has

M.M. Beyerlein (ed.), Work Teams: Past, Present and Future, 131–155.

often been recognized, the theory benefited a great deal from collaborative work with many colleagues and graduate students, especially at Teacher's College at Columbia University, where beginning in 1963 he headed the social psychology program. The resulting extensive empirical research base gives the theory credibility and power uncommon in the social sciences.

The authors of this chapter are part of this team. David Johnson was one of Deutsch's first graduate students at Teachers College in 1966. Dean Tjosvold is an extended member in that he completed his graduate work with David in 1972 at the University of Minnesota. The chapter will focus on how the authors working together and with their own teams of researchers have extended the theory and practice of cooperation and competition.

Our collaboration with each other and other scholars has been characterized by a common commitment to developing theory and research-based knowledge to strengthen teams that in turn promote full individuality and effective organizations. With this important cooperative goal, we have taken independent paths and approaches. David has theorized and developed meta-analyses to clarify the nature of interaction in cooperation and competition and their consequences. Based in a college of education, he and his brother Roger have validated procedures for cooperative learning in schools and universities. Based in a business faculty, Dean has conducted research into the implications of the theory for understanding group problem solving, leadership, and power in organizations. Together they have specified that open-minded interaction, constructive controversy, complements, and cooperative goals in effective group problem solving. Our diversity has enriched and extended our research.

We will emphasize our own work not only because we know it best, but also because too few others are incorporating the theory in their ongoing research. A recent edited handbook on work group psychology failed to refer Deutsch's theory of cooperation and competition (West, 1996). Few management, educational, family, and social work books show how to use the theory to improve professional practice. We have felt privileged and advantaged to use Deutsch's theory to understand the complexities of interdependence. We want researchers with diverse perspectives to join with us in using cooperation theory to develop practical knowledge of work teams.

This chapter provides an historical account of cooperation theory. It first outlines social interdependence theory, offering clear definitions of cooperation, competition, and independence with an explication of the hypothesized underlying dynamics. The second section summarizes the meta-analyses of research on the powerful impact of interdependence on interaction patterns within teams and their effects on achievement and productivity, relationships, and psychological health. Social interdependence theory has proved very useful in understanding conflict, defined as incompatible activities. Whether the conflict is experienced within a cooperative or competitive context has been found very much to affect its dynamics and its constructiveness. The fourth section reviews the empirical development of constructive controversy, which has been found to characterize effective, cooperative group problem solving. Cooperation theory is hypothesized to be universal. The final section reviews recent research on social power and conflict in

China as examples of the utility of the theory to understand the many faces of interdependence.

Theory of Social Interdependence

Theorizing on social interdependence began in the early 1900s, when one of the founders of the Gestalt School of Psychology, Kurt Koffka, proposed that groups were dynamic wholes in which the interdependence among members could vary. One of his colleagues, Kurt Lewin, refined Koffka's notions in the 1920s and 1930s while stating that (a) the essence of a group is the interdependence among members (created by common goals) which results in the group being a "dynamic whole" so that a change in the state of any member or subgroup changes the state of any other member or subgroup, and (b) an intrinsic state of tension within group members motivates movement toward the accomplishment of the desired common goals. Lewin's students and colleagues, such as Ovisankian, Lissner, Mahler, and Lewis, contributed further research indicating that it is the drive for goal accomplishment that motivates cooperative and competitive behavior.

Morton Deutsch (1949, 1962) extended Lewin's reasoning about social interdependence and formulated a theory of cooperation and competition. He argued that behavior depended not just on whether individuals were in a group but how they believed their goals were related to each other. Perceived goal interdependence was hypothesized to have a pervasive impact on underlying dynamics and expectations and thereby interaction which in turn affects the outcomes of group work. The basic premise of social interdependence theory is that the type of interdependence structured in a situation determines how individuals interact with each other which, in turn, determines outcomes.

Social interdependence exists when individuals have overlapping goals and each individual's outcomes are affected by the actions of the others (Deutsch, 1949, 1962; Johnson & Johnson, 1989). It may be differentiated from social dependence (i.e., the outcomes of one person are affected by the actions of a second person but not vice versa) and social independence (i.e., individuals' outcomes are unaffected by each other's actions). There are two types of social interdependence cooperative and competitive. The absence of social interdependence and dependence results in individualistic efforts.

Goal Interdependence

Group members can believe that their goals are cooperatively or competitively related or unrelated (Deutsch, 1949, 1962; Johnson & Johnson, 1989):

1. In cooperation, individuals' goal achievements are positively correlated; individuals perceive that they can reach their goals if and only if the others in the group also reach their goals. Thus, individuals seek outcomes that are beneficial to all those with whom they are cooperatively linked.

2. In competition, individuals work against each other to achieve a goal that only one or a few can attain. Individuals' goal achievements are negatively correlated; each individual perceives that when one person achieves his or her goal, all others with whom he or she is competitively linked fail to achieve their goals.

Thus, individuals seek an outcome that is personally beneficial but detrimental to all others in the situation.

3. In independence, there is no correlation among participants' goal attainments. Each individual perceives that he or she can reach his or her goal regardless of whether other individuals attain or do not attain their goals. Thus, individuals seek an outcome that is personally beneficial without concern for the outcomes of others.

Of course, most situations are mixes of these pure forms. We hypothesized that how group members believe their goals are predominately related very much affects how they work together.

Underlying Dynamics

Deutsch proposed that goal interdependence has its powerful effects by its impact on underlying expectations and reactions. In particular, goal interdependence affects substitutability (i.e., the actions of one person substitute for the actions of another), cathexis (i.e., the investment of psychological energy in objects and events outside of oneself), and inducibility (i.e., openness to influence). Without interdependence, there is no basis for substitutability, cathexis, or inducibility. However, cooperative and competitive goals have profoundly diverse effects on them.

In cooperative situations, the effective actions of one group member substitute for those of others. If one member completes a sub-task well, others need not perform it. Participants positively cathect to each other's effective actions as they help them achieve their goals. There is high inducibility because group members expect to influence and help each other to perform effectively to accomplish their cooperative goal. Cooperators have a vested interest in each contributing because that helps them all reach their goals.

In competitive situations, another's ineffective actions, not effective, substitute. A competitor is more likely to win if the other performs ineffectively and more likely to lose if the other performs well. Participants negatively cathect to each other's effective actions. Mutual influence is low because competitors suspect others are trying to have them perform ineffectively.

Interaction Patterns

Substitution, catharsis, and inducibility are in turn hypothesized to affect interpersonal interactions. Although typically the logic proposed is that goal interdependence affects action, the relationship between the type of social interdependence and the interaction pattern it elicits is assumed to be bi-directional. Each may cause the other.

Between 1898 and 1989, over 575 experimental and 100 correlational studies of interesting patterns were conducted by a wide variety of researchers in different decades with different age participants and tasks, and in different settings. Results of these studies when taken together in meta-analyses strongly support the generalization that positive interdependence creates promotive interaction (Johnson & Johnson, 1989). Promotive interaction occurs as individuals encourage and facilitate each other's efforts to reach the group's goals (such as maximizing each member's learning). Group members promote each other's success by:

1. Giving and receiving help and assistance (both task-related and personal).

2. Exchanging resources and information. Group members seek information and other resources from each other, comprehend information accurately and without bias, and make optimal use of the information provided. There are a number of beneficial results from (a) orally explaining, elaborating, and summarizing information and (b) teaching one's knowledge to others. Explaining and teaching increase the degree to which group members cognitively process and organize information, engage in higher-level reasoning, attain insights, and become personally committed to achieving. Listening critically to the explanations of group mates provides the opportunity to utilize other's resources.

3. Giving and receiving feedback on taskwork and teamwork behaviors. In cooperative groups, members monitor each other's efforts, give immediate feedback on performance, and, when needed, give each other help and assistance.

4. Challenging each other's reasoning. Intellectual controversy promotes curiosity, motivation to learn, reconceptualization of what one's knows, higher quality decision making, greater insight into the problem being considered, and many other important benefits (Johnson & Johnson, 1979, 1995b).

5. Advocating increased efforts to achieve. Encouraging others to achieve increases one's own commitment to do so.

6. Mutually influencing each other's reasoning and behavior. Group members actively seek to influence and be influenced by each other. If a member has a better way to complete the task, group mates usually quickly adopt it.

7. Engaging in the interpersonal and small group skills needed for effective teamwork.

8. Processing how effectively group members are working together and how the group's effectiveness can be continuously improved (Johnson & Johnson, 1989).

Negative interdependence typically results in oppositional interaction. Oppositional interaction occurs as individuals discourage and obstruct each other's efforts to achieve. Individuals focus both on increasing their own success and on preventing anyone else from being more successful than they are. No interaction exists when individuals work independently without any interaction or interchange with each other. Individuals focus only on increasing their own success and ignore as irrelevant the efforts of others. Each of these interaction patterns creates different outcomes.

Outcomes

Social interdependence is a generic human phenomenon that has impact on many different outcomes simultaneously. Over the past 95 years, researchers have focused on such diverse dependent variables as individual achievement and retention, group and organizational productivity, higher-level reasoning, moral reasoning, achievement motivation, intrinsic motivation, transfer of training and learning, job satisfaction, interpersonal attraction, social support, interpersonal affection and love, attitudes toward diversity, prejudice, self-esteem, personal causation and locus of control, attributions concerning success and failure, psychological health, social competencies, and many others. These numerous outcomes may be subsumed within three broad categories (Johnson & Johnson, 1989): (a) effort to achieve, (b) positive relationships, and (c) psychological health (see Table 1).

If research is to have impact on theory and practice, it must be summarized and communicated in a complete, objective, impartial, and unbiased way. In an age of information explosion, there is considerable danger that theories will be formulated on small and nonrepresentative samples of available knowledge, thereby resulting in fallacious conclusions that in turn lead to mistaken practices. A quantitative reviewing procedure, such as meta-analysis, allows for more definitive and robust conclusions. A meta-analysis is a method of statistically combining the results of a set of independent studies that test the same hypothesis and using inferential statistics to draw conclusions about the overall result of the studies. The essential purpose of a meta-analysis is to summarize a set of related research studies, so that the size of the effect of the independent variable on the dependent variable is known.

TABLE 1. Conflict in cooperation and competition

Interdependence		Interaction		Outcomes	
Cooperative Goals	→	Constructive Controversy Mutual Exchange	→	Quality Decisions Relationships Productivity	Affirmation Mutual Success Confidence
Competitive Goals	→	Avoid Discussion Closed-Minded Coercion Attempts	→	Low Quality Decisions Fragmented Relationships Low Productivity	Frustration Hostility Revenge

Achievement and Productivity

Achievement both in the sense of the learning of individual group members and in the development of an effective solution for the group is a critical dependent measure. Students in cooperative learning groups and employees in work teams must continuously update their knowledge, have the ability to think critically use higher-level reasoning, and are committed to life-long learning.

The investigation of the relative impact of the three types of social interdependence on achievement is the longest standing research tradition within American social psychology. Between 1898 and 1989, researchers conducted over 375 experimental studies with over 1,700 findings on social interdependence and productivity and achievement (Johnson & Johnson, 1989). And that does not count the research on social facilitation and other related areas where implicit competition may be found. Since research participants have varied widely as to sex, economic class, age, and cultural background, since a wide variety of research tasks and measures of the dependent variables have been used, and since the research has been conducted by many different researchers with markedly different orientations working in different settings and in different decades, the overall body of research on social interdependence has considerable generalizability.

A meta-analysis of all studies (Johnson & Johnson, 1989) found that the average person cooperating performed at about 2/3 a standard deviation above the average person learning within a competitive (effect size = 0.67) or individualistic situation (effect size = 0.64). Not all the research, however, has been carefully conducted. The methodological shortcomings found within many research studies may significantly reduce the certainty of the conclusion that cooperative efforts produce higher achievement than do competitive or individualistic efforts. When only studies with high internal validity were included in the analysis, the effect sizes were 0.88 and 0.61, respectively. Further analyses revealed that the results held constant when group measures of productivity were included, as well as individual measures, for short-term as well as long-term studies, and when symbolic, as well as tangible rewards were used.

Kurt Lewin often stated, "I always found myself unable to think as a single person." Most efforts to achieve are a personal but social process that requires individuals to cooperate and to construct shared understandings and knowledge. Competitive and individualistic structures, by isolating individuals from each other, tend to depress achievement.

Interpersonal Relationships

Since 1940, over 180 studies have compared the impact of cooperative, competitive, and individualistic efforts on interpersonal attraction and social support (Johnson & Johnson, 1989). Cooperative efforts, compared with competitive and individualistic experiences, promoted considerable more liking among individuals (effect sizes = 0.66 and 0.62 respectively). The effects sizes were higher for (a) high quality studies and (b) the studies using pure operationalizations of cooperative learning than for studies using mixed operationalizations. The weighted effect sizes for cooperation versus competition and cooperation versus individualistic efforts are 0.65 and 0.64, respectively. When only the methodologically high quality studies are examined, the effect sizes go up to 0.77 and 0.67. "Pure" cooperation results in greater effects than do mixtures of cooperative, competitive, and individualistic efforts (cooperative vs. competitive, pure = 0.75 and mixed = 0.48; cooperative vs. individualistic, pure = 0.67 and mixed = 0.36).

Much of the research on interpersonal relationships has been conducted on relationships between white and minority persons and between nonhandicapped and handicapped persons in educational settings (Johnson & Johnson, 1989). There have been over 40 experimental studies comparing some combination of cooperative, competitive, and individualistic experiences on cross-ethnic relationships and over 40 similar studies on mainstreaming of handicapped students (Johnson & Johnson, 1989). Their results are consistent. Working cooperatively creates far more positive relationships among diverse and heterogeneous students than does learning competitively or individualistically.

The positive relationships among members promoted by cooperative efforts have considerable impact on a wide variety of variables. Generally, the more positive the relationships among group members (i.e., the more cohesive the group), the lower the absenteeism, the fewer the members who drop out of the group, and the more likely students will commit effort to achieve educational goals, feel personal responsibility for learning, take on difficult tasks, feel motivated to learn, persist in working toward goal achievement, have high morale, feel willing to endure pain and frustration on behalf of learning, listen to and be influenced by group members and leaders, commit to each other's learning and success, and achieve and produce (Johnson & F. Johnson, 1997).

Besides liking each other, cooperators give and receive considerable social support, both personally and academically (Johnson & Johnson, 1989). Since the 1940s, over 106 studies comparing the relative impact of cooperative, competitive, and individualistic efforts on social support have been conducted. Social support may be aimed at enhancing another person's success (task-related social support) or at providing support on a more personal level (personal social support). Cooperative experience promoted greater task-oriented and personal social support than did competitive (effect size = 0.62) or individualistic (effect size = 0.70) experiences. Social support tends to promote achievement and productivity, physical health, psychological health, and successful coping with stress and adversity.

Psychological Health

Psychological health is the ability to develop, maintain, and appropriately modify interdependent relationships with others to succeed in achieving goals (Johnson & Johnson, 1989). To manage social interdependence, individuals must correctly perceive whether interdependence exists and whether it is positive or negative, be motivated accordingly, and act in ways consistent with normative expectations for appropriate behavior within the situation.

Four studies have directly measured the relationship between social interdependence and psychological health. The samples studied included suburban high-school seniors (Johnson & Norem-Heibeisen, 1977), juvenile and adult prisoners (N. James & Johnson, 1983), step-couples (S. James & Johnson, 1988), and Olympic hockey players (Johnson, Johnson, & Krotee, 1986). The results indicated that (a) working cooperatively with peers and valuing cooperation result in greater psychological health than does competing with peers or working independently and (b) cooperative attitudes are highly correlated with a wide variety of indices of psychological health. Competitiveness was in some cases positively and in some cases negatively related to psychological health, and individualistic attitudes were negative related to a wide variety of indices of psychological health. Cooperativeness positively correlates with psychological health, such as emotional maturity, well-adjusted social relations, strong personal identity, ability to cope with adversity, social competencies, and basic trust in and optimism about people. Personal ego-strength, self-confidence, independence, and autonomy are all promoted by being involved in cooperative efforts. Individualistic attitudes tend to be related to a number of indices of psychological pathology, such as emotional immaturity, social maladjustment, delinquency, self-alienation, and self-rejection. Competitiveness is related to a mixture of healthy and unhealthy characteristics. Whereas inappropriate competitive and individualistic attitudes and efforts have resulted in alienating individuals from others, healthy and therapeutic growth depends on increasing individuals' understanding of how to cooperate more effectively with others. Cooperative experiences are not a luxury. They are absolutely necessary for healthy development.

Since the 1950s, there have been over 80 studies comparing the relative impact of cooperative, competitive, and individualistic experiences on self-esteem (Johnson & Johnson, 1989). Cooperative experiences promote higher self-esteem than do competitive (effect size = 0.58) or individualistic (effect-size = 0.44) experiences. Our research demonstrated that cooperative experiences tend to be related to beliefs that one is intrinsically worthwhile, others see one in positive ways, one's attributes compare favorably with those of one's peers, and one is a capable, competent, and successful person. In cooperative efforts, students: (a) realize that they are accurately known, accepted, and liked by one's peers, (b) know that they have contributed to own, others, and group success, and (c) perceive themselves and others in a differentiated and realistic way that allows for multidimensional comparisons based on complementarity of own and others' abilities. Competitive experiences tend to be related to conditional self-esteem based on whether one wins or loses. Individualistic experiences tend to be related to basic self-rejection.

Competitive and Individualistic Efforts

The hundreds of studies conducted indicate that under most conditions, cooperation has more powerful effects on the variables studied than do competitive or individualistic efforts. Under most conditions, cooperative efforts are more effective than are competitive and individualistic efforts. There is some evidence that on very simple, over-learned, repetitive motor tasks, competition may produce higher achievement than does cooperation (Johnson & Johnson, 1989). It is unclear whether individualistic efforts have any advantage over cooperative efforts. More research is needed to clarify the conditions under which competitive or individualistic efforts may have more powerful effects than cooperation.

Conflict as a Complement to Cooperation

Research reviewed has documented the considerable value of cooperative teams for individuals and organizations. However, maintaining cooperative groups and systems at a high level requires considerable effort. Group members and leaders must continually renew their cooperative goals and interactions or face the prospect of decline (Tjosvold, 1991). Cooperative teams do not run automatically; they need continual nurturing. This section argues that well-managed conflict renews cooperative teams.

However, an enduring confusion has been that effective, cooperative teams work without conflict. As they have common goals, they are on the same side with strong relationships and avoid the chaos and destruction of conflict. However, cooperation is not the opposite of conflict. Project team members committed to the common task of building a cost-effective new transmission line disagree over the means, such as the best route for the line, to reach their shared goal. They may also disagree about an effective division of labor, their treatment of each other, and how to divide the benefits fairly. To work cooperatively is to manage conflict.

Indeed, cooperators often confront a great deal of meaningful and intense conflict. As people work cooperatively, they become highly invested in their task and relationships. They take considerable satisfaction from their achievement and become more emotionally involved with each other. They want to be treated in a fair way that affirms their personal identity (Deutsch, 1984). Although competition escalates conflict, cooperation does not minimize conflict but rather enlarges the areas of possible conflict. Our most intense conflicts that challenge our ability to manage them are with persons with whom we have at least some cooperative goals.

Conflict's Definition

The theory of cooperation and competition has proved highly useful for understanding constructive conflict management (Deutsch, 1973, 1990). Critically, it has provided an unconfounded definition of conflict as incompatible activities; one person's actions interfere, obstruct or in some way get in the way of another's action. Conflict has traditionally been defined as opposing interests involving scarce resources and goal divergence and frustration (Tjosvold, 1998). In addition to denying the reality that people with cooperative, highly overlapping goals often are in conflict, conflict as opposing interests confounds conflict with competition defined as incompatible goals. It is not clear whether the theorized effects of conflict are due to conflict or to competition. This issue of definition is not simply a technical one for researchers. The belief that the conflict is competitive and involves incompatible interests makes its management difficult.

Conflict in Cooperation and Competition

Cooperative goals and their resulting orientation toward promoting each other make it more likely that conflicts will be dealt with in ways that increase benefits and reduce costs (Deutsch, 1973). Cooperative goals are fundamental to positive conflicts whereas competitive goals very much interfere with conflict handling and productive conflict. Little research has explored the links between independent goals and conflict dynamics.

Studies affirm that cooperative goals produce the promotive interaction that aids managing conflict (Deutsch, 1973; Tjosvold, 1998). Table 1 summarizes that the cooperative or competitive interdependence impacts outcomes by fostering much different dynamics. Specifically, cooperative goals lead to mutual exchange and an open-minded discussion of diverse positions that in turn strengthen the quality of the negotiated decision and productivity and reaffirms the relationship between the protagonists resulting in mutual affirmation, success, and confidence in future collaboration. Competitive goals heighten the tendency to avoid a direct discussion or alternatively a tough, closed-minded discussion and attempt to coerce the other to do one’s bidding--including at times threats and actual violence--dynamics that undermine decision making, getting the job done, and relationships and result in frustration, aggression, hostility, and revenge.

Conflict is not the opposite of cooperation; it aids realizing the benefits of working cooperatively. Although popular, the assumption of the incompatibility of conflict and cooperation is unrealistic and destructive. Rather group members can use their conflicts to identify problems and create solutions. Managing conflict is a practical way for groups to change and renew.

Conflict's Contribution to Cooperative Group Problem Solving

Researchers have emphasized the value of conflict for promoting productive teamwork and effective organizational problem solving. The theory of cooperation and competition identifies the processes by which conflict can be constructive and the conditions under which it is.

Constructive Controversy Dynamics

Deutsch's theory of cooperation and competition provides a powerful way to understand conflict and identify the conditions that impact its management. The theory was the basis for constructive controversy research that we began in the mid 1970s. Our experimental research has documented not only that discussion of opposing positions can contribute to group problem solving but also the dynamics by which controversial discussions can be so useful. It also helps to specify the nature of promotive interaction that cooperative goals induce. Considerable field research has shown that controversy dynamics can be highly useful for solving a wide array of complex problems for organizations.

Constructive controversy is used to characterize the dynamics induced by cooperative goals that contribute to effective group problem solving (Johnson, Johnson, Smith, & Tjosvold, 1990; Johnson & Tjosvold, 1989; Tjosvold, 1991a, 1985). Controversy occurs when persons discuss their opposing views about how a problem should be solved. Proposing opposing positions interrupts at least temporarily their making a decision and resolving the issue. Controversy emphasizes the intellectual disagreement that occurs as people cope with their incompatible activities and try to resolve their conflicts. It occurs as scientists debate the validity of a theory but is not restricted to debates over ideas and truth. Negotiating over wage agreements and unfriendly behavior have characteristics of intellectual disagreement as protagonists develop and propose alternative solutions to resolve their conflict.

The hypothesis that controversy heightens the value of cooperative goals for relationships and productivity is derived from the work of a number of social psychologists and cognitive developmentalists as well as Deutsch's theory (Berlyne, 1966; Deutsch, 1973; Jan's, 1982; Kohlberg, 1969; Maier, 1970; Piaget, 1950, 1948). Develop and express, question and understand, integrate and create, and agree and implement are the hypothesized, mutually reinforcing dynamics of controversy (Figure 1). Figure 1 identifies the four major processes of develop and express, question and understand, integrate and create, and agree and implement as four major processes by which controversy contributes to effective problem solving. These processes occur and reoccur, as managing conflict is reiterative. Especially in complex conflicts, discussants may cycle through these processes several times before reaching a final conclusion.

Develop and Express

Considerable social and cognitive developmental research support the first hypothesized dynamic of controversy. People have been found to develop positions based on incomplete information, an inadequate analysis of the problem, and failure to consider all proper alternatives (Corner, Kinicki, & Keats, 1994; Innami, 1994; Tversky & Kahneman, 1974).

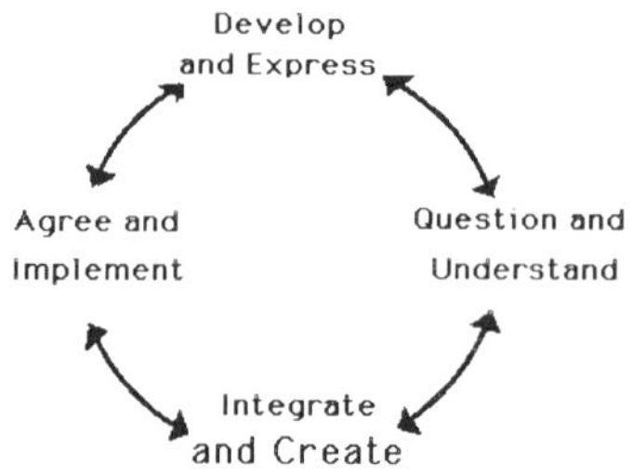

Figure 1. Constructive Controversy Dynamics

Question and Understand

Experimental studies have documented the causal links between controversial discussions and creative problem solving (Tjosvold, 1985). Direct controversy can contribute to full exchange of perspectives and understanding of issues. When confronted with an opposing view, people have been found to feel uncertain about the most adequate solution; they doubt that their own position is correct. Given this uncertainty about the adequacy of their own positions, they have been found to be curious and to seek to understand opposing views (Tjosvold, 1982; Tjosvold & Deemer, 1981, 1980; Tjosvold & Johnson, 1977, 1978; Tjosvold, Johnson, & Fabrey, 1980; Tjosvold, Johnson, & Lerner, 1981).

Participants who disagreed directly compared to those in agreeable discussions indicated higher levels of internal uncertainty and asked their protagonists more questions that demonstrated greater interest in understanding the opposing perspective. They recalled more opposing arguments, identified the reasoning others were using, and predicted the kind of reasoning--as measured by Kohlberg's (1969) stages of cognitive development--that their protagonist would use on new issues more accurately than participants who discussed similar views (Tjosvold & Johnson, 1977, 1978).

Field experiments in schools also support theorizing on controversy's effects on epistemic curiosity. Students involved in controversy versus those who were to seek agreement read and reviewed more relevant material, used free time to gather more information, and requested information from others (Lowry & Johnson, 1981). Students in controversy, compared to those striving for agreement, used more relevant material and worked outside of class, gave up free time to search for more information, and understood their opponent's perspective more thoroughly (Johnson, Johnson, & Tiffany, 1984; Smith, et al., 1984, 1981).

Integrate and Create

The expression of various views and the defending and articulating their rationales and the internal uncertainty and search for new, more complete information and understanding are hypothesized to lead to the development of new, useful solutions to the problem at hand. Experiments have shown that protagonists, compared to participants with similar positions, integrate several points of view. They are not only aware but are willing to consider and incorporate opposing views (Johnson & Johnson, 1985; Tjosvold, 1982; Tjosvold & Deemer, 1980; Tjosvold & Johnson, 1978; Tjosvold, et al., 1980; Tjosvold, et al., 1981).

Agree and Implement

The open-minded discussion and the creation of new alternatives are expected to result in agreement to solutions that the protagonists accept and implement. Constructive controversy is critical for full, effective participation and mutual influence (Tjosvold, 1987). Laboratory and field experiments have shown that individuals involved in controversial participation reach agreement and carry out that agreement (Richter & Tjosvold, 1980; Tjosvold & Deemer, 1980).

Contribution of Cooperative Goals

As suggested by Deutsch's theory, cooperative goals, but not competitive ones, have been found to facilitate the full dynamics of constructive controversy. The value of controversy for learning another's position appears to hold for competitive as well as cooperative situations. However cooperative, but not competitive goals, induced the willingness to incorporate opposing views and reach an agreement. Protagonists in cooperation used their discussion of opposing views to integrate several points of view. They combined the information and ideas to make a high quality decision they were willing to implement (Tjosvold, 1982; Tjosvold & Deemer, 1980; Tjosvold & Field, 1984).

External Validity of Controversy Research

Questionnaire studies have documented that cooperative, constructive controversy dynamics generalize to decision making in organizations (Tjosvold & Tsao, 1989). For example, effective project managers both engaged in open discussion of conflict and discussed issues in cooperative ways; ineffective project managers both avoided conflict and tried to win (Barker, Tjosvold, & Andrews, 1988).

Cooperative goals and constructive controversy were found to contribute greatly to effective self-managing teams (Alper, Tjosvold, & Law, 1998). Teams characterized by highly cooperative goals were found to discuss their opposing views openly and skillfully. These cooperative-constructive controversy teams were also rated by themselves and their managers as more careful, productive, and innovative than were teams with more competitive and independent goals and less open discussion of conflicting positions. The strong fit with the structural equation model suggests that cooperative goals and constructive controversy very much contributed to strengthened teamwork and improved performance of these self-managing teams.

Organizational Effectiveness

Studies have extended research to show the vital role of the dynamics and outcomes of cooperation and constructive controversy on a wide range of issues critical for organizational success. All organizations must serve their customers or face the prospect of reduced support. To market high technology effectively, for example, service, training, engineering and technical personnel must coordinate with each other and with salespersons (Tjosvold & Wong, 1992; Wong & Tjosvold, 1995). Cooperative goals promote the open, lively discussions that result in integrated, creative solutions that solve problems and create value for customers (Tjosvold, Dann, & Wong, 1992; Tjosvold & Wong, 1994).

Organizations must innovate so that they are prepared to serve customers in the future with quality products at competitive prices. Faculty members and employees of a large post-secondary educational institution were able to develop innovative solutions and consider all views when they discussed their opposing views openly and forthrightly (Tjosvold & McNeely, 1988). Cooperative employees of a retail chain were able to use new scanning technology efficiently, because they exchanged information and hammered out ideas about how to solve the many problems the technology created (Tjosvold, 1990).

Experimental, questionnaire, and field interview studies have documented and developed the cooperative goals-constructive controversy framework. Together results are convincing that cooperative goals induce open-minded, constructive controversy that in turn results in high quality, implemented solutions and that these dynamics occur in a wide range of organizational contexts.

The Theory's Universal Aspirations

Deutsch has characterized his theorizing as grand. Cooperation theory is expected to apply at different levels (within and between groups and organizations) with different issues (conflict, power) and across cultures (collectivist and individualistic). It analyzes interdependence as a key characteristic of groups, but interdependence also characterizes organizations and society within which work teams operate. In contrast, group research has tended to be more focused. For example, group models provide a broad framework to identify the antecedents, interaction, setting, and other variables that affect team performance (Hackman, 1983).

The theory's aspirations offer the potential of a powerful analysis of social life and application to central, complex organizational issues. It can help understand the context in which work teams operate and the relationships outside the group that promote team effectiveness. Research already reviewed demonstrates the potential of cooperation theory to analyze conflict within and between groups. This section reviews studies on power and in China as examples of how the theory can be applied to critical issues relevant but typically not considered in group research.

The Faces of Power

Power has long been recognized as central to organizations but research has largely ignored its impact on the internal and external dynamics of groups (McClelland, 1975; Pfeffer, 1982). Power, a highly negative force in many companies, is associated with coercion, intimidation, dominance, and arrogance. However, power can have a highly positive face where all persons feel powerful and invigorated to pursue important goals (Frey, 1993; Kouzes & Posner, 1987). Employees are better served by powerful leaders who are confident and skilled enough to empower their employees and protect them from unwanted interference (Kanter, 1983).

Cooperation theory helps understand when power takes a constructive or a destructive course.

Power has traditionally been defined as the capacity to make another do what he would not otherwise do; powerful leaders are able to overcome resistance to get those subject to power to do their bidding (Dahl, 1957; Emerson, 1962). In addition to problems in measuring and observing, this kind of definition assumes that there is an incompatibility between the person with power and the person subject to it; low power persons are "forced" to do what is not in their self-interest. Indeed, the sociologist Max Weber (1947) explicitly argued that power occurs when persons are in competition.

Power is more usefully defined as the capacity to affect outcomes, or equivalently as the control over valued resources (Thibaut & Kelley, 1959). A leader has power over a group member to the extent that the member sees that her leader has resources that she values. She might value her leader's kindness and compassion, knowledge and suggestions on how to get work done, the ability to assign people to projects, and performance ratings and bonuses. Knowledge, assistance, and emotional support have been found to be prevalent bases of power whereas funding, evaluation, and authority were less (Tjosvold, 1981, 1989, 1990).

Power is a measure of the extent of how dependent people are; cooperation and competition measure the kind or direction of their interdependence. Experiments and field studies indicate that even with unequal power, people with cooperative goals exchange resources and productively complete tasks whereas unequal power in competition arouses suspicion, a refusal to exchange resources, and frustrated tasks and relationships (Tjosvold, 1975a, 1975b, 1981, 1989, 1990).

These initial studies suggest that power can promote effective teamwork within and between groups and with organizational leaders, when it operates within a cooperative context. Feeling united in a common effort and that they are in this together, group members build up each other's power and use it to help them achieve their common goals. Individuals and teams recognize and appreciate their abilities, are open to influence as they influence others, and exchange information and resources for mutual benefit. Power need not be an instrument of control and disruption but can strengthen cooperative relationships and make them more productive.

Cross-Cultural Validity: Evidence from East Asia

Western theories cannot be assumed to generalize to Chinese and other collectivist cultures (Hofstede, 1993). However, in today's diverse and global marketplace, theories that can be applied in various cultures are needed to understand and facilitate cross-cultural teamwork and conflict.

Experiments indicate that controversy when discussed in a cooperative context promotes open-mindedeness and integrated views in China as in the West. Open controversy, compared to avoiding conflict strengthened relationships, and induced epistemic curiosity where Chinese people asked questions, explored opposing views, demonstrated knowledge, and worked to integrate views (Tjosvold, Hui & Sun, 1998). Cooperative goals and persuasive influence attempts were found to communicate respect and promote an open-minded exploration of opposing views and an integration of them (Tjosvold & Sun, 1998).

In a study of 39 groups and their supervisors in Hanzhou, China, findings indicate that work teams in China can use open-minded, constructive discussion with opposing teams to promote product quality and cost reduction and these discussions are more likely with cooperative than competitive goals (Tjosvold & Wang, 1998). The measures of product quality and cost reduction were taken independently of the measures of goal interdependence and interaction.

Studies conducted in Hong Kong indicate that cooperative, open-minded discussions helped restaurant employees work together to serve their customers and manufacturers work with their suppliers in China to improve quality (Tjosvold, Moy, & Sasaki, 1996; Wong, Tjosvold, Wong, & Liu, in press). Cooperative goals also promoted the open-minded discussion that helped teams of mass transportation employees obtain organizational support they needed to reduce costs and improve quality (Tjosvold, 1998). Structural equation analyses support that the dynamics of cooperative controversy helped develop the commitment of Chinese staff to their Japanese companies (Tjosvold, Sasaki, & Moy, 1998).

Although research provides good support for the theory in China, results do not imply that goal interdependence is operationalized in a highly similar way in the East as in the West. The actions that develop cooperative goals or communicate an attempt to discuss different positions open-mindedly may be quite different as may the general level of goal interdependence and open-minded discussion. A future challenge is to show how group members from the West and the East can together use cooperation research to develop their teams and discuss their differences open-mindedly and productively.

Applying the Theory

The documented value of cooperative goals and constructive controversy demands that the theory be applied. Placing people in the same room, seating them together, telling them they are a cooperative group, and advising them to "cooperate," does not make them a cooperative group. Project teams, committees, task forces, departments, and councils are groups, but they are not necessarily cooperative.

Almost everyone has been part of a group that wasted time, was inefficient, and generally produced poor work. Pseudo and traditional groups are characterized by a number of dynamics that impair their effectiveness (Johnson & F. Johnson, 1997), such as group immaturity, uncritically and quickly accepting members' dominant response, social loafing, free-riding, and group-think. Even formally assigning the group a common goal does not insure that group members believe that their important goals are cooperative or give them the skills and wherewithal to work together and manage their conflicts constructively. Helping teams work cooperatively requires structured, ongoing effort.

Fortunately, the theory suggests the discipline needed to promote true cooperation. As with our research, we have developed distinct, complementary approaches to applying cooperation theory. David's model of five elements is directed toward a wide range of educational settings (Johnson & Johnson, 1997). It indicates what cooperative learning teams look like and provides clear, practical, and validated procedures for action. Many thousands of teachers are using this model, and their feedback has made the model both more comprehensive and useable. Dean's team organizational model specifies the social psychological characteristics needed for cooperative teams and organizations in a wide variety of settings (Tjosvold, 1991; Tjosvold & Tjosvold, 1993). It offers a range of procedures that can be modified to fit the diverse situations of organizational teams.

The Basic Elements of Cooperation

The basic components of effective cooperative learning are positive interdependence, face-to-face promotive interaction, individual and group accountability, appropriate use of social skills, and group processing. The integrated application of these elements results in effective cooperative learning.

Positive interdependence exists when group members believe that they are linked with each others in a way that they cannot succeed unless they all work and that they must coordinate their efforts to complete a task (Johnson & Johnson, 1989). The discipline of using cooperative groups begins with structuring positive interdependence. Group members have to know that they "sink or swim together," that is, they have two responsibilities: to maximize their own productivity and to maximize the productivity of all other group members.

There are two major categories of interdependence: outcome interdependence and means interdependence (Johnson & Johnson, 1989). When persons are in a cooperative or competitive situation, they are oriented toward a desired outcome, end state, goal, or reward. If there is no outcome interdependence (goal and reward interdependence), there is no cooperation or competition. In addition, the means through which the mutual goals or rewards are to be accomplished specify the actions required on the part of group members. Means interdependence includes resource, role, and task interdependence (which are overlapping and not independent from each other).

Individual accountability and personal responsibility for contributing are critical for successful cooperative groups. Group members are responsible for completing their own share of the work and facilitating the work of other group members. Members will reduce their contributions to goal achievement when the group works on tasks where it is difficult to identify members' contributions, when there is an increased likelihood of redundant efforts, when there is a lack of group cohesiveness, and when there is lessened responsibility for the final outcome (Harkins & Petty, 1982; Ingham, Levinger, Graves, & Peckham, 1974; Kerr & Bruun, 1981; Latane, Williams & Harkins, 1979; Moede, 1927; Petty, Harkins, Williams, & Lantane, 1977; Williams, 1981; Williams, Harkins, & Latane, 1981). If, however, there is high individual accountability and it is clear how much effort each member is contributing, if redundant efforts are avoided, if every member is responsible for the final outcome, and if the group is cohesive, then the social loafing effect vanishes. In addition, the smaller the size of the group the greater the individual accountability may be (Messich & Brewer, 1983). Research recently confirmed that individual accountability contributes to the effects of positive interdependence (Archer-Kath, Johnson, & Johnson, 1994).

Promotive interaction occurs when group members encourage and facilitate each other's efforts to complete tasks and achieve in order to reach the group's goals. Promotive interaction is characterized by the following.

1. Providing others with efficient and effective help and assistance.
2. Exchanging needed resources, such as information, materials, and processing information more efficiently and effectively.
3. Providing each other with feedback in order to improve their subsequent performance on assigned tasks and responsibilities,
4. Challenging each other's conclusions and reasoning in order to promote higher quality decision making and greater insight into the problems being considered.
5. Advocating exerting efforts to achieve mutual goals and influencing each other's efforts to achieve mutual goals.
6. Acting in trusting and trustworthy ways.
7. Being motivated to strive for mutual benefit.
8. Feeling less anxiety and stress (Johnson & Johnson, 1989).

Group members should continually learn and build the interpersonal and small group skills needed for high quality cooperation. To coordinate efforts to achieve mutual goals, group members must (a) get to know and trust each other, (b) communicate accurately and unambiguously, (c) accept and support each other, and (d) resolve conflicts constructively (Johnson, 1997; Johnson & Johnson, 1997). Interpersonal and small group skills form the basic nexus among individuals, and if individuals are to work together productively and cope with the stresses and strains of doing so, they must have a modicum of these skills. Long-term field studies confirmed that value of teaching social skills (Lew, Mesch, Johnson, & Johnson, 1986a, 1986b; Mesch, Johnson, & Johnson, 1993; Mesch, Lew, Johnson, & Johnson, 1986).

In group processing, members periodically reflect on how well they are functioning and plan how to improve their work processes. A process is an identifiable sequence of events taking place over time, and process goals refer to the sequence of events instrumental in achieving outcome goals. Group processing may be defined as reflecting on a group session to describe what member actions were helpful and unhelpful and to make decisions about what actions to continue or change. The purpose of group processing is to clarify and improve the effectiveness of the members in contributing to the joint efforts to achieve the group's goals. Research has directly documented the value of group processing for cooperative groups (Johnson, Johnson, Stanne, & Garibaldi, 1990; Putnam, Rynders, Johnson, & Johnson, 1989; Yager, Johnson, & Johnson, 1985).

Team Vision

There is no one step or hurdle that itself makes a team productive. In a team organization, people throughout the organization are committed to their common vision, believe they are united behind the vision, are empowered to work together to realize it, explore issues and decisions through debating opposing views, and reflect on their conflicts and progress for ongoing improvement. The Team Organization model (Figure 2) summarizes these central aspects of developing an effective team (Tjosvold, 1993, 1991; Tjosvold & Tjosvold, 1991).

A clear, engaging direction is central to developing a team and organization. All members are fully aware of the team's strategic plan, code of ethics, and organization structure. They know what they are expected to accomplish and how they will work together to achieve it. They understand the importance of this vision for themselves and others, and are committed to pursuing it. This vision motivates and directs.

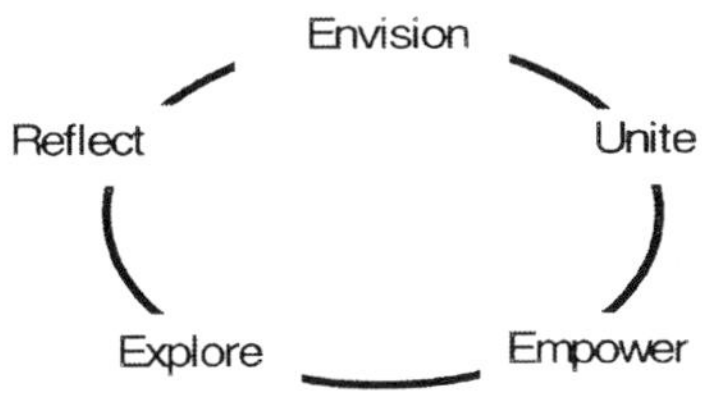

Figure 2. Team Organization

Visions must be created; they do not just appear. Leaders are pioneers who challenge the status quo, and are willing to risk failure to search for a better way (Kouzes & Posner, 1987). Yet, leaders cannot create the vision alone. They listen to employee concerns and ideas to help them create the group's vision. They enlist employees to help them mold the vision. They realize they cannot command commitment, they must inspire it. Leaders are "keepers of the dream," as Steve Jobs said, but they must inspire others to share this dream.

An effective vision convinces team members they are cooperatively united in a common effort. Sensing they are moving in the same direction, they communicate openly and understand each other. They realize they need the information, knowledge, ideas, support, and energy of others to get their jobs done and to contribute successfully to the company.

Cooperative unity cannot be taken for granted nor decreed. Team members must come to their own conclusion that what is good for one is good for all; success for one is success for all. One person can not cooperate alone. Everybody sees the positively related goals and is willing to work together to accomplish them.

Feeling united in a common effort contributes to confidence that the team can realize its vision. But that is insufficient. Team members do not exert themselves fully unless they believe that they have the technical resources, organizational mandate, and the skills to combine their ideas and efforts successfully. Empowering, like envisioning and uniting, cannot be done to people; they themselves must believe that they can do it.

Teams are not islands. They need the organization's mandate, permission, and support to be highly effective. Believing that team members have the necessary technical skills and resources to reach the group goal is central to a sense of power and confidence. Interpersonal and social skills are also vital. Working together requires sensitivity, empathy, and confrontation. Individual responsibility and team accountability empower a group. Team members want to divide the labor fairly and effectively. They feel a sense of personal accountability to complete their tasks so that other team members can complete theirs. They do their own jobs and whatever else it takes so that the team as a whole is successful.

Working together and feeling empowered do not mean smooth sailing and inevitable success. Every group needs the ability to explore issues, and overcome barriers to move toward its vision.

Issues and decisions come in such a great variety that teams must be flexible and use the approach appropriate for the situation. However, for central, critical issues, the team should dig into issues, create alternatives, and chose a high quality solution that solves the problems and strengthens the group. This controversy must reaffirm the team's unity and empowerment to be successful.

Teams need to be able to assess their present state of functioning, celebrate and build upon their accomplishments, learn from mistakes, and manage their conflicts. The team assesses its strengths and successes, as well as its frustrations and limitations.

An essential first step is to create valid, useful information about the group's present functioning (Argyris, 1970). Organization development specialists have created a rich array of methods to collect data. The team organization model identifies envisioning, uniting, empowering, and exploring as areas to assess and develop and suggest how conflicts can be used to promote team effectiveness.

The five components and team organization models summarize a great deal of research on goals, cooperation and competition, power, controversy, group processing, and conflict management. The parts of the models complement and supplement each other and form a coherent whole. Cooperative teamwork requires a great deal from leaders and team members. But this spirited teamwork gives much to organizations and people. Through it, teams can improve their value to their customers and members, providing the challenging tasks and rich rewards of serving others, as well as oneself.

Summary and Conclusions

Over the past 100 years researchers have focused on such diverse outcomes as achievement, problem solving, higher-level reasoning, retention, achievement motivation, intrinsic motivation, transfer of learning, interpersonal attraction, social support, friendships, prejudice, valuing differences, self-esteem, social competencies, psychological health, moral reasoning, and many others. These numerous outcomes may be subsumed within three broad categories: achievement and productivity, positive interpersonal relationships, and psychological health. Cooperative efforts, compared with competitive and individualistic ones, tend to result in higher levels of these outcomes, especially when carried out in a disciplined, integrated manner.

The research on social interdependence has an external validity and a generalizability rarely found in the social sciences. The more variations in places, people, and procedures the research can withstand and still yield the same findings, the more externally valid the conclusions. The research has been conducted in ten different historical decades. Research subjects have varied as to age, sex, economic class, nationality, and cultural background. A wide variety of research tasks, ways of structuring the types of social interdependence, and measures of the dependent variables have been used. The research has been conducted by many different researchers with markedly different theoretical and practical orientations working in different settings and countries. The diversity of subjects, settings, age levels, and operationalizations of social interdependence and the dependent variables give this work wide generalizability and considerable external validity. The theory can be applied with confidence in many kinds of group and organizational settings.

The theory has guided our research. We have found it liberating, not at all a straightjacket. It has helped us develop an empirical base to understand conflict, power, and other intricacies of group and organizational life. Interdependence is fundamental to organizational life, and the theory can provide an integrated way to understand its complexities.

It has also guided our research collaboration. We have cooperated directly on streams of research and used our disagreements to proceed. (We barely glimpsed at the dramatic scenery in the drive over the Atlas Mountains in Morocco as we hotly debated our original controversy studies.) But we are also independent researchers with our own understanding, research agenda, and applied focus. We know that cooperative goals and constructive controversy facilitates individuality, as well as team development, and that diversity strengthens cooperative work.

Frank Schmidt (1996) has reminded us that applied researchers, frustrated with the lack of replicated theories and main effects, too often conduct research historically, pursuing new leads without building upon existing knowledge. The theory of cooperation and competition is, albeit imperfect, a highly useful basis upon which to continue to develop valid, useful knowledge about groups. The theory is parsimonious, elegant, powerful, and empirically developed. We invite you to bring your diverse perspectives and interests and join us in using the theory of cooperation and competition to strengthen our knowledge base about work teams and their organizations.

For centuries, groups have accomplished the ordinary and the extra-ordinary for organizations; in all likelihood the demands on groups will intensify. Teams increasingly include experts trained in different disciplines, stationed around the world, with diverse cultural backgrounds, who must meet tight deadlines. For example, Jeff Felt, frustrated that he could only offer total knee-replacement surgery to his patients suffering from cartilage defects and osteoarthritis, built a team to fulfill his dream of an out-patient, minimally invasive arthroscopic procedure as an alternative. Ph.D. trained polymer researchers, mechanical and biological testers, animal clinical specialists, rheumatologists, orthopedic surgeons, and venture capitalists assembled in Minneapolis must work with clinical surgeons and regulators in Norway, Mexico, Germany, Australia, and the United States. Their investors demand that the dream turns into marketable products.

Jeff Felt and the millions of others, who are and will be striving to make their diverse, dispersed teams synergistic need knowledge about the conditions that promote productive teamwork. It may well be that the demands on teams will continue to outstrip our knowledge about groups. Although considerable research has developed Deutsch's theory, much more needs to be done. Studies are needed to show managers and employees how they can apply the theory to solve various problems. Fortunately, we know that cooperative goals and the procedures and skills to discuss opposing views open-mindedly contribute in vital, powerful ways to making teams work. We cannot predict future challenges, but we know that this knowledge can help us meet them.

Acknowledgements

The first author appreciates the financial support of the Research Grants Council of Hong Kong, RGC grant project No: LC890/96H.

References

Alper, S., Tjosvold, D., & Law, S. W. (1998). Interdependence and controversy in group decision making: Antecedents to effective self-managing teams. *Organizational Behavior and Human Decision Processes*, 74, 33-52.

Archer-Kath, J., Johnson, D. W., & Johnson, R. (1994). Individual versus group feedback in cooperative groups. *Journal of Social Psychology*, 134, 681-694.

Argyris, C. (1970). Intervention theory and method: A behavioral science view. Reading, MA: Addison-Wesley.

Berlyne, D. (1966). Curiosity and education. In J. Krumbolz (Ed.), *Learning and the educational process*. Chicago: Rand-McNally.

Berlyne, D. (1965). Notes on intrinsic motivation and intrinsic reward in relation to instruction. In J. Bruner (Ed.), *Learning about learning*. (Cooperative Research Monograph No. 15). Washington, D. C.: U.S. Department of Health, Education, and Welfare, Office of Education.

Corner, P. D., Kinicki, A. J. & Keats, B. (1994). Integrating organizational and individual information processing perspectives on choice. *Organization Science*, 5, 294-308.

Dahl, R. P. (1957). The concept of power, Behavioral Science, 2, 201-218.

Deutsch, M. (1949). A theory of cooperation and competition. *Human Relations*, 2, 129-152.

Deutsch, M. (1962). Cooperation and trust: Some theoretical notes. In M. R. Jones (Ed.), *Nebraska symposium on motivation* (pp. 275-319). Lincoln, NE: University of Nebraska Press.

Deutsch, M. (1973). The resolution of conflict. New Haven, CT: Yale University Press.

Deutsch, M. (1980). Fifty years of conflict. In L. Festinger (Ed.), *Retrospections on social psychology* (pp. 46-77). New York: Oxford University Press.

Deutsch, M., & Krauss, R. M. (1962). Studies of interpersonal bargaining. *Journal of Conflict Resolution*, 6, 52-72.

Emerson, R. M. (1962). Power-dependence relations. *American Sociological Review*, 27, 31-41.

Frank, M. (1984). A comparison between an individual and group goal structure contingency that differed in the behavioral contingency and performance-outcome components (Doctoral dissertation, University of Minnesota). *Dissertation Abstracts International*, 45/05, 1341-A.

French, J. R. P., Jr., & Raven, B. (1959). The bases of social power. In D. Cartwright (Ed.), *Studies in social power* pp. 150-167. Ann Arbor: University of Michigan Press.

Frey, R. (1993, Sept - Oct.). Empowerment or else. *Harvard Business Review*, 80-94.

Hackman, J. R. (1983). *A normative model of work team effectiveness*. Technical Report No. 2, Research Program on Group Effectiveness, Yale School of Organization and Management.

Harkins, S. G., & Petty, R. E. (1982). The effects of task difficulty and task uniqueness on social loafing. *Journal of Personality and Social Psychology*, 43, 1214-1229.

Hofstede, G. (1993). Cultural constraints in management theories. *The Academy of Management Executive*, 7, 81-94.

Innami, I. (1994). The quality of group decisions, group verbal behavior, and intervention. *Organizational Behavior & Human Decision Processes*, 60, 409-430.

Ingham, A., Levinger, G., Graves, J., & Peckham, V. (1974). The Ringelmann effect: Studies of group size and group performance. *Journal of Personality and Social Psychology*, 10, 371-384.

James, N., & Johnson, D. W. (1983). The relationship between attitudes toward social interdependence and psychological health within three criminal populations. Journal of *Abnormal and Social Psychology*, 121, 131-143.

James, S., & Johnson, D. W. (1988). Social interdependence, psychological adjustment, orientation toward negative life stress, and quality of second marriage. *Journal of Social Psychology*, 128(3), 287-304.

Janis, I. (1982). *Groupthink: Psychological studies of policy decisions and fiascoes*. Boston: Houghton-Mifflin.

Johnson, D. W. (1970). *Social psychology of education*. New York: Holt, Rinehart, & Winston.

Johnson, D. W. (1997). *Reaching out: Interpersonal effectiveness and self-actualization* (6th Ed.). Needham Heights: Allyn & Bacon.

Johnson, D. W., & Johnson, F. (1997). *Joining together: Group theory and group skills* (6th Ed.). Needham Heights: Allyn & Bacon.

Johnson, D. W., & Johnson, R. (1974). Instructional goal structure: Cooperative, competitive, or individualistic. *Review of Educational Research*, 44, 213-240.

Johnson, D. W., & Johnson, R. (1979). Conflict in the classroom: Controversy and learning. *Review of Educational Research*, 49, 51-70.

Johnson, D. W., & Johnson, R. (1981). Effects of cooperative and individualistic learning experiences on interethnic interaction. *Journal of Educational Psychology*, 73(3), 454-459.

Johnson, D. W., & Johnson, R. (1989). *Cooperation and competition: Theory and research*. Edina, MN: Interaction Book Company.

Johnson, D. W., & Johnson, R. (1995a). *Teaching students to be peacemakers*. Edina, MN: Interaction Book Company.

Johnson, D. W., & Johnson, R. (1995b). *Creative controversy: Intellectual challenge in the classroom*. Edina, MN: Interaction Book Company.

Johnson, D. W., & Johnson, R. (1995c). Teaching students to be peacemakers: Results of five years of research. *Peace and Conflict: Journal of Peace Psychology*, 1(4), 417-438.

Johnson, D. W., Johnson, R., & Holubec, E. (1992). *Advanced cooperative learning* (2nd ed.). Edina, MN: Interaction Book Company.

Johnson, D. W., Johnson, R., & Holubec, E. (1993). *Cooperation in the classroom*, (6th ed.). Edina, MN: Interaction Book Company.

Johnson, D. W., Johnson, R., & Krotee, M. (1986). The relationship between social interdependence and psychological health within the 1980 United States Olympic ice hockey team. *Journal of Psychology*, 120, 279-292.

Johnson, D. W., Johnson, R., Stanne, M., & Garibaldi, A. (1990). Impact of group processing on achievement in cooperative groups. *Journal of Social Psychology*, 130, 507-516.

Johnson, D. W., Skon, L., & Johnson, R. (1980). Effects of cooperative, competitive, and individualistic conditions on children's problem-solving performance. *American Educational Research Journal*, 17(1), 83-94.

Kanter, R. M. (1983). *The change masters*. New York: Simon & Schuster.

Kerr, N. (1983). The dispensability of member effort and group motivation losses: Free-rider effects. *Journal of Personality and Social Psychology*, 44, 78-94.

Kerr, N., & Bruun, S. (1981). Ringelmann revisited: Alternative explanations for the social loafing effect. *Personality and Social Psychology Bulletin*, 7, 224-231.

Kerr, N., & Bruun, S. (1983). The dispensability of member effort and group motivation losses: Free-rider effects. *Journal of Personality and Social Psychology*, 44, 78-94.

Kohlberg, L. (1969). Stage and sequence: The cognitive-development approach to socialization. In D. A. Goslin (Ed.), *Handbook of socialization theory and research*. (pp. 347-480). Skokie, IL: Rand McNally.

Kouzes, J. M. & Posner, B. Z. (1987). *The leadership challenge*. San Francisco: Jossey-Bass.

Latane, B., Williams, K., & Harkins, S. (1979). Many hands make light the work: The causes and consequences of social loafing. *Journal of Personality and Social Psychology*, 37, 822-832.

Lew, M., Mesch, D., Johnson, D. W., & Johnson, R. (1986a). Positive interdependence, academic and collaborative-skills group contingencies and isolated students. *American Educational Research Journal*, 23, 476-488.

Lew, M., Mesch, D., Johnson, D. W., & Johnson, R. (1986b). Components of cooperative learning: Effects of collaborative skills and academic group contingencies on achievement and mainstreaming. *Contemporary Educational Psychology*, 11, 229-239.

McClelland, D. C. (1975). *Power: The inner experience*. New York: Irvington.

Mesch, D., Johnson, D. W., & Johnson, R. (1988). Impact of positive interdependence and academic group contingencies on achievement. *Journal of Social Psychology*, 128, 345-352.

Mesch, D., Lew, M., Johnson, D. W., & Johnson, R. (1986). Isolated teenagers, cooperative learning and the training of social skills. *Journal of Psychology*, 120, 323-334.

Mesch, D., Lew, M., Johnson, D. W., & Johnson, R. (1993). Effects of cooperative learning on isolated teens. In J. Cohen & M. Fish (Eds.), *Handbook of school-based interventions*. (pp. 404-405). San Francisco, CA: Jossey-Bass.

Moede, W. (1927). Die richtlinien der leistungs-psycholgie. *Industrielle Psychotechnik*, 4, 193-207.

Petty, R., Harkins, S., Williams, K., & Latane, B. (1977). The effects of group size on cognitive effort and evaluation. *Personality and Social Psychology Bulletin*, 3, 575-578.

Pfeffer, J. (1992). Understanding power in organizations. *California Management Review*, 34, 29-50.

Pfeffer, J. (1981). *Power in organizations*. Boston: Pittman.

Piaget, J. (1950). *The psychology of intelligence*. New York: Harcourt.

Piaget, J. (1948). *The moral judgment of the child*. Glencoe, IL: Free Press.

Putnam, J., Rynders, J., Johnson, R., & Johnson, D. W. (1989). Collaborative skill instruction for promoting positive interactions between mentally handicapped and nonhandicapped children. *Exceptional Children*, 55(6), 550-557.

Schmidt, F. L. (1996). Statistical significance testing and cumulative knowledge in psychology: Implications for training of researchers. *Psychological Methods*, 1, 115-129.

Skon, L., Johnson, D., & Johnson, R. (1981). Cooperative peer interaction versus individual competition and individualistic efforts: Effects on the acquisition of cognitive reasoning strategies. *Journal of Educational Psychology*, 73(1), 83-92.

Smith, K., Johnson, D. W., & Johnson, R. (1981). Can conflict be constructive? Controversy versus concurrence seeking in learning groups. *Journal of Educational Psychology*, 73, 651-663.

Thibaut, J. W. & Kelley, H. H. (1959). *The social psychology of groups*. New York: John Wiley & Sons.

Tjosvold, D. (1998). The cooperative and competitive goal approach to conflict: Accomplishments and challenges. *Applied Psychology: An International Review*.

Tjosvold, D. (1993). *Teamwork for customers: Building organizations that take pride in serving*. San Francisco: Jossey-Bass.

Tjosvold, D. (1991). *Team organization: An enduring competitive advantage*. Chichester: Wiley.

Tjosvold, D. (1990). Power in cooperative and competitive organizational contexts. *Journal of Social Psychology*, 130, 249-258.

Tjosvold, D. (1989). Interdependence and power between managers and employees: A study of the leader relationship. *Journal of Management*, 15, 49-62.

Tjosvold, D. (1986). *Working together to get things done*. Lexington, MA: D. C. Heath.

Tjosvold, D. (1985a). Implications of controversy research for management. *Journal of Management*, 11, 21-37.

Tjosvold, D. (1985b). Power and social context in superior-subordinate interaction. *Organizational Behavior and Human Decision Processes*, 35, 281-293.

Tjosvold, D. (1985c). The effects of attribution and social context on superiors' influence and interaction with low performing subordinates, *Personnel Psychology*, 38, 361-376.

Tjosvold, D. (1981). Unequal power relationships within a cooperative or competitive context, *Journal of Applied Social Psychology* 11, 137-150.

Tjosvold, D., Andrews, I. R., & Jones, H. (1983). Cooperative and competitive relationships between leaders and their subordinates. *Human Relations*, 36, 1111-1124.

Tjosvold, D., Dann, V., & Wong, C. L. (1992). Managing conflict between departments to serve customers. *Human Relations*, 45, 1035-1054.

Tjosvold, D., & Deemer, D. K. (1981). Effects of control or collaborative orientation on participation in decision-making. *Canadian Journal of Behavioural Science*, 13, 33-43.

Tjosvold, D., & Deemer, D. K. (1980). Effects of controversy within a cooperative or competitive context on organizational decision-making. *Journal of Applied Psychology*, 65, 590-595.

Tjosvold, D., Hui, C., & Law, K. S. (in press). Empowerment in the leader relationship in Hong Kong: Interdependence and controversy. *Journal of Social Psychology*.

Tjosvold, D., & Moy, J. (1998). Managing employees in China from Hong Kong: Interaction, relationships, and productivity as antecedents to motivation. *Leadership & Organization Development Journal*, 19, 147-156.

Tjosvold, D, Moy, J., & Sasaki, S. (1996). Managing for customers and employees in Hong Kong: The quality and teamwork challenges, *Journal of Market-Focused Management*, 1, 339-357.

Tjosvold, D., Sasaki, S., & Moy, J. (1998). Developing commitment in Japanese organizations in Hong Kong: Interdependence, interaction, relationship and productivity. *Small Group Research*, 29, 560-582.

Tjosvold, D., & Tjosvold, M. M. (1991). *Leading a team organization: How to create an enduring competitive advantage*. Lexington Books.

Tjosvold, D., & Tsao, Y. (1989). Productive organizational collaboration: The role of values and cooperative goals. *Journal of Organizational Behavior*, 10. 189-195.

Tjosvold, D., & Wang, Z. M. (1998). *Cooperative goals and constructive controversy in work teams in China: Antecedents for performance*. Paper, Academy of Management Meetings, San Diego, CA, August, 1998.

Tjosvold, D., & Wong, C. L. (1994). Working with customers: Cooperation and competition in relational marketing, *Journal of Marketing Management*, 10, 297-310.

Tversky, A., & Kahneman, D.,(1974). Judgment under uncertainty: Heuristics and biases. Science, 185, 1124-1131.

Weber, M. (1947). *The theory of social and economic organization*. New York: Oxford University Press.

West, M. A. (1996) *Handbook of work group psychology*. Chichester: Wiley

Williams, K. (1981). *The effects of group cohesiveness on social loafing*. Paper presented at the annual meeting of the Midwestern Psychological Association, Detroit.

Williams, K., Harkens, S., & Latane, B. (1981). Identifiability as a deterrent to social loafing: Two cheering experiments. *Journal of Personality and Social Psychology*, 40, 303-311.

Wong, A., Tjosvold, D., Wong, W., & Liu, C. K. (in press). Relationships for quality improvement in the Hong Kong-China supply chain: A study in the theory of cooperation and competition. *Journal of Quality & Reliability Management*.

Wong, C., & Tjosvold, D. (1995). Goal interdependence and quality in services marketing. *Psychology & Marketing*, 12, 189-205.

Yager, S., Johnson, D., & Johnson, R. (1985). Oral discussion, group-to-individual transfer, and achievement in cooperative learning groups. *Journal of Educational Psychology*, 77(1), 60-66.

Chapter 9

Allan Mogensen (1901-1989)

A Pioneer with Work Teams and His Impact on Yugoslavian Teams

Matjaž Mulej
University of Maribor, Maribor, Republic of Slovenia

Abstract

Work teams can be called an interesting method of organizational development. With "Work Simplification" Allan Mogensen became a forerunner of organizational development by building a bridge from Taylorism to organizational development, including work teams, for over 50 years. He found what topics can better be covered by worker and work teams than bosses, and what managerial rather than technological innovation is their precondition, i.e., the managers' trust of subordinates' capability to be creative, professional, serious, and reliable. His influence over my work in Slovenia (and other areas of Yugoslavia, then) regarding work teams and innovation helped produce very substantial savings, and even change the Slovene (but not Yugoslav) Constitution before Slovenia became a country of its own, toward support for innovation. Mogensen is hence worth calling a celebrity and a pre-pioneer of organizational development and work teams.

The Selected Topic and Viewpoint

In the 1993 National Organizational Development Network Conference in San Francisco, the profession of Organizational Development was said to be thirty years old, and its main pioneers were pictured and recognized. Nobody seemed to know of Allan Mogensen from whom many of us have learned a lot on change management, on topics most employees can be successfully asked to work on, as creative persons and potential innovators, and on preconditions for workers to do it. I also learned from him a lot for my work on and with my "USOMID" methodology of "Creative Cooperation of the Many." I want this contribution to help the world, especially the USA, to give up their oversight of Mogensen. It is my view that Allan Mogensen (Mogy) is worth calling a celebrity and a pre-pioneer of Organizational Development, and work teams.

M.M. Beyerlein (ed.), Work Teams: Past, Present and Future, 157–168.

Mogensen's "Work Simplification" as a Bridge from Scientific Management to Organizational Development

One of America's most distinguished Industrial Engineers, Allan Mogensen was the Father of Work Simplification. He was educated in the teachings of Frederick Taylor who created the paradigm of scientific management. Mogy was a protege of Lillian Gilbreth, the first female industrial engineer in the USA and a woman revered internationally. Mogy died in 1989 after an extremely fruitful career of 65 years, of which over 50 years were devoted to his creativity-of-the-many enhancing method which was obviously an organizational development method, although not called so, until 1987.

It all started in a real-world situation. In 1926, Mogy worked for the Kodak Company in Rochester, New York. He was tasked with optimizing the movements of a shop floor worker and used a motion picture camera to film him at his labors. Upon seeing the film (incidentally!), the worker asked Mogy not to use the film because, "I can do the job better." This was a defining moment for Mogy. This experience made him realize that the best source for innovation - the best new way of doing a job - can be learned from the very person doing that job. From that time on Mogy was transformed from a Taylorist ("we think - they work") to an aggressive advocate of what today is called Organizational Development. This means the individuals doing the work are asked for suggestions and cooperation aimed at improving the way the task is done and overcoming its difficulties. For example, the worker is to be found a capable and serious professional, expert of their own job, not just living tools which need to be ordered every movement. In the next more than half a century Mogy directly contributed to the success of many companies, as well as the USA Army during World War II and later by helping them implement their own creativity toward innovation through his Work Simplification.

Mogy found out and believed that the Tayloristic managers made a big mistake when they asserted, "We think, they work." He was convinced that "nobody knows the characteristics, problems and opportunities of any process better than the experienced doers, but they are rarely asked their opinion or even a creative contribution." In short, Mogy declared, "the single best person to improve the way a job is done, is the person already doing the job."

In three decades after World War II, Art Spinanger, Mogy's protege and in later years teammate, went even further with Procter and Gamble. He switched from seeking and implementing improvement on the basis of trusting the worker's creative capabilities to Deliberate Method Change: thus, there are no limits to a better productivity and competitiveness. Dr. Ben Graham Jr., also a Mogy's protege and later long years team mate, is still working on the same lines in "Paperwork Simplification." He is now very international, and linking Paperwork Simplification with Re-engineering which actually reconfirms much of Mogy's work. How rare this is still today can be concluded from the fact that the Wall Street Journal found the case of a company "asking workers who make the products to write their how-to manuals," worth mentioning on the first page on October 4th, 1994.

In the mid-1930s, Mogy found out that he could no longer serve all companies seeking his help. He started educating groups of delegates from different companies in his "Work Simplification Conferences" held in Lake Placid, NY, first, and later in Sea Island, GA. They were outstanding forums for learning for more than 50 years. In addition, Mogy kept being a consultant. His greatest challenge was to defeat the behavioral trait known as "resistance to change." Fighting this attitude via "Work Simplification" is what makes Mogy an organizational development person, his distinguished results in this battle make him an outstanding organizational development pioneer and personality. He found the topic on which work teams could do their best job, as well as the way for their brains and hearts, not only hands, to open up and be employed for the common benefit: their own/shared *work process improvement*.

In 1982, Mogy appeared on the famous American TV program, "Today." His opening statement was: "Ninety percent of the presidents and chief executive officers of American companies don't give a damn about their people." That's quite an accusation, but few in the field of management would dispute it. Too many managers believe that subordinates are not able or willing to think, because they do not have enough education or investment in the company, or desire to pursue the company's goals. On the other hand, the other ten percent of the companies who do care about their people - and therefore listen to their improvement suggestions - inevitably prosper. (General Bill Creech in his 1994 book *The Five Pillars of TQM* argues that they are not even ten percent, but only two percent. Creech speaks on the basis of 46 years of experience in improving the quality of work in the USA Air Force and business as well as observation of others, both in the USA and around the world, and his own many successes.) At any rate, it seems to be an overwhelming majority which poorly use creativity and commitment of the many, their "hidden capital," as we call it in Slovenia (Gabrijelcic, 1993, 1995; Ursic 1993, 1996).

The logic of managers who do not want to listen to their subordinates is a consequence of the 19th century reality and its (quite primitive) labor intensive technology addressing much more hands than heads and hearts. Its source was a lack of skills, knowledge and experience on the part of lower-level workers. But the efforts for competitiveness caused the need for more advanced equipment and labor force. Hence this lack was less true in Mogensen's early days, and it was even less true when organizational development became established as an important discipline over the last thirty years. It is even less true today, but the managerial mistrust is still around.

To learn more about Mogy's work read his book *Mogy: An Autobiography* by Allan Mogensen with Rosario "Zip" Rausa's *Father of Work Simplification.*[1] The book also contains some cases. Its basic message is based on Mogy's experience and life long belief:

1. in order to be competitive and survive we need improvement;
2. for it we need change management;
3. for it to work we need to consider the doers of any process
4. as knowledgeable and creative experts on it;
5. for their creativity to be employed we must offer suitable methodologies
6. such as Work Simplification;
7. for this to happen managers must cooperate with workers.

This is what makes Mogy an organizational development pioneer before organizational development had ever been mentioned, including the work teams method. Cases in his book and in his conference materials demonstrate that he frequently found teams much more capable of solving the problem than individuals, and had the habit to work in groups of job mates (Mogensen, 1980).

We could of course talk also about other pre-pioneers who applied other methods, but adhered to the same underlying statement of respect for the subordinates' capacities, all way to the shop floor. Like J. Lincoln's "this company has had the highest paid workers in the world and the lowest labor cost for turning out their products, due to their incentive system enhancing creativity of many" (Henderson, 1985, p. 513). But it seems that nobody has done more toward the liberation of human creativity on the lower (as well as upper) levels of the organizational hierarchical structure, and hence toward a successful change management, such as organizational development, and over so many decades as Mogy did.

My Discovery and Application of Work Simplification in the Fictitiously Self-Managerial Yugoslavia

I learned about Mogy, his ideas, and his methods in the late 1970s from Dr. Robert Massey, President of Progress Management Services, Arlington, VA. He is a Mogensen's disciple who is mentioned several times in Mogy's autobiography. He visited Maribor, Slovenia (part of Yugoslavia at the time), in 1978 to take my international summer course on "New Aspects of Self-Management in Yugoslavia." Unlike Yugoslavs, Dr. Massey expected self-management to be a Mogy-style worker participation and to provide a hospitable environment for innovation to flourish. Importantly, the model of self-management included participation of lower-level workers, they were supposed to be part of both the managerial and the working process and to be listened to by senior officials (but not about innovation concerning their daily job, the agenda was to control managers in their most general decision making).

However, the Yugoslav bureaucracy discovered the democratic essence of this trend toward self-management early on.[2] They found it dangerous to their own privileges and centocratic thinking (as Creech calls it). They quite soon contrived ways to destroy the very core of self-management by imposing excessive legalistic formality on it, etc. Thus the empowerment of workers, a necessary condition of continuous participative improvement, was emasculated and the workers lost interest in this "alleged participation." They were inhibited by superiors who wanted to fully control all information related to the work involved in Tayloristic style, whose followers' reading of Taylor is different from Taylor's writing in one essential sentence. In his book, F. W. Taylor suggested managers listen to their workers in order to learn from them (Taylor 1967; centocrats do not accept and miss this message).

Then the obsolence of this governmental (and managerial) impact over Yugoslavia was not clear to many. Self-management was actually fictitious instead of being a source of innovation and prosperity. The centocratic turf dragons won their battle for their power again, but country was losing its chances. An internationally respected model became a bad reality.

Dr. Massey was disappointed, but he did not give in. He kept feeding me information on Work Simplification and encouraging me to study it. I kept working on Systems Theory professionally, and found the holism and depth aimed at by the systems thinking (and needed by mankind and every individual equally) unattainable without interdisciplinary creative cooperation. This caused a few more incentives for me to learn more about enhancing creativity. Some activitists of the Suggestion

Systems in Slovenia felt that my *Dialectical Systems Theory* (Mulej, 1974, 1976, 1979 & 1998; Devetak & Mulej, 1985; Mulej, et al., 1987; Mulej, et al., 1992; Dyck, Mulej, et al., 1998) was so well oriented toward reaching holism and creative results of people by incentives and by creative cooperation methods, that we could and should share the effort to bring the innovation movement out of the blind alley of the time. I learned also about Systematic Heuristics (Mueller, 1970), TEK Circles (Potter & Kaufman 1980), experience with trusting the subordinates (Graham Jr. & Parvin 1979; Lehrer, 1981; NYSE, 1982; Peters & Waterman, 1982) and Mogensen's method (Mogensen, 1980).

In 1979 and 1980, I first successfully applied creative cooperation of many. It was in preparation and sponsoring of three Davis Cup matches, as the secretary of my tennis club in Maribor. In teams made of experienced club members working for living in different fields which could be related to their field of activity in our club, we listed 880 activities to be taken care of by about 50 persons, in one Davis Cup performance. The Work Simplification approach worked well in both designing and featuring of the competition. It helped us to dig out experience and innovative ideas, thus to produce memos on lists of activities and process flow charts including all essential activities for the competition to run smoothly. This took place without any imposition, but resulted from the experiences of individuals trusted and involved. In the process, they/we all were teammates per topics, and I was the facilitating methodologist. Later on, the same notes were employed for preparation of a number of further competitions in tennis and skiing (including a part of the Winter Olympic Games in Sarajevo 1984). The same experience has later on become also an essential basis for my work with innovative teams in enterprises. (Unfortunately, we have never been able to have a contract in governmental offices.)

In 1981, I was a Fullbright visiting professor in the USA for four months. I devoted my free time to Work Simplification. As a development economist (by M.A.) with a doctorate in Systems Science, I believed that Mogensen's philosophy could lead the way to change, or at least positively impact, Yugoslavia's negative economic trends. The country was then lagging behind other countries in West Europe (it was no member of the Soviet Bloc since 1948 and different from it and from the West for its attempt to have self-management, on the surface, at least). It was plunging deeper and deeper into a crisis of international competitiveness. It needed ideas to resurrect itself. The "Mogensen way" offered a possible solution.

A country run by more or less the same persons in government and party bureaucracy for too long was unable to see such a way on its own. As we know from many analyses in the 1960s and 1970s, even in the USA which used to be a role model for many things in Slovenia, the centralistic paradigms of management were prevailing over the decentralistic models in the name of savings, consolidation, avoiding the unnecessary duplication of work, etc. (Reich, 1984; Creech, 1994). Such a centralization of management was not friendly to the application of Work Simplification or self-management or any other empowerment of subordinates, including work teams. On the other hand, the general level of democratization was growing in Slovenia, so did the general level of education, urbanization of population etc., which was making the deployed precepts of governing less and less useful.

Today we can even find out that Yugoslavia's decline and ultimate disintegration was not caused by diversity of its (over 30) nationalities, or ethnic issues, but rather by the lack of modernization of attitudes at the core of the ruling bureaucracy, especially the one in federal bodies and the Army. Their power used to lay in their possibility and ability to redistribute existing resources.[3] They did not care for the (more demanding) support and enhancement of creation of new resources through innovation. It would require the bureaucracy to give up a lot of power if it hoped to free the creativity of the 'lower levels'. Moreover, there was growing disparity between the people who were becoming better educated (and were hence inclined to do work more creatively) than before and/or in early Tito's times, on one hand, and the state, army and political bureaucracy.[4] It might have been just an example of what Creech puts: "There is a permanent fight between those who want to do the work, and those who want to prevent them from doing it in a wrong way." The real economic consequence was a chronic misuse of human resources, and ultimately the country's disintegration. In economic terms, instead of a governmental support to the transition from a suppliers market to a buyers market, a state supported suppliers market was reinforced.[5] The few followers of Mogensen as well as the few other organizational development persons and (not so very few) democratic individuals, on the other hand, realized it was time for more people to be empowered to use their creativity. It would be beneficial to themselves, their organizations, and their country, if they could innovate, make full use of the workers' ability to improve the way of doing their job.[6] The Mogensen philosophy made great sense to me in terms of its own, as well as in terms of my understanding of the self-management model on the basis of systems thinking. I did not see a tool of political abuse of people in self-management, on this basis, but rather a means for digging out human creativity and cooperation in order to help democracy develop as a means toward holism, innovation and prosperity. (Mulej, 1981) I found Mogy's work also a tool of enhancing creativity (like self-management in Japan), rather than of bluffing people (which was actually being done by the fictitious self-management in Yugoslavia), and I wanted to take advantage of both of them for the benefit of my fellow country/wo/men.

In 1981, immediately after returning from the USA, I had my first chance to practically use what I learned and developed from Work Simplification (and other sources mentioned). I call it USOMID as the Slovene acronym for "Creative Cooperation of the Many." It worked quite well. But it needed a long time to be more broadly accepted. Like every innovative idea, it came across obstacles called the established habits/culture, which were also objectively supported by the suppliers market. Hence, it actually was imposed by us (and our supporters such as The Chamber of Economy of Slovenia). It was much easier to be contracted for courses and seminars than for practical work at changing the organizational habits. We would support their own effort aiming at improvement and other types of innovation by USOMID. Eventually, my group developed to six full time associates (plus me as their part time mentor). In 1989, we dismissed our group, because I had new duties at my university and had no more time to support the group. My group members became managers, or internal or independent consultants.

With some of them, we are resuming the work now again. After becoming independent, in 1991, Slovenia had to pay too much attention to the legal aspect of its transition for old and new companies to have time, energy, and interest in work teams, etc. Too many new entrepreneurs and managers surfaced and too many small companies were established anew or from parts of the old ones for the bosses not to think that they had to depend on themselves rather then on their subordinates, at least for the time being. But in January 1996 an agreement was signed by 20 plus nongovernment organizations, including the Slovene Academy of Sciences and Arts, both Universities, Chamber of Economy, and several professional societies such as Engineers, Inventors etc., determined to share effort for Slovenia to become an Innovative Society. At the moment, in May 1998, this agreement is rather a piece of forgotten paper than causing activities. But they are taking place anyway, the infrastructure has emerged, competition presses for quality and hence for innovation).

In 1983, again at the mediation of Dr. Massey, Dr. Don Cole of the Organizational Development Institute in Cleveland, Ohio, invited me to address his Third Organizational Development World Congress in Dubrovnik, Croatia (part of Yugoslavia at the time, too). I was found to be an organizational development person before I knew what it was. Since then I have learned about organizational development and inserted my own ideas alongside with those contained in Mogy's Work Simplification program. I joined the International Organizational Development Association (IODA) in 1985 and was chair of its small chapter in Slovenia.

Over the years, the ideas and experiences continued to evolve. We have helped generate many innovations in companies around Yugoslavia resulting in tremendous savings. (If all organizations in Yugoslavia made one third of the average result of our client companies, all international and internal debts of Yugoslavia could be paid off in two years. The hidden capital - the creativity of the many - was poorly employed, unfortunately their lives remained rather poor with no real need.) The common denominator of our results was that we "modernized" attitudes, so to speak, and influenced the managerial and workers behavior in organizational development style. We found that change management begins with *innovation of management*, only afterwards innovation management and innovation can result. Work teams, called USOMID circles in our version, have been a usual part of our consulting work. Now-a-days they are here and there integrated into the efforts of Slovene companies to gain the ISO 9000 certificates, although not in all cases. Companies that involve some +30% of employed persons already possess this international certificate of high quality of business, in Slovenia, in May 1998. We still have no right to be satisfied. Centocratics are still in power a lot, like all around the world. They tend to love power more than other individuals, and have a quite free way to it, in the modern democratic times, like they have had earlier, or even more because there are many more organizations around, about 230,000 compared to less than 20,000 of 1989, in Slovenia; a big majority are small private companies. The creativity of subordinates is still underused.

Inclusion of Innovation into the Constitution of Slovenia: An Impact of Work Simplification

Yugoslavia consisted of six Socialist Republics. In the 1980s, Slovenia was the only one to grant "entry to political bodies and impacts" to advocates of organizational development and innovation of management, such as myself.[7] A member of the Presidency (a collective president) of Slovenia was then even officially (although not publicly) delegated the duty to support innovating in the Republic's policy. In March 1990, the last period before the legal switch of Slovenia to a many-party political democracy and then to becoming a country of its own after Yugoslavia's disintegration in 1991, the Slovene Constitution was amended. By one amendment the notion of socialism was omitted from the official name of the Republic of Slovenia. The second one made the phrase "innovation-based economy" become a constitutional term. These changes are two sides of the same coin. This happened only in Slovenia, too, no other Yugoslav republic, nor Yugoslavia as a country (there have always been constitutions per all six republics and one for the entire country). In the independent Slovenia's constitution, the word "innovation" no longer appears, but its preconditions do (Ovin & Borak, 1997).

Thus, Allan Mogensen, a key player in the development of organizational development in the USA and Japan, had his impact, through influence of his Work Simplification, through our personal contact and through his and my friendship with Dr. Robert Massey, in the development of Slovenia toward a modern and free European country. Mogy and organizational development were vital (although indirect) elements in the transformation of Slovenia after seven decades of a rigid rule imposed by Kingdom Yugoslavia (1918-1941), Hitler's and Mussolini's occupation (1941-45) and Tito (1945-1991). Of course, the previous centuries of Habsburg's Austria was no better; then the economy was based on the tradition of agriculture and handicraft rather than industries of an innovative type. There was no buyers market's prevalence, in general.[8]

Since 1981, many students, while pursuing B.A., M.A., MBA, and Ph.D. degrees at the University of Maribor in Slovenia have studied Systems Thinking, Innovation and organizational development as a part of their curricula. We also offer an M.A. in innovation management, since 1995. Work teams are a permanent part of our teaching, students have to write some of their papers in small teams in at least one course per year. In recent years, similar courses have been offered to students of economics, social sciences, traffic, and sports, which is still much less than needed.[9]

At this moment, the major part of changes of an organizational development type takes place under the flag of Total Quality Management, Reengineering, and Project Management, less with USOMID directly. A driver of the most part is the aim of gaining the ISO 9000 certificate in order to be an internationally acceptable business partner. But it is my fear, that given the "centocratic" tradition and the frequent complacency of the old and new entrepreneurs and managers, it might well be that formalities rather than the usual organizational development and Mogy kind of changes will take place (like in other countries). In the ISO 9000 there is no explicit aim of "innovation," although a total or any better quality can no way be attained without both non-technological and technological innovation. Those who confine their understanding of "innovation" to the technological one only (unlike documents of OECD, WIPO and EU), are hardly able to see the historic importance of the non-technological innovation proven critical by economic historians Rosenberg and Birdzell (1986).

The business's care for Suggestion System (as a method of incremental innovation) has diminished a lot, too. Some of the newly passed legislation is supportive again. Innovation also entered the new law on support for an accelerated development of the lagging regions of Slovenia. The most important support for creativity enhancement and employment, including work teams method, comes from a relatively high openness of the Slovene economy to international competition and markets. Slovenia is too small to be a closed-in economy, and has learned very well how short-sighted such a policy would be, in its own earlier experience.[10]

Much work remains to be done, like in other countries. Mogy's influence is still not sufficiently strong and broad (as Tom Peters, Bill Creech and many others demonstrate in other cases, too; see: Peters 1997).

Concluding Remarks

In terms of work teams history, Alan Mogensen is important for two basic reasons. First, he pioneered a major field of work teams' *work contents*: improving their members' own daily work practices by both technological and non-technological innovation; according to experience, these innovations are incremental improvements of work processes, mostly, but not exclusively. Success follows and produces a better appreciation of workers' creativity, causes their moral and self-esteem to grow, as well as their personal and their bosses' commitment to have a natural basis.

Second, he showed that the basic precondition for such organizational and business results is an innovation in the inherited managerial style, which general Creech (1994) calls the transition from managership to leadership. I translate his words as the *transition from a commanding management style to a cooperative one.*

It is important, as this brief presentation shows, that Alan Mogensen (Mogy), Father of Work Simplification, be remembered and honored for his role in making Organizational Development, including work teams, a beneficial tool for many people. It is also or even more important to remember that "centocracies" are still killing rather than supporting and reinforcing the development and beneficial use of creativity of many, especially lower-level citizens and workers. The Organizational Development profession must hence keep being a movement toward democracy in management and on the shop floor, not only in politics, general economics, and life in local communities and families. Hence, work teams must keep developing as a type of organizational development effort.

Acknowledgements

I wish to thank Dr. Robert Massey and Rosario "Zip" Rausa for their great help in my work on this contribution, as well as over many years in general.

Notes

1. The book is available from Jim Denyes at Idea Associates, 1241 Kingsway Drive, Chesapeake, VA 23320, (804) 445-8778.

2. Legally, self-management was introduced after Tito's breaking away from Stalin in 1948. It became constitutional in 1953 and developed further in constitutional changes of 1963 and 1974.

3. It is well known that Yugoslavia did not deploy the direct commanding central planning model like the Soviet block countries did, but its federal government kept control over essential prices, foreign currency funds, imports and money emission. Market was a constitutional term since 1963, but legislation supportive of it such as the one making entrepreneurship, deregulation, demonopolisation, and privatization

possible and normal, started being passed only 25 years later. This was too late for the country to survive.

4. For the sake of honesty, one must admit, that the international and local Yugoslav knowledge and science of economic theory has been based on Keyness rather than Schumpeter. Keyness does not ascribe any importance to innovation. See Rihtaric 1997, and earlier.

5. Closed border should provide jobs, economic development, etc., but without innovation and making room for the individual creativity to be used for innovation this aim is unattainable. Bureaucracy was obviously unable to perceive this fact. They were also unable and unwilling to see what they were causing. At the universities, there were only two graduate courses in development economics, none speaking of innovation management. Our book *Innovative Business*, 1987, *Gospodarski vestnik Ljubljana* (in Slovene) was the first one. So was our book on linking creative cooperation, systems thinking, and marketing, called *Creative Cooperation from Conceptualization to Successful Marketing of a Product*, 1985, *Gospodarski vestnik, Ljubljana* (in Slovene).

6. It was only in Slovenia, that professionals supportive of innovation were able to receive public support from the League of Communists which performed its conference *The Way toward an Innovative Society* and published proceedings, in 1984. It was only in Slovenia, that the parliament of the Republic passed a resolution supportive of innovation, in 1985 and later on legislation on this basis. A strong Quality Control Circles movement followed, but not for very long, since it was not sufficiently needed by the business policy of the enterprises in the current state-supported suppliers market.

7. It was only in Slovenia, in late 1980s, that the head of the Inventors Association was made a member of the Republican Assembly's Commission for the New Constitution.

8. Of course, Austria had Maria Theresia and her son Joseph as emperors who brought so much new that their period is called the enlightened absolutism. In basic socio-economic contents, Tito's period was so, too. The areas of Yugoslavia who never had lived under Austria, experienced this governmental way of accelerating their transition from a pre-industrial to a modern kind of life and work under Tito for the first time, Slovenia for the second time. This also explains why it was easier for us to have echoed with USOMID in Slovenia that in other republics. It also says a lot about the socio-economic reasons for Yugoslavia's falling apart: the developmental differences were too big for the same governmental measure to suit all areas.

9. The consideration of topics on innovation, systems thinking, teamwork and organizational development is found to be poor also by bodies of the European Union. See Miege & Mahieux, 1989; Green Paper on Innovation, 1995; Green Paper on Living in Information Society, 1996.

10. Currently, Slovenia exports beyond 70% of its industrial products, mostly to European Union countries. Details reach beyond the topic of this book.

References

Creech, B. (1994). *The five pillars of TQM: How to make total quality management work for you.* Dutton, NY: Truman Talley Books.

Devetak, G., & Mulej, M. (1985). *Ustvarjalno sodelovanje od zasnove do uspesne prodaje izdelka [Creative cooperation from conceptualization to successful marketing of a product].* Gospodarski vestnik, Ljubljana

Dyck, R., Mulej, M. and coauthors (1998). *Self-transformation of the forgotten four-fifths.* Dubuque, IA: Kendall/Hunt.

Editorial (1994, Oct. 4). Firms ask worker who make the products to write the how-to manuals. *The Wall Street Journal*, 1.

European Union (1995). *Green paper on innovation.* Commissions of the European Union.

European Union (1996). *Green paper on living in an information society: People first.* Commissions of the European Union.

Gabrijelcic, J. (1993). *Organizacijski razvoj kot vir nevidnega kapitala [Organizational Development as a source of the invisible capital].* Dissertation, University of Maribor, School of Business and Economics, Maribor, Slovenia

Gabrijelcic, J. (1995). *Od kakovosti k odlicnosti. Z organizacijskim razvojem [From quality to excellence by organizational development].* Dolenjska zalozba, Novo mesto, Slovenia

Graham, B. Jr., & Parvin, T. S. (1979). *The amazing oversight: Total participation for productivity.* New York: Amacom.

Henderson, R. I. (1985). *Compensation management: Rewarding performance.* Fourth Edition. Reston, VA: Reston Publishing Co., Inc. A Prentice-Hall Co.

League of Communists (1984). *Na poti v inovacijsko druzbo. Zbornik problemske konference [The way toward an innovative society].* Komunist, Ljubljana.

Lehrer, R. (1981). *Participative productivity and quality of work life.* Reston, VA: Prentice Hall Inc.

Lincoln, J. F. (1961). *A new approach to industrial economics.* New York: The Devin-Adair Company.

Lincoln, J. F. (1951). *Incentive management.* Cleveland, OH: Lincoln Electric Company.

Mogensen, A., Rausa, R. (1989). *Mogy: Father of work simplification an autobiography.* Chesapeake, VA: Idea Associates.

Mogensen, A., (Ed.) (1980). *Work simplification. executive conference material.* Lake Placid, NY.

Mueller, J., (1970). *Grundlagen der Systematischen Heuristik.* Dietz Verlag, Berlin

Mulej, M. (1974). *Dialekticna teorija sistemov [Dialectical systems theory].* Unpublished lecture to graduate students, University of Ljubljana, School of Physical Education

Mulej, M. (1976). Towards a dialectical systems theory. In R. Trappl (Ed.), *Proceedings of the third European meeting on cybernetics and systems research.* Austrian Cybernetics Society, Vienna

Mulej, M. (1979). *Ustvarjalno delo in dialekticna teorija sistemov [Creative work and dialectical systems theory].* Razvojni center Celje

Mulej, M. (1981). *O novem jugoslovanskem modelu druzbene integracije [On the new Yugoslav model of social integration].* Zalozba Obzorja, Maribor

Mulej, M., & Devetak, G. (1985). *Ustvarjalno sodelovanje od zasnove do uspesne prodaje izdelka [Creative cooperation from conceptualization to successful marketing of a product].* Gospodarski vestnik, Ljubljana

Mulej, M., et al. (1986). *Usposabljanje za ustvarjalnost. Metodologija USOMID [Training for creativity: The USOMID Methodology].* (4th rev. ed) Ekonomski Center Maribor

Mulej, M., et. al. (1987). *Inovativno poslovanje [Innovative Business].* Gospodarski vestnik, Ljubljana

Mulej, M., et al. (1992). *Teorije sistemov [Systems theories].* University of Maribor, School of Business and Economics, Maribor

Mulej, M., et al. (1994). *Inovacijski management, I. del: Inoviranje managementa [Innovation management: Part I innovation of management].* University of Maribor, School of Business and Economics, Maribor

Mulej, M. (1994). *Organizational development in Slovenia and beyond.* Paper to: NODN 1994 Conference, Baltimore, MD.

Mulej, M. (1998). *Mehke teorije sistemov [Soft systems theories].* University of Maribor, School of Business and Economics.

NYSE (1982). *People and productivity: A challenge to corporate America.* A Study from the N. Y. Stock Exchange Office of Economic Research. New York Stock Exchange, New York.

Ovin, R., & Borak, N., (Eds.) (1997). *Prehod in prestrukturiranje slovenskega gospodarstva. [Transition and restructuring of the Slovene economy].* Zveza ekonomistov Slovenije, Ljubljana.

Peters, T., & Waterman, R. (1982). *In search of excellence: Lessons from America's best-run companies.* New York: Harper and Row.

Peters, T. & Austin, N. (1985). *A passion for excellence.* New York: Random House.

Peters, T. (1997). *Innovation circle.* New York: A. Knopf.

Potter, K. (1980). *Circles guidelines.* Beaverton, OR: Tectronix.

Reich, R. (1984). *The next American frontier.* New York: Penguin Books.

Rihtaric, M. (1997). Paradoksi globalizacije (Keyness ali Schumpeter?). (Paradoxes of Globalization). *Nase gospodarstvo* (Maribor) Vol. 43, n. 1-2

Rosenberg, N., & Birdzell, L. E. (1986). *The past: How the west grew rich.* New York: Basic Books, Inc.

Tajlor, F. V. (1967). *Naucno upravljanje [Scientific management].* Izd. Pod. Rad, Beograd, Serbia, Yugoslavia

Ursic, D. (1993). *Inoviranje podjetja kot poslovno-organizacijskega sistema [Innovating of an enterprise as a business organizational system].* Dissertation, University of Maribor, School of Business and Economics, Maribor, Slovenia

Ursic, D. (1996). *Inoviranje podjetja [Enterprise innovating].* Studio Linea s.p., Maribor, Slovenia

Chapter 10

Modern Socio-Technology
Set by De Sitter

Jos Benders, Hans Doorewaard, and Erik Poutsma
Catholic University of Nijmegen, Nijmegen, The Netherlands

Abstract

Paradoxically, the notion of new work organizations has a long history, in particular in the Netherlands. To understand this, it is necessary to make a distinction between the accidental experiments with new forms of work, such as team-based working, on the one hand, and the acceptance of these ideas among the business community at large on the other. For at least since the 1960s, team-based working has been a central issue in workplace reform and is even older as an idea. However, it took a considerable period before the concept broke through, perhaps because for a long time it had the image of good for people but bad for business. However, for the last decade or so, probably on the wings of received understandings of highly efficient Japanese team-based organizations, team-based working has been and still is intensely advocated as an effective way of working that is sure to pay off handsomely.

The importance of team-based working has traditionally been stressed by proponents of the Dutch brand of socio-technical systems design, commonly referred to as Modern Socio-technology or MST. Emeritus professor Ulbo de Sitter, now *éminence grise*, is widely regarded as its founding father. As described below, MST resulted out of several decades of organizational renewal in practice and theory.

First, we describe the predecessors of the modern socio-technical approach in the Netherlands, focusing on experiments in the early sixties and seventies. The next sections deal with the historical development of modern socio-technology and the current state of the art, respectively. Conclusions are drawn after discussing contemporary theoretical developments and MST's diffusion.

Early Developments

As in other countries, throughout most of the twentieth century the majority of Dutch organizations were characterized by a high degree of division of labor. Throughout much of the century this was accepted as the only economically feasible way of organizing, but it had been criticized for its negative social consequences as early as the beginning of the century. Yet until 1960 such criticisms never resulted in actual changes. In that year, an experiment was started in Eindhoven at a television assembly plant of Philips, the large Dutch electronics company. The Philips researchers sought to investigate the impact of three different lay-outs on what was at that time called output,

M.M. Beyerlein (ed.), Work Teams: Past, Present and Future, 169–180.

quality and morale. The major invention was splitting a long assembly line into five segments, which were operated by better-structured groups of about 20 persons. In addition, whereas the original line had only one quality inspection station at its end which complicated feedback, each line segment had its own quality inspection station.

Compared to the long line, the new system led to shorter waiting times, to smaller balancing and system losses, and less disruptions caused by a lack of material supply. A more even production flow and the faster feedback improved quality. Morale in the new setting was compared to that in the original line and to that of smaller groups producing channel selectors. For most indicators, the score of the segmented line was in between the scores of the other two production settings (Van Beek, 1964).

These positive findings had a not to be underestimated influence on the development of so-called work structuring within Philips. The term work structuring was introduced in 1963 (Fontijne, 1970, p. 32) and covered a large variety of changes in the conventional organization designs. About 1965 the importance of work structuring became more officially recognized at the corporate level, job design experiments began to flourish and "gradually the practical notion became more influenced by the theoretical notions and ideas. The theoretical framework was eclectic in character; ideas from different schools such as the orthodox job enrichment school, the socio-technical system approach and organizational development school were included", according to Den Hertog (1979, p. 152). By 1968, at least 36 experiments at Philips had been carried out. In 1972, Philips' work structuring activities were assessed critically by the company's Central Workers' Council (a works' council represents employees, is legally compulsory for companies as of a minimum size, and is composed of employees who are elected). It was concluded that the movement had scarcely come off the ground, only involving 3.5 per cent of Dutch Philips workers, and that change projects were often restricted to small and isolated parts of organizations. However, the Council had a favorable opinion about the experiments, and recommended so-called `preventive work structuring', meaning to apply these ideas to the design of new production systems, plants and technical systems, which is especially relevant in case of heavily mechanized work settings. Den Hertog (1979) mentions some measures to stimulate work structuring after 1972, including:

1. Social marketing: the stimulation of work structuring by corporate management.
2. An attempt to approach the organization as a whole in contrast to the limited scope of former experiments.
3. Increased worker participation.
4. Developing preventive work structuring.

Apart from the Philips experiments, other experiments with new work forms were carried out in the 1960s. As in the Philips cases, these experiments aimed both at organizational goals and/or workers' interests. Kuipers (1972) mentions 37 cases of task structuring, a term which he uses as a synonym for work structuring. The approach spread beyond Philips and the electronics industry, as evidenced by the fact 18 out of these 37 cases were not in that sector. Kuipers' data were collected between September 1969 and August 1971, and refer to task structuring and work consultation. Unfortunately, both the description of the data as well as the analysis are superficial, although the results were comparable to those of Philips.

The Protestant employers union VPCW initiated six experiments among its members. These were motivated by "the thought, that responsibility in its religious/ethical meaning is a factor of sufficient importance to justify experiments with a greater responsibility" (Ramondt, 1968, p. 13), rather than by changing business conditions, as was the case with work structuring. Ultimately, only two of the six organizations involved managed to increase employee responsibility by giving them more control over their own work situation. In one organization, the result was not lasting while in the remaining three cases the reform attempts were stopped within a few months. Overall, the results were disappointing, both from organizational and ideological points of view. "The process has a sobering effect on those who expect that idealistic motives - more humane work relations - as such can induce organizational change"(Ramondt, 1974, p. 110).

Ramondt (1974, p. 76-79) also describes an experiment at the Pernis oil refinery of Chevron. In several departments, tasks of different natures were added to functions. Management reported favorable results with respect to productivity, organizational transparency and absenteeism. Staff was cut back by 49 per cent. The experiment claimed to be motivated by McGregor's theory, but Ramondt dismisses this idea as a social desirable, ex post legitimization of a reorganization, and motivated by economic concerns.

Towards Modern Socio-Technology

The term socio-technical was first used in The Netherlands in 1965, when a field experiment was carried out in the cheque-clearing department of a large bank. Main researcher Hans van Beinum had been working at the London-based Tavistock Institute, so that socio-technical notions came to influence the 1965 experiment.

The department's main task was clearing large numbers of cheques. An important reason for conducting the experiment was the tight labor market. Only by the creation of complex tasks instead of the former simple jobs one expected to be able to attract new workers for the department. Joint optimization of the technical and social system was assumed to lead to the most effective organization. The old organization was characterized by individual, independent and homogeneous tasks, and task specialization. Employees were not able to take over each other's work, and close supervision was felt to be necessary. Four changes were implemented: group tasks, task variation, promoting the knowledge about work coherence, and giving more responsibility. The results were that job satisfaction, work morale, and productivity increased. It remains unclear whether the rising productivity can be attributed to the experiment, as only one (out of two) of the control groups showed a similar development (Van Beinum, Van Gils and Verhagen, 1968). Table 1 summarizes the basic assumptions of this approach.

The previous organization was seen as too complex: the high division of labor not only resulted in simple work, but also required much co-ordination and supervision, and hence additional sub-units. By forming groups and assigning them more responsibility, the organization could become simpler.

Allegro's study (1973) in a textile mill is influenced both by the ideas of the traditional socio-technical approach and by emerging perspectives of organizational development. Allegro found out that after two and a half years, 40 employees worked in "small group tasks for 2 persons [...] which had the characteristics of an autonomous

TABLE 1. Summary of field experiment in check clearing department

Old System	New System
Simple individual tasks	Complex task groups
Complex organization	Simple organization
External control	Internal control

Source: Van Beinum, Van Gils and Verhagen, 1968, p. 46. Used with permission.

group task'. Productivity had not decreased, employee involvement had increased, and absenteeism was down. These changes were attributed to the qualifications of the newly hired personnel, as well as to the new policy of creating complex jobs. "However, the most important result seemed to be that the organization is actively involved in a learning process" (Allegro, 1973, p. 210).

Evaluating the 1960s and 1970s

Although many experiments had been conducted in the 1960s and 1970s, these failed to break through. When at the end of the 1970s Huijgen was looking for firms that actively pursued a policy to break way with the existing ways of organizing, he only found two, a very small number given that his research focused on branches that were considered to face major problems in this respect (1984, p. 13-14). Statistical surveys conducted around 1980 point in the same direction, showing that there were few semi-autonomous workgroups (Loontechnische Dienst, 1979; Muffels, Heinen and Van Mil 1982). Despite the facts that - all in all - some 54 experiments had been conducted within Philips (Den Hertog, 1975, p. 107), and that repeated efforts were made to revitalize and extend the approach, ultimately the movement of work structuring has not taken root (Dankbaar, 1990, p. 14). Management interest in new forms of work organization had increased, but remained selective. The approaches used were meant to mitigate negative effects of conventional organization structures. Projects tended to be small-scale, and were generally initiated by management.

More qualitative judgements adopted a pessimistic tone as well. Van Hoof and Huiskamp (1989) found that from the point of industrial democracy the results were meagre:

> "Only the creation of (semi-) autonomous groups (and to an ever more limited degree, job enrichment) contributed to a greater influence of workers on their own work. However, this autonomy was generally exercised within strict limits." (p. 158)

But an evaluation of the 1960s and 1970s is complicated because of the relationship between economic and organizational goals on the one hand, and social goals on the other. The very first Philips-experiment (Van Beek, 1964) had already included both types of goals, but it appears as if in the course of time social goals came to dominate. Especially in the 1970s the buzzwords were quality of work and humanization of work. The debate focused more than ever on job content, job requirements and working conditions (Van Hoof and Huiskamp, 1989, p. 159), and according to Pot et al., "work structuring failed due to single sided interest for quality of working life" (1991, p.

23-24). Especially if this interest was seen by managers as motivated solely by ethical rather than by economic concerns, it is not surprising that work structuring ultimately failed. Although Ramondt stated that at Philips organizational goals were more or less met (1974, p. 48-76), work structuring's success in these terms was apparently not sufficient to keep the approach alive within the company, let alone elsewhere. In conclusion: neither from an economic nor from a social perspective had large-scale results been reached.

However, indirectly the experiments of the 1960s and 1970s were important for setting the scene for what was to come. Theoretically, they had been informed by different streams of thought, among which socio-technical work. Work structuring, pioneered within Philips and later used elsewhere, became the overarching label, yet there had never been a solid theoretical background, which was felt as a major impediment.

Modern Socio-Technology

At the beginning of the 1970s the distinction between socio-technical work and work structuring was blurred. Even De Sitter (see box 1 for some personal details), who was to become the leading exponent of Dutch socio-technical thinking, called work structuring an "applied form of socio-technique" (1974a, p. 65). In his Ph.D.-thesis, he found that the leadership style was not so much a personal characteristic of leaders, but instead to an important extent dependent on the organization structure. Both social leadership, which allows for changing the rules of the game, and instrumental leadership, which stresses obeying existing rules, proved to be dependent on structural characteristics: if the workload could be dealt with within predetermined rules, instrumental leadership would suffice, but if employees could not cope with the workload within such rules, one finds social leadership (De Sitter, 1995). In his later work, structural characteristics are constantly emphasized, for which cybernetics and social systems theory provided vital insights.

After his appointment in 1970 as a full professor at the Eindhoven University of Technology, De Sitter and his associates started working on developing a theoretical approach (De Sitter 1974a and 1974b; Van der Zwaan, 1975) for what was initially called *sociotechniek* and defined as:

> “the study and explanation of the manner in which both the technical strumentation and the division of labor are related to environmental conditions and the operation, capacity and output of production systems, as well as the application of this analytical insight into the design of production systems.” (De Sitter, 1974a, p. 81).

De Sitter's hallmark study *Op Weg naar Nieuwe Fabrieken en Kantoren* (*On the Road towards New Factories and Offices*; 1981) brought the approach to the attention of a large public, and can be seen as a catalyst for the development of Dutch socio-technical thinking. In it, extensive use was made of Swedish (and German) engineering and organizational design traditions (cf. De Sitter, Den Hertog and Dankbaar, 1997: 499-500). In the 1970s, De Sitter repeatedly visited his native Sweden, where he became well-acquainted with the organizational renewal programs set up by the Swedish Employers' Confederation SAF. De Sitter even translated two summarizing books from Swedish into Dutch (De Sitter, 1975; Agurén, Edgren and De Sitter, 1982).

Among others, these books stressed the way different manufacturing operations were combined into physical layouts (see Figure 1 with the three different basic structures; also see Engström's contribution in this volume).

Professor Ulbo de Sitter

Ulbo de Sitter was born on April 2, 1930 in Jönköping, Sweden. Both his grandfather and father were professors in astronomy and geology respectively. Although raised in an intellectual environment (rumor has it that he once sat on Einstein's lap), he de Sitter began his career as a machinist on merchant ships. After his military service, he began his studies and accepted his first research job in 1962 with the Dutch PTT (national mail and telecom company). From 1966 till 1970, he worked at the University of Amsterdam, where he completed his PhD-thesis on leadership. As of 1970, he has been a full professor, subsequently at the Eindhoven University of Technology, the University of Limburg and the University of Nijmegen, from where he retired in 1995.

As a ship's mechanic, De Sitter was confronted with the hierarchical chain of command. Detailed company prescriptions prevented creating safe working conditions at sea. He called such experiences "the concrete start of a study in sociology," which in his view has to be `design-oriented,' i.e. it must be actively engaged in improving social condtions.

Sources: Van Eijnatten and Van der Zwaan (1995); De Sitter (1995)

At that time, the functional structure, which organizes operations by type, and the line structure, in which operations are organized sequentially along the product flow, were increasingly being criticized for having negative consequences on organizational outcomes and human well-being. In the mid-1970s, Burbidge's work on group technology offered an alternative for the functional structure, which often leads to substantial coordination difficulties and hence losses (see Benders and Badham in this volume for a more elaborate discussion). In the same period, Wild (1975) criticized line structures for various inefficiencies such as system and balance losses. In addition, line structures have almost traditionally been viewed as detrimental for worker well-being. In the Netherlands, like De Sitter, Jan in 't Veld advocated such ideas in *Organisatie-structuur en arbeidsplaats* (1981); the book had an engineering focus, and became an important source of inspiration for socio-technical proponents.

In *Op Weg naar Nieuwe Fabrieken en Kantoren* De Sitter combined such engineering insights with social points of view. De Sitter paid much attention to Karasek's views on job design (1979) and the notion of job decision latitude, which are still cornerstones of Modern Socio-technology (MST). Essentially, MST equates quality of working life with job decision latitude (*regelcapaciteit* in Dutch), which is seen as an objective view of quality of working life in the sense that it can be assessed by measuring job attributes rather than asking employees how they feel about their work, which is a subjective approach. However, job decision latitude alone does not suffice: there must be something to make decisions about, i.e. the working situation must pose challenging job demands to the job holder. Only jobs that combine a sufficiently high job decision latitude with such job demands reduce strain and enhance learning (Karasek, 1979).

Both job decision latitude and production structures are expressions of more fundamental insights derived from cybernetics and systems theory, which forms the core of the scientific basis of MST. MST sees work stations as interrelated elements in a network. Often due to external changes, disturbances and interferences occur which need to be resolved. This requires local capacity to control, so appropriate interactions can be selected to solve distrubances. This self-organization is necessary for effective problem solving. Furthermore, following Ashby's law of requisite variety, a system's possibilities for control must match the need for control due to environmental changes.

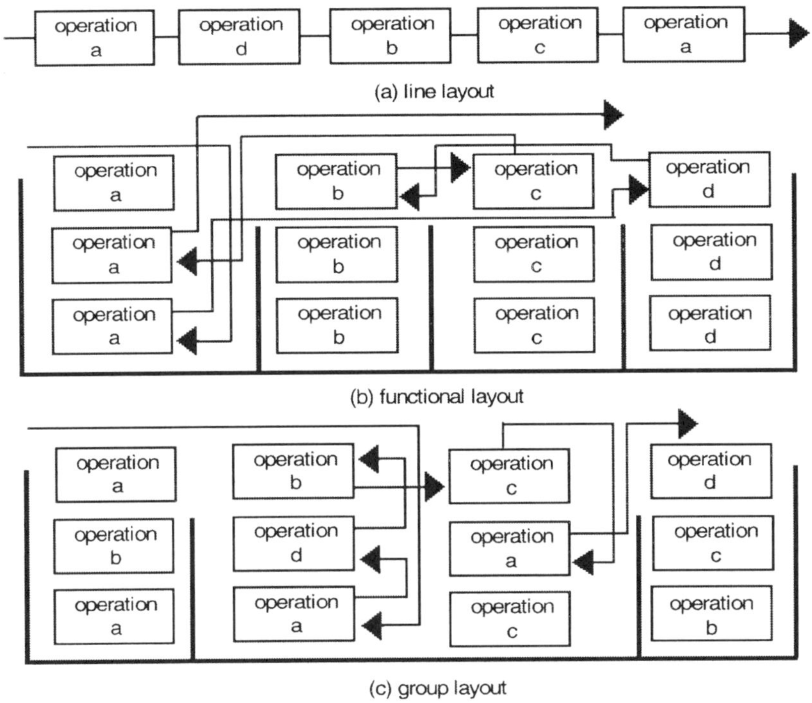

Figure 1. Basic Forms of Layout

In the case of a high degree of division of labor, there are many elements and hence interrelations. Together these form a complicated network that is not only sensitive to disturbances, but at the same time has few possibilities to deal locally with these disturbances. Thus, the more complex the organization, the harder it is to control. This affects organizational effectiveness negatively, and at the same time means that job holders have little control over their own work. From this perspective, at the core of the problem of the functional structure is the large number of possible interactions and relations between the workstations making it hard to control, whereas the line structure is problematic for its tight couplings between elements, leading to a high sensitivity for disturbances. In other words: the functional structure is too complex, and the line structure has little control capacity.

Whereas *Op Weg naar Nieuwe Fabrieken en Kantoren* can be seen as the diagnosis of what was wrong in Dutch factories and offices, the follow-up study *Het flexibele bedrijf* (The Flexible Company; 1986), written by De Sitter and a large number of associates under the name "Groep Sociotechniek", provided some recipes and solutions. In 1994, at the end of his academic career, De Sitter summarized his work in *Synergetisch produceren* (*Producing Synergetically*), published in 1994.

Design Theory

MST's conceptual foundation underlies a worked-out design methodology. This consists of a number of steps, which have to be followed subsequently. Figure 2 is a visual display of MST's design process.

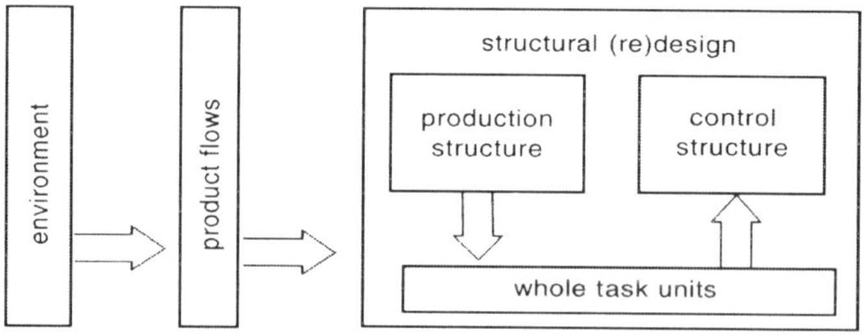

Figure 2. The Design Process in Modern Socio-Technology

The first step is analyzing the environment, which has to result in a list of requirements or design criteria that the new organization has to meet. These include market objectives, but other criteria such as the quality of working life and labor relations may also be on the list. The next step involves analyzing the flow patterns of the products to be made, which serves as input for designing the production structure, first roughly and then in detail. This involves (semi-)autonomous production units creating via parallellization (making parallel production flows) and segmentation (splitting up production flows). These production units are operated by so-called whole task - groups. The design of the control structure starts by allocate control tasks to the lowest possible level: first workstations, then whole task-groups, and only then to higher hierarchical levels. So-called operational groups, which combine several support and line functions, may be created to assist a number of whole task-groups. Such operational groups would typically include maintenance and quality control specialists.

Contemporary Theoretical Developments

MST provides a number of design principles and a design methodology. Applying MST expertise in practice inevitably leads to all the difficulties inherent in organizational change. Whereas Allegro (see above) already emphasized the importance of attention for organizational change in 1973, the articulation of a detailed design methodology appears to have worked in the opposite direction, and MST has been criticized for being an expert-driven approach, paying insufficient attention to employee participation in developing and implementing new organization designs (cf. Huijgen and Pot, 1995). Van Eijnatten's history of the development of socio-technical thought (1993), which received considerable attention in the Dutch academic community, shows that early socio-technical work inspired the development of socio-technical approaches in other countries, most notably in Sweden and Australia (see Emery's contribution in this volume). However, such socio-technically-informed approaches tend to see expert knowledge as undesirable as it would distort the participative character of the design process. Informed by such writings and practical experiences several Dutch authors try to reconcile the expert and participative views (f.i. Fruytier, 1996). Whereas the importance of employee participation is uncontested, many different models circulate how to deal with it and no consensus about how to incorporate participation in designing and implementing new plans into MST has yet been arrived at. A recent development is the use of `roundtable' or `group' conferences, in which socio-technical facilitators work with large groups of organization members to design new structures in relatively short periods of time (Van Amelsvoort, 1996).

A second area of development concerns human resource issues, especially designing and implementing work teams, and performance and reward systems. Guidelines for the design, implementation, and development of teams were published by Van Amelsvoort and Scholtes (1994) in a booklet targeted at practitioners. Their team development model appears to be used widely and to have become somewhat of a standard in the Netherlands (Van Amelsvoort and Benders, 1996).

Although performance measurement and payment systems receive considerable attention in the mid-1990s, little seems to happen in practice. There are some experiments catching the originally American model of PROMES to teams by developing so-called goal matrices. These weight the scores on a number of performance criteria to calculate an overall performance score.

In addition, several companies are experimenting with new payment systems (Simonse, Scholtes and Van Amelsvoort, 1995). Skill-based wage systems, which stimulate employees to develop their skills, appear to be gaining some popularity. Linking wages to performance, however, is still a sensitive topic. Unions tend to be against it, especially at the team level. Van Amelsvoort and Scholtes recommend that the team bonus be a small part of total wages to foster the team spirit and cooperation within the team (1994, p. 39).

Whereas the importance of issues such as change management and HRM-practices is uncontested, there remains somewhat of a controversy whether or not these should be incorporated in socio-technical theory or in contrast should be seen as complementary. Other areas in which work is being done include the control structure and applying socio-technical thinking to product development.

Diffusion

Given that by the mid-1990s key socio-technical notions such as flow production and team-based working appear to be considered as proper rather than awkward and suspect ways of organizing, and that MST derived its insights from many sources, the question arises what this organization concept has to offer?

For practitioners, what matters is whether or not insights work in their particular settings (Eccles and Nohria, 1992). Although the MST failed to break through internationally, it is a proven concept in the Netherlands. Practitioners elsewhere may want to profit from these insights and put MST to their own tests. One particularly important point that other concepts promoting team-based working either neglect or underplay is the stress MST puts on the structural environment: these define the limits and therefore the opportunities for teams to work in, an insight for which De Sitter coined the term human resource mobilization (1994). Implementing teams has to start by looking at the organization.

Knowledge about socio-technical design is disseminated through various channels such as academic curricula (most notably at the universities of Eindhoven, Groningen and Nijmegen), consulting agencies, publications and conferences, and through change projects. De Sitter co-founded the foundation *Stichting NKWO* to provide socio-technical courses. As of 1985 several socio-technical consulting agencies were founded, among which *KOERS* and the *ST-Groep*.

In practice, socio-technical insights appear to be increasingly applied and, unlike the situation in the beginning of the 1980s, teams are no longer exceptions but, on the contrary, a model of good practice. Large and renowned companies such as DAF Trucks, Akzo Nobel and Philips are among its adopters. Nevertheless, there is still much work to be done in further diffusing it, not just by extending the approach by developing complementary views on issues such as employee participation, change management and HRM, but also by trying to increase its reputation and therefore legitimacy as an effective organization concept. MST is a well-grounded approach, which in some ways works to its disadvantage: the academic focus and theoretical underpinning make Dutch-language publications on MST often hard to read, and practitioners are easily put off by socio-technical jargon. This may have not only have been an important obstacle in MST's diffusion, but also have given it more of a stuffy image as an approach out of an ivory tower inhabited by societally engaged academics rather than that of a business approach to redesigning organizations. As of approximately 1993, the originally American concept of Business Process Reengineering (BPR) has become fashionable in the Netherlands, as well. This appears as somewhat of a surprise if one accepts the claim of MST adherents that BPR's basic ideas are roughly similar to those of MST, yet that BPR is less sophisticated as a design approach. BPR is thus typically commented on by MST adherents as some sound ideas, "which we have been applying for the last twenty years" (De Sitter, 1994: VIII). Yet, as Van Veen notes, BPR is mainly a consultancy product whereas MST has a firm basis in Dutch academia (1998: 52-53), making MST less vulnerable to the capriciousness which is characteristic for management fashions.

Conclusion

As shown above, MST did not develop in a vacuum. It built forth on theoretical work as well as field experiments. As early as 1960, the interconnectedness of organizational and work design and their consequences for organizational effectiveness had been recognized at Philips. Whereas many experiments followed under the title of work structuring, a coherent view on these issues did not start developing until De Sitter and his companions started their work on socio-technical design in the early 1970s. By combining insights from different technical and social sciences as well as practical experiences they worked out a systematic, integral approach to redesign organizations. This approach strongly stresses the production environment in which teams operate: these determine the conditions under which teams have to work. Unless the organization is designed properly, there is no use implementing teams.

What can we learn from this history of MST? Perhaps the most important lesson is that whereas it already takes a long time to work out such a design-oriented approach, it even takes longer to get it accepted. And even now, when its content is not disputed any more, the ideas are often implemented under another label. Thus, a well worked out theoretical foundation alone does not guarantee that an approach is picked up. It must also appear legitimate in the eyes of key organizational decision-makers. Unless they perceive an approach as attractive, it will not get adopted. MST adherents may claim that MST makes money, but these claims were and are not generally accepted. This point may have long been overlooked by the rational academics that founded and developed MST. Yet, the fact that De Sitter's book *Synergetisch produceren*, which summarizes his life's work, was awarded a prize for the best business book of 1994 by the National Association of Management Consultants, however, is an important recognition of his, and MST's, contribution to organizational design and may help in the future diffusion.

Acknowledgements

We are indebted to Pierre van Amelsvoort and Mike Beyerlein for their comments on earlier draft of this paper.

References

Agurén, S., J. Edgren and L.U. de Sitter (1982), *Nieuwe fabrieken*, the Hague: NIVE.

Allegro, J.T. (1973), Socio-technische organisatieontwikkeling, Leiden: Stenfert Kroese.

Dankbaar, B. (1990), *Prospects for Anthropocentric Production Systems in the Netherlands*, FAST-paper 256, Brussels: Commission of the European Communities.

den Hertog, J.F. (1975), *Werkstructurering*, Alphen aan de Rijn\Brussels: Samsom.

den Hertog, J.F. (1979), New Leads in Job Design: The Philips' Case, in: Davis, L. and J.C. Taylor (eds.), *Design of Jobs* (second edition), Santa Monica: Goodyear Publishing Company, pp. 148-160.

de Sitter, L.U. (1974a), Sociotechniek, *M&O*, 28(2), pp. 65-83.

de Sitter, L.U. (1974b), Sociotechniek 2; Aantekeningen bij een sociotechnisch model v7an een produktiesysteem, *M&O*, 28(3), pp. 163-176.

de Sitter, L.U. (1975), *Werkoverleg en werkstructurering in Zweden; Een verslag van 500 bedrijfsexperimenten op de werkvloer*, the Hague: NIVE.

de Sitter, L.U. (1981), *Op weg naar nieuwe fabrieken en kantoren*, Deventer: Kluwer.

de Sitter, L.U. (1994), *Synergetisch produceren; Human Resources Mobilisation in de produktie: een inleiding in de structuurbouw*, Assen: van Gorcum.

de Sitter, L.U. (1995), De onzichtbare hand, in: van Eijnatten, F.M. (ed.), *Als het maar stroomt! Ulbo de Sitter; Laveren tussen simpel en complex*, Assen: van Gorcum, pp. 121-138.

de Sitter, L.U., J.F. den Hertog and B. Dankbaar (1997), From Complex Organizations with Simple Jobs to Simple Organizations with Complex Jobs, *Human Relations*, 50(5), pp. 497-534.

Eccles, R.G. and N. Nohria (1992), *Beyond the Hype; Rediscovering the Essence of Management*, Boston: Harvard Business School Press.

Fontijne, J. (1970), Evolutie, experiment en evaluatie in de produktie-organisatie van een televisiefabriek, in: van Dijck, J.J.J., J.L.J.M. van der Does de Willebois and M.J.M. Daniëls (eds.), *Organiseren rondom mensen (Technologie, economie, autonomie)*, Leiden: Stenfert Kroese, pp. 32-42.

Fruytier, B. (1996), The Redesign Dialogue: Organizational Change and the Theory of Autopoietic Systems, *Economic and Industrial Democracy*, 17(3), pp. 327-358.

Groep Sociotechniek (1986), *Het flexibele bedrijf; Integrale aanpak van flexibiliteit, beheersbaarheid, kwaliteit van de arbeid en produktie-automatisering*, Deventer: Kluwer Bedrijfswetenschappen.

Huijgen, F. (1984), *Management en arbeidsbeleid*, Nijmegen: ITS.

Huijgen, F. and F.D. Pot (eds.) (1995), *Verklaren en ontwerpen van produktieprocessen : het debat over arbeidsprocesbenadering en sociotechniek*, Amsterdam: SISWO.

in't Veld, J. (1981), *Organisatiestructuur en arbeidsplaats; De organisatie van mensen en middelen; theorie en praktijk*, Amsterdam/Brussels: Elsevier.

Karasek, R.A. (1979), Job Demands, Job Decision Latitude and Mental Strain; Implications for Job Redesign, *Administrative Science Quarterly*, 24(2), pp. 285-308.

Kuipers, J.H. (1972), *Verantwoordelijkheidsverruiming in de direkte werksituatie*, Amsterdam\The Hague: SWI-VU\COP-SER.

Loontechnische Dienst (1979), *Werkoverleg en werkstructurering in Nederland 1978*, the Hague: Loontechnische Dienst.

Muffels, R., T. Heinen and G. van Mil (1982), *Werkoverleg en werkstructurering en de subsidieregeling arbeidsplaatsverbetering; Een onderzoek bij bedrijven met meer dan 100 personeelsleden*, Tilburg: IVA.

Pot, F.D., M.H.H. Peeters, P. van Amelsvoort and J. Middendorp (1991), *Functieverbetering en integraal ontwerpen; Richtlijnen voor het verbeteren van het aspect welzijn bij de arbeid in ontwerpprojecten*, NIPG publication 91.010, Leiden: NIPG-TNO.

Ramondt, J.J. (1968), *Verantwoordelijkheid in het werk: verslag van experimenten in zes industriële bedrijven*, Alphen aan den Rijn\Brussels: Samsom.

Ramondt, J. (1974), *Bedrijfsdemocratisering zonder arbeiders; Een evaluatie van ervaringen met werkoverleg en werkstructurering*, Alphen aan de Rijn\Brussels: Samsom.

Simonse, L., G. Scholtes and P. van Amelsvoort (1995), *Loont het?; Beoordelen en belonen van zelfsturende teams*, Vlijmen: ST-Groep.

van Amelsvoort, P. (1996), *Het programmeren en regisseren van veranderingsprocessen*, Vlijmen: ST-Groep.

van Amelsvoort, P. and J. Benders (1996), 'Team time; a model for developing self-directed work teams, *International Journal of Operations and Production Management*, 16(2), pp. 159-170.

van Amelsvoort, P. and G. Scholtes (1993), *Zelfsturende teams; Ontwerpen, invoeren, begeleiden*, Oss: ST-Groep.

van Beek, H.G. (1964), The Influence of Assembly Line Organization on Output, Quality and Morale, *Occupational Psychology*, 38(4-5), pp. 161-172.

van Beinum, H.J.J., M.R. van Gils and E.J. Verhagen (1968), *Taakontwerp en werkorganisatie; Een socio-technisch veldexperiment*, Leiden: NIPG-TNO.

van der Zwaan, A.H. (1975), The Socio-technical Systems Approach; A Critical Evaluation, *International Journal of Production Research*, 13(2), pp. 149-163.

van Eijnatten, F.M. (1993), *The Paradigm that Changed the Work Place*, Stockholm\Assen: Arbetslivscentrum\van Gorcum.

van Eijnatten, F.M. and A.H. van der Zwaan (1995), Werk en Leven van Ulbo de Sitter, in: van Eijnatten, F.M. (ed.), *Als het maar stroomt! Ulbo de Sitter; Laveren tussen simpel en complex*, Assen: van Gorcum, pp. 11-20.

van Hoof, J.J. and R. Huiskamp (1989), New Forms of Work Organization in the Netherlands, in: Grootings, P., B. Gustavsen and L Héthy (eds.), *New forms of work organization in Europe*, New Brunswick: Transaction Publishers, pp. 155-174.

van Hooft, M.C.G., P.J.L.M. van Amelsvoort and L.U de Sitter (1996), in: Hooft, M.C.G. van (ed.), *Synergetisch produceren in praktijk; Toepassingen van structuurbouw in industrie en dienstverlening*, Assen: Van Gorcum, pp. 7-24.

van Veen, K. van (1998), Een vergelijking tussen BPR en MST; Twee productieconcepten en hun context, *Bedrijfskunde*, 70(2), pp. 47-54.

Wild, R. (1975), On the selection of mass production systems, *International Journal of Production Research*, 13(5), pp. 443-461.

SECTION III.

DEVELOPING WORK TEAMS AROUND THE WORLD

Chapter 11

Work Teams in Australia

John Cordery
University of Western Australia, Nedlands, Perth, Western Australia

Abstract

This chapter provides a brief history of the development of team-based approaches to work organization within Australia over the past three decades. Early experiments with teams in the seventies are described, and factors leading to their limited success identified. The next decade is seen as a developmental phase, during which time organizations sought to develop the necessary skills and flexibility in the workforce, which would permit teams to flourish, and when innovative techniques for the management of productivity and quality were adopted. Finally, in recent years, an eclectic mix of quality movement-inspired management techniques and traditional team design has begun to bear fruit for many organizations, centering on the re-engineering of work processes and team empowerment.

Introduction

Australian industry was a late adopter of many of the behavioral and social science interventions used in other countries to address organizational problems and modify managerial practices. "Many Australian managers in the late sixties and early seventies were working in an industry climate which reinforced authoritarian attitudes and promoted hierarchical distinctions between managers and the managed, leaders and the led" (Griffiths, 1995, p. 14).

The history of team-based work organization in Australia over the past three decades is characterized by initial cautious experimentation, by frequent frustration and failure and, in more recent times, by a growing degree of comfortable success. The approach of this paper will be to characterize the history of the use of work teams within Australia over recent times by reference to particular examples, attempting to draw conclusions about the reasons underlying Australian organizations' experiences and to make predictions for the future. Three phases in the development of teamwork are identified, roughly corresponding with the past three decades. These are described as (a) experiments with participation and democracy, (b) Multi-skilling and productivity improvement, and (c) Re-engineered work processes and team empowerment.

M.M. Beyerlein (ed.), Work Teams: Past, Present and Future, 183–192.

Experiments with Participation and Industrial Democracy

Prior to 1970, it is generally asserted that Australian organizations had little experience with or interest in what we would now recognize as team-based work organization (Griffiths, 1995; Derber, 1970). Early in the decade, however, this situation began to change, influenced by three main factors. The first of these was the gradual diffusion of innovative perspectives on management and work organization within multi-national companies operating in Australia. Second, Australian academic researchers began to work with Australian organizations to set up experimental trials of new forms of work organization. Finally, formal institutional structures began to emerge to encourage the development of increased worker participation and industrial democracy, supported largely by governments and the trade union movement.

An early example of the diffusion of ideas within Australian subsidiaries of multinational companies, leading to the introduction of work teams occurred between 1972 and 1975 in several Australian plants owned and operated by the Netherlands-based Philips Industries (Dunphy, Andreatta & Timms, 1976). Throughout the 1960s, stimulated by the work of the Tavistock Institute of Human Relations, the parent company had experimented in its European operations with work structuring approaches. These frequently centered on the formation of small product teams containing vertically-loaded work roles. Thus it was in one Australian Philips plant, where 2-way radio equipment was manufactured, that an assembly line was replaced by teams responsible for assembling an entire product. Similar initiatives took place in an established cabinet factory and in a new color television manufacturing plant, following models of work organization then operating in Philips' European plants. Dunphy et al., (1976) reported that the new models of work organization were seen as contributing to substantial gains in efficiency, quality and profitability in all plants. They also reported that employees appeared to have positive attitudes to the changes in work organization and, though no direct evidence of employee job satisfaction was available, absenteeism in all plants was at historically low levels. The experimentation with teams at the Philips factories was however short-lived. Griffiths (1995) reports that Philips closed their factories, not because of problems with the new work structures, but following a reduction in tariff barriers and a resultant increase in competition from low cost manufacturing based in Asia.

Another early Australian teams experiment by a multinational corporation was that conducted at ICI Welvic in Melbourne (Andreatta, 1974; Robinson & McCarroll, 1976; Gibbons & McCarroll, 1978; Andreatta, 1981; Finnie, 1987). This PVC plant began operating in 1973, with its 13 operations employees organized into small semi-autonomous work groups from the outset. These teams operated without foremen, and were collectively responsible for a range of decisions, including determining shift rosters, organizing their work, housekeeping and initiating maintenance requests. Teams also participated in human resource management activities such as the selection and training of new operators, and in team-building sessions designed to improve production knowledge and to generate process improvement ideas (Finnie, 1987). Within three years the size of the operating workforce had grown to 21, operating continuous shifts and with the semi-autonomous team working still largely intact researchers reported general satisfaction on the part of employees and management with the team concept, steadily improving productivity and low absenteeism (Robinson & McCarroll, 1976; Andreatta, 1981). On the negative side. it was reported that team members were not highly motivated to carry out routine and mundane housekeeping activities, contributing to quality problems - of concern to management at a time of rapidly increasing competition.

Towards the end of the decade, researchers reported that a change in plant management, a downturn in the market, and continuing management concerns about communication, quality and housekeeping had led to some significant changes to the work organization and how the teams operated (Gibbons & McCarroll, 1978). Responding to the market, production in some areas had been curtailed and a strong push for improved quality initiated. This saw, amongst other things, the introduction of standard operating procedures, teams became directly responsible to the production planner, and formal job descriptions were developed. In addition, the plant manager instituted daily plant inspections, and assumed responsibility for recruiting new operators (Finnie, 1987). Not surprisingly, these responses were seen by operators as leading to a decline in the autonomy of the teams, and questions were raised about management's commitment to teaming (Finnie, 1987; Griffith, 1995). Despite this, teams continued at Welvic, and were still the basic form of work organization some 16 years following plant start-up. Finnie (1987) reported that, in 1986, quality and productivity issues were still of concern to management and had placed stress on the teams, ultimately leading to the appointment of additional supervisory and specialist technical support personnel and a perceived reduction in the teams' autonomy.

The long-term survival of teams at Welvic appears to have been the exception, rather than the rule as far as Australian organizations are concerned in the seventies. Even in another ICI plant (ICI Botany) early experiences with team-based work redesign ended in failure. The key to the persistence of Welvic's teams appears to be the ability of management to adapt the concept to suit changing market and economic conditions, despite the occasional conflict and resentment that this generated between teams and management.

The second major impetus for the development of work teams in the seventies occurred through the involvement of a number of key academic researchers concerned with the democratization of work. Particularly influential was the work of Fred Emery, whose concern with work democratization and experience with Scandinavian industrial democracy programs led to the development of the participant design workshop as a means of more readily diffusing an understanding of socio-technical work design concepts within organizations, and of freeing the work redesign process from an over-reliance on external consultants and experts. The work of Fred Emery is discussed in detail elsewhere in this volume, but suffice it to say here that his approach was adopted by a number of Australian organizations, such as CSR, ICI, ALCOA and Australia Post, and the semi-autonomous work group or self-managing team was a frequent conceptual outcome of these workshops. Other academic researchers who were influential in the advocacy of semi-autonomous work teams at this time included Dexter Dunphy and Hollis Peter.

The third avenue of support for team-based interventions at this time came from institutional programs, set up expressly to encourage forms of worker participation and industrial democracy. A number of the early experiments with teams in Australia were fostered and maintained by the desire of governments and unions to support such initiatives as model approaches to organizational management. The State Government of South Australia formed an Industrial Democracy Unit, soon to be followed by a Unit for the Quality of Working Life. Through its Working Environment Branch, the Australian Government's Department of Employment and Industrial Relations offered Employee Participation Research Grants to encourage research into forms of participation in decision-making which included participative teams. Illustrative of the type of project that this program encouraged is a study carried out in a South Australian food factory by researchers from Flinders University from 1975 to 1981 (O'Brien, 1983). Here workers in one section of the factory were formed into small teams which met over a period of six to identify and discuss work problems with management. In what was an early experiment with quality or process improvement teams, O'Brien (1987) reported that

> "...employees who attended the work groups rated them favorably. They felt on the whole that the work groups were useful, allowed them to communicate their problems, were enjoyable and improved their knowledge of the work of the section. However, only two out of three lines voted to adopt work groups, and of those lines which had work groups, only 40 per cent of employees attended one or more meetings...The groups were not extended to other sections of the factory because of production needs, limited managerial manpower, relatively poor employee responses, and the need to have a forum where cross-sectional problems could be discussed." (pp. 19-20)

By the end of the decade, the first flush of enthusiasm and support for semi-autonomous work groups and teams as a means of jointly promoting productivity, industrial democracy, and employee quality of working life had given way to feelings of frustration as initial experiments were seen to falter in the face of a number of pressures. Worsening economic conditions, changes to tariff regulations, and increased competition from other manufacturing nations in the region translated into increased managerial pressure for efficiency, quality and productivity (as illustrated in the case of ICI Welvic), pressure which led to the closure of some firms and to a retreat to traditional management practices in others. In reviewing Australian socio-technical systems-based teamwork interventions of the seventies, Griffith (1995) concludes:

> "These interventions were fragile, and were swamped within months or years by dominant organizational cultures that were static and hierarchical in nature.... where changes did result in productivity improvements, it was not long before these innovations gave way to more traditional work systems compatible with the dominant management mindsets." (p. 63)

Another reason that these interventions were frequently unable to survive pressures for productivity improvement arose from the nature of the Australian industrial relations system. First, an inflexible system of occupational and job demarcations enshrined in industry-level collective union-management agreements or "awards" acted as a barrier to effective teamwork, as well as impeding the development of new skills needed for team members to effectively respond to pressures for increased quality and efficiency. Second, the emphasis in work democratization shifted, away from more immediate forms of worker participation (e.g. job enrichment, semi-autonomous work groups) to more distant representative forms of participation (e.g. codetermination, joint consultative committees), reflecting both the preferences of peak union and management organizations and Australia's tradition of a highly "institutionalized" approach to industrial relations (Lansbury & Prideaux, 1987).

Multi-Skilling and Productivity Improvement

Despite these initial setbacks, early in the 1980s a number of Australian companies (many of them influenced by participant design seminars run by the Emerys through the Center for Continuing Education at the Australian National University)) began to seek solutions to the problems of flexibility, skill and productivity which had dogged earlier team experiments, in an attempt to ensure that the potential benefits of teamwork were more fully realized and lasting. These largely centered on, first, the development of firm-level representative structures and collective agreements which supported the erosion of traditional narrow job demarcations through "broad-banding" and multiskilling (Cordery, 1989) and, second, the development of productivity management techniques (such as TQM) which would provide the means for regulating and improving quality and efficiency within devolved work structures.

In the early 1980s, Woodlawn Mines was a pioneer of multiskilling as a pre-cursor to the introduction of semi-autonomous group working. Whereas in some of the early experiments with autonomous group working, rotation of tasks was constrained by the rigid system of job demarcations proscribed by industrial agreements or awards, Woodlawn Mines sought to set in place a number of arrangements which would facilitate the long-term viability of group work. First, a collective agreement was reached with the three unions on site which limited the number of job demarcations which existed, and which provided a monetary incentive for employees to broaden the range of skills they possessed and used on the job. Second, the roles of the traditional mine foreman and supervisor were replaced by that of a shift coordinator in the mine and mill and technical adviser in the engineering department, with the aim of putting in place a pattern of supervision and management which would support the development of semi-autonomous work groups (Lansbury & Prideaux, 1987; Lansbury & Davis, 1992). The ultimate fate of Woodlawn's semi-autonomous work groups is not a matter of published record, though a film made by one of the unions concerned in the early 1980s reports early teething troubles as mine teams sought to clarify the extent of their responsibilities and to develop appropriate self-regulatory skills (AMWSU, 1983).

Following Woodlawn's example, ALCOA of Australia took the multi-skilled team concept one step further. In the early eighties, a new bauxite refinery was built at Wagerup in Western Australia, based upon socio-technical systems design. Here, multi-skilling was also encouraged by means of skill-based pay and the self-managing team was the basic unit of work, with 10 operating teams of between 10 and fifteen employees responsible for running the plant in a continuous 3-shift operation. A longitudinal comparative study of the operation of these teams reported that team members were more satisfied with their jobs than their counterparts in traditionally organized jobs at a sister refinery (Cordery, Mueller & Smith, 1991), and provided indirect evidence of productivity gains. Here, finally, the context for teamwork appeared to be right, and the refinery has continued to operate self-managing teams to the present day, through several expansion projects. Following the early success of Wagerup. ALCOA also extended the team concept to its local bauxite minesites and to its alumina smelter in the state of Victoria.

Following the pioneering attempts of Woodlawn and ALCOA, large numbers of Australian organizations began to develop multiskilling programs as the platform for work redesign and teamwork. Mining giant CRA, for example, at its Argyle Diamond Mine (the world's largest diamond mine) developed a skills extension program (skills-based pay), and used this as the platform for developing both enlarged individual jobs and self-managing operating teams. In the public sector, similar moves began to take place. Williams (1994) reports:

> "In 1987 the Australian Government introduced its Office Structures Implementation (OSI) policy to simplify and broaden job classifications, reduce levels of supervision, enlarge the scope for work redesign, and provide for participation by employees in decisions about how their jobs and work organization are organized." (p. 269)

The Western Australian State Government similarly "broad-banded" all its clerical, administrative and word-processing job classifications and instituted pilot multiskilling programs designed to provide a platform for future work redesign (Cordery, Sevastos, Mueller & Parker, 1993).

Alongside these moves to reduce some of the earlier job flexibility barriers to developing effective teamworking, Australian companies also began to mimic their North American counterparts in adopting a range of so-called Japanese management practices, particularly aimed at improving product and service quality. As in the U.S., TQM techniques and Quality Circle teams were popular initiatives, and were implemented at companies such as Bendix/Mintex, CIG, Ford, Reckitt & Coleman, Kodak, Mitsubishi and Otis Elevator (Dunford & McGraw, 1986; Smart, 1985; Kriegler & Wooden, 1985; Coombes, 1985; Griffiths, 1995). As with their US counterparts, experience showed these "voluntary" teams to have a limited lifespan (Cordery, 1996), though the quality philosophy, the development of standard operating procedures and the problem-solving skills and orientation developed through TQM and QCs were to provide, along with new flexibility in processes of skill formation and application, a platform for the next wave of successful team interventions. An early experimental intervention which combined the problem-solving, process improvement approach of quality circles with some of the decision-making responsibilities of autonomous work groups is described by Pearson (1992).

Re-Engineered Work Processes and Team Empowerment

The development of sophisticated tools and techniques which would enable teams to manage quality effectively, to diagnose and solve performance problems, as well as the increasingly flexible industrial relations system, laid the foundation for a dramatic resurgence in teamworking in the nineties, centering on programs of process re-engineering, the flattening and functional integration of organizational structures, and the creation of empowered teams (Mathews, 1994). As in other countries (e.g. Osterman, 1994), self-managing teams are rapidly increasing in popularity in the nineties (Cordery, 1995), though many Australian organizations still prefer to quality teams with their proscribed decision-making responsibilities (Griffiths, 1995).

A recent illustration of how Australian organizations have built upon the quality and flexibility initiatives of the previous decade to develop high performance self-managing teams is provided by TransWater, a subsidiary of the Sydney Water Corporation (Sydney Water Board, 1994). Prior to 1994, TransWater (then known as the Bulk Water & Waste Water Division) employed 569 employees; with just under 300 of these in low skill blue collar jobs and the remainder in administrative or technical support roles, to operate 29 waste water treatment plants. The operation of these plants had changed little over nearly one hundred years, and a rigid system of job demarcations (21 non-managerial job classifications, split into white and blue-collar occupations) was reinforced by a rigid hierarchical organization structure (9 levels from base to top). The plants were characterized by relatively low level of operator skill, little success in introducing new technology, and an industrial relations climate that could best be described as hostile. Much of this disputation occurred as employees sought to reinforce demarcations between blue collar and technical/engineering staff. Over recent years, there had been increasingly intense political, market and community pressure on the organization to improve the performance of its aging plants, which were frequently unable to handle peak loads leading to the unintended release of untreated effluent and subsequent environmental degradation.

In 1994 TransWater responded to these pressures by "re-engineering" its operations. This involved either automating or outsourcing low skill or "non-core" tasks, and upgrading the skills of its production workforce. In a cooperative union-management initiative 21 blue and white collar job classifications were collapsed into 4 production officer roles and these roles organized into self-managing teams, each bearing the collective responsibility for operating either a plant or a shift, as well as developing and implementing standard operating procedures and quality improvement initiatives. Operator skill and knowledge levels were raised by virtue of a selection process, in which all jobs were declared vacant and employees who wished to applied for one of the new team-based roles were tested against a new set of competencies. This process, along with the outsourcing and some voluntary retrenchment, resulted in a reduction in the numbers of operating employees from 294 to 191 and an increase in the proportion of operations employees with post-secondary school qualifications from 32% to 72%. Over the 12 months following the introduction of teams, externally monitored improvements in the levels of key pollutants in treated effluent were observed of between 11 and 30 percent (Wright &

Cordery, 1996). In the corresponding time period, there had also been a significant reduction in absenteeism, in injury frequency, and in industrial disputation (with no recorded disputes).

The new generation of team-based organizational interventions spans all sectors of the Australian economy, facilitated by the fashion for benchmarking and best practice, and appears to have overcome the problems of robustness which characterized earlier interventions. For example, Williams (1994) describes how the introduction of electronic lodgement of taxation returns and a re-engineering of work processes facilitated moves to self-managing work teams, and generated significant performance improvements within the Australian Tax Office. Researchers from the University of New South Wales have documented similar team successes in companies such as Alcan, Bendix Mintex, Colonial Mutual, CIG Gas cylinders, and in one of the organizations in which teamwork initially failed - ICI Botany (Dunphy & Berggren, 1992; Mealor, 1992; Mathews, 1994). The key to these new types of team is the re-engineering of fundamental work processes; frequently involving new advanced forms of automation, a quality and productivity improvement orientation, and the empowerment of teams though upgraded skills and responsibilities.

Conclusions and Future Directions

In many ways, the historical pattern of work teams in Australia is similar to that seen in other countries. We have seen initial social science experiments with teams viewed with suspicion and mistrust, patchy early success and highly publicized failure, and the slow development of eclectic approaches to teams within changed economic, political and technological contexts. However, Australia was a relatively late starter down this path and it has taken longer to get to the current stage of development because of the additional constraints provided by the country's unique industrial relations system. What, then, does the future hold for Australian organizations in this area? It seems appropriate to defer to one of the pioneers of work team interventions in this country in this matter. Based on his recent experience in a wide variety of Australian firms, Dexter Dunphy has argued that there is now an urgent need to refine models of team design, to focus beyond the operating team to other parts of the organization, to improve our understanding of team performance and to develop more cost-effective approaches to team development (Dunphy & Bryant, 1996). This will assist in ensuring that team designs continue to play a central role within leading Australian organizations well into the next decade.

References

AMWSU. (1983). *Not Just a Number, Part One*. Film produced by Amalgamated Metal Workers and Shipwrights Union (New South Wales State Council).

Andreatta, A. J. (1981). Organizational effectiveness through semi-autonomous groups. In W. M. Ainsworth & Q. F. Willis (Eds.), *Australian organizational behavior: Readings*. South Melbourne: Macmillan, pp 349-356.

Andreatta, H. & Rumbold, B. (1974). Organization development in action: Job design and development. *Personnel Practice Bulletin*, 30, 342-356.

Coombes, P. (1985). Quality circles: No longer flash, but effective if given an Aussie accent. Rydges, 58, 50-51.

Cordery, J. (1996). Autonomous work groups and quality circles. In M. West (Ed.), *Handbook of Work Group Psychology*. Chichester: John Wiley & Sons, pp 225-248.

Cordery, J. (1995). Work redesign: Rhetoric vs reality. *Asia Pacific Journal of Human Resources*, 33, 3-19.

Cordery, J. L., Sevastos, P., Mueller, W. S. and Parker, S. (1993) Correlates of beliefs towards functional flexibility within a white-collar public sector organization. *Human Relations*, 46, 705-723.

Cordery, J. L, Mueller, W. S. and Sevastos, P. (June 1992). Multi-skilling within a minerals processing firm: A case study. *Journal of Industrial Relations*, 268-283.

Cordery, J. L., Mueller, W. S. and Smith, L. M. (1991). Attitudinal and behavioral outcomes of autonomous group working: A longitudinal field study. *Academy of Management Journal*, 34, 464-476.

Derber, M. (1979). Advancing Australian industrial democracy. Industrial Relations, 17, 112-116.

Derber, M. (1970). Cross currents in worker participation. *Industrial Relations*, 9, 123-136.

Dunford, R. & McGraw, P. (1986). Abandoning simple recipes and benefiting from quality circles: An Australian study. *Work and People*, 12, 22-25.

Dunphy, D. & Bryant, B. (1996). Teams: Panaceas or prescriptions for improved performance? *Human Relations*, 49, 677-699.

Dunphy, D. & Berggren, C. (1992). Industrial renewal at Alcan Sheet Division, Granville. *CCC Paper No. 032*. Center for Corporate Change: University of New South Wales.

Dunphy, D., Andreatta, H. & Timms, L. (1976). Redesigning the work organization at Phillips. *Work and People*, 2, 3-11.

Finnie, E. G. (1987). Semi-autonomous work groups at the Welvic plant of ICI Australia. In Department of Employment and Industrial Relations (Eds.), *Industrial democracy and employee participation: Digest of case studies*, Vol. 1, 2nd Edition. Canberra: Australian Government Publishing Service, pp 115-123.

Gibbons, A. R. & McCarroll, G. (1978). Welvic revisited. *Work and People*, 4, 23-26.

Griffiths, A. (1995). Socio-technical interventions and teams in Australia: 1970s - 1990s. *Economic and Labor Relations Review*, 6, 73-93.

Kreigler, R. & Wooden, M. (1985). Japanese management practices in Australia: The case of Mitsubishi. *Work and People*, 11, 3-8.

Lansbury, R. D. & Davis, E.M. (1992). Employee participation: Some Australian cases. *International Labor Review*, 131, 231-248.

Lansbury, R. D. & Prideaux, G. (1984). Industrial and organizational democracy: The Australian experience. In B. Wilpert & A. Sorge (Eds.), *International yearbook of organizational democracy* (Vol. II), Chichester: John Wiley & Sons.

Main Roads Department, Queensland (1987). The reorganization of the Queensland Motor Vehicle Registration Branch. *Industrial democracy and employee participation: Digest of case studies*, Vol. 1, 2nd Edition. Canberra: Australian Government Publishing Service, pp 167-183.

Mathews, J. (1994). *Catching the wave: Workplace reform in Australia*. Sydney: Allen & Unwin.

Mealor, T. (1992). ICI Australia: The Botany Experience. *Studies in Organizational Analysis and Innovation*, No.8, Industrial Relations Research Center, University of New South Wales.

O'Brien, G. E. & Stevens, L. (1981). The relationship between perceived influence and job satisfaction among assembly line employees. *Journal of Industrial Relations*, 23, 33-48.

O'Brien, G. E. (1983). Employee participation in an assembly line factory: *Employee Participation Research Report No. 1*. Canberra: Australian Government Publishing Service.

O'Brien, G. E. (1987). Success and failure of employee participation: A longitudinal study. *Industrial democracy and employee participation*, Vol. I (2nd Ed.). Canberra: Australian Government Publishing Service. pp 17-25.

Osterman, P. (1994). How common is workplace transformation and who adopts it? *Industrial and Labor Relations Review*, 47, 173-188.

Pearson, C. A. (1992). Autonomous work groups: An evaluation at an industrial site. *Human Relations*, 45, 905-936.

Robinson, A. & McCarroll, G. (1976). A work group approach at Welvic. *Work and People*, 2, 32-36.

Salen, M. A. & Banner, D. K. (1992). Self-managing work teams: An international perspective. *Leadership & Organization Development Journal*, 13, 3-8.

Smart, D. C. 91985). Total quality in Kodak (Australasia). *Practicing Manager*, 6, 21-23.

Sydney Water Board (1994). New ways of working at Sydney's sewage treatment plants. Paper presented at conference *Beyond Best Practice*, University of Western Sydney, Nepean, 27 September 1994.

Williams, T.A. (1994). Information technology and self-managing work groups. *Behavior and Information Technology*, 13, 268-276.

Wright, B. M. & Cordery, J. L. (1995). An organizational transition to self-managing production teams: The case of Sydney Water. *Discussion Paper No. 8/95*, Department of Organizational & Labor Studies, University of Western Australia.

Wright, B. M. & Cordery, J. L. (1996). Organizational & behavioral outcomes of self-directed work teams: A field study. *Discussion Paper No. 3/96*, Department of Organizational & Labor Studies, University of Western Australia.

Chapter 12

Three Kinds of Autonomy at Work in Norway

Jon Gulowsen
Bodo College, Bodo, Norway

Abstract

This chapter gives a brief description of three kinds of work autonomy. What kind of decisions were the workers involved in? What were the institutional and technological bases of their autonomy? Do they belong to different periods of technological development? With these questions in mind, I will discuss the Norwegian Participation Programme, and re-examine some of the assumptions on which it was based. The relationship between autonomy and rate of technological change will be paid special attention.

Introduction

This century has witnessed at least three categories of autonomous workers (a) the descendants of the artisans, (b) autonomous groups of unskilled workers, and (c) highly skilled specialists in technologically advanced industries. Are we dealing with one phenomenon dressed for different occasions or with three entirely separate phenomena?

Although trivial to some people, this question has been of importance in Norwegian work sociology. In the 1960s the Trade Union Congress and the Norwegian Confederation of Employers jointly sponsored an action research project called the Participation Programme or the Industrial Democracy Programme. The concept of autonomous work groups was in the core of this programme.

The basic aim of the project was to increase worker participation, to improve work conditions, to create more meaningful work and to fight alienation. The research team argued that increased participation, development of more flexible forms of work organization, job rotation, job enlargement and development of autonomous work groups would improve work satisfaction and at the same time increase the flexibility of the work organization and stimulate productivity. This kind of a process was coined socio-technical, or joint optimization. Emery (1959) suggested that once it was possible to demonstrate that such anti-Taylorian principles of work organization were efficient as well as motivating, these principles would diffuse into leading industrial sectors and gradually change industry into a more humane direction. The international Quality-of-Working-Life movement grew out of these experiments.

M.M. Beyerlein (ed.), Work Teams: Past, Present and Future, 193-199.

In order to test these assumptions, the researchers and the sponsors started a number of field experiments from 1964 and onwards. The experimental departments included workers from a wide range of skills, but were dominated by workers with low or no formal industrial training at all. Another objective was to start a process of social diffusion and gradually change industrial society. Being aware of the complexity of work relations in industry, Emery argued that it would be impossible to measure and evaluate the social diffusion caused by the experiments. A programme aiming for such dramatic transformations of industry as well as society could only be validated historically (Emery & Thorsrud 1968, 1972; Gulowsen, 1974). However, the researchers who were involved neither agree what actually happened during the experiments, nor did they agree about the extent to which the ideas behind the experiments actually diffused into other areas of working life.

The Participation Programme also included a study of eight autonomous work groups, which had developed spontaneously in Norwegian working life. The purpose of the study was to develop an operational concept of work group autonomy and to clarify some technological conditions for different kinds of autonomy. For the purpose of this chapter, I have returned to these groups and looked into their later development. This provides us with a new platform and gives us an opportunity to reach a better, and hopefully, less controversial understanding of the social diffusion of autonomy.

The Artisans: Undivided Autonomy

The artisans dominated industry until the last part of the 19th century. According to the traditions they controlled every aspect of work, from the design phase to the selling of the product. They owned the means of production, they recruited and trained the apprentices, and collectively they set the standards of work, quality and design. The whole structure was supported by strong trade unions. The influence of the artisans was sufficiently wide to call it *undivided autonomy*.

After a century of Taylorism, descendants of the artisans are still to be found in a number of traditional industries such as ship and boat building, book binding, furniture production, sail-making etc. Much of the work style and autonomy which was typical for the early phase of industrialization has survived, probably due to the very demanding character of the work. The degree of division of work is low or at least very moderate. The manager and the owner are often one and the same person, and he often takes part in the manual work himself together with members of his family. The tasks differ from day to day and are very difficult to plan in detail making a flexible work organization very important. Some expert work also demands quite a bit of creativity, and creativity is not very likely to flourish without autonomy. Under such conditions the principle of economics of scale becomes dubious, in fact small is not only beautiful, it becomes efficient as well.

Nevertheless, in spite of some obvious exceptions, students of industrial sociology seem to agree that the artisans and the skilled craftsmen have lost most of their position. Braverman (1974) has argued that they stood in the way for modern industrialists who were eager to apply scientific methods of management and to integrate science and production in order to increase their competitive power. Stone (1975) has described this process in the American steel industry. After a fierce and bloody battle, the craftsmen lost in 1892. Their strong union never managed to get on its feet again. Generally the artisans have been forced out of the main stream of industrial development and into the backwaters.

Unskilled Workers: Autonomy in the Work Process

The concept of work group autonomy was spelled out in *A Measure of Work Group Autonomy* (Gulowsen, 1972). This article was based on empirical studies of eight autonomous work groups which were identified in different industrial and semi-industrial sectors.[1] For the purpose of this chapter, it is important to notice that these groups had typical manual work, often heavy and exhausting. They did not include any artisans; in fact it is very difficult to trace any link between the work culture of the artisans and these specific autonomous work groups. The workers had low formal skills, and generally belonged to a semi-rural working class culture. Their autonomy was somehow related to the formal and informal institutions of such a culture.

Almost three decades have passed since the groups were described. What actually happened to the groups? Did they manage to preserve their level of autonomy or were they run over by "the development?" To answer very briefly, very few have survived. By looking into their death history, we get an understanding of the motives behind and the strength of this kind of autonomy. Since detailed descriptions of the groups have been published elsewhere (Gulowsen, 1971), in this chapter I will limit myself to the testimony on the death certificates.

The coal miners in Durham traditionally had a very high degree of autonomy (Trist 1963). After the nationalization of the coal mining industry during the last part of the 1940s, the British Coal Board invested in advanced and expensive production equipment, and introduced some modern scientific principles of management as well. Thus the coal miners lost most of their autonomy. In the following competition with other sources of energy coal mining has gradually lost out and most of the industry, including the mines in Durham, have been closed.

For many decades the Norwegian National Railways used a special type of springs in order to fix the rails to the ties. These springs were manufactured by a group of four workers who were employed by a large company in Oslo. In the middle of the 1970s, the National Railways started substituting such rail springs with other products. As a result the production was stopped and the members of the autonomous work group were placed in other types of work.

Hommelvik, a subsidiary of a mechanical firm in Trondheim, manufactured electrical panel heaters. The production was organized as a system of highly autonomous work groups, until the whole production department was moved to a nearby town. There a new system with somewhat less autonomy was set up after local negotiations between management and the workers. This agreement, which included a joint bonus, a certain level of job rotation and working without foremen, was voted down by the workers in 1977. This was a response to an all over manpower reduction scheme in the corporation. Many workers found that individual piece rates would give them a maximum of security the way conditions seemed to develop.

The Alfa Lime Works was operated by two highly autonomous work groups until they were closed when the local manager retired at the age of 67. The basic reason for the closure was, however, high costs and old fashioned technology. In fact the closure was long overdue. Ten years previously, a rival technology producing five times as much lime in about a quarter of the space had become available.

A major steel company in Oslo included a small galvanizing department. On evening shifts this department was operated by a work group without a foreman, granting the workers a limited amount of autonomy. The department stuck to this kind of organization for three decades. However, during the summer of 1989 the whole group was fired. A total reorganization of the company included the firing of 400 workers. The principle of seniority was strictly followed on company level, and none of the members of the galvanising group had worked for the company long enough to keep their jobs.

The remaining two groups are still operative. A group of lumbermen operating with semi advanced technological equipment, works according to the same patterns as previously in areas where hilly terrain makes it difficult to introduce more advanced technology. In flat terrain logging has become totally mechanised and work has become specialized leaving little room for work group autonomy.

A plant belonging to a major Norwegian manufacturer of ferro alloys used to organize the production as a system of autonomous work groups. However, the production has witnessed a steady technological development and a number of changes in the work organization. Some of the shift groups still practice job rotation, but no work group autonomy worth mentioning is left. The management had introduced major organizational changes without consulting the workers or the trade union.

To sum up, only two out of the eight groups have survived, and only one of these has preserved a significant level of autonomy. The other six disappeared when the production units to which they belonged were stopped or reorganized for technological or economical reasons.

The fates of these eight autonomous work groups provide us with some clues regarding the basis for autonomy among unskilled workers. We notice that all the groups have operated within mature industries. Such industries are sooner or later faced with a choice between (a) closure, (b) investment in new technology, or (c) minimization of all costs and total cut in investments. It seems as if all the groups we have studied belonged to these categories, waiting for the inevitable decision to close down or to invest into new technology and thus remove the basis for work group autonomy. The study gives us reason to believe that laissez-faire management including a high degree of autonomy for the workers, may be an optimal managerial strategy if a production system is highly mature. This way costs related to administration and conflict management are probably at a minimum. This level of autonomy, *work process autonomy*, is no challenge to the establishment. It is a way to simplify management, not to give workers an active share in it. Granting autonomy to unskilled workers may be a way of prolonging the economic viability of a production system which is about to become outdated.

New Skilled Workers: Expert Autonomy

Rapid technological advances during the last 10-20 years have fostered a new generation of workers, highly skilled and often with a significant degree of autonomy. These *new skilled workers* (Gulowsen 1988) are in charge of specially advanced tasks such as programming, instrumentation, robotization, process control, etc. in different kinds of industry. The workers often work in close cooperation with other highly skilled people such as scientists and engineers. While the latter are more theoretically oriented, the function of the new skilled workers is to handle the practical side of real and often very complex technological problems. *Expert autonomy* is descriptive for this level of worker influence.

Conclusion

In this chapter I have discussed three different kinds of autonomy in the work place. The artisans had undivided autonomy. They were autonomous with respect to every part of the work process. Unskilled autonomy was limited to intra-group decisions and decisions related to work methods. Finally, the autonomy of new skilled workers in modern industry is connected to technological issues, making the term expert autonomy appropriate.

These kinds of autonomy rest on different institutional conditions. The artisans' autonomy at work was based on their collective control of the technology and the norms of their trade. It was frequently supported by ownership of the means of production, occasionally by close family relationships as well. Finally, at the height of their power their autonomy was not challenged by managerial or professional groups.

Unskilled autonomy is related to a high degree of division of work in industry. Management, technological supervision and practical work are separate roles. To the extent that workers have any degree of autonomy, this is likely to be supported by the institutions of the working class culture. This autonomy is often limited to relatively trivial issues, that is issues where management, represented by engineers and foremen, do not find it work while to control the workers.

Expert autonomy differs clearly from the two preceding categories. While the two former kinds of autonomy were overpowered by rapid technological development, the expert autonomy connected to the new skills is a product of the same development. This kind of autonomy is delegated form management and based on the value of their skills and the scarcity of such qualifications in the labor market.

Thus, the three kinds of work autonomy are entirely separate phenomena. They differ in kind as well as in cause and effect. The one does not stand on the shoulders of the other. The fact that they rest on different institutional and technological foundations and ideally belongs to different historical epochs supports this conclusion.

Some Implications for Socio-Technical Theory

Diffusion of Principles of Organization

The preceding arguments, in one respect, support the socio-technical perspective that was the basis for the Norwegian Participation Programme. They demonstrate that industrial work mirrors the technological progress in industry.

However, the hope that organizational principles giving workers increased autonomy would diffuse and change large parts of industry does not seem to be well founded. The expansion of the new skills and corresponding expert autonomy is no indication that unskilled autonomy has developed and diffused into new fields. In short, wide spread expert autonomy is no historical validation of the Industrial

Democracy Programme. In an era of rapid technological transformation, there is no alternative for capital management but to grant the pioneers of this technology a significant degree of autonomy.

Different types of autonomy reflect technological growth and maturation, trade union strength as well as managerial attitudes and ownership structures. Looking for explanations for continuity and transformation in industry, we are better advised to look at this kind of variables, than to pay much attention to degrees and kinds of autonomy at the work level.

Work Autonomy and Rate of Technological Development

Emery has expressed two views about the relationship between work autonomy and the rate of technological development. In an early phase of the Participation Programme, together with Thorsrud he suggested a set of conditions for work group autonomy including the following.

1. The group shares a common and unified task and works within easily definable boundary conditions.

2. The task does not vary unexpectedly or in ways which the group itself cannot control or cope with.[2]

However, at a later stage in the Programme, he argued that autonomy at the work level is necessary in order for a work organization to respond to technological change (Emery & Trist, 1965).

As long as we operate with only one category of autonomy at the work level, clearly these two views contradict each other. But, recalling that we are actually confronting entirely different kinds of autonomy, this contradiction becomes less puzzling. The autonomy of the unskilled workers seems to be highly dependent on stable boundary conditions. Our case studies indicate that it tends to collapse once faced with rapid changes. But we have also seen that the expert autonomy connected with the new skills depend on technological change, or vice versa.

So, in a way, my arguments in this chapter clarify Emery's dilemma. The problem was that he, or rather we, did not distinguish properly between the different kinds of autonomy.

Notes

1. A more detailed study of these groups is published in Norwegian (Gulowsen, 1971).

2. These conditions were introduced in a mimeo from 1964, and reproduced in Gulowsen 1970, p. 188.

References

Braverman, H. (1974). *Labor and monopoly capital.* Monthly Review Press.

Emery, F. E. (1959). *Socio-technical systems*, London: Tavistock.

Emery, F. E. (1968), *The historical validity of the industrial democracy project.* Oslo: Work Research Institute.

Emery, F. E., & Trist, E. L. (1965). The causal texture of the environments. *Human Relations*, 18, 21-32.

Gulowsen, J. (1971), *Selvstyrte arbeidsgrupper*. Oslo: Tanum.

Gulowsen, J. (1972), A measure of work group autonomy. In L. Davis (Ed.), *Design of jobs*. London: Penguin.

Gulowsen, J. (1988), Skills, options, and unions. R. Hyman & W. Streek (Eds.), *New technology and work organization*. Oxford: Blackwell.

Stone, K. (1975), The origins of job structures in the steel industry. In R. C. Edwards, M. Reich, & D. M. Gordon (Eds.), *Labor market segmentation*. Lexington, MA: Heath and Company.

Trist, E. L. (1963), *Organizational choice*. London:Tavistock.

Chapter 13

Group Fabrication to Self-Designing Work Teams

The Development of Work Teams in Germany

Conny Antoni
University of Trier, Trier, Germany

Abstract

The discussion of work teams in Germany as an alternative to the tayloristic division of labor and functional specialization can be traced back to the beginnings of the 20th century. At a Daimler factory group fabrication was introduced, integrating different parts, machines, and professionals in a group. They completely finished a product such as a water pump or a gearing although work specialization even increased. However it took more than sixty years that group technology and manufacturing cells found broader interest in industry. The main reasons for this renewed interest were changing market characteristics demanding a higher amount of flexibility, quality and productivity than the traditional tayloristic work structures could achieve. In particular the upcoming discussion of lean production at the beginning of the 90's furthered the spread of work teams in German industrial and service companies significantly. In contrast the discussion of quality of work life and industrial democracy in the 70's remained restricted to the scientific community and a few government sponsored pilot projects. In the 90's work teams were primarily perceived as a means to increase productivity and flexibility. Nevertheless many companies integrated ideas from the discussion about quality of work life from the early 70's, such as self regulation, job enrichment, and election of the team speaker. However the current focus on short term share holder value will put even more pressure on work teams to increase productivity. This might endanger group self-regulation and continuous improvement and strengthen traditional cost cutting strategies such as overhead reduction.

The Renaissance of Work Teams in Germany

Since the beginning of the 90's there has been a renewed interest in work teams both in industry and science. The discussion started in industry triggered by the MIT study about the international competitiveness of the auto industry (Womack, Jones and Roos, 1990). At first many auto and supplier companies implemented work teams. With a short delay many other industrial and service companies followed this

M.M. Beyerlein (ed.), Work Teams: Past, Present and Future, 201–217.

trend. It took some years until industrial and organizational psychologists realized that their futile call for new work structures in the 70's seemed now to be fulfilled. However a closer look revealed that conditions for self-regulating work teams had changed over time. No longer industrial democracy (Emery and Thorsrud, 1982) were the key words but total quality management (Zink, 1994), Kaizen (Imai, 1986) and lean production (Womack et al., 1990).

What factors caused this development? The reception of the MIT study fell in a time where German companies lost market shares to Japanese competitors. This increased the awareness of three already existing trends. The most influential was the change from seller to buyer markets. This implied that increasing international competition caused a change in the power relations between sellers and buyers in favor of the buyers in many markets. Typical symptoms were an increasing number of customer specific product developments or product requirements as well as shorter product cycles. Customers required just-in-time delivery or even just-in-time production. For example companies in the auto supplier industry are told what they have to produce just a couple of hours before they have to deliver it just in time to the point at the assembly line where their parts are assembled. Traditional standardized mass production was profitable due to the economies of scale. Smaller batches, individualized products, and shorter product cycles together with higher cost pressure, quality and flexibility requirements demanded a more flexible production paradigm.

In the 80's German companies tried to cope with this emerging development by automation and computer integrated production. However, their vision of a fully automated and manless production was doomed to fail. To meet the flexibility and cost requirements even flexible manufacturing technology needed higher skilled workers. Furthermore they have to cooperate effectively to keep the costly machinery running 24 hours a day and 7 days a week. Low skilled blue-collar workers and a strict division of labor between direct and indirect functions caused too many standstills and productivity losses.

The increasing demand for skilled work fitted well to the increasing number of skilled young workers. They expected not only qualified work but also job autonomy, responsibility, and cooperative leadership. This change from materialistic to post-materialistic work values alone would not have been strong enough to change existing work structures. But changing work values together with technological requirements for skilled and responsible work combined with market demands for flexible and high quality production supported the renaissance of qualified cooperative work structures.

In the following we will look at the historical development of work teams in Germany. At first a predecessor of group technology called group fabrication dating back to the 20ies will be described. The next step in the development of work teams in Germany was the discussion about quality of work life and industrial democracy in the beginnings of the 70's. Finally, the concept of quality circles in the 80's paved the way for the upcoming work teams in the early 90's.

Early Beginnings: Group Fabrication

Group technology and manufacturing cells are an important technological basis for self regulating work teams in modern manufacturing. Successful pilot projects in companies such as Mannesmann-Boge, Ekato or YMOS (Antoni, 1994) contributed significantly to the spread of work teams in Germany. Group technology means to integrate technical similar parts, the required manufacturing tools and workers in a work team to build a manufacturing cell. Manufacturing cells also comprise engineering, production planning and control (Brödner, 1985). Group technology is regarded as a modern approach to work organization. It can provide substantial savings in areas such as set-up times, scrap, rework and inventories (Cummings & Blumberg, 1987). The principle of completing a part or product in a group or cell can also be applied to assembly work. A group may even encompass engineering, production planning, manufacturing, final assembly, and quality control functions.

Although the concept of group technology is regarded as a modern form of work organization it can be traced back to the second decade of the 20th century. The concept of group fabrication was invented at a factory of Daimler Benz at Untertürkheim and was based on the same principles. Lang and Hellpach (1922) give the following description of group fabrication (translation by the author):

> "... fabrication groups were designed like small mechanical workshops consisting of all kinds of shop machines and besides engine operators, mechanics and other kinds of workers. The task of such a group is to complete a certain number of different but related parts which form together an independent significant part of the complete product. Such a fabrication group is self-contained and independent of other work departments, and hence there are many options for its location. The transport of in-process parts is reduced to its utmost within the group; only raw material is delivered and leaves the group completely finished and assembled. The advantages of group fabrication are manifold: Parts are checked before they are handed on to the next process step and leave the shop only after they are completely finished. If the worker experiences perhaps a somewhat greater monotony at work, he has on the other hand the opportunity to watch the ongoing progress of work or to see how his part is used, which will instigate his work motivation, strengthen his responsibility..." (Lang & Hellpach, 1922, p. 2).

Despite these early industrial experiences group fabrication did not have much impact on the development of work structures in Germany in the years to follow. Functionally oriented plant design with specialized manufacturing workshops dominated the development. The reason for the failure of group fabrication might be that inventory and transport costs as well as total time to delivery was not as crucial as they are today. At least they could be limited due to a rather small range of parts and products. Later on work teams were neither in the focus of industry nor of industrial and organizational psychology until the discussion of quality of work life and industrial democracy reached Germany in the late 60ies and early 70's.

Quality of Work Life: The Approach of the 70's

The discussion of work teams in Germany at the end of the 60ies and the beginning of the 70's was influenced by the quality of work life program in the US (Davis & Cherns, 1975), and in particular by the Scandinavian approach to industrial democracy. The experiments in Norway (Emery & Thursrud, 1982) and especially those in the Swedish car industry, such as the Volvo plant in Kalmar (Berggren, 1991), became widely known in Germany. At that time a coalition of the social-democratic and liberal party formed the government and adopted the Norwegian industrial democracy approach. The German chancellor Will Brandt became famous for his pleading to "dare" more industrial democracy. An important political reform was the "Betriebsverfass-ungsgesetz" from 1972, which defined the rights of the works council. In particular it specified their rights to participate in management decisions concerning pay, working time, suggestion schemes, selection and training, as well as changes in work structure. Its importance lies in the fact that any organizational development and personnel training since then, has to be agreed upon by management and the works council. In order to strengthen industrial democracy and to enhance quality of work life the huge research program "humanization of work life" was started. Almost all projects to implement work teams in the 70's and early 80's were sponsored by this program (Gaugler, Kolb & Ling, 1977; Rohmert & Weg, 1976).

One of the most well known projects to implement semi-autonomous work teams was launched at a VW motor assembly plant at Salzgitter (BMFT, 1980; Ulich, 1989). In this project, four self-regulating work teams were compared to traditional assembly line work structures (classical assembly line and transfer line assembly). The traditional motor assembly was characterized by task fragmentation and short work cycles lasting up to one or two minutes. In contrast, a complete motor was assembled in about 35 minutes by seven workers in the self-regulating work teams. Besides the motor assembly, they also adjusted and run in the motors, and did the material handling, disposition of parts and quality control. It was possible to qualify all participating workers for this complex task. The team did it's own work assignment. They also elected a speaker, and had regular meetings to discuss work related topics every two weeks.

At the beginning of the project the teams were coached by a supervisor without disciplinary power. However, at a later phase of the project, work assignment and disciplinary power was conferred upon the supervisor again. This can be interpreted as a symptom for the occurring conflicts about group autonomy, performance standards and wage questions between management, works council and the research team. These conflicts contributed significantly to the failure of the project. All self-regulating work teams were dissolved after the government sponsored research project ended.

It is no surprise that the parties evaluated the project differently: the company estimated 250 percent higher costs of mass production in the work teams, compared to the traditional assembly line, and even more compared to a transfer line assembly. Work teams were said to have lower costs only, if less than to 300 motors per day were produced. The researchers and the trade union criticized this calculation as inadequate, because many factors in favor of the work teams were not included in the traditional analytical controlling methods. Furthermore they argued that the working conditions in the self-regulating teams were much better, with respect to criteria of quality of work life such as ergonomic standards, action latitude, social and cognitive work requirements, and progressive job satisfaction.

The processes and conflicts occurring in this project were typical for most of the projects about self-regulating work teams at that time. The researchers focused on the humanization of working life, implying existing conditions were inhuman. This provoked resistance on the side of the management, particularly as they feared uncontrollable bottom-up democratic processes, endangering both power relations and productivity. The trade unions followed the primary strategy to improve employee qualification as a way to raise the average wage level. On the other hand, the trade unions and the works councils kept a critical eye on group autonomy, as they feared their new participatory rights being restricted. The companies were highly hierarchical and had a predominant authoritarian, distrusting leadership culture. These circumstances were obviously conflicting with the principles of delegation, participative decision making, trust and responsibility required for the implementation of self-regulating work teams. This cultural background influenced not only management behavior, but also that of the works council, trade unions and last but not least of the employees. For these reasons it often proved impossible to resolve conflicts constructively. Obviously the time was not ripe enough to implement self regulating work teams successfully. The concept of self regulating work teams was discarded and another concept was adopted by industry: Quality circles.

Quality Circles: An Ice-Breaker for Work Teams in the 80's

At the end of the 70's and the beginnings of the 80's the success of Japanese companies led to a first wave of adoption of Japanese management techniques (Ouchi, 1981; Crocker, Charney & Chiu, 1984; Bungard & Wiendieck, 1986). Quality circles were regarded as one of the most promising methods to increase productivity. Like in other western countries large numbers of companies started to implement quality circles. In a survey we did in 1985 already 40 percent of the 100 largest industrial companies in Germany had implemented quality circles. This percentage rose to 50 percent in 1990 and 56 percent in 1994 (Antoni, 1995). Quality circles were predominantly introduced in the production departments, but were also implemented in the service departments or even in service companies, although to a smaller percentage.

Top management drove the spread of quality circles. Top managers visited Japanese companies and were told that employee participation in problem solving and continuous improvement processes would raise job satisfaction, cooperation, quality and productivity. Consequently they told their middle management to implement quality circles. Others saw their competitors introduce quality circles and followed this route. Trade unions were very critical as the momentum of the quality circle grew. They argued that quality circles are a means to get a hold on the gold in the heads of the employees. Finally employees would loose their jobs due to their own suggestions. Especially in the metal industry trade unions advised the works councils to agree only to the introduction of quality circles, if they could participate in the crucial decision committees, and if the employees could participate financially in the savings, and if their jobs were guaranteed.

Due to this standpoint, the implementation process of quality circles became highly political in many companies. We know of companies struggling for years to find an agreement between management and the works council. It is easy to imagine that those models were prone to fail. Other factors worsened the situation even more. Quality circles met similar problems like the work teams in the 70's. This time however, top management pushed the implementation process. Furthermore employees could be more easily convinced to participate, since no structural changes were required to introduce quality circles. Consequently lower and middle management came into a sandwich position: their employees developed problem solutions and improvements, which they regarded as their own genuine business and top management expected them to support this. Sometimes they were even asked, why they did not have such good ideas on their own, especially since they were paid for it. Some staff functions, such as industrial engineering experienced the same. Furthermore, in some companies quality circles could present their suggestions directly to a joint top management and works council committee, which decided upon their approval. Thus quality circle suggestions could pass by all hierarchical levels in between.

In this situation staff personnel and middle management felt threatened by quality circles. Employee participation in problem solving was inconsistent with their role perception; it weakened their control and even questioned their position as an expert. Since top management wanted the success of the quality circles, open resistance seemed not adequate. Consequently the opponents fell back to rational objections: they found ways to prove that the suggested solutions could not work or they referred to time and money constraints. For example, to meet customer demands all time was needed for manufacturing, and hence no time was left for circle meetings; or they could not support quality circles due to their workload; or there was no spare money to implement quality circle solutions, etc. When circle members experienced this resistance and realized that their suggestions were futile, they soon lost their motivation. In return middle management could prove that their employees had nor more ideas and lacked motivation in the long run.

These strategies were used to isolate and block quality circle activities in many companies. They probably would not have worked if top management had behaved differently. It was not enough to demand the quick implementation of quality circles. A successful implementation process would have required the development of a more participative leadership culture, starting with top management leadership behavior. It happened in a lot of companies that top management demanded a quick implementation of quality circles within a couple of weeks. No discussion was allowed about the organizational prerequisites or about the requirements for the concerned persons. In these companies quality circles were introduced but with a rather limited effect.

However there were also successful projects operating even until today. One reason might be that these projects could evolve and were supported by personnel and organizational development processes. One example is the BMW "Lernstatt" model which can be subsumed under the quality circle concept (Reichart, 1984; Antoni, 1986).

The "Lernstatt" was development by BMW and a consultant company in 1973. At the beginning it was designed as a participative learning instrument for teams on the shop floor using team working methods (Klebert, Schrader & Straub, 1980). "Lernstatt" is an acronym formed out of the words "lernen" (learning) and "Werkstatt" (workshop) to symbolize that it is an approach suitable to the shop floor. The "Lernstatt" was started to teach German to foreign workers. Language teachers who had received special training acted as first line supervisors. In this training they had developed their own teaching material that focused on daily working routines. It happened that in the "Lernstatt" not only language was taught, but also daily problems and conflicts were solved. After some time the German colleagues complained that they were given no time to meet, and to talk to their supervisors. This was the beginning of the development of the "Lernstatt" as a general organizational learning and problem-solving instrument.

Like in a quality circle employees can participate in the "Lernstatt" voluntarily. They can elect a team participant to act as moderator or ask their first line supervisor. His task is to co-ordinate the learning or problem solving process, to suggest adequate problem solution techniques, and to control the group dynamic processes. To be able to fulfill his task, the moderator needs the respective training in group dynamics, and in problem solving skills. If special know-how is needed to solve a problem, experts for specific topics can be invited. The "Lernstatt" is supposed to suggest solutions to work related problems, and if they are approved of, to implement them, if possible.

Several other companies such as Hoechst or Bosch implemented the "Lernstatt" as well. Today some have changed the name of their "Lernstatt" or of their quality circle model, because "Kaizen" or continuous improvement processes (CIP) became the keywords in the 90's. Whether they are called "Lernstatt", "CIP"- or "Kaizen-Teams" or quality circles does not matter. For the first time, many employees on the shop floor had the opportunity to work and learn in teams, and to participate in work related improvement processes. In many companies this paved the way for the team concept in the 90's.

Work Teams as a Means for Rationalization in the 90's

In the 80's many companies tried to implement new information technology and computer integrated manufacturing. Doing these projects some companies, such as Mannesman-Boge, realized that not the lack of information technology were their primary problem, but rather the way organizational processes were designed (Büth, 1994). Other companies such as YMOS (today belonging to Magna) experienced that traditional overhead reduction or industrial engineering programs for cost cuttings reached their limits, and new work processes and structures were needed (Antoni & Eyer, 1997). Again other companies such as Mettler Toledo became aware that they even had to change their manufacturing technology to be able to implement flexible work structures to meet the market requirements (Hüser & Kaun, 1995).

Companies such as Mannesmann-Boge, YMOS or Mettler-Toledo started projects to implement process oriented flexible work and organization structures at the end of the 80's. As a part of this reorganization process they implemented self-regulating work teams successfully. In 1990 already 23 percent of the largest (in respect to turnover) German industrial companies tested self regulating work teams. These companies could already present successful models of a lean company and of effectively running self-regulating work teams as the discussion about lean production started in Germany at the end of 1990 (Antoni, 1994; Binkelmann, Braczyk, & Seltz, 1993; Zink, 1995). Pushed by the MIT study these models found wide recognition. In 1994 the number of companies having self-regulating work teams implemented increased up to 32 percent. Further 12 percent already wanted to implement them (Antoni, 1996).

Although it soon became fashionable to have work teams as a symbol for modern work structures, fortunately many companies analyzed their specific requirements before they designed and implemented them. Some older managers or industrial engineers might have still remembered their first tries and failures to introduce work teams in the 70's. A wide range of models was developed. Some resembled more the Japanese team concept, having Toyota as a model, some were more oriented to the concept of self-regulating work teams, made known by the Volvo plants in Kalmar or Uddevalla (Berggren, 1991; 1992). However, most models shared many common characteristics, placing them somewhere in between these Japanese or Scandinavian models (Antoni, 1996; Kaune, 1996).

Teams at Toyota have a high technological interdependence, due to assembly line and just-in-time manufacturing. Even though team members are multi-skilled, workstations have average work cycles less than 1 or 2 minutes, reflecting a strong division of labor. Work procedures are highly standardized and controlled by first line supervisors and foremen. They are responsible for work assignment, training and performance appraisals; employees experience high performance pressure, and motivating employees to participate in Kaizen activities to eliminate all kinds of disturbances and waste. The pursuit of company goals dominates all other interests.

The Toyota team model is often contrasted to the work team approach of the Volvo plant at Uddevalla. In Uddevala parallel teams are located in workshops and assemble independent of each other complete automobiles. The average work cycles last several hours, providing large degrees of freedom to the individual worker and the team, and requiring substantial professional training. The first line supervisor acts as a coach, and co-ordinates his teams with the help of elected or rotating team leaders. Employee participation in decision making, company suggestion schemes, collective bargaining, and defined performance limits to prevent stress are further characteristics of the Uddevalla concept (Berggren, 1991; Jürgens, Malsch & Dohse, 1989; Kashima & Callan, 1994; Womack et al., 1990).

Particularly the German auto industry oriented their team model in the assembly departments closer to the Toyota than to the Uddevalla team model. For example, at a Ford plant even so called Japanese assembly lines were implemented. Similar to Japan, teams at these lines were led by foremen. Members were qualified to perform direct and indirect tasks, and to rotate between workstations. Many worked on assembly platforms moving automatically parallel to the assembly line back and forth between work stations. All parts needed for assembly were stored on the platform, thus reducing unnecessary walking to get parts and allowing assembly at a steady position. The works council and the employees accepted this approach not at least, because they could participate in a thorough ergonomic work redesign process, before the new work structure was implemented. Furthermore teams were trained in technical and social skills. As work cycles, like in other German car assemblies, lasted up to a couple of minutes qualification level was significantly increased by job rotation. Nevertheless it was still rather a multi-skilling than neo-craftsmanship approach.

Other Ford plants and other companies such as Audi, BMW, Daimler-Benz, Opel and VW favored a more participatory approach. They had their team leaders or better speakers elected by team members. However, they usually did not change assembly line manufacturing and short work cycles. Instead they intensified just-in-time delivery and manufacturing, and reduced buffers even more, thus increasing group interdependence, and reducing action latitudes. Manufacturing or product cells were tested only in parts manufacturing, such as in the stamp-shop. Furthermore they were implemented in pre-assembly areas, such as the pre-assembly of doors, or if differing assembly times for product variants slowed down line speed too much. Changes in work structure at the assembly lines were confined to the integration of indirect functions, such as quality control, logistics (parts supply) and minor repairs. Furthermore work assignment and the scheduling of vacancies within defined standards were delegated to the work teams. Finally "Kaizen" played a central role. All companies tried to complement their so far extremely slow and inefficient traditional suggestion schemes by team based continuous improvement processes. One way used to speed up the implementation of suggestions was to empower first line supervisors to accept, to reward and to implement suggestions, if less than a certain tax relevant amount of money (800 DM) was needed (Gerst, Hardwig, Kuhlmann & Schumann, 1994; Kaune, 1996).

In the supplier industry more autonomous team models were developed. For example at YMOS or Mannesmann-Boge manufacturing or product cells were implemented. They comprise almost the complete process chain of a product. The teams are responsible for disposition, manufacturing control, industrial engineering, manufacturing and assembly, work assignment, quality control and logistics. Customer orders arrive online at a team terminal, and the team adjusts its manufacturing control respectively. Logistics are based on the "Kanban" principle. The manufacturing of the desired products up to the point of shipment is completed within the team. If product complaints should occur, they are handled by the team itself in direct contact with the customer. To be able to meet customer demands, teams can adjust their working time correspondingly. For adjustment purposes, they have yearly time budgets, allowing more or less work depending on customer and employee needs. They are restricted only by legal and company specific regulations. For example the YMOS specific agreement says, employees having a regular 36 hours per week contract are allowed to accumulate 50 hours plus or minus (20 hours plus being the monthly maximum), under the condition that they balance their work record once a year. Regular working time ranged from Sunday 9.30 p.m. to Saturday 6.00 p.m., 24 hours a day.

Team flexibility and productivity are rewarded by bonus systems. For these purposes a completely new wage system was developed. A group performance bonus, depending on scrap and output in relation to direct and indirect working time is topped on a constant basis, and on individual performance assessment. The latter reflects such criteria as qualification, job and working time flexibility. At a Mannesman-Boge plant qualification level of team members is even assessed by the group. The first line supervisor lost his disciplinary power, and has become member of a service team, supporting and coaching work teams if needed. 12 work teams totalling about 400 employees report directly to the manager of the manufacturing department, reducing hierarchy to two management levels. To sum up, in these companies implementing self-regulating work teams did not on only change work and leadership structure, but also time and wage systems. Eventually a change process in organizational culture was triggered from hierarchical, external control to team self-regulation, trust and responsibility (Büth, 1994; Antoni & Eyer, 1997).

These case studies give an idea of the diversity of the team models. To get a more representative overview over the characteristics of work teams in the German industry, we interviewed experts in charge of team implementation in the survey mentioned above.

Most companies formed product oriented teams, for example, their task was to finish a product or at least a significant part of it. They had direct and indirect tasks. In almost all companies teams were responsible for quality control, after-work, process improvements, set up work, preparation of tools, in-process transport, fine tuning of the production control and planning. In terms of group autonomy, teams in most companies could elect their team speaker, do their work assignment, decide to do additional tasks, schedule their team meetings, plan their breaks during work, and schedule their days off work, taking customer demands into account. Out of control were usually personnel decisions, such as to engage new group members, or to lend group members to other teams. The same holds for decisions concerning the speed of work and the working time. In these respects, teams were only informed about management decisions. Nevertheless most teams had significantly more autonomy than work teams at Toyota.

In the average, a work team had 10 members comprising both skilled and unskilled workers. Most of them (62 percent) were co-ordinated by a team member without disciplinary power. Team meetings were regularly once a week. Work flexibility was quite high: in 72 percent of the company's team members could perform at least half of the workstations within the group. In most companies the first line supervisor remained the direct supervisor of the employees. However, due to group autonomy, his role had changed significantly. Many daily routines had been delegated to the work teams. His new task was to coach his teams, and to train them in their new duties. Furthermore he had to co-ordinate several self-regulating teams. In case of disciplinary problems a team could not handle, he was still in charge of work discipline. Finally, he had more time to spend on production planning and industrial engineering tasks. However, about every fifth company had cancelled the position of the first line supervisor, in order to get a flatter hierarchy.

With respect to the role of first line management, the team model in most German companies resembles more the Uddevalla than the Toyota team model. In terms of job content and qualification level, team models are difficult to compare based on the results of this survey, but most German team models seem to be in between the Uddevalla and Toyota team model.

The primary purpose of German companies for implementing work teams was to raise productivity. The companies named other objectives as well, such as the increase of quality, flexibility, and work motivation, but to a much lesser degree. Interestingly, they reported as team successes productivity increases, as well as flexibility and quality improvements. But at first place they named higher work motivation, and to a somewhat lesser degree higher qualification. On the other hand, the three biggest problems were lacking employee acceptance, middle management support, and the implementation process of work teams itself.

These problems indicate that it was still difficult to implement self-regulating work teams in the existing organizational culture. One reason might have been that in many companies the implementation process was designed by industrial engineers and other experts without direct involvement of the respective employees and supervisors. Eventually, some companies embedded work team implementation in an organizational development process, in order to give supervisors and employees the opportunity to participate and to design their own work structure.

Towards Self Designing Work Teams

Hackman (1987) differentiates self-regulating and self-designing work groups. While the former are responsible for task performance and process control, the latter are as well responsible for group structure and development. Management responsibility is in this case restricted to the design of the organizational context variables. A third type being groups regulated by their supervisor without own responsibility. This typology is of course only a rough sketch of alternative group models, but it is helpful in the process of team design and development. Although it does not mean that one moves necessarily from externally regulated, to self-regulating, and finally to self-designing work teams, many companies follow this path of increasing group autonomy and responsibility. The development towards self-designing work teams might be best described by taking a case study.

At Daimler Benz the MIT study (Womack et. al, 1990) was taken seriously and several consequences were drawn at the executive board. One of them was to implement work teams in the whole company. Consequently the central industrial engineering department developed a manual, how to implement work teams in the production departments. This manual outlined a detailed project management procedure of the implementation process. Steering committees and project groups were defined to involve top management, the works council and the relevant staff departments. However, first line supervisors and their respective employees were not involved. Consequently, work teams were implemented out of a staff perspective, which often did not meet the specific and various requirements of the shop floor. This provoked resistance by lower management and the respective employees. At best it caused friction, manufacturing problems and demotivation. In some cases the implementation process was blocked, and nothing did change actually, but the labeling of the work structure. Sometimes existing team spirit and cooperation processes even deteriorated, after so called work teams were introduced.

In a pilot project a different approach was tested. Its objective was to develop and implement works teams participatively, involving shop floor workers and first line supervisors. This concept was implemented in a stamp shop, supplying the autobus assembly with metal parts. The stamp shop operated on a three-shift schedule, employing 48 workers and two first line supervisors. The technology level ranged from simple stamping machines to computer controlled laser cutters. This department had been under severe cost pressure. In comparison to external stamp shops it was too expensive. Hence outsourcing was a constant threat. An earlier attempt of the manager in charge to establish a computer-integrated manufacturing was refuted as too expensive, because investments would have been necessary, amounting up to several million dollars. As a low cost alternative, self regulating work teams should be implemented to meet the flexibility and cost targets.

Based on the participative approach a project team was formed, consisting out of two representatives from the shop floor, two first line supervisors, a representative from the works council, an industrial engineer, a person from the training department, and the department manager. If needed the team was supplemented by the respective people from production planning, or control, or the personnel department. Company management and the works council had decided on an external process evaluation, hence a member of our research team participated in the project team as an external consultant.

The two representatives of the shop floor workers were elected after a first introductory information about the project objectives by the department head. Later the elected team speakers took their role. The project started with a status quo analysis. In a workshop all employees were asked to list their work related problems. These problems were clustered and rated according to their priority. This problem list was compared to a problem list done by management and a joint decision was made to tackle the top priority problems in both lists. Small task force teams were formed to develop problem solutions and to implement them. Team members were volunteering employees and members of the project team, or staff departments if necessary. The task forces reported to the project team, and later to the work teams. The task of the project team was to co-ordinate the task forces, and to support them especially if the cooperation of staff departments was needed. Furthermore the project team defined the necessary milestones, monitored project progress and developed conceptual ideas, which were then discussed and agreed upon in weekly team meetings on the shop floor and then reported back to the project team.

This procedure allowed employees to participate in the design and implementation process on three levels: to begin with, they could discuss their ideas, and decide on solutions in workshops, and later on in their weekly team meetings; secondly, they could elaborate and implement problem solutions in special task forces; and finally they could participate in the project team, at least with the help of their elected representatives. Of course employees could not design their teams irrespective of management and internal customer expectations. But they could participate in the design process of their team, its boundaries, and its future development. In this respect it seems justified to call them self-designing and not only self-regulating work teams. The results of the self-design process can be best illustrated by some examples.

The employees discussed and decided on their team structure. At start they preferred a complete shift to be taken as a team and wanted no technology, or product based team structure. Two years later they changed to product and machine based teams, comprising all three shifts. They reorganized their manufacturing processes, allowing just in time production and delivery to the assembly lines, thus reducing inventories and costs dramatically. They changed their layout, so that one person could operate several machines simultaneously. They integrated quality control and product design for customer specific product modifications. With the help of the personnel department, they developed a new wage system that required higher job flexibility with increasing wage levels. In line with this, they developed an on-the-job training program to qualify people for different jobs. Last but not least, they constantly improved machine programming thus reducing scrap significantly.

For these reasons this project was ultimately a big economic and motivational success. Productivity and flexibility increased significantly, as well as working conditions, team spirit and qualification level. However, it was not an easy way.

Especially the integration of indirect tasks, such as quality control, and product design, was very difficult. The respective departments did everything, but to cooperate. There was no open resistance, but the processes were slowed down extremely. For example it took months, to install a barcode reader, in order to be able to do in-process quality control. These process losses caused huge motivational problems, especially since expectations were high on the side of the blue-collar workers. Due to their participation from the very start of the project, expectations for significant changes rose early in the process. Thus they were frustrated for a long time, due to the hidden resistance of indirect departments. This situation was aggravated, because their a priori beliefs about the reactions of the indirect functions, and their disbelief that changes could happen, were confirmed at first. The Gordian knot could only be undone, as the plant top management and the works council intervened in favor of the work teams. Another critical factor was that management kept its promise that manufacturing time standards would not be changed, and that the focus would lie on process losses and overhead costs. Project success proved that the big points could be won by this strategy, and not by walking on old beaten paths. Finally it was helpful that not only productivity oriented decisions were made, but that also working conditions were improved. It would have been much easier if top management had taken a clearer and more decisive stand from the very beginning. This proved once more that change processes need supportive power structures in order to be successful.

This dependence on top management might be one reason, why self-designing and even self-regulating work teams are still not the common type of work team. To get into top management one usually has to play the rules better than everybody else, and one needs to have a strong power motive. Both factors contribute to stabilize the existing authoritarian culture in organizations, which conflicts with self-regulating and self-design principles.

Self-regulating and even more self-designing work teams restrict management influence to some degree, and demand cooperation and delegation. Self-control and management by objectives require management to keep out of group processes, and dispense with detailed process information if goal attainment is not endangered. If however, top management expects middle management to have detailed process information, and consequently, if managers at every level try to have the same degree of information, delegation and self-regulation will finally collapse. The same is true, if top management gives detailed directions into a team, skipping all levels in between. Self-regulating and self-designing work-teams require self-control and trust, both no typical attributes for hierarchical and authoritarian organizations.

On the other hand, self-regulating teams allow greater top management control, as they help to reduce hierarchical levels, and increase organizational transparency. Transparency increases, because self-regulation requires goal, information, and feedback systems starting from top management down to the work team level and vice versa. These factors reduce of course lower and middle management power as informational gatekeepers, one reason why they often oppose self-regulating work teams.

Another perspective on the limits of self-designing teams is that it does not make sense in the long run, to participate people in team design, if customer orientation is not increased. It must be kept in mind that work design is not an end in itself, as well as employee satisfaction is not the single purpose of organizations. The primary purpose of profit organizations is to make profit, as it is the purpose of employees to earn money. However, functionally structured organizations tend to optimize functional and not process goals. For this reason, especially self-designing teams in quality control, industrial engineering, and other service departments might optimize their own processes and goal attainment, but not their service. Parkinson´s law is a well-known description of this tendency. For these reasons it is advisable to start self-design processes with those who are close to the customer in order to enhance organizational productivity and not to optimize sub-unit goals as an end in itself.

Customer focus as the key word in the beginning of the 90's is nowadays step by step substituted by the term shareholder value. This symbolizes a shift in stakeholder focus. As a consequence, returns on investment and stock performance are predominant management goals. However, increases in productivity in already lean companies often imply increasing work intensity. The reason is simple: processes are already restructured and most of the waste has already been eliminated. Consequently, increasing work intensity above a certain limit will strangulate group processes. There is less time for training, team meetings and problem solving. The pressure, to get ones growing daily business done, limits time and willingness for mutual support, continuous improvement, and strategic planning. As a result, process losses might occur again, reinforcing the pressure in a vicious circle. This would promise poor chances for the further development of self-regulating or self-designing teams. However, a shortsighted shareholder value will be detrimental to all stakeholders in the long run. There is no doubt that shareholder value is an important goal, and that a strategy to strengthen it will be beneficial both for the company and the economy, but it has to be balanced with the other goals, such as customer focus and employee orientation. If this happens, self-regulating and self-designing work teams will have a fair chance for their further development in Germany.

References

Antoni, C. H. (1986). Qualitätszirkel und Lernstatt - Ein Vergleich soziotechnischer Systeme japanischer und deutscher Herkunft. In W. Bungard & G. Wiendieck (Ed.), *Qualitätszirkel als Instrument zeitgemäßer Betriebsführung* (pp. 163-184). Landsberg/Lech: Verlag Moderne Industrie.

Antoni, C. H. (1990). *Qualitätszirkel als Modell partizipativer Gruppenarbeit. Analyse der Möglichkeiten und Grenzen aus der Sicht betroffener Mitarbeiter*. Bern: Huber.

Antoni, C. H. (Ed.) (1994). *Gruppenarbeit in Unternehmen - Konzepte, Erfahrungen, Perspektiven*. Weinheim: Psychologie Verlags Union.

Antoni, C. H. (1995). Gruppenarbeit in Deutschland - eine Bestandsaufnahme. In K. J. Zink (Ed.), *Erfolgreiche Konzepte der Gruppenarbeit* (pp. 23-37). Neuwied: Luchterhand.

Antoni, C. H. (1996). *Teilautonome Arbeitsgruppen. Ein Königsweg zu mehr Produktivität und einer menschengerechten Arbeit.* Weinheim: Psychologie Verlags Union.

Antoni, C. H. & Eyer, E. (1997). Kunden- und prozeßorientierte Arbeitsorganisation bei der YMOS AG. C. H Antoni, E. Eyer & J. Kutscher (Eds.), (1998), *Das flexible Unternehmen: Arbeitszeit, Gruppenarbeit, Entgeltsysteme*, (*chapter 08.01.*, pp. 1-28). Wiesbaden: Gabler.

Berggren, C. (1991). *Von Ford zu Volvo. Automobilherstellung in Schweden.* Berlin: Springer.

Berggren, C. (1992). *Alternatives to lean production. Work organization in the swedish auto industry.* Ithaca, NY: Cornell ILR Press.

Binkelmann, P., Braczyk, H. & Seltz, R. (Eds.) (1993). *Entwicklung der Gruppenarbeit in Deutschland.* Frankfurt: Campus Verlag.

BMFT (Bundesminister für Forschung und Technologie). (1980). *Gruppenarbeit in der Motorenmontage. Ein Vergleich von Arbeitsstrukturen.* Frankfurt: Campus.

Brödner, P. (1985). *Alternative Entwicklungspfade in die Fabrik der Zukunft.* Berlin: edition sigma.

Büth, P.(1994). Erfahrungen mit der Einführung von Produktinseln in der BOGE GmbH. In C. H. Antoni (Ed.) (1994a). *Gruppenarbeit in Unternehmen - Konzepte, Erfahrungen, Perspektiven* (pp. 191-208). Weinheim: Psychologie Verlags Union.

Bungard, W. & Wiendieck, G. (Eds.), *Qualitätszirkel als Instrument zeitgemäßer Betriebsführung* (pp. 163-184). Landsberg/Lech: Verlag Moderne Industrie.

Crocker, D. L., Charney, S., & Chiu, J. S. L. (1986). *Quality circles. A guide to participation and productivity.* New York: Mentor.

Cummings, T. G. & Blumberg, M. (1987). Advanced Manufactoring Technology and Work Design. In T. D. Wall, C. W. Clegg & N. J. Kemp (Eds.), *The Human Side of Advanced Manufacturing Technology* (pp. 37-60). Chichester: John Wiley & Sons.

Davis, L. E. & Cherns, A. B. (Eds). (1975). *The quality of working life. Vol. I & II.* New York: Free Press.

Emery, F. & Thorsrud, E. (1982). *Industrielle Demokratie - Bericht über das norwegische Programm der industriellen Demokratie.* Bern, Stuttgart, Wien: Huber.

Gaugler, E., Kolb, M. & Ling, B. (1977). *Humanisierung der Arbeitswelt und Produktivität.* Ludwigshafen: Kiehl.

Gerst, D., Hardwig, T., Kuhlmann, M. & Schumann, M. (1994). Gruppenarbeit in der betrieblichen Erprobung - Ein Modell kristallisiert sich heraus. *Angewandte Arbeitswissenschaft, Nr.142*, pp. 5-30.

Hackman, J. R. (1987). The Design of Work Teams. In J. W. Lorsch (Ed.), *Handbook of Organizational Behavior* (pp. 315-342). Englewood Cliffs, NJ: Prentice-Hall.

Hüser, M. & Kaun, R. (1995). Wer wa(a)gt, gewinnt Wägetechnik nach Kundenwusch von der MettlerToled GmbH. In H.-J. Warnecke (Ed.), *Aufbruch zum fraktalen Unternehmen* (pp. 315-337). Heidelberg: Springer.

Imai, M. (1986). *Kaizen. The key to Japan's competitive success.* New York: McGraw-Hill.

Jürgens, U., Malsch, T. & Dohse, K. (1989). *Moderne Zeiten in der Automobilfabrik.* Berlin: Springer.

Kashima, Y. & Callan, V. J. (1994). The japanese work group. In M. D. Dunnette & L. M. Hough (Eds.). *Handbook of industrial and organizational psychology* (pp. 609-645). Palo Alto: Consulting Psychologists Press.

Kaune, A. (1996). Gruppenarbeit in der Automobilproduktion Standortbestimmung, Gestaltungsmöglichkeiten und Weiterentwicklungsansätze. *Angewandte Arbeitswissenschaft, 150*, pp. 1-15.

Klebert, K., Schrader, E., & Straub, W. (1980). *Moderationsmethode.* München: Preisinger Studio und Verlag für Kommunikation.

Lang, R. & Hellpach, W. (1922). *Gruppenfabrikation.* Berlin: Julius Springer.

Ouchi, W. G. (1981). *Theory Z: How American business can meet the Japanese challenge.* Addison: Wesley.

Reichart, L. (1984). Lernstatt - die deutsche Alternative. *Personal, 36* , 231-234.

Rohmert, W. & Weg, F. J. (1976). Organisation teilautonomer Gruppenarbeit: Betriebliche Projekte - Leitregeln zur Gestaltung, Bd.1. In RKW (Ed.), *Beiträge zur Arbeitswissenschaft, Reihe I, Bd. 1* (pp. 12-13). München, Wien: Carl Hanser.

Ulich, E. (1989). VW-Projekt: Gruppenarbeit in der Motorenmontage. In S. Greif, H. Holling & N. Nicholson (Eds.), *Arbeits- und Organisationspsychologie: Internationales Handbuch in Schlüsselbegriffen* (pp. 527-533). München: Psychologie Verlags Union. (Neuauflage 1995).

Womack, J. P., Jones, D. T. & Roos, D. (1991). *Die zweite Revolution in der Automobilindustrie.* Frankfurt: Campus.

Zink, K. J. (Ed.) (1994). *Qualität als Managementaufgabe.* Landsberg: Verlag Moderne Industrie.

Zink, K. J. (Ed.) (1995). *Erfolgreiche Konzepte zur Gruppenarbeit.* Neuwied: Luchterhand.

Chapter 14

Group Work Concepts in Germany

Developments During the Past Three Decades

Sabine Sonnentag
University of Amsterdam, Amsterdam, The Netherlands

Sabine Remdisch
University of Giessen, Giessen, Germany

Abstract

This chapter presents an overview over the development of group work in Germany and German-speaking countries. First, this chapter describes action theory as a major theoretical contribution relevant for group work. Then practical implications of group work concepts will be discussed. These group work concepts implemented in work organizations range from autonomous group work in the seventies and quality circle implementations in the eighties to the adoption of lean production concepts in the nineties. In a concluding section these various concepts are compared with one another, discussed with respect to action theory and put into an international context.

Introduction

This chapter describes the history of group work in Germany and other German-speaking countries since the seventies. In this historical survey both developments with respect to theory and implementations of group work in companies will be covered. A main original development that was brought forward with respect to theory was action theory (Hacker, 1986; Frese & Zapf, 1994) an English overview). With respect to group work implementations in companies three decades will be differentiated. In the seventies much attention was paid to autonomous work group concepts that were discussed in the context of quality of work life. These quality of work life-discussions had been put into practice by the German government which implemented a research program called humanization of the work place (Humanisierung des Arbeitslebens). In the eighties quality circles and related concepts were put into practice on a large scale. Group work in the nineties mainly centered around the idea of lean production.

M.M. Beyerlein (ed.), Work Teams: Past, Present and Future, 219–235.

Theory Development: Group Work in the Context of Action Theory

In the past decades there has been a substantial academic discussion on group work in Germany and German-speaking Switzerland. Parallel to this discussion, theory development has taken place. Very influential within that development has been action theory (Frese & Zapf, 1994; Hacker, 1973, 1986; Volpert, 1987). Action theory can be regarded as a grand theory (Frese & Zapf, 1994) that is both cognitive- and behavior-oriented. Action theory has been influenced both by the cybernetic framework of Miller, Galanter, and Pribram (1960) and by Soviet psychology. There is some overlap with control theory that is better known in the Anglo-American tradition (Carver & Scheier, 1982; Lord & Levy, 1994).

First conceptualizations of action theory were published around 1970 (Hacker, Skell, & Straub, 1968; Volpert, 1971). Basic ideas within this theory have been formulated as a framework for describing actions of individuals. Later, action theory concepts were applied and extended to cooperative work processes (Cranach, Ochsenbein, & Valach, 1986; Oesterreich & Resch, 1985). With respect to group work two aspects within action theory are relevant: the definition of cooperation (Hacker, 1986) and the conceptualization of groups as self-active systems (Cranach, et al., 1986). Furthermore, concepts within the action theory framework offered important criteria for evaluating group work practice.

Basic Concepts within Action Theory

Action theory focuses on work as a goal-directed activity realized through actions (Hacker, 1985). Actions are defined through their orientation towards a conscious goal and are regarded as the central constituents of work (Hacker, 1985, 1986). Action theory describes how actions are regulated by taking up both a process and a hierarchical perspective. The action process is comprised of the development of goals, orientation including prognosis, generation of plans, decision among available plans, execution and monitoring of plans, and feedback processing. With regard to the hierarchical perspective, four levels of action regulation are distinguished: sensorimotor level; level of flexible action patterns; intellectual level; heuristic level (cf., Frese & Zapf, 1994 for a detailed description of the process and hierarchical perspective). Furthermore, action theory conceptualizes a general action related mental model that comprises knowledge of central features of the work process. Such an action related mental model includes representations of goals, of situational conditions and cues, as well as of possible actions for achieving the goal. The availability of an appropriate action related mental model is regarded to be essential for effective actions. Von Cranach and his coworkers described how these general concepts of human action could be applied to groups and their regulation (Cranach, et al., 1986; Tschan & Cranach, 1996). Recently, also Badke-Schaub and Frankenberger (1996) referred to action theory concepts for analyzing and discussing group level functioning.

Conceptualizing Group Work

One important issue within action theory has been the question about central aspects of good work design (Hacker, 1986; Volpert, 1990). It has been pointed out that besides other aspects (i.e., completeness of actions with respect to both their sequential and hierarchical aspects, control at work, and opportunity for learning), the opportunity for cooperation is essential for good work design. Furthermore, various grades of cooperation have been differentiated and a specification of group work has been provided. Hacker (1986) pointed out that not every situation in which several persons work in physical closeness deserves the term group work. Crucial for group work is joint task accomplishment whereby group members share a common goal, show coordinated activities, and communicate with each other. Thus, without a common external task that group members redefine as their common internal group task, there is no real group work. Therefore, many forms of cooperation that might naively be called group work are excluded from this conceptualization of group work.

The influence of this theoretical clarification on practical purposes was twofold. First, it provided a basis for the development of job analysis instruments. One of these instruments is the Tätigkeitsbewertungssystem (TBS) developed by Hacker and his colleagues (Hacker, Iwanowa, & Richter, 1983; cf. Frese & Zapf, 1994 for a short English summary of the TBS). One dimension of the TBS refers to cooperation and communication and offers a procedure that allows a job analyst to evaluate the grade of cooperation needed in a specific task environment.

The second practical implication of the theoretical clarification of group work refers to the provision of an unambiguous criterion in order to evaluate group work situations. By referring to an action theory background mainly lean production concepts have been criticized for resulting in Tayloristic work organization with low decision latitude at the group level, short cycle times, and a high amount of overtime (Ulich & Weber, 1996; Weber, 1994; cf. paragraph on group work in the nineties).

Groups as Self-Active Systems

The conceptualization of groups as self-active systems was put forward by von Cranach and his colleagues (Cranach, et al., 1986). The central idea of this approach is that there is a basic parallel between the action regulation of an individual and that of a group. Similarly to an individual's action, a group's action can be described from both a process and a hierarchical perspective. Additionally, also a group needs to have an understanding, a mental model, of the task and the task situation. However, above these parallels between the individual and group level action regulation, the group level processes comprise not only the group level processes but also the processes of all the individual members that have to be coordinated towards a common goal (cf., also Tschan & Cranach, 1996). Empirical support for such an action theory approach to group work was provided by Tschan (1995).

Group Work in the Seventies: Humanization of the Work

In this section, the humanization of the work place program promoted by the then West German government will be presented. The most prominent group work implementation within this humanization program at Volkswagen will be described.

The Humanization of the Work Place

During the seventies, lively discussions on work and the need for a humanization of the workplace took place both on an academic and a political level. The demand of employees for self-determination, participation, autonomy, and a higher involvement in decision-making was increasing (Ulich, 1991). The German government reacted to these recent developments by establishing a supportive government program for the humanization of the work place (Regierungsprogramm zur Humanisierung der Arbeit). Semi-autonomous work groups and new concepts of job-rotation, job-enlargement, and job-enrichment were implemented on the shop floor. The most popular case of a new group work design within Germany was probably the implementation in the automobile company Volkswagen.

The developments in Germany were based on the so-called socio-technical systems theory that was developed at the Tavistock Institute in Britain during the forties and fifties (Emery & Trist, 1969) and was subsequently elaborated by Scandinavian researchers such as Thorsrud (1972). The basic idea was to structure work in such a way that it satisfied both the technical needs of an industrial society and the social needs of an educated work force. Putting emphasis not only on the technical but also on social aspects of work had become necessary to reduce high turnover and absenteeism rates (Emery & Trist, 1969; Thorsrud, 1972). The traditional work practices seemed inappropriate for matching the social and the technical aspects of the workplace. Work groups provided an alternative approach for redesigning and improving work systems (Cummings, 1978). Consequently, individual work places were more and more replaced by group structures (Hofmeister, 1991) and extensive experimentation with innovative work group designs started in European manufacturing settings. On the whole, the most far-reaching concepts of group work were implemented in Scandinavia, which can be explained by Scandinavia's long tradition of human-centered work practices and by the problem Scandinavian companies faced in recruiting workers due to the high workers' surplus in the labor market (Wölm & Rolf, 1991). In Sweden at the car companies VOLVO and SAAB far-ranging experiments with semi-autonomous groups were done (Berggren, 1991) which "resulted in a truly democratic change process" (Rehder, 1992, p. 62). The single concepts of group work differed slightly between the companies, but as a crucial element the assembly line was replaced by single work stations and production platforms on which groups often assembled the complete car. As a consequence, work cycle-times increased substantially. Furthermore, the groups controlled their own pace of work, decided about work distribution within the group, elected their group speaker, and met regularly in group meetings.

The Case of Volkswagen

In Germany, especially the automobile industry with its high degree of repetitive and simplified working tasks on the assembly line was strongly criticized for not taking care of the human needs of the workers. In 1975 a huge three-year research project supported by the government program for the humanization of the work place started at Volkswagen (Volkswagen AG, 1980). A concept of semi-autonomous work groups was implemented in the production area (engine assembly). The evaluation of the implementation process should show if the new group concept could meet the expectations of the workers without loss in productivity. It should test whether semi-autonomous work groups could be regarded as a real alternative to traditional assembly line work.

Within the research project four semi-autonomous work groups, each of them consisting of seven employees, were compared to employees still working in the traditional way on the assembly line with fragmented, repetitive working tasks. The newly installed work groups were responsible for a variety of tasks, and the employees could undertake larger units of work resulting in work cycle times of 35 minutes. Each of the groups elected a group speaker and held regular group meetings.

The results of the research project at Volkswagen showed that the way of organizing work in-groups was intrinsically motivating and enhanced employee satisfaction (Ulich, 1983). The workers described their new work as more meaningful, because it had enabled them to bring in their experience and technical know-how. On the whole, there was an increase in employees' competency levels. Concerning stress and strain, an increase in cognitive and social strain as a consequence of the group system was found. A new reward system adapted to the group structure was introduced one year after the project had started. However, performance rates and productivity results of the semi-autonomous group implementation were not totally convincing.

After the research project was officially finished, the management of Volkswagen decided to stop the group concept, because the former fragmented task organization was more in line with the company's rationalization goals. Obviously, there was skepticism about the cost effectiveness of an extensive humanization of work approach (Volkswagen AG, 1980). One can speculate that another reason for the end of the group concept simply was the fact that nobody within the Volkswagen Company felt responsible for continuing the project after the researchers had left the company. Not until five years later, the workers' council of Volkswagen wanted the group concept to be renewed.

The project at Volkswagen has influenced the German discussion about the humanization of the work place and the development of new group work concepts since the seventies. If one takes into consideration that altogether no more than 28 workers took part in the research project the popularity and the far-reaching consequences of the project are impressive. They show the high ground of ideals for human-centered work organization and the widespread interest in organizational reform and socio-technical engineering in Germany.

Group Work in the Eighties: Quality Circles and Related Concepts

In this section, quality circle implementations in the German industry will be presented. The section starts with an overview over the historical background and then introduces the two main concepts, quality circles and Lernstatt. Typical implementations in organizations will be summarized and evaluated.

Historical Background

While in the seventies much attention was paid to group work in the context of humanization of the work place, discussions and implementation processes in the eighties concentrated on quality circles and related concepts such as the Lernstatt (learning circle, learning place) concept. There are several reasons for the increased interest in quality circles and Lernstatt activities since the end of the seventies.

First, as companies in other western countries, German industry became aware of the economic growth and high quality standard in Japan and the implication that might have for their own economic situation. When looking for possible reasons for Japan's economic power, also Japanese management techniques including quality circles were analyzed. Since at least part of the success of Japanese organizations were attributed to their management techniques, quality circles were adopted in German companies as in other western countries.

Second, during the economic growth of the German industry in the sixties and seventies, foreign workers were recruited at a large scale. Typically, these workers came from countries such as Italy, Spain, Greece, and Turkey. In some companies 90 percent of the industrial workforce was comprised of foreign workers (Antoni, 1986). In their work situations these workers, as well as their German speaking coworkers, were confronted with language problems that often could not be overcome in the everyday work process but threatened productivity and integration. Thus, big organizations such as BMW and Hoechst started specific qualification activities. These activities became well known under the term Lernstatt.

Bungard (1992) discusses changes in work-related values as a third reason for the growing interest in quality circles during the eighties. Surveys indicated a decrease in work motivation and work-related values, especially among un- or semi-qualified workers. Therefore, companies had to look for new concepts for increasing work motivation of their employees.

Main Concept

Strictly speaking when describing quality circles within German companies, two concepts have to be distinguished: the quality circle concept (in the original sense, adopted from Japan) and the Lernstatt concept developed in German companies in order to cope with the problems foreign workers were confronted with.

Quality Circle

According to Bungard and Wiendieck (1986) the essential characteristics of quality circles in the eighties can be described as follows: Quality circles were discussion meetings (Gesprächsrunden) of 5 to 10 persons from lower organizational levels. All members of a quality circle came from the same organizational division or department. The circle met regularly (every two or four weeks) on a voluntary basis in order to discuss and solve job-related problems. The group decided on the topics to discuss - independently from higher organizational levels. The discussion was facilitated by the workers' supervisor, an external agent, or an ordinary group member. Product quality was only one - although important - topic within the discussions. Additionally, topics such as safety, work procedures, equipment, and cooperation with the supervisor were covered. The discussion meetings took one to two hours and were scheduled during regular working time. If this was not possible, the meetings were scheduled otherwise and workers were paid additionally. Discussion facilitators informed a coordinator regularly about the discussed topics. Solutions produced by the quality circle could be rewarded with a bonus.

Despite this rather convergent description provided by Bungard and Wiendieck (1986), the way of implementing quality circles within companies differed substantially between organizations (Zink & Ackermann, 1988). In large organizations even differences between departments were reported (Antoni, 1994).

Quality circles differed form work groups in the context of humanization of the work place in that they concentrated on additional tasks and in that they were only indirectly related to the production process, whereas work groups in the context of the humanization idea accomplished tasks in the actual production process. Furthermore, quality circles' direct impact on the way work was organized and jobs were designed was less straightforward. While the work groups concepts in the context of humanization of the work place often clearly implied a reorganization of the work process, quality circles could exist irrespective of the traditional Tayloristic work structures and procedures (Antoni, 1990).

Lernstatt

The Lernstatt concept was developed in the seventies in order to overcome problems associated with the work situation of foreign workers employed in the German industry. The main reason for this initiative taken in some major companies were language difficulties but also other problems such as turnover and absenteeism associated with the work situation of these foreign workers. More traditional language course concepts had failed.

The main idea of the Lernstatt concept was to face and solve the problems in small groups close to the everyday work situation. Therefore, German first-line supervisors and workers were recruited and got some basic pedagogical training. It was their task to teach their foreign colleagues basic language skills necessary for coping with daily problems inside and outside the company. The groups were small and comprised six to eight workers and two trainers. Typical methods included role-plays and discussions of everyday problems. Thus, social competencies increased additionally through this kind of training. By working with these groups, German supervisors and coworkers got a better understanding of their foreign colleagues' situation.

German workers, who were not involved in these groups on a regular basis, became aware that they might also benefit from the participation in such a group discussing work-related problems. Therefore, subsequently the Lernstatt concept developed from a language course into a more general learning concept. Topics discussed in Lernstatt groups were often similar to those of quality circles. However, the Lernstatt concept focused more on learning and personal development processes of the individual than was the case within quality circle groups. Furthermore, Lernstatt groups often followed an approach in which the group processes were considered central while quality circles tended to apply more formalized procedures (Antoni, 1986).

Typical Implementations in Organizations

Since the beginning of the eighties, the implementation of quality circles in organizations increased visibly. In 1985 and 1986, Bungard and Antoni (Antoni, 1990) conducted a telephone survey in 100 big, successful industrial companies. It was found that in 1985 already 40 percent of the companies had implemented quality circles, the percentage increased to 48 percent in 1986, and reached the 50 percent level in 1989/90 (Antoni, Bungard, & Lehnert, 1992). However, the occurrence of quality circles in smaller companies was substantially smaller (Lehnert, 1994). In the beginning, quality circles were predominantly implemented in production areas (Antoni, 1990). However, positive experiences were also reported in other areas, such as service (Klaus & Bednarek, 1988). Parallel to the development in companies, since 1982 nation-wide quality circles congresses were organized. These congresses became an important forum for discussing and promoting the quality circle concept.

When comparing the implementation of quality circles in German industry with the corresponding processes in other western countries, many parallels become evident (Barrick & Alexander, 1987; Cordery, 1996). However, one specific issue typical for the development in Germany was policy-oriented discussions within unions and workers' councils in which the quality circle concept was related to other forms of employee participation. Central in this discussion was the question whether quality circles were compatible or in conflict with unions' policies (Breisig, 1990; Schultz, Selzner, & Wachsmuth, 1992).

Evaluation

A great deal of the German literature on quality circles and related concepts concentrated on practical issues. There were many articles and books published offering guidelines and suggestions for practitioners interested in the quality circle concept (e.g., Rischar & Titze, 1984; Schmidt-Brabe, 1994). With respect to empirical studies, descriptions of implementation processes, general assessments of a concept's success, and identification of typical problems encountered dominated the literature. These general evaluations of quality circles and related concepts mainly arrived at positive conclusions (Antoni, 1990; Bungard & Wiendieck, 1992; Heeg, 1985). For example, when summarizing results from 401 companies, Antoni (1990) found that persons directly involved in and responsible for quality circles reported increased quality of cooperation, job satisfaction, product quality, better work situation, better communication and cost reduction. However, no effects with respect to absenteeism, turnover, and accidents were reported. Quasi-experimental studies offering methodologically sound evaluations of quality circles or related concepts were rare (Antoni, 1990; Bednarek, 1985). These studies supported findings of the more general evaluations -- although at a less optimistic level. With respect to theory, some authors related the quality circles concept to other theoretically based concepts of group work and participation processes (e.g. Antoni, 1990; Schultz-Gambard & Bungard, 1992). However, a specific theoretical approach was not formulated (Bungard, 1992).

Group Work in the Nineties Under the Label Lean Production

In this section lean production systems originating from Japan will be contrasted with their implementations in Germany. It will be described how lean production concepts were put into practice during the nineties. An evaluation of the lean production concepts realized within the German industry will be provided.

The Success of the Japanese Lean Production System

During the nineties the discussion of new production concepts in Europe was dominated by the concept of lean production. A significant number of European business organizations were taking action in order to increase employee involvement on the shop floor. The driving forces for these organizational changes, especially in the automobile industry, were changes in the world markets with intensified competition, spread of new technologies and workers demands for more interesting and varied work. The latest Japanese lean production models seemed to be a successful answer to the challenges of the world market.

In the discussion of why Japanese lean production systems had proven to be superior to Western mass production, the importance of group work was intensively emphasized (Womack, Jones, Roos, & Sarpenter, 1990). Especially after the publication of the MIT study (Womack et al., 1990) the topics of lean production were discussed by managers as the most promising management strategy for meeting the so-called Japanese challenge. The MIT study had compared 90 automobile companies from 15 different countries for a time period of 5 years. The results were impressive: Compared to Japanese factories both in Japan and in North America, European and partly the American automobile companies showed about half of the productivity and a lower quality level (Womack et al., 1990). Additionally, Japanese companies needed only half the time for the development of new products; they were quicker in their reactions to consumer demands, and showed an increased variety of products and services (Womack et al., 1990).

Within lean production the employee was regarded as the decisive production factor (human capital). The Japanese lean production concept tried to fully utilize the know-how, the past experiences and qualifications of the employees. A further essential basic element was the purposeful inclusion of the employees in problem-solving processes. Employees were expected to have a high level of competence and problem-solving capabilities, as well as being very cooperative and responsible (Bullinger, 1993). Within the lean production system the employees were organized in work groups. The processes of group dynamics and group responsibilities were systematically made use of.

According to the MIT study, in 1989 approximately 70% of all Japanese production companies had implemented work groups compared to 0.6% in Europe (Womack, 1991). In the following years, the European companies, inspired by the great success of the Japanese, step by step tried to catch up by also introducing work groups and other lean production elements. It turned out that the Japanese lean production system could not simply be copied, but had to be adapted to the specific European prerequisites and characteristics. Historically, Europe had its own trajectory of organizational design programs, highly influenced by the humanization of the work place - idea implemented in the seventies.

The definition of group work within the Japanese lean production concept differed considerably from the European concept of semi-autonomous work groups (Weber, 1993). The Japanese lean production system could not at all be regarded as group work in the sense of humanization of the work place. Although workers rotated jobs within the groups, included inspection and some minor repair and machine maintenance within the groups and had the possibility to meet regularly for half an hour to discuss production problems and to look for improvements, most workers still did repetitive routine work in short cycles, suffered from high stress and had only limited independence. The Japanese concept of group work was severely criticized in the German-speaking literature, for example it was referred to as management by stress (Jürgens, 1993; Weber, 1993). And also Berggren (1992) regarded lean production as only an intensified assembly production, which is an understandable view from Europe's focus on ideals and practices of human work organization.

The More Human-Centered Current German Group Work Concepts

In Germany the metalworkers' union and the workers' councils turned the introduction of lean production into an important policy issue, whereas in Japan the idea of unions was nearly dead. The German unions actively negotiated for their own concepts of group work, continuing the campaigns for the humanization of work from the seventies (Roth & Kohl, 1988). Most of the aspects of lean production in Japan were introduced for efficiency purposes. Human-centered concerns, such as longer cycle times, more autonomy for work groups, and elected group leaders, were not part of the Japanese lean system. But these elements were developing in Germany (Turner & Auer, 1992). In Germany, progress toward group work in the car industry has been slower and more deliberate. Here, the union has played a strong proactive role in developing and promoting its own concepts of new work organization. Labor and management have been negotiating the substance of group work, including some elements that could be considered lean and others that came from the union's orientation toward humanization (Turner & Auer, 1992). German automobile companies did not just replace their old production system with elements of the Japanese lean system that did not much improve the quality of work life, but continued to experiment with other new models of management, that claimed high levels of quality, flexibility and productivity while trying to improve employees' development. The metalworkers' union argued that group work could serve management interests in cutting costs and raising productivity while at the same time raising skill levels and making work more interesting and human. It was argued that the high skill level in the German workforce, promoted by an extensive, national vocational education system already in place, would make the widespread introduction of skilled group work possible (Turner & Auer, 1992).

Further differences between western countries and Japan concerning the cultural background have to be mentioned. Large Japanese firms offered, in contrast to European companies, employment security to their employees, predictable seniority-linked wages and promotion systems, and full membership in the company community (Berggren, 1992). On the whole the Japanese employees showed a higher cooperative attitude and a stronger identification with the destiny of their company. Therefore, the Japanese management had more or less a free hand in shop-floor organization.

Taking all these differences in the cultural background between western countries and the Japanese culture into account, it became obvious that the lean production system could not simply be copied from the Japanese model. As a consequence the new work organization in Germany looked different in many ways.

Implementation in Organizations

In 1991 in Eisenach, an East German town, General Motors started building up a transplant explicitly modelled on its Japanese joint ventures in North America, CAMI and NUMMI. Similarly, Volkswagen tried to implement lean production elements in its east German plant in Mosel. Beside these greenfield approaches, traditional companies in the German automobile industry were restructed, as well. For example, the General Motor-plants Opel-Bochum and Opel-Rüsselsheim have been experimenting with work groups since 1989. In early 1991, the first German auto industry agreement for the firm-wide implementation of group work was signed at Opel between management and the general workers' council. Porsche and also Mercedes Benz started implementing lean production elements and group work in their production halls in 1992.

In the end, the actual shape of group work in the German industry that had emerged from negotiation processes between the union's maximal approach and employer notions, turned out to be:

1. The broad assignment of varying tasks for the group, including long cycle times.
2. Group competence in decision making in such areas as job rotation, division of work, quality control and training needs.
3. Elected group speakers.
4. Regular group meetings.
5. A joint steering committee at the firm level, with equal labor and management representation to coordinate the implementation of group work (Muster & Wannöffel, 1989, pp.39-54; Betriebsvereinbarung Nr 179: Gruppenarbeit, Adam Opel AG, 1991).

Evaluation

An evaluation study done at the Opel plant at Rüsselsheim showed that the introduction of the group work concept and other lean production elements on the shop-floor had been effective to some extent (Remdisch, 1993). After a period of 12 to 18 months considerable changes of the workers' jobs and their working situation had taken place. The workers reported more opportunities for qualification, more responsibility, higher task requirements, but also more strain and stress than before (Brodbeck & Remdisch, 1993). Concerning economic aspects it could be shown that workers' problem-solving behavior had increased, their multiskilling rate had doubled, and the number of industrial accidents had significantly been decreased, which could be explained by the fact that the maintenance of industrial safety was an often discussed topic within the group meetings. According to the management, the involvement of the workers in the continuous improvement process had significantly increased the productivity (Remdisch, 1993).

Further remarkable evaluation data are provided by Womack and Jones (1996) about the automobile company Porsche: "Under the new system, the number of suggestions per employee per year has risen to twelve, which is among the highest in Europe for European-owned firms" (p. 200). "After the fully lean system was in place for example in the engine assembly, the amount of space for inventories was reduced from 40 percent of the assembly area to zero, the amount of parts on hand was reduced from 28 days to essentially zero, and parts were in the assembly area for only about 20 minutes before the completed engine was sent to the final assembly area" (p. 203). Womack and Jones (1996) also described Porsche as a good example for the successful combination of Japanese and German thinking. This combination was able "to create something better than either" (p. 217).

Obviously, the European strategies for the synthesis of both lean and human-centered practices so far seem to have turned out well. On the one hand, workers' needs were achieved. On the other hand, the concepts seemed to be also economically convincing. According to Womack and Jones (1996), there is "already evidence that when lean concepts are married to the strengths of the German tradition, ..., a remarkably competitive hybrid form can emerge" (p. 189). Further evaluation of long-term outcomes is of course needed. Especially, it has to be checked in how far these hybrid concepts meet the human-centered goals of group work.

While the European concepts were succeeding, the limits of the Japanese lean production system became more and more evident. Japanese employees were moaning about the high stress level at work. As a consequence, Japanese firms started looking for new, so-called post-lean concepts that aspire to fit productivity to human needs (Jürgens, 1992). It looked as if the current European concepts were more future-oriented than the Japanese lean production, and that this time Japan could learn from Europe (Weber, 1993).

Conclusion

The implementation of work group concepts in companies over three decades represents a rather broad range of work group practices. However, common to all implementation processes was the assumption that problems both in productivity and workers' job satisfaction and well-being could be overcome with the specific group work implementations. The group work concept put into practice during the seventies was developed in the context of the humanization of work movement while the group concepts pursued in the nineties paid more attention to productivity aspects. However, this does not imply that in the seventies productivity was neglected (Volkswagenwerk AG, 1980). There is just as little ground for saying this as for concluding that concern for workers' attitudes have been completely abandoned in the nineties.

One major difference between group work concepts pursued in the seventies and nineties on the one hand and quality circles on the other hand refers to their respective closeness to the production process. Establishing groups in the seventies and nineties aimed at a direct involvement of these groups in the production process. Thus, the goods were produced by the groups and some degree of cooperation was required in order to fulfill the tasks. In contrast, groups meeting as quality circles or in a Lernstatt setting were no immediate agents in the production process. Of course, it could be the case that quality circle members were co-workers at an assembly line, but the quality circle as a unit was only indirectly linked to the production process. For example, problems occurring in the production process became discussion topics in the quality circles meetings and suggestions formulated by the quality circles were implemented in the production process. Nevertheless, the quality circles remained dissociated from the direct production process.

One feature realized in all group work concepts was the implementation of group discussion meetings. Such group discussions were the main activity of quality circles, but also occurred in the other two group work practices. Thus, meeting as a group, discussing problems, and developing possible solutions turned out as one crucial aspect of group work in the companies. This is noteworthy because in these group discussions workers who were often not familiar with expressing themselves in such a setting were asked to participate. As a consequence, group discussions often were only moderately efficient and a need for more training became obvious.

With respect to theory the question raised whether the three group work practices fulfil the group work criteria put forward by Hacker (1986) and how these group work practices can be described in action theory terms. The group work concept of the seventies came rather close to the group work criteria presented above. Besides joint task accomplishment, group members cooperated in setting subgoals for their work and planning task execution. Furthermore, it was attempted to realize a high degree of work group autonomy - an issue of crucial importance within action theory.

Also within the quality circle concept crucial features of group work had been put into practice, such as pursuing a common goal, showing coordinated activities and communication. However, quality circles were mainly busy with identifying problems, searching for possible solutions and, sometimes, evaluating the implemented solution. In action theory terms, quality circle activities were limited to goal formulation, orientation, planning, and feedback processing. But plans formulated by quality circles were executed by other stakeholders within an organization. Thus, quality circles activities did not cover the complete action process. Members of quality circles spent only a very little proportion of their working time in these circles implying that the participation in the circles per se did not change much in the degree members cooperated in their everyday work situation.

Finally, group work concepts of the nineties only partially met group work criteria formulated within action theory (Weber, 1994). Especially, Japanese group work structures of the nineties were often characterized by rather flexible work organization with at the same time short-cyclic tasks for the individual group members. This implied reduced opportunities for joint task accomplishment and communication. However, a first evaluation of European group work practices in the nineties with their higher task variety and opportunities for group decision making suggests that these groups potentially could meet the group work criteria.

Although we focused in our overview on history of group work in Germany and German-speaking countries during the past three decades, we want to stress that most of the developments were not at all unique for these countries. Parallel developments took place in other western industries: a focus on semi-autonomous group work practices inspired by the Swedish experiences during the seventies (e.g., Wall & Clegg, 1981); quality circles implementations during the eighties (cf. Cordery, 1996); lean production-oriented group work practices during the nineties. Nevertheless, these developments took place in a specific historical and political context with such essential features as the humanization of the work place program initiated by the German government, a relatively high rate of foreign shopfloor workers, a highly developed vocational education system, and specific union policies. Taken together, the developments presented in this chapter give a good example of more general tendencies with respect to group work practices and their implementation under specific background conditions during the past twenty-five years.

References

Adam Opel AG and the Opel General Works Council Rüsselsheim (1991). Betriebsvereinbarung Nr 179: Gruppenarbeit. *European Industrial Relations Review*, 210, p.11-12.

Antoni, C. (1986). Qualitätszirkel und Lernstatt - ein Vergleich soziotechnischer Instrumente japanischer und deutscher Herkunft. In W. Bungard & G. Wiendieck (Eds.), *Qualitätszirkel als Instrument zeitgemäßer Betriebsführung* (pp. 163-184). Landsberg /Lech: Verlag Moderne Industrie.

Antoni, C. H. (1990). *Qualitätszirkal als Modell partizipativer Gruppenarbeit. Analyse der Möglichkeiten und Grenzen aus der Sicht betroffener Mitarbeiter.* Bern: Huber.

Antoni, C. H. (1994). Gruppenarbeit - mehr als ein Konzept. Darstellung und Vergleich unterschiedlicher Formen der Gruppenarbeit. In C. H. Antoni (Ed.), *Gruppenarbeit im Unternehmen. Konzepte, Erfahrungen, Perspektiven* (pp. 19-48). Weinheim: Beltz.

Antoni, C., Bungard, W., & Lehnert, E. (1992). Qualitätszirkle und ähnliche Formen der Gruppenarbeit in der Bundesrepublik Deutschland: Eine Bestandsaufnahme der Problemlösegruppen-Konzepte bei den 100 umsatzgrößten Industrieunternehmen. In W. Bungard (Ed.), *Qualitätszirkel in der Arbeitswelt. Ziele, Erfahrungen, Probleme* (pp. 109-138). Göttingen: Verlag für Angewandte Psychologie.

Badke-Schaub, P., & Frankenberger, E. (1996). *Von den Daten zum Modell: Eine empirische Untersuchung von Gruppenarbeit in der Konstruktionspraxis* (Memorandum No. 14). University of Bamberg: Department of Psychology.

Barrick, M. R., & Alexander, R. A. (1987). A review of quality circle efficacy and the existence of positive findings bias. *Personnel Psychology*, 40, 579-592.

Bednarek, E. (1985). *Veränderungen der Arbeitsmotivation durch Qualitätszirkel und Lernstatt.* Dissertation, Technical University of Munich. Faculty for Economy and Social Scienes.

Berggren, C. (1991). *Von Ford zu Volvo: Automobilherstellung in Schweden.* Berlin: Springer.

Berggren, C. (1992). *Alternatives to lean production: work organization in the Swedish auto industry.* Cornell University: ILR Press.

Breisig, T. (1990). It's team time. *Kleingruppenkonzepte im Unternehmen.* Köln: Bund-Verlag.

Brodbeck, F. C., & Remdisch, S. (1993). Implementing group work in the car manufacturing industry. The foreman as a focal factor. In M. J. Smith & G. Salvendy (Eds.), Human-Computer-Interaction. *Proceedings of the 5th International Conference on Human-Computer-Interaction*, Orlando, Florida, August 8-13 (p.32-37). New York: Elsevier.

Bullinger, H. J. (1993). Human computer interaction and lean production: The shop floor example. *Proceedings of the Fifth International Conference on Human Computer Interaction*, Orlando, Florida, August 8-13.

Bungard, W. (1992). Qualitätszirkel als Gegenstand der Arbeits- und Organisationspsychologie- Einleitung und Überblick. In W. Bungard (Ed.), *Qualitätszirkel in der Arbeitswelt. Ziele, Erfahrungen, Probleme* (pp. 1-21). Göttingen: Verlag für Angewandte Psychologie.

Bungard, W., & Wiendieck, G. (1986). Zusammenfassende Diskussion: Definition und Abgrenzung des QZ-Konzepts. In W. Bungard & G. Wiendieck (Eds.), *Qualitätszirkel als Instrument zeitgemäßer Betriebsführung* (pp. 53-57). Landsberg/Lech: Verlag Moderne Industrie.

Bungard, W., & Wiendieck, G. (1992). Qualitätszirkel in einem Großbetrieb der metallverarbeitenden Industrie-Ergebnisse einer Befragung von Vorgesetzten, Moderatoren und Mitarbeitern. In W. Bungard (Ed.), *Qualitätszirkel in der Arbeitswelt. Ziele, Erfahrungen, Probleme* (pp. 139-180). Göttingen: Verlag für Angewandte Psychologie.

Carver, C. S., & Scheier, M. F. (1982). Control theory: A useful conceptual framework for personality-social, clinical, and health psychology. *Psychological Bulletin*, 92, 111-135.

Cordery, J. L. (1996). Autonomous work groups and quality circles. In M. A. West (Ed.), *Handbook of work group psychology* (pp. 225-246). Chichester: Wiley.

Cranach, M. v., Ochsenbein, G., & Valach, L. (1986). The group as a self-active system: outline of a theory of group action. *European Journal of Social Psychology*, 16, 193-229.

Cummings, T. G. (1978). Self-regulating work groups: A socio-technical synthesis. *Academy of Management Review*, 1(3), 625-634.

Emery, F., & Thorsrud (1982). *Industrielle Demokratie*. Bern: Huber.

Frese, M., & Zapf, D. (1994). Action as the core of work psychology: A german approach. In H. C. Triandis, M. D. Dunnette, & L. M. Hough (Eds.), *Handbook of industrial and organizational psychology* (pp. 271-340). Palo Alto, CA: Consulting Psychologists Press.

Hacker, W. (1973). *Allgemeine Arbeits- und Ingenieurpsychologie: Psychische Struktur und Regulation von Arbeitstätigkeiten*. Berlin: VEB Deutscher Verlag der Wissenschaften.

Hacker, W. (1985). Activity: A fruitful concept in industrial psychology. In M. Frese & J. Sabini (Eds.), *Goal directed behavior: The concept of action in psychology* (pp. 262-284). Hillsdale, NJ: Erlbaum.

Hacker, W. (1986). *Arbeitspsychologie*. Bern: Huber.

Hacker, W., Iwanowa, A., & Richter, P. (1983). *Tätigkeitsbewertungssystem*. Berlin: Diagnostisches Zentrum.

Hacker, W., Skell, W., & Straub, W. (Eds.) (1968). *Arbeitspsychologie und wissenschaftlich-technische Revolution*. Berlin: Deutscher Verlag der Wissenschaften.

Heeg, F. J. (1985). *Qualitätszirkel und andere Gruppenaktivitäten: Einsatz in der betrieblichen Praxis und Anwendung*. Berlin: Springer.

Hofmeister, G. (1991). *Gruppenarbeit und Aspekte normativer Steuerung in Wirtschaftsorganisationen* (Dissertation). Köln: Universität Köln, Wirtschafts- und Sozialwissenschaftliche Fakultät.

Jürgens, U. (1992). *Mythos und Realität von lean production in Japan* (Zwischenbericht). Berlin: Wissenschaftszentrum für Sozialforschung.

Jürgens, U., Malsch, T., & Dohse, K. (1989). *Moderne zeiten in der automobilfabrik*. Berlin: Springer.

Klaus, F., & Bednarek, E. (1988). Qualitäts-Zirkel im Dienstleistungsbereich - Ergebnisse einer Pilotstudie mit 46 Ingenieuren. *Zeitschrift für Arbeits- und organisationspsychologie*, 32, 92-94.

Lehnert, E. (1994). Gruppenarbeit in mittleren Industriebetrieben. In C. H. Antoni (Ed.), *Gruppenarbeit in unternehmen: Konzepte, Erfahrungen, Perspektiven* (pp. 285-307). Weinheim: Beltz.

Lord, R. G., & Levy, P. E. (1994). Moving from cognition to action: A control theory perspective. *Applied Psychology: An International Review*, 43, 335-398.

Miller, G. A., Galanter, E., & Pribram, K. (1960). *Plans and the structure of behavior*. New York: Holt, Rinehart & Winston.

Muster, M., & Wannöffel, M. (1989). *Gruppenarbeit in der Automobilindustrie*. Bochum: IG Metall Verwaltungsstelle Bochum.

Oesterreich, R., & Resch, M. (1985). Zur Analyse arbeitsbezogener Kommunikation. *Zeitschrift für Sozialisationsforschung und Erziehungssoziologie*, 2, 271-291.

Rehder, R. R. (1992). Building cars as if people mattered: the Japanese lean system vs. Volvo's Uddevalla system. *Columbia Journal of World Business*, 27(2), p.56-70.

Remdisch, S. (1993). *Group work in the automobile industry: The new role of the supervisor.* (Diploma thesis). Giessen: University of Giessen.

Rischar, K., & Titze, C. (1984). *Qualitätszirkel: Effektive problemlösung durch gruppen im betrieb.* Grafenau: Expert Verlag.

Roth, S., & Kohl, H. (1988). *Perspektive: gruppenarbeit.* Köln: Bund Verlag.

Schmidt-Braße, U. (1994). Qualitätszirkel in organisationen. In E. Gros (Ed.), *Anwendungsbezogene arbeits-, betriebs- und organisationspsychologie* (pp. 359-386). Göttingen: Verlag für Angewandte Psychologie.

Schultz, F., Selzner, J., & Wachsmuth, R. (1992). Organisationspsychologie und interessenvertretung: wege zur weiterentwicklung des QZ-Konzepts. In W. Bungard (Ed.), *Qualitätszirkel in der arbeitswelt: Ziele, erfahrungen, probleme* (pp. 89-106). Göttingen: Verlag für Angewandte Psychologie.

Schultz-Gambard, J., & Bungard, W. (1992). Qualitätszirkel aus kontrolltheoretischer perspektive. In W. Bungard (Ed.), *Qualitätszirkel in der arbeitswelt: Ziele, erfahrungen, probleme* (pp. 51-70). Göttingen: Verlag für Angewandte Psychologie.

Tschan, F. (1995). Communication enhances small group performance if it conforms task requirements: The concept of the ideal communication cycles. *Basic and Applied Social Psychology*, 17, 371-393.

Tschan, F., & Cranach, M. v. (1996). Group task structure, processes and outcome. In M. A. West (Ed.), *Handbook of work group psychology* (pp. 95-121). Chichester: Wiley.

Turner, L., & Auer, P. (1992). *The political economy of new work organization.* WZB - research papers, No. FSI92-4. Berlin: Wissenschaftszentrum WZB.

Ulich, E. (1983). Alternative arbeitsstrukturen - dargestellt am beispiel der automobilindustri. *Zeitschrift für Arbeits- und Organisationspsychologie*, 27, 70-78.

Ulich, E. (1991). Arbeitspsychologie. Stuttgart: Poeschel.

Ulich, E., & Weber, W. G. (1996). Dimensions, criteria and evaluation of work group autonomy. In M. A. West (Ed.), *Handbook of work group psychology* (pp. 247-282). Chichester: Wiley.

Volkswagenwerk A. G. (1980). *Gruppenarbeit in der motorenmontage: EIn vergleich von arbeitsstrukturen.* Frankfurt/Main: Campus.

Volpert, W. (1971). Sensumotorisches lernen: Zur theorie des trainings in industrie und sport. Frankfurt/M.: Limpert.

Volpert, W. (1987). Psychische regulation von arbeitstätigkeiten. In U. Kleinbeck & J. Rutenfranz (Eds.), *Arbeitspsychologie: Enzyklopädie der psychologie, D III, Band 1* (pp. 1-42). Göttingen: Hogrefe.

Volpert, W. (1990). Welche arbeit ist gut für den menschen? Notizen zum thema menschenbild und arbeitsgestaltung. In F. Frei & I. Udris (Eds.), *Das Bild der Arbeit* (pp. 23-40). Bern: Huber.

Wall, T. D., & Clegg, C. W. (1981). A longitudinal field study of group work redesign. *Journal of Occupational Behavior*, 2, 31-49.

Weber, W. (1993). Auswirkungen der ‚lean production' auf die produktionsarbeit und humane alternativen aus arbeitspsychologischer sicht. In E. Ulich (Ed.), *Mensch - Technik - organisation.* Zürich: Verlag der Fachvereine.

Weber, W. G. (1994). Autonome und restriktive gruppenarbeit in der produktion. Anmerkungen zu einer arbeitspsychologischen unterscheidung. *Zeitschrift für Arbeitswissenschaft*, 48, 147-156.

Wölm, J., & Rolf, A. (1991). Zur geschichte der gruppenarbeit. In H. Oberquelle (Ed.), *Kooperative abeit und computerunterstützung,* (pp. 129-147). Göttingen: Verlag für Angewandte Psychologie.

Womack, J. P., & Jones, D. T. (1996). *Lean thinking: banish waste and create wealth in your corporation.* New York: Simon & Schuster.

Womack, J. P., Jones, D. T., & Roos, D. (1990). *The machine that changed the world.* New York: Rawson Associates.

Womack, J. P., Jones, D. T., & Roos, D. (1991). *Die zweite revolution in der Automobilindustrie*. New York: Campus Verlag.

Zink, K. J., & Ackermann, M. (1988). Quality circles und qualität der arbeit. *Zeitschrift für Arbeits- und Organisationspsychologie*, 32, 72-79.

Chapter 15

The Formation of Work Teams in Russia

Commanding Methods of Labor Organization in the Czarist Russia

Yuri Alexandrov, Alexander Karyakin, and Andrey Tseshinsky

Ivanovo State Power University, Ivanovo, Russia

Abstract

Collective (team) methods of labor organizations have been present in every period of world history. The popularity of the teamwork concept in the United States is not an unexpected invention, but rather a natural development of the science of management. The collective (team) form of work is historically inherent to every nation, and Russia has one of the richest experiences in the development to collective forms of work. This chapter discusses the historical steps of collective forms of work development in Russia and the Soviet Union, with examples from the past as points of focus.

Introduction

The work team concept that is widely spread in the USA now has deep historical roots in Russia. Labor team organization in Russia and in some oriental countries originated from the tribal life. The team or "artel," as it was earlier called in Russia, was strengthened by mutual responsibility, the use of joined labor and common capital. An artel can be defined today as an autonomous production organization with the complete pecuniary responsibility for the final results of collective labor and the collective ownership of production means. Artels became very common in Russia in the middle of the seventeenth century among peasants involved in fishery. Other kinds of artels, such as dairy products, manufacturing, gold mining, building, and gunsmiths were also known. These artels had various approaches to team organization, wages and labor distribution, leader selection, fixed capital investment and management. For instance, wages in different artels could be distributed: (a) equally among all artel members, (b) depending on the experience and the qualification of the worker (without estimation of the labor contribution), (c) proportionally to the individual labor contribution, or (d) with regard for the invested pecuniary means.

Mostly, the character of the performed work caused peculiarities in each team. The common features for all artels were complete responsibility of the artel members for the labor results and the property, a wide range of independently solved problems, as well as the important role of the agreement in regulating internal and external relationships.

M.M. Beyerlein (ed.), Work Teams: Past, Present and Future, 237–246.

One of the first industrial artels appeared in the Urals at the Nickolayev small arms factory in the 1860s. It numbered originally 60 people and later increased to 150. Active labor activities, self-management, and constant production instruments improvement caused a 10% increase in labor productivity over a three-year period. The main principles of artel formation were:

1. Every artel member was obliged to work in the artel himself.
2. It was not allowed to participate only financially.
3. Every artel member was obliged to pay an entrance fee.
4. It was allowed to use a credit or to pay in installments.
5. All artel members were equal in management without regard for the wages and the profit.
6. The wage was fixed depending on the qualification and the received profit.
7. Responsibilities for debts and liabilities extended only to the artel property.

A leader elected for one year and his four assistants performed management of the artel. There were certain requirements for the educational level of the leader. The scope of problems solved by the leader was restricted; for instance, in the financial sphere they could make decisions only within certain limits. More important problems were solved at the meetings of the artel representatives (one for every five people). The meeting was authorized to cancel any decision from a leader. Profit and wages distribution was done according to the results of the collective labor with regard for the individual contribution.

A manager distributed work according to a specific order and the skills of a definite artel member. Part of the profit came to the common artel fund. Similar artels were organized in other regions of Russia as well. However, with the development of industry, self-supporting organizational structures like artels lost their importance.

Teams of 1917-1945

After the 1917 Revolution the principle change in the development of industry was done in favor of absolute centralization of planning and financing on the government level. A definite weakening of the directive-management took place in the middle of the 1920s. However, starting with 1929 management of enterprises again became directive and centralized, and it retained such characters until 1965. Of course, organization of a self-directed teamwork type was out of the question during that period, although attempts to realize some principles of teamwork were often undertaken. The commanding style of management in industry produced a negative effect on teamwork.

The first teams of workers appeared in 1920. Uniting into small groups, the most active young workers tried to solve some production problems together. Such groups took on obligations to strengthen discipline, to achieve wasteless material expenditures, neatness and order at the work place. Teams like that were called "shock teams" because their functioning was based on the enthusiasm of the workers seeking to increase to maximum labor productivity by means of their active shock work. For instance, the following requirements of the charter of a shock team for one of the workshops at Zlatoust metallurgical plant included:

1. A member of the team works honestly and consciously.
2. A member seeks to produce more high quality metal.
3. A member struggles against shirking and slipshodness at work.
4. A member always tries to increase his qualification and political literacy.
5. A member actively participates in the production meetings.
6. A member of the team should be progressive in everything.
7. A member should be an example at work and also in his public and private life.

A considerable impetus was given to the development of teamwork in 1928 by the appeal of the Communist party leadership to communists and workers. The appeal summoned them to develop creative activities of the working class and to stimulate its wide involvement in state management.

The 16th Communist Party Congress of 1931 had a great influence on the teamwork movement. Its documents stated that the most important factor of the successful development of the country was an upsurge of labor activity and creative enthusiasm of workers expressed in the mass transition to the new forms of labor organization. This influence of the Communist party was especially evident in large industrial centers where workteams were actively developing. For example, the first shock team in Leningrad was formed in July 1928, at the knitted-goods factory "Ravenstvo" (Equality). This team had 49 members. For eight months of work the team achieved a 13% decrease of raw material processing prime cost and a 17% increase of labor productivity.

In the 1930s, the most common types of teams were: (a) shock teams which grouped workers of several professions; (b) rationalization teams, a prototype of the "quality society;" and (c) public "tow" teams in which experienced workers rendered active help to the younger generation.

In 1931, the first non-financing by the state teams appeared in Leningrad: it was the first attempt to solve some management problems inside the teams. The main point of self-supporting basis was in the following: (a) the team made an agreement with the plant administration for the fulfillment of a certain task during a 10-15 day period; (b) the team itself scheduled the fulfillment of the task; and (c) within the provided finance limits.

Unfortunately, the rigid and directive management considerably restricted the independence of such teams. The idea of competition arose at the same time and stimulated the increase of labor productivity. Many enterprises began to introduce the idea of counter-planning. Having been given the task from the administration, teams analyzed their resources and put forward their own increased plans for the production output.

One of the interesting initiatives belonged to the teams at "Krasnaya Zarya" (The Red Dawn) plant in Leningrad. They fixed the amount of goods to be produced after every hour of work and put forward a new increased plan for the next hour. The media covered the work and the initiatives of teamwork very widely, the most active teams being morally and materially supported.

However, forming and functioning of the teams caused many problems. They could be explained first of all by (a) shortcomings in the setting of rates and wages, (b) by the lack of well-thought methods of wage distribution, (c) by the lack of financial means, (d) the deficiency of commercial goods, and (e) complicated consideration of personal labor contribution of team members. Labor rates didn't take into account technical equipment of the plant; there was no differentiation between qualified and non-qualified, easy and heavy labor. In some places, particularly in the Urals, it was a common practice to do all the work together and to distribute wages equally, which caused wage levelling. As a result, the workers were not interested in increasing their qualifications. Many qualified workers left the teams for other enterprises. A great drawback was in the fact that labor productivity in the teams was measured by the total number of work hours.

As a result, with labor productivity in hours up to 150-200 percent, the teams didn't fulfill the plan for the total volume of output. The low level of labor discipline and fluctuation of manpower prevented production development. Very often team initiatives grew into a political propaganda campaign to the detriment of rational methods of management. Serious deviations from the technological norms were committed for the sake of fulfillment of the task ahead of schedule and showy reports to the party leadership. It took place when Stalingrad tractor works and Gorky automobile works were set working. In 1935, the Communist Party leadership made another attempt to stimulate the teamwork movement. Some restrictions of the wages increase were abolished, rates were fixed for longer terms; these measures promoted a labor productivity rise and stirred workers activity.

A new stakhanov movement (named after the initiator Alexey Stakhanov) also marks this time -- "stakhanovizm." It spread widely over the country. The leader played the principle role; the other members of the team were in the shadow and had mostly auxiliary functions. This movement appeared, of course, not by chance, it was the result of efforts of the communist leaders to strengthen industry by means of another forcing of a competition campaign. It was essentially a political movement, which was supported by Stalin who always favoured political decisions of the problems over economic ones. The Stakhanov movement started with the record in coal mining set up by A. Stakhanov in Donbas on August 31, 1935. The record was promoted mostly by creation of special favorable industrial and later moral and material conditions. The Stakhanov movement developed only in some professional groups favoured by the communist leaders and available for setting up records. Administration and communist leadership of enterprises were only formally interested in having several stakhanov workers; it confirmed their political loyalty. Some workers, on the contrary, sincerely wanted to join this movement; they tried their best to be among the Stakhanov followers, to have a profitable working place. Progressive forms of wages stimulated their interest in increasing labor productivity, especially as industrial conflicts, directives, rules, and technical norms were not taken into account in this case.

Stakhanov workers strongly resisted regulations from management, which implied transfer of many plenary powers to the workers who, unfortunately, had neither the necessary knowledge nor the wish to go deep into economical, engineering and organizational problems. But management still possessed a very rigid form of responsibility. After some economic failures in 1936, a number of large lawsuits were organized against representatives of management who were accused of anti-Communist activities. In many cases stakhanov workers were the main prosecutors. Hypertrophied attention to team leaders or separate workers led to many contradictions and problems.

1. Development of disproportion in production and interruptions in supply. Range of goods considerably decreased: they produced mostly the goods that were available for setting up records.
2. Increase of workers exploitation and occupational injuries. Maintenance and technical control were ignored in order to increase productivity. Equipment was being destroyed. Ignoring the rates led to over-expenditure of raw materials.
3. Decrease of the quality of goods. In many cases when setting up records, they often ignored the quality.
4. Fast and unreasonable wage expenses increased. The system of wages was destroyed.

During the war years of 1941-1945, the commanding style of management became even stronger. Sometimes they ran to extremes. For example, in some enterprises teams had not only a leader but also a military-like political adviser. Workers sometimes went to their working places dismounts. It was an attempt to substitute the initiative activities of workers by use of a commanding system.

Post-War Period in Team Development

While in some fields of industry a labor productivity rise was achieved by additional manual efforts of workers, by improving their labor skills, in machine-building and metallurgy production, the rise depended on the better application of the equipment. It required reorganization of the principles of team formation. In 1948, the first teams including not only workers but also engineers and scientists started to appear. They had a wide range of activities, such as technical consultations, exchange of experience, technical documentation and production samples, training the second profession, and excursions to the best enterprises.

In 1958, a new attempt to stir up a team movement by means of ideological slogans was made. Some teams were given the rank of "The Team of Communist Labor." Unfortunately, the influence of the commanding style of management was still too great. Very often, competitions for the rank "The Team of Communist Labor" admitted a good deal of bureaucratise and formalism, especially when drawing-up pledges and summing up. Awarding honored ranks turned into an end in itself.

In 1965, the leaders of the enterprises received more independence and rights. But the measures intended to improve the economy were inadequate and were not successful. Beginning with the 1970s, some enterprises started to introduce methods of non-financing by the state management which gave the possibility of independent solutions of some production problems in the enterprise on the level of small groups of workers. Thus, in accordance with the resolution of the Communist Party Central Committee of the USSR of July 12, 1979, *"On Improvement in Planning and Strengthening the Executive Mechanism Impact on the Production Level and Labor Efficiency,"* work teams are to be the major form of the initial labor groups.

This resolution entitles work teams to arrange their labor activities independently, including:

1. Determining the amount of salaries, wages and bonuses paid for the bulk of work done by the whole team, the contribution of each individual worker to the collective labor especially being taken into account.

2. Allowing team members to distribute the bonuses and premiums given for professional craftsmanship and for performing different related functions.
3. Recommending the Administration and the Trade Union Committee of an enterprise to make amendments to the workers' classification system, guiding in this matter by law in general and by the by-laws of the organization in particular, and promote workers, who proved their high qualifications in practice, to high positions.
4. Electing socialist competition winners within a work team and determining their awards.
5. Selecting among the members of team candidates for pecuniary of moral awards in the all-plant socialist competition.

The resolution also led to the spreading of teams in the industry of the 1980s. They gained definite independence and could be considered as a prototype of teamwork in socialist Russia. Teams like that were mostly common in industry. What is the merit of the work team organization system, its main advantage that enabled it to survive for such a long period of time? The answers to this question include:

1. Coincidence of personal and public interests.
2. The socialist principle "From each according to his abilities, to each according to his labor."
3. Fair and complete rewarding of workers in accordance with their individual participation and contributions.

These factors cause high productivity among people grouped in work teams; they stimulate their initiative and produce high labor outcomes at a low expense. In work teams, that are the initial production links, labor cooperation can be obtained most completely. Work teams are grouped for performing different kinds of work, such as:

1. Working with and maintaining large-size and complex assemblies demanding labor co-ordination of many workers from adjacent teams.
2. Performing production tasks that cannot be easily distributed among individuals.
3. Performing similar technological processes when, though having the same volume and field of work, one individual cannot yet do this production task alone.
4. Performing such kinds of work, when either the outcome of a particular team directly depends on the work of the auxiliary and servicing personnel, or on workers who have no permanent workplaces. In the latter case, it is not possible to determine the range of their duties and obligations, either.

What are the differences between a team and an ordinary group of people engaged in manufacturing? Usually the following main principles of team formation are distinguished.

1. Creating of the working association with the purpose of producing some final result (a finished product, a half-finished product and the like), according to which the evaluation of the teamwork is performed.

2. Establishing the payment to the members of the team (completely or partially) taking into account the final results of the teamwork and individual participation of each member.
3. Appointing equipment, instrumentation and production space to the team.
4. Combining of administrative and collective management.
5. Concluding an agreement between the administration of the enterprise and the team.
6. Organizing of the system of planning, accounting, evaluation and material stimulation for teams.

In other words, a team is formed on the basis of the agreement between the leaders and the workers with the purpose of manufacturing a product with payment according to the final result. This agreement stipulates the terms of accounting and evaluation of the team participants' labor, providing of the team the means of production and work area, as well as the system of management and planning.

According to the agreement, a team is given a certain degree of independence in solving production problems and sometimes in distributing payment. Financing by the state, the team works for the final result on the common order (rated task)l its activities are planned.

TABLE 1. The number of workers and teams in industry

Year	Number of teams in thousands	Including those working on self-supporting basis	The number of workers teams	
			Thousands of people	%
1980	1,068	--	10,765	42.9
1985	1,510	438	19,227	73.6
1986	1,505	469	19,887	77.1
1987	1,442	497	19,684	75.7
1988	1,397	533	19,266	74.6
1989	1,326	530	18,060	73.5

In the advanced teams working on a self-supporting basis, the plans are determined not only for the production volume and the labor quality improvement but also for the salary fund, the expenditure of materials, fuels, power and other resources. Various publications on this subject treat the theoretical fundamentals of creating teams differently, and it found its practical realization in our enterprises, as well.

The team leader selected among the workers was both nominated by the chief executives of the enterprise and further approved at a team meeting or appointed by the workers at a meeting and later agreed upon by the management. At many enterprises special preparatory courses for training the selected candidates and potential team leaders were arranged. Besides the leader, team members, when numbering more than 10-12 people elected the team council to which the best qualified and most active workers were promoted. The team council or the team meeting, if the number of team members were small, made decisions about the problems concerning the team vitality such as:

1. Labor planning and equipment distribution.
2. Task distribution among team members.
3. Labor fulfillment supervision.

4. Supervision of labor safety, equipment maintenance, and technological process performance.
5. Determination of each team member's contribution to the total labor outcome and, on this basis, determination of the rate which is taken into account in distributing salaries and wages.

At the same time questions of production improvement, team member' selection, penalizing, etc. required managerial co-ordination at different levels of hierarchy, and limited the team independence and flexibility in decision making. Five to six stages were required for co-ordination of some questions.

The Structure and Management of Teams at the Enterprise

In accordance with the task done and professional qualifications, workers were divided into two types of teams: special task teams and complex task teams. Special Task Teams grouped workers of one or several related professions performing technologically similar functions together (i.e., production line conveyors). Complex task teams grouped workers of various professions performing different main or auxiliary functions together (i.e., engineers and technicians). Very often complex task teams were about 70-100 people in number. The question of number of workers in the teams has been considered many times and has not been agreed upon yet. Those who are in favour of enlarging teams to prove their stand, state three points. First, in small teams close personal relations dominating business ones are formed, a corporate spirit and group exclusiveness are developed, and the team tends to become a company of close friends. Second, large teams promote favourable conditions for making the technological process complete, for planning and controlling the bulk of work done. Third, large teams simplify the problem of inter-changeability among workers. However, large teams lack collective cohesion, their workers do not feel responsible for the work done, for the ultimate product.

Russian psychologists consider that 15-25 members should be the maximum numbers of workers in a team. This will result in multi-channel interdependence of workers, their interaction, and integration. On the basis of these factors collective motivation of high labor productivity will be developed.

But this quantity is, by no means, obligatory. Under some circumstances, a work team numbering more than 50 people may obtain the greatest outcome results. For instance, in the Sumskaya Region a large work team of 75 workers at the Promsvyaz Plant was in charge of the whole one-item production cycle.

For the fist three years the team at the Promsuyaz Plant had 49.3% production outcome growth, 40.3% productivity level rise and 18% wages rate increase. In addition to these, waste in the working hours, including loafing and truancy, and in metals and instrumentation expenses decreased greatly. The essential point in teamwork is control and evaluation of individual contribution to a team's outcome on the whole.

Wages

It should be noted that wages of workers were formed from several parts: (a) the main salary which was determined by norms and a defined task; (b) bonuses, for example, for the fulfillment of the task ahead of schedule, for the quality, for the fulfillment of the planned or for the important task and so on; and (c) additional payment for the work at night, on holidays, or for unhealthy conditions of work. Approaches to the distribution of wages in teams included:

1. The *main salary* was distributed with regard for the work time and qualifications (which was determined by a special plant committee by the presentation of a team-leader or a manager).

   Bonuses were distributed according to a coefficient (i.e., percentages); additional payment was determined by a manager according to the working conditions of a concrete worker.

   Shortcoming: with a bonus being small, concrete contribution of each member of the team was considered very little.

2. The *main salary* and the bonus were distributed with regard for coefficients, but the salary was not to be lower than a certain minimum which took into consideration a worker's qualifications and working hours.

   Shortcoming: it is difficult to create a well thought-out system of coefficients. As all the money earned by the team is distributed according to this system, there can be some members of the team not satisfied by the coefficient determined for them, and the team can lose highly qualified workers. The contradiction is in the fact that if the system of coefficients is too complicated, it is difficult to apply it; if it is too simple, it becomes subjective.

3. The *main salary* consists of two parts. The rate of the first part is defined with regard for some additional operations not stipulated by the profession or the norms which workers have to fulfill. It gives the chance to decrease the number of people in the team. This part of the salary is distributed with regard for the contribution of each worker in the process of mastering additional professions. The second part is distributed with regard for working hours and qualifications.

   Bonuses were distributed according to a coefficient.

   Shortcoming: This approach complicates the system of accounting and, similar to the first approach, it considers personal contribution very little.

Coefficients: One of the applied methods is a purely empirical, subjective determination of the coefficient. There is statistical data that in 1984, in 40% of the cases, the team council determined the coefficient in 21.7% by the team-leader, in 8% by the common meeting.

The second method implies application of a certain basic coefficient assigned to each worker on the basis of the results of the preceding work (e.g., taking into account the salary for the previous year or six months). The basic coefficient is later corrected according to the results of a month is work with regard for the previously formed list on increasing and decreasing factors.

Some of the factors have a subjective character. However, in any case a manager or a supervisor confirmed coefficients. The shortcoming of this approach in the specific conditions of Russia is in the fact that a decrease of the coefficient of one team member could influence the extra material interests of the whole team, because the factors (see Table 2) were often taken into consideration when distributing benefits (e.g., like receiving free-of-charge accommodations in a sanatorium or buying goods which were in high demand).

TABLE 2. Coefficient factors

Increasing Factors	Decreasing Factors
High personal productivity	Not fulfilling the task
Mastering new profession	Low labor quality
Economical material expenditures	Shirking, tardiness
Assistance to other team members	Unlimited breaks in work
Complexity of the work done	Breach of the public peace (breaking laws)
High quality of labor and others	Others

It is only natural that the problems regarding team vitality are not limited by the ones mentioned above. Such problems as (a) interaction with high authorities; (b) determination of the individual decision making sphere; (c) teamwork organization and team members' functions; (d) inter-changeability and holding more than one profession; (e) cooperation with engineering, technical, promotion, and adjacent groups; (f) quality guarantee; and (g) many others are not considered in this article at all. One should mention here that, despite the above problems in teamwork organization, teams proved vital and conductive to further theoretical research and practical realization.

However, the bossy and directive style of management at our enterprises limited the possibilities of team development and independence. Numerous forms of control and reporting prevented normal teamwork organization. Very often teams were arranged formalistically, with lack of interest about tasks being done and without the workers' consent. Problems of psychological matching among team members, their qualification improvement, and training for new professions were not investigated thoroughly.

Acknowledgements

Interpreted by E. Kazarova.

References

Andreyev, B. J., and Chterevan, V. P., (1986). Industrial teams of new type. *Misl*, 265.

Bronshtein, V.V., (1989). Collective contract: Problems and perspectives. *Moscow Economics*, 140.

Meier, R. (1993). About wonders and monsters: Stakhanov's movement and stalinizm. *Native History*, N 3.

Shor, F. D. and Romanenko, J. P., (1988). Team contract and production efficiency. *Mashinostroyenie*, 87.

Umanski, V. A., (1989). The role of teams in production efficiency rise. *Technika*, 158.

Vorozheikin, I. E. (1990). Competition: from the past to the present. *Sovjetskaya Rossia*, 330.

Chapter 16

Yugoslav Self-Management

The World's Largest Experiment in Work Teams

Monty Lynn
Abilene Christian University, Abilene, Texas, United States

Matjaž Mulej and Karin Jurše
University of Maribor, Maribor, Republic of Slovenia

Abstract

Under Josip Tito's leadership (1945-1980), Yugoslavia broke away from Stalin in 1948 and developed the world's largest experiment in work teams, called self-management. Its focus was not on incremental innovation *a la* Japanese total quality management, nor on production as in North American quality of work life initiatives, but on leadership issues. Workers were supposed to replace owners and state bureaucracy in running firms. The experiment failed, in large part because the state bureaucracy did not trust workers' capabilities and did not want to give up their own authority. The result was that two critical elements of self-management--responsibility and vision--were undermined rather than developed. A state-supported neo-Taylorism with a "thinking tank" and a separate "working tank" evolved which represented little responsibility behind a facade of self-management. By the 1980s, worker councils had become a formality rather than real, professional leadership within Yugoslav firms.

Introduction

The federally legislated system of Yugoslav self-management holds the record as the world's largest experiment in work teams and worker democracy, as well as one of the longest lasting--over forty years. The vision was that every Yugoslav adult citizen--roughly 15 million in 1991--would have director-level voice in their companies and communities through a variety of representative councils which could advise and, after 1963, direct management. In contrast to team-based production, Yugoslav self-management created team-based leadership.

Only a few examples of this democratic organizational structure exist in the West. The producer co-ops in Spain's northern Basque region and a few companies dotted around the globe share similarities with the Yugoslav structure but on a much smaller scale. Self-management was unique inside Central and Eastern Europe as well. It presented to the East and the West, a bold and promising model. But even

M.M. Beyerlein (ed.), Work Teams: Past, Present and Future, 247–253.

before the break-up of Yugoslavia in 1991, self-management, disappointingly, had died on the vine.

While the story of Yugoslav self-management is a complex one, our focus is on the work teams themselves--the so-called workers' councils and management councils--and what we believe kept their promise from becoming reality. Yugoslav self-management may be unique, but the lessons learned from its failure are not. They speak to any attempt to establish functional work teams within organizations. To see the creation and dissolution process of these groups, we have to travel back forty years before the birth of self-management.

Work Structures in Yugoslavia Prior to Self-Management

In an effort to catch-up with the West's advancing economies, the Kingdom of Yugoslavia (1919-1941) made attempts to catalyze capitalism domestically, principally by way of large infusions of external capital and equipment. For a variety of reasons, the development efforts failed and there was little visible economic change by the time the Second World War began. Perhaps prematurely, the conclusion that many Yugoslavs drew was: "Capitalism doesn't work, at least not in Yugoslavia."

The Yugoslav king and government fled the country within two weeks of the time that Hitler and Mussolini's forces marched into Yugoslavia in 1941. Nazis and Fascists expanded their empires easily, although beginning in July 1941, Tito's Yugoslav partisan movement began resisting them. After two years, the partisans won the Allies' support. Over a period of four years of war, factories, roads, railways, and private property were badly destroyed, and many intellectuals and leaders were killed, taken to concentration camps, or deported to Bosnia, Serbia, and other areas. When the war ended, what little economic value remained from the capitalistic efforts was destroyed. In terms of economic history, the period of enlightened absolutism was a natural next step. Tito was the person who won the war, so he formed the government.

Having lost most everything--personally and economically--the diverse Yugoslav citizenry united around the Communist Party and pulled together to rebuild their destroyed economy. The existing scarce resources would be marshaled more efficiently, they reasoned, if private property was nationalized. Then, government leaders could concentrate investments and human resources where they were economically most critical. Property and industry was nationalized. But with private owners removed, it was soon discovered that the state could not operate firms effectively. As the sole Eastern European state to do so, Yugoslavia, under President Tito's leadership, broke relations with Stalin in 1948 and abandoned centralized planning.

The idea of self-management had existed in theoretical form for some time and was functioning in a few small international experiments (see Bošković & Dašić, 1980). But its specifics were undeveloped in large part, and untested on a countrywide basis. To the economists, philosophers, educators, and other intellectuals who helped craft it, Yugoslav self-management represented the next natural step (before the real end of enlightened absolutism) in the march toward a functional, socialistic society.

But what structure would replace Stalinistic organization? The economy needed a system that would be consistent with the ideals of the new communist government, help Yugoslavia catch-up with the West, and provide leadership and innovation, which were critically needed in industry. Trailblazing their own path, a bold plan was drafted in 1949 by intellectuals and the Communist Party which called for workers to be given democratic rule over company operational plans, strategy, and policies through a structure of various representative councils. The councils were generally: cross-functional; composed of between 15 and 20 employees for workers' councils in large firms, all the employees in small firms, and 3 to 11 for the management board; constituted by employees elected by their peers, and; not paid extra for their efforts.

In theory, self-management seemed a promising democratic road between what national experience and the challenge of the country's ethnic diversity suggested to be ditches on the right and the left--capitalism and central planning. In the early 1980s, writers were claiming that self-management had created a "no-party system," and that self-management freed political decision-making "from monopolism and bureaucratic subjectivism." But behind the scenes, another story was developing.

Where Things Went Wrong

The crafters of self-management frequently alluded to employee development as an outgrowth of effective workers' councils. They also were aware that external groups and the organizational setting itself could limit the work groups' effectiveness. Yet in spite of much writing on the subject and numerous warning flares fired about the dangers of encroaching threats, self-management steered directly into two traps--an inability to catalyze responsibility and vision among workers, and; an external control of and resistance to workers' councils. Four self-management developments illustrate these pitfalls:

1. Council tasks were often meaningless. Although markets were constitutionally introduced into Yugoslavia in 1963, most industries were dominated by monopolies that supported a sellers rather than a buyers market. Demand generally exceeded supply, so there were few incentives for enhancing competitiveness, few reasons to improve processes, products, or services. Thus, group tasks--even those taken quite seriously by the workers' council members--were often of little import in firm operations.

2. Council autonomy was not protected. Increasingly, the control over how work teams operated and what decisions they undertook, were controlled by federal

law. The same law that breathed life into workers' councils later suffocated them. Whether designed to aid work teams or diminish their influence, outside regulations served to complicate and frustrate council members and group process.

3. The operational environment was inconsistent with the workers' councils. The workplace was not changed when self-management was implemented, even though the two differed dramatically. Production continued to be top-down, structured according to domineering interpretations of Frederick Taylor, Max Weber, and Henry Fayol. Workers were assigned to fragmented, de-skilled, and segmented jobs and operated under the authority of a managerial hierarchy. The bottom-up workers' councils were often inconsistent with and unable to evoke change in organizational structure and culture.

4. There was little de facto support for the on-going development of workers' councils. Professionals and management could easily monopolize information due to differences in knowledge between them and the workers. Invention and innovation were treated like hobbies--things not to be taken seriously. From the reward system, there apparently was little value placed on developing effective group practice or workers' council knowledge. Additionally, council members were asked to deal with tasks which were beyond their areas of expertise and training (e.g., approve the final balance sheet and regular business plans, appoint executives, and oversee salaries and safety).

There are multiple possible explanations why little decentralization occurred and why self-management became increasingly impotent. One is that political and corporate power-holders wanted to retain power rather than share it with workers, so they intentionally sterilized the process, keeping the form of self-management but removing its influence. After 25 years, since bringing the concept of "market" into the federal constitution, no laws were passed to reinforce markets via private property, demonopolization, deregulation, or easy entrepreneurship. Central control over foreign exchange, import, some export, and prices remained in place because of the powerholders.

A second, less malevolent explanation is that self-management represented a radical experiment whose support could not overtake the centuries of culture and practice embedded in Yugoslav minds and institutions (cf., Kelly, 1996). A third interpretation favors the structural life cycle of organizations, indicating that the encrustation of dynamic processes is a constant tendency--an iron law of oligarchy (Michels, 1962) and democracy where organizational governance is a pendulum which swings between control by the many and control by a few. There are arguments for each of these cases. But whether one looks at the workers' councils from a power, innovation, or structural perspective, one theme is the same--

Yugoslav self-management was not sufficiently under-girded by responsibility and vision.

At the Heart of the Problem

Responsibility and vision are critical elements in work groups, because they are the ones that are so desperately needed in times of transition, and the ones most easily undermined. As self-regulating mechanisms, individual vision and responsibility help organizations make needed rapid changes in adjusting to a dynamic environment. Their absence often leads to organizational Balkanization and drift, which later undermines effective organizational change. Even though they were only advisory at first, from the beginning, the intent of the workers' councils was to develop workers into manager-like employees, endowing them with an increased measure of vision and responsibility. In other words, self-management was:

> an opportunity not only to acquire a better insight into the work and problems of the enterprise but also to exert a direct influence on production and the management of the enterprise. Workers will thus gain enormous experience, and every opportunity will be provided for executive cadres of the enterprise to be drawn from the ranks of the workers (Bošković & Dašić, 1980, p. 59).

Through its democratic structure, self-management was designed to move workers toward "independent-interdependence," that is, toward democratic self-rule.

In large part, it was this aspect of self-management that threatened to diminish the role and power of the government and political bureaucracy. Government and company power-holders did not bend their authority far enough in exerting influence over the still state-owned monopolies. The motives of the government bureaucrats, politicians, and company management may be debated, once again, as prudently cautious or selfishly malevolent. But, power-holders' actions, the organizational setting, and the mismatched tasks and lack of authority entrusted to the workers clearly and consistently show how limited the federal practice of self-management actually was.

The lessons learned in Yugoslavia were echoed by scholars and practitioners in the 1970s, 80s, and 90s writing on different kinds of work groups--quality-of-work-life/job enrichment, socio-technical systems, and workplace democracy. These studies confirm the importance of meaningfulness and autonomy in work tasks, the criticality of team-organization fit, the benefits of empowering work teams, and the pivotal role of vision and responsibility in team functioning.

What About Today?

Today's ex-Yugoslavia--the countries of Slovenia, Croatia, Yugoslavia (Serbia and Macedonia), Bosnia and Herzegovina, and Montenegro--are engaged in yet another period of radical economic change. Where economic and legal transition is taking place in the former Yugoslav republics, the nature of workplaces is being changed significantly. Privatization, entrepreneurship, foreign alliances and investment, and legislative changes have brought a market that increasingly favors buyers rather than sellers, economic incentives for innovation, and change in organizational structures and processes.

Some firms--especially in Slovenia where the number of business and other legal entities grew from 18,000 in 1991 to beyond 230,000 in 1997, and where 75% of manufactured products are exported--are experimenting with various versions of total quality management and international quality standards. Employee buyouts represent a sizeable share of firm privatizations in some parts of ex-Yugoslavia, however, worker ownership does not *de facto* lead to democratic work team structures. Self-management is no longer practiced except in a handful of firms that are still organized in the old style. Vision and responsibility are left to individual organizations and their leadership. Very few companies are known to deploy work teams as a measure of enhancing productivity, rationality, quality, or competitiveness by making room for workers' creativity to flourish to the benefit of their organizations and countries. The period of enlightened absolutism used to live under the label of self-management. Its next era may be a very liberal capitalism. If, when, and how the international experience of the more advanced parts of the world will accelerate this phase toward modern Western capitalism remains to be seen.

Most eyes are focused on the West again and on leveraging resources in such a way that will accelerate economic development once more. Regardless of the particular structures which will emerge in the future, two lessons regarding teams are clearly illustrated from the history of Yugoslav self-management--responsibility and vision are key team ingredients under democratic work structures, and; effectiveness can be undermined from outside teams as easily as it can be from within.

References

Bošković, B. & Dašić, D. (1980). *Socialist self-management in Yugoslavia: 1950-1980. Documents*. Belgrade: Socialist Thought and Practice.

Kelly, M. (1996, Sept/Oct). Rebels without a clue: A company experiment in democratic capitalism hits a wall. *Business Ethics*, 8.

Lynn, M. L., Jurše, K., & Mulej, M. (1996). *Responsibility and vision in Yugoslav self-management: Two critical omissions*. Paper presented to the 8th Conference of the International Association for the Economics of Participation, Prague, Czech Republic.

Michels, R. (1962). *Political parties: A sociological study of the oligarchical tendencies of modern democracy*. (E. & C. Paul, trans). New York: Free Press.

Mulej, M. (1981). *O novem jugoslovanskem modulu druzbene integracije*. Maribor, Slovenia Yugoslavia: Zalozba Obzorja.

Mulej, M. (1994). Dimensions of change during development from a preindustrial to a modern society. *Cybernetics and Systems*, 25(3), 911-930.

Mulej, M., Sruk, V., & Majerič, A. (1991). What about self-management after the political reorganization of Yugoslavia. In J. Svejnar, et al. (Eds.), *Proceedings of the Sixth International Conference on Workers' Self-Management.* Ithaca, NY: International Association for the Economics of Self-Management.

Mulej, M., de Zeeuw, G., Espejo, R., Flood, R., Jackson, M., Kajzer, Š., Mingers, J., Rafolt, B., Rebernik, M., Suojanen, W., Thornton, P., and Uršic, D. (1992). *Teorije sistemov.* Maribor, Slovenia: Economics and Business School (EPF), University of Maribor.

Chapter 17

When the Teams Came Marching Home

U.S. Military Team Research Since World War II

Elizabeth Blickensderfer
Naval Air Warfare Center, Orlando, Florida, United States

Eduardo Salas
University of Central Florida, Orlando, Florida, United States

Janis Cannon-Bowers
Naval Air Warfare Center, Orlando, Florida, United States

Abstract

Use of teams has become prevalent throughout our late 20th century society, and the U. S. military is no exception. From operating high tech equipment to accomplishing complex field maneuvers, military personnel face challenging tasks that demand a team oriented atmosphere. The purpose of this chapter is to describe the stream of team performance research accomplished for the U.S. military. The emphasis of the review is Navy related research, as that is our speciality area.

Introduction

Use of teams has become prevalent throughout our late 20th century society, and the U. S. military is no exception. From operating high tech equipment to accomplishing complex field maneuvers, military personnel face challenging tasks that demand a team oriented atmosphere. The U.S. military has been relatively fortunate in terms of resources to direct toward understanding teams: it has access to a streamlined R & D effort focused on understanding the nature of crews, groups, and teams. The purpose of this chapter is to describe the stream of team performance research accomplished for the U.S. military (for detailed review of this topic, see also Denson, 1981; Dyer, 1984; Salas, Bowers, & Cannon-Bowers, 1995). The emphasis of the review is Navy related research, as that is our specialty area. We organized the material by decade (the latter half of the 20th century).[1]

Before beginning this review, a description of military teams is in order. Many characteristics of military teams are highly similar to those of teams found in the civilian world, however, the reader unfamiliar with military environments may find a review of military team characteristics useful. Gill (1977) listed multiple characteristics of military teams. These include: some military teams have a history

M.M. Beyerlein (ed.), Work Teams: Past, Present and Future, 255–273.

together, while others are ad hoc; all military teams face a degree of turnover; the size of military teams varies by task; levels of required interdependency vary, with some team members highly interdependent and others less so; the formal structure of the military impacts the nature of team member interactions; prior to joining an active unit, members receive extensive individual training; almost all military teams work with some type of equipment; and some military teams must train for a situation they hope never to face--combat (Dyer, 1984). We will now turn to a description of the military team research.

The 1940s, 1950s and 1960s: The Beginning

Ironically, while the military was facing a growing necessity for effective teams during the 1940s, 50s, and 60s, little research on military team training and performance occurred during this time period. Perhaps the most significant contribution of the 1950s was the acknowledgement that a need to study team performance (as opposed to groups) existed. Although researchers had already been examining questions relating to group environments (for review see Lorge, Fox, Davitz, & Brenner, 1958), few if any researchers addressed the issue of *team* performance. In the 1950s, however, more than one work was produced that was concerned with the need to study teams in military environments (Borgatta, Lanzetta, McGrath, & Strodbeck, 1959; Glanzer & Glaser, 1955). This work became a jumping off point for the next decade when the amount of team research began to increase considerably. The 1960s brought some research which began to indicate a differentiation of team characteristics from task characteristics as well as a differentiation of individual skills and team skills (a distinction that was not made explicit until the late 1980s). The remainder of this section will be organized into team characteristics and task characteristics.

Team Characteristics

Some work from this time period focused on developing a better understanding of various team characteristics. Many of the topics examined are still popular today in team research. For example, Glaser, Glanzer, and Morten (1955) touched on a behavioral issue that continues to be examined today: measuring team communications. Glaser et al. developed indices to describe the nature and extent of communication links among Navy team members (Dyer, 1984). This included link frequency, communication frequency, concurrent activity, sequence, and predictability. This work was perhaps the first to identify specific behaviors as potentially important to team performance.

Other researchers took an attitudinal approach to team characteristics and were concerned with topics such as team cohesion (i.e., "stick togetherness") (Fieldler & Meuwese, 1962) and cooperation (Jordan, Jensen, & Terebinsky, 1963). Much of this research indicated an influence from the group literature, as team researchers utilized the group literature to formulate hypotheses for team performance. For example, Tuckman (1965) advocated that good interpersonal relationships between small group members must be formed before they are able to focus effectively on performance of the team task. Although Tuckman focused on "groups" as opposed to "teams," this proposition directed research attention to "team" concepts such as coordination, interaction, and communication. Many of Tuckman's ideas were later incorporated into models of team development (Morgan, Glickman, Woodard, Blaiwes, & Salas, 1986).

Task Characteristics

Other efforts in this time period focused on task characteristics. For example, one research interest was the relationship between team size and performance (George, Hoak, & Boutwell, 1963; Kidd, 1961; Kincade & Kidd, 1959). George, et al. (1963) manipulated task distribution among 5-person laboratory teams and investigated which distribution was most effective. The results indicated that concentrating the bulk of the team's strength on three of the five team members, as opposed to concentrating it on only two members or distributing it among more than three members, produced the best task performance. This research brought the realization that adding more people to the team does not necessarily increase productivity of the team; distribution of labor is also critical.

One pocket of military team research in the 1960s came from Ohio State researchers (Briggs & Johnston 1966a, 1966b, 1967; Johnston, 1966; Johnston & Briggs, 1968). Among other points, this group highlighted how teammates can both help and hinder performance under high workload conditions. First, Johnston and Briggs (1968) demonstrated the importance of teammates backing each other up during high workload conditions. Using a simulated air traffic control task, Johnston and Briggs found that fewer flight errors occurred under high load conditions when a team member was allowed to compensate for a partner's behavior (Dyer, 1984). The study also demonstrated that, with non-compensatory teams under high workload conditions, communication among teammates disrupted performance (Dyer, 1984). Thus, teammates who compensate for each other boost the team performance, but if they don't compensate for each other, any extra communication hurts the team's performance. In related work examining aircraft/bomber crews, Roby and Lanzetta (1957a, 1957b) investigated the impact of variations in workload and work distribution on team communications. The results indicated that having even one overloaded team member could impact the performance of the team as that individual was as likely to neglect obligations to fellow team members as he or she was to neglect his or her own control responsibilities (Dyer, 1984).

Summary

As illustrated in Tables 1 and 2, the 1950s and 1960s brought a recognition that research was needed in the area of team performance, the introduction of some methods to study teams, and a first look into some task and team characteristic issues. This work paved the way for a gradual expansion of team research throughout the next few decades.

1970s & 1980s: A Growth Period

Only a small amount of team research came out of these decades. However, the research that did appear added considerable to the knowledge base. The two major topic areas of this research were (a) the impact of individual ability on team performance and (b) team development.

TABLE 1. Team Research in the 1950s

Significant Findings or Events	Authors
• Stated a need for team research existed.	Borgatta, Lanzetta, McGrath, & Strodbeck (1959); Glanzer & Glaser (1955)
• Developed indices to describe the nature and extent of communication links among Navy team members.	Glaser, Glanzer, & Morten (1955); Glanzer & Glaser (1959)
• Found group-task motivation was related to pride in group performance and a perception of interdependence among group members with respect to the attainment of reward.	Berkowitz & Levy (1956)
• Found that even one overloaded team member could impact the performance of the team: overloaded individuals neglect obligations to fellow team members.	Roby & Lanzetta (1957a, 1957b)
• Found that bomber crews with four or fewer membership changes during the 10 month period performed better than those with more changes.	Forgays & Levy (1957)
• Reviewed studies of group performance done in the years 1920 - 1957. Identified different types of groups.	Lorge, Fox, Davitz, & Brenner (1958)
• Demonstrated changes in team performance from crew experience.	Biel, Chapman, Kennedy, & Newell (1957); Chapman, Kennedy, Newell, & Biel (1959)

TABLE 2. Team Research in the 1960s

Significant Findings or Events	Authors
• Found that group productivity is not a linear function of group size; a negatively accelerated function exists between performance and team size.	Kidd (1961)
• Demonstrated that adding more people to the team does not necessarily increase productivity of the team.	George, Hoak, & Boutwell (1963)
• Study suggested that a developmental process (including developing a shared understanding of the task and team) leads to the development of co-operation.	Jordan, Jensen, & Terebinsky (1963)
• Examined team member turnover. Found that changes in key or central positions had the greatest effect upon team performance.	Ziller (1963); Trow (1964)
• Proposed that teams learn differently in established situations versus emergent situations.	Alexander & Cooperband (1965)
• Found that aircrew communication content and communication patterns varied with the mission.	Siskel, Lane, Powe, & Flexman (1965)
• Presented a model of small group development	Tuckman (1965)
• Found that frequency of communications sent during Ranger patrols varied with mission phase and team members involved.	Brown (1967)
• Examined the role of knowledge of results and how knowledge of results should be applied by instructors to achieve desired team performance.	Briggs & Johnston (1967)
• Demonstrated the importance of teammates backing each other up during high workload conditions.	Johnston & Briggs (1968)
• Defined collaboration and coordination and developed indices to describe task structure.	O'Brien (1968)
• Posited that team performance is a function of task structure, work structure, and communication patterns among team members.	Naylor & Dickinson (1969)
• Attempted to model team behavior with a computer simulation of Naval crews.	Siegel, Wolf, &Fischl (1969)

Individual Ability and Skills: Individual Training or Team Training?

In the 1970s, the influence of variables relating to individual ability and skill on team performance began to attract research attention. This was part of a gradual shift in attention away from interpersonal skills and toward the effects of individual skills and abilities on team performance. Several studies indicated that teams with members who had higher task proficiency, abilities, and skills performed better than teams made up of individuals with less ability (Kabanoff & O'Brien, 1979; Steiner, 1972). For example, researchers found that the accuracy and speed of team performance were positively related to the average skill level (Kabanoff & O'Brien, 1979: Klaus & Glaser, 1970; Terborg, Castore, & DeNinno, 1976). One manner in which having high ability team members seems to help is that those individuals learn the task more quickly than lower ability individuals. Research has found that teams with high individual skill levels reached criterion performance with less training than did teams with average or poor individual skill levels (Bouchard, 1969; George, Hoak, & Boutwell, 1963; Hall & Rizzo, 1975; Klaus & Glaser, 1965; Tziner & Eden, 1985).

Team Development

Another area of emphasis in the mid-1980s examined the evolution and maturation of operational teams (Glickman, Zimmer, Montero, Guerette, Campbell, Morgan, & Salas, 1987; Guerette, Miller, Glickman, Morgan, & Salas, 1987; McIntyre, Morgan, Salas, & Glickman, 1988; Morgan, Glickman, Woodard, Blaiwes, & Salas, 1986). The focus was to investigate how teams perform in the "naturalistic" environment, and the research examined real U.S. Navy command and control teams. McIntyre et al. (1988) described the evolutionary process through which the teams progressed. Briefly, the teams progressed through six phases, which ranged from exploring roles to achieving a fully functioning level of team performance. Morgan et al. (1986) presented a model of these developmental phases. The model suggested that the phases depend to a certain extent upon members' experience as a team, individual expertise, task characteristics, and the environmental context. In other words, not all teams are expected to pass through all phases. This model incorporated Tuckman's (1965) ideas concerning group development by including stages labeled: forming, storming, norming, and performing. Importantly, this model also differentiated between task-oriented skills and team skills training (i.e., "taskwork skills" and "teamwork skills"). Taskwork skills training aimed to foster task skills such as understanding task requirements, discovering operating procedures, and acquiring task information and other task oriented issues. Teamwork skills training aimed to develop behavioral interactions and attitudinal responses of team members such as coordination, adaptation to varying situational demands, mutual performance monitoring, and effective communication.

Summary

As summarized in Tables 3 and 4, the 1970s and 1980s brought a small amount of team research focused on a variety of team performance topics. Major works focused on individual ability and team development.

TABLE 3. Research in the 1970s

Significant Findings or Events	Authors
• Demonstrated that teams with members who had higher individual task proficiency, abilities, and skills performed better than teams made up of individuals with less individual ability.	Kabanoff & O'Brien (1979); Klaus & Glaser (1970); Terborg, Castore, & DeNinno (1976)
• Found that teams with high individual skill levels reached criterion performance with less training than did teams with average or poor individual skill levels.	Bouchard (1969); George, Hoak, & Boutwell (1963); Hall & Rizzo (1975); Klaus & Glaser (1965); Tziner & Eden (1985)
• Identified characteristics of tasks that teams perform.	Steiner (1972); Shaw (1976); Dieterly (1978)
• Demonstrated changes in helicopter crew communication as a function of crew training.	Siegel & Federman (1973)
• Posited a conceptual model of team performance that emphasized the individual skills/team skills question.	Nieva, Fleishman, & Reick (1978)
• Used techniques for analyzing the flow of work within teams.	Boldovici (1979); Thurmond & Kribs (1978)
• Analyzed aircrew communication and found four types of communications.	Siegel & Federman (1973)
• Measured timing, accuracy, and brevity of messages in aircrew performance. Recommended that a standard vocabulary be used to reduce message length.	Obermayer, Vreuls, Muckler, Conway, & Fitzgerald (1974)
• Demonstrated changes in team performance from crew experience.	Root, Hayes, Word, Shriver, & Griffin (1979)
• Identified problems in measuring team performance variables including process and outcome variables.	Connelly, Comeau, & Steinheiser (1980); Kubala (1978)
• Identified multiple contingencies inherent to team feedback.	Pritchard & Montagno (1978)
• Examined turbulence within tank crews. Found that change in duty positions reduced crew performance more than did changes in crew membership or change in assignment to a particular tank.	Eaton & Neff (1978)
• Examined the relationship between team performance and member turnover. Found that team performance declined when teams were composed of 40% or more untrained individuals.	Morgan, Coates, Alluisi, & Kirby (1978)

TABLE 4. Team Research in the 1980s

Significant Findings or Events	Authors
• Identified skills of small-unit leaders which affect team processes: management, communication, problem-solving, tactical and technical skills.	Henriksen, Jones, Hannaman, Wylie, Shriver, Hamill, & Sulzen (1980)
• Conducted a review of the field of team training as it relates to military teams.	Dyer (1984)
• Investigated the use of artificial intelligence techniques to simulate a team member in a combat information center for use in training simulations.	Johnston & Obermayer (1984)
• Discussed the potential of simulation for team training.	Hansen & Wulff (1985)
• Developed the Team Evolution and Maturation Model suggesting the developmental stages that teams tend to progress through. The model provided important implica-tions for the design and development of team training.	Morgan, Glickman, Woodard, Blaiwes, & Salas (1986)
• Began to differentiate between task-oriented skills and team skills training (i.e., "task-work skills" and "teamwork skills").	Morgan, Glickman, Woodard, Blaiwes, & Salas (1986)
• Found that function overlap compaired with restriction of communication impedes problem solving.	Eimer (1987)
• Presented a description of the evolutionary process of teams observed in a naturalistic environment.	McIntyre, Morgan, Salas, & Glickman (1988)
• Found that familiar flight crews (those that have flown together recently) have better communication patterns and made fewer errors than non-familiar flight crews.	Kanki & Foushee (1988)
• Found that team building training results in more stable, cohesive teams.	Kahan (1989)
• Identified basic components of teamwork.	McIntyre & Salas (1995)

1990s: New Understanding

Team researchers made dramatic gains in the 1990s. Integrative models of team performance that linked situational, task, and team characteristics appeared. From the behavioral standpoint, new understanding of team competencies and team performance measurement systems appeared. At the same time, team researchers opened the door to cognitive theory and its implications for team training. Finally, theoretically based team training interventions began to receive empirical investigation.

Models of Team Performance

Efforts to develop comprehensive models of team performance began to appear in the second half of the 1980s and the early 1990s. For example, Gladstein (1984) presented a descriptive model of group performance. This model indicates that group performance is a product of the interaction between group and organizational elements with group process. The Gladstein model was one of several (i.e., Gersick, 1988; Hackman, 1983; Morgan et al., 1986; Nieva, Fleishman, & Reick, 1978) that Salas, Dickinson, Converse, and Tannenbaum (1992) integrated into their comprehensive model of team performance. This model was later refined by Tannenbaum, Beard, and Salas (1992) and named the "Team Effectiveness Model" (TEM). The model describes the multiple pieces of team effectiveness including: organizational and situational characteristics, task and team characteristics, individual characteristics, work structure, team processes and team outcomes. As described in the next few sections, a growing number of these factors have been examined empirically. The model provided team researchers a framework for their research and was a welcome addition to team research.

Task Characteristics

Some research examined task characteristics and the implications for team performance. These include effects of workload, time pressure, and structure. Briefly, recent research directed at the workload construct (e.g., Bowers, Urban, & Morgan, 1992; Kleinman & Serfaty, 1989) has led to the notion that cognitive load may serve as a moderator of the team process-team performance relation (Salas et al., 1995). That is, level of workload may determine which team processes are necessary for effective team performance, and in turn, which team training interventions will be most useful for those situations. In a related area, Adelman, Zirk, Lehner, Moffett, and Hall (1986) examined the effects of time pressure in a tactical team decision making task and found that the higher degree of time pressure, the more unreliable team decision making became. While more work is needed in this area, the Adelman et al. (1986) study gave empirical evidence that time pressure can impact team performance. Finally, renewed effort in examining team structure appeared in the 1990s (Bowers et al. 1992; Kleinman & Serfaty, 1989; Urban, Bowers, Monday, & Morgan, 1995). Perhaps most important for military teams are the results from Bowers, et al. (1992). This study suggested that regardless of workload, hierarchically arranged teams showed lower performance than non-hierarchical teams. Follow-up work is needed to gain a better understanding of this problematic area and design training interventions to diminish it.

Individual Characteristics

The 1970s research raised questions relating to the role that individual abilities of team members play in team performance. While little research on this topic has occurred since then, Stout, Salas, and Carson (1994) provided some recent data in this area. Stout and colleagues assessed the degree to which subtask performance influenced team process and overall team performance. While, the results revealed no relationship between individual skill and team process, the results did show that teamwork behaviors predicted variance in team performance beyond that explained by individual task competence. This indicates that individual ability is a portion of team performance but is not alone responsible for team performance.

Team Characteristics

While some 1990s researchers examined task issues, considerably more work has focused on team characteristics. These characteristics can be classified as attitudes, behaviors, or cognitions (Salas & Cannon-Bowers, in press).

Attitudes

While some interest in the impact of team attitudes on team performance has continued to appear in military team literature during the 1990s, more work on team attitudes has appeared in non-military literature than in the military research. For example, Navy researchers (Salas and colleagues) have focused their work on behaviors instead of attitudes and personality constructs (Prince & Salas, 1993). Army researchers have also been concerned with behaviors (Leedom & Simon, 1995). The military related research that has appeared in this area includes the work of Driskell and Salas (1992, 1997). This work indicated that collective orientation (the disposition to receive and value inputs from others) plays a critical role in facilitating teamwork. In this work, when performing an interdependent task, the collectively-oriented team members performed more effectively than did the individual oriented team members. The next step in this work is to identify potential training methods to foster collective orientation.

Behaviors

In order to fulfill goals and missions, teams coordinate, communicate, strategize, adapt, and synchronize task relevant information (Salas & Cannon-Bowers, in press). Considerable work has gone into identifying behaviors and actions that teams exhibit as teams accomplish their tasks (for full review see Dyer 1984; Modrick, 1986; Salas, Bowers, & Cannon-Bowers, 1995). Briefly, military researchers have uncovered a variety of behaviors which effective teams tend to exhibit. These include employing implicit or explicit coordination activities (Kleinman & Serfaty, 1989), performance monitoring (Hackman, 1990), providing tasks and motivational reinforcement (Oser, McCallum, Salas, & Morgan, 1989), adapting to unpredictable situations (Prince & Salas, 1993), exhibiting flexibility (Prince & Salas, 1993), identifying and making corrective actions (McIntyre & Salas, 1995), using closed-loop communication (McIntyre & Salas, 1995); exhibiting assertiveness (Smith-Jentsch, Salas, & Baker, 1996), and predicting each others' behavior (Volpe, Cannon-Bowers, Salas, & Spector, 1996).

Multiple authors have proposed schemas and frameworks of teamwork behaviors. This work has generated a variety of team skill listings. An effort to synthesize these listings, Cannon-Bowers, Tannenbaum, Salas, & Volpe (1995) consolidated a number of the teamwork skill definitions found in the literature into the following competencies: adaptability, shared situational awareness, performance monitoring and feedback, leadership/team management, interpersonal, coordination, communication, and decision making. Associated subskills were also generated for each skill competency. Adaptability, for example, was defined as, "The process by which a team is able to use information gathered from the task environment to adjust task strategies through the use of compensatory behavior and reallocation of intra-team resources" (p. 344). The list of alternate labels for adaptability were flexibility, compensatory behavior, and dynamic reallocation of function. In this definition alone, the authors drew from a number of works (Alexander & Cooperband, 1965; Johnston & Briggs, 1968; McCallum, Oser, Morgan, & Salas, 1989; McIntyre & Salas, 1995). By sorting through the multitude of definitions and synthesizing them into one succinct list, Cannon-Bowers et al. demonstrated the links between the different approaches to team skill classification and helped clarify the behavioral definition of "teamwork" (Salas, Cannon-Bowers, & Blickensderfer, 1993). Researchers are now testing methods to foster these behaviors among team members.

Cognitions

Along with attitudes and behaviors, teamwork also has a cognitive component, as team members need a set of knowledges to perform team tasks. In response to this realization, researchers have begun to utilize constructs and findings from the cognitive psychology literature to understand team performance. One cognitive construct that has received considerable attention by military team researchers is the notion that teams who develop a shared mental model of the task, their teammates' roles, and the situation perform more effectively (Cannon-Bowers, Salas, & Converse, 1993; Orasanu, 1990). Shared mental models allow team members to develop expectations and generate predictions concerning how to perform during routine situations as well as when the team encounters a novel or stressful situation. A complaint with this line of thought is the lack of measurement attempts (Klimoski & Mohammed, 1994). However, military researchers from both the Army and Navy have begun testing measures of shared understanding (Blickensderfer, Cannon-Bowers, & Salas, 1997; Minionis, Zaccaro, & Perez, 1995; Stout, 1995).

An aspect of shared mental models that Cannon-Bowers and colleagues (Cannon-Bowers et al., 1993, 1995) have emphasized is the importance of cue-strategy associations for teams functioning in complex, knowledge-rich environments. It is argued that patterns of cues in the environment trigger team members to perform in certain manners. For example, one team member may recognize cues that indicate another team member is overloaded and needs help. Team members build up mental associations between particular cues and required responses. This knowledge allows teams to adapt, reallocate functions, and perform without overt communications (Cannon-Bowers, et al., 1993, 1995; Orasanu, 1990).

Team Training Strategies

In the 1990s, several successful team-training interventions were established. These had strong theoretical bases as well as laboratory tests to support them. The training interventions listed in Table 5 are a product of decades of team research. Indeed, the appearance of these interventions is highly satisfying, as they are evidence of the knowledge gained over the past decades. Although full descriptions of these programs are beyond the scope of this chapter, interested readers are recommended to read the sources listed in Table 5.

TABLE 5. Military Team Training Strategies

Team Training Strategy	Description	Method	Sources
Aircrew Coordination Training, Cockpit Resource Management and related programs	Builds specific behavioral skills to improve team coordination in the cockpit.	Use lecture, behavioral modeling and practice to teach team members to use specific behavioral skills in the cockpit.	Brown (1987); Leedom (1990); Prince, Chidester, Bowers, & Cannon-Bowers, (1992); Prince & Salas (1993); Simon & Grubb (1993); Simon & Pawlik (1993); Wiener, Kanki, & Helmreich (1993)
Cross-Training	Emphasized building shared understanding and improving team performance.	Using positional rotation, train team members in the basic duties of their teammates.	Cannon-Bowers, Salas, Blickens-derfer, & Bowers, (1998); Volpe, Cannon-Bowers, Salas, & Spector (1996)
Team Leader Training, Team Dimensional Training	Trained team leaders to debrief using input from the whole team and focus on specific behaviors rather than the traditional one-way debrief.	Use lecture, behavioral modeling and practice to teach team leaders how to debrief effectively.	Tannenbaum, Jentsch, & Behson (1998); Smith-Jentsch, Zeisig, Acton, & McPherson (1998)
Team Self Correction Training	Trained team members to engage in lessons learned discussions following task performance with the goal being to build shared mental models and improve performance.	Use lecture, behavioral modeling and practice to teach team members how to participate effectively in a team discussion.	Blickensderfer, Cannon-Bowers, & Salas (1997a,b)
Team Model Trainer	Computer-based training package designed to build shared understanding of the task among teammates.	Use a computer-based training program to teach team members how the team operates and the roles of all team members.	Duncan, Rouse, Johnston, Cannon-Bowers, Salas, & Burns (1996)

Technology

The 1990s also saw the birth of a number of tools and simulations for use in team research and training settings. Many of these were the fruition of decades of work. A primary focus of team oriented simulations has been to network individual computer stations (or simulators) together to create a team environment. These simulations range from low tech systems adapted from commercially available software to high tech systems sponsored by the Defense Advanced Research Projects Agency (DARPA). Low-fidelity simulations include: the Low-Fidelity Aviation Research Methodology (Bowers, Salas, Prince, & Brannick, 1992), the Team Performance Assessment Battery (Bowers, Urban, et al., 1992), the Tactical Naval Decision Making System (Dwyer, Hall, Volpe, Cannon-Bowers, & Salas, 1992), the Team Interactive Decision Exercise for Teams Incorporating Distributed Expertise (Hollenbeck, Sego, Ilgen, & Major, 1991), and C^3 Interactive Task for Identifying Emerging Situations (Wellens & Ergener, 1988). These simulations gave team researchers test-beds which are relatively low-cost and portable, provide interdependent tasks, give sufficient experimental control, and provide a method for testing and generating team performance theory (Weaver, Bowers, Salas, & Cannon-Bowers, 1995).

Along with low-tech simulations, high tech simulations are also flourishing. One of the most prominent network simulation projects is SIMNET (Alluisi, 1991). In 1983 DARPA sponsored a proof of concept technology demonstration of interactive networking for real-time, person-in-the-loop battle engagement simulation and war-gaming (Alluisi, 1991). The technology from this project (simulator networking project, i.e., "SIMNET") later became the basis for another DARPA initiative to demonstrate advanced distributed simulation technology (Alluisi, 1991). Furthermore, the SIMNET technology has been deployed at Ft. Knox as part of the Mounted Warfare Test-Bed. Researchers in differing branches of the armed forces have begun to use this system to examine questions concerning distributed team performance (Bell, 1995; Moses, 1996; Oser, Dwyer, & Fowlkes, 1995). For example, using this simulated environment, researchers tested an event based approach to training including scenario design, performance measurement, and after-action review (Oser et al., 1995). Tests of this nature are crucial, as they allow researchers to assess the performance of teams in distributed field settings.

Summary

Table 6 summarizes some of the team research that transpired in the 1990s. Indeed, considerable progress has occurred. Models of team performance emerged, and a number of variables impacting team performance have been tested. Team researchers also made progress in identifying the attitudes, cognitions, and behaviors, which constitute effective team performance. Finally, the 1990s saw the fruition of networking simulation technology, which has created numerous new test-beds useful for researching team performance.

Concluding Remarks

The history of military team research is rich and extensive. Multiple significant findings have appeared, and many of these findings should generalize beyond the military to teams in the private sector. Numerous individual researchers and government agencies contributed time, energy, and resources into this research agenda. In particular, the Army Research Institute, the Air Force Human Resource Laboratory, National Aeronautics and Space Administration, and the Naval Air Warfare Center Training Systems Division have worked to ensure that science remains a major focus of the efforts to solve the team performance problems encountered by the U.S. military. With this knowledge base, the future looks bright. Investments by the military will continue to be made in understanding the nature of teams. One focus will remain on how cognitive theory may help explain teamwork

TABLE 6. Team Research in the 1990s

Significant Findings or Events	Authors
• Identified problems in collective training research (e.g., inadequate definitions of collective concepts, lack of team development models, and difficulties in distinguishing individual and collective skills).	Turnage, Houser, & Hofman (1990)
• Demonstrated that team process behaviors can be separated from task related behaviors. Furthermore, teamwork behaviors are correlated with task outcomes.	Stout, Cannon-Bowers, Morgan, & Salas (1990); Oser, McCallum, Salas, & Morgan (1989)
• Described the use of Petri-nets, a mathematical modeling technique, as a means to model complex team functioning and as a basis to develop team performance measures.	Coovert & Cannon-Bowers (1990)
• Developed a comprehensive model of team performance: the "Team Effectiveness Model". The model describes the multiple pieces of team effectiveness including: organizational and situational characteristics, task and team characteristics, individual characteristics, work structure, team processes and team outcomes.	Salas, Dickinson, Converse, and Tannenbaum (1992); Tannenbaum, Beard, & Salas (1992)
• Findings led to the idea that the level of workload may determine which team processes are needed for team performance, and in turn, which team training interventions will be most useful for those situations.	Bowers, Urban, & Morgan (1992); Kleinman & Serfaty (1989)
• Demonstrated that regardless of workload, hierarchically arranged teams showed lower performance than non-hierarchical teams.	Bowers, Urban, & Morgan (1992)
• Showed that teamwork behaviors predicted variance in team performance beyond that explained by individual task competence.	Stout, Salas, & Carson (1994)
• Collectively-oriented team members performed more effectively than did egocentric team members.	Driskell & Salas (1992)
• Consolidated a number of the teamwork skill definitions found in the literature and into the following competencies: adaptability, shared situational awareness, performance monitoring and feedback, leadership/team management, interpersonal, coordination, communication, and decision making.	Cannon-Bowers, Tannenbaum, Salas, & Volpe (1995)
• Introduced the notion of Shared Mental Models as a theoretical framework to study teams.	Cannon-Bowers, Salas, & Converse (1993); Orasanu (1990)
• Presented a measurement model that links coordination processes to team performance and mission outcome. Model assumes that team coordination is necessary for mission success, a multidimensional property of the team, and emerges over time in response to training.	Spiker, Tourville, Silverman, & Nullmeyer (1996)
• Principles, lessons learned and specifications began to be outlined from the research based in earlier decades.	Salas, Cannon-Bowers, & Blickensderfer (1997); Cannon-Bowers & Salas (in press)
• Validation of team training strategies began to show their ability to improve teamwork in complex environments.	Salas, Cannon-Bowers, & Johnston (1997); Stout, Salas, & Fowlkes (1997); Spiker et al., 1996.

(e.g., What cognitive elements are important to team performance? How do we measure team cognitions?). Another focus will be distributed team training (e.g., What is the nature of distributed teams? How can we train distributed teams to coordinate most effectively?). A third focus will remain on transitioning the findings from all these decades into behavioral technology (e.g., automated team performance measurement, intelligent tutoring for teams, and team performance modeling). Overall, military team performance has proven to be a fruitful research area with many intriguing avenues examined and others open for discovery.

Notes

1. Please note that many of the works reviewed in this chapter were difficult to access (e.g., technical reports). Hence, some of the information presented is based on secondary sources (e.g., Dyer, 1984).

Disclaimer

The views expressed herein are those of the authors and do not reflect the official position of organization with which they are affiliated.

References

Adelman, L., Zirk, D. A., Lehner, O. E., Moffett, R. J., & Hall, R. (1986). Distributed tactical decision-making: Conceptual framework and empirical results. *IEEE Transactions on Systems, Man, and Cybernetics*, SMC-16, 794-805.

Alexander, L. T., & Cooperband, A. S. (1965). *System training and research in team behavior* (TM-2581, DTIC No. AD 620 606). Santa Monica, CA: System Development Corporation.

Alluisi, E. A. (1991). The development of technology for collective training: SIMNET, a case history. *Human Factors*, 33(3), 343-362.

Bell, H. H. (1995). The engineering of a training network. *Proceedings of the Seventh Annual International Training Equipment Conference*, Arlington, VA, 365-370.

Berkowitz, L., & Levy, B. I. (1956). Pride in group performance and group-task motivation. *Journal of Abnormal and Social Psychology*, 53, 300-306.

Biel, W. C., Chapman, R. L., Kennedy, J. L., & Newell, A. (1957). *The systems research laboratory's air defense experiments* (P-1201, DTIC No. AD 606 273). Alexandria, VA: Human Resources Research Organization.

Blickensderfer, E., Cannon-Bowers, J. A., & Salas, E. (1997a). Fostering shared mental models through team self-correction: Theoretical bases and propositions. In M. Beyerlein, D. Johnson, & S. Beyerlein (Eds.), *Advances in interdisciplinary studies in work teams* (Vol. 4, pp. 249-279). Greenwich, CT: JAI Press.

Blickensderfer, E., Cannon-Bowers, J. A., & Salas, E. (1997b, April). Training teams to self-correct: A laboratory investigation. Paper presented at the 12th annual meeting of the Society for Industrial and Organizational Psychology, St. Louis, MO.

Boldovici, J. A. (1979). *Analyzing tank gunnery engagements for simulator-based process measurement* (ARI Research Report 1227. Performed by Human Resources Research Organization). Alexandria, VA: U. S. Army Research Institute for the Behavioral and Social Sciences.

Borgatta, E. F., Lanzetta, J. T., McGrath, J. E., & Strodbeck, F. L. (1959). *Report of the task group on team functions* (Report submitted to the Office of Science, Director of Defense Research and Engineering, DTIC No. AD 283 329). Washington, DC: Smithsonian Institution, Research Group in Psychology and the Social Sciences.

Bouchard, T. J. (1969). Personality, problem-solving procedure, and performance in small groups. *Journal of Applied Psychology Monographs*, 53, 1-29.

Bowers, C. A., Salas, E., Prince, C., & Brannick, M. (1992). Games teams play: A methodology for investigating team coordination and performance. *Behavior Methods, Instruments, and Computers*, 24, 503-506.

Bowers, C. A., Urban, J. M., & Morgan, B. B., Jr. (1992). *The study of crew coordination and performance in hierarchical team decision making* (TR No-92-01). Orlando, FL: University of Central Florida Team Performance Lab.

Briggs, G. E., & Johnston, W. A. (1966a). Influence of a change in system criteria on team performance. *Journal of Applied Psychology*, 50, 467-472.

Briggs, G. E., & Johnston, W. A. (1966b). *Laboratory research on team training* (NAVTRADEVCEN 1327-3, DTIC No. 485 636). Columbus, OH: Ohio State University.

Briggs, G. E., & Johnston, W. A. (1967). *Team training* (NAVTRADEVCEN-1327-4 AD-660 019, Technical Report No. 1327-4). Orlando, FL: Naval Training Device Center.

Brown, R. L. (1967). *A content analysis of communications within Army small-unit patrolling operations* (HumRRO Technical Report 67-7). Alexandria, VA: George Washington University, Human Resources Research Office, Division No. 4, Fort Benning, GA.

Brown, D. (1987). Introduction to MAC CRM training. In H. W. Orlady & H. C. Foushee (Eds.), *Cockpit resource management training: Proceedings of the NASA* / MAC workshop (pp. 132-134). Moffett Field, CA: NASA Ames Research Center.

Cannon-Bowers, J. A., & Salas, E. (1998). Making decisions *under stress: Implications for individual and team training*. Washington D.C.: American Psychological Association.

Cannon-Bowers, J. A., Salas, E., & Converse, S. A. (1993). Shared mental models in expert team decision making. In N. J. Castellan, Jr. (Ed.), *Individual and group decision making: Current issues* (pp. 221-246). Hillsdale, NJ: LEA.

Cannon-Bowers, J. A., Tannenbaum, S. I., Salas, E., & Volpe, C. E. (1995). Defining team competencies and establishing team training requirements. In R. Guzzo & E. Salas (Eds.), *Team effectiveness and decision making in organizations* (pp. 333-380). San Francisco, CA: Jossey-Bass.

Cannon-Bowers, J. A., Salas, E., Blickensderfer, E., & Bowers, C. A. (1998). The impact of cross-training and workload on team functioning: A replication and extension of initial findings. *Human Factors*, 40(1), 92-101.

Chapman, R. L., Kennedy, J. L., Newell, A., & Biel, W.C. (1959). The system research laboratory's air defense experiments. *Management Service*, 5, 250-269.

Connelly, E. M., Comeau, R. F., & Steinheiser, F. (1980) *Team performance measures for computerized systems* (Contract No MDA-903-79-C-0274). Vienna, VA: Performance Measurement Associates.

Coovert, M. D., Cannon-Bowers, J. A., & Salas, E. (1990). Applying mathematical modeling technology to the study of team training and performance. *Proceedings of the 12th Annual Interservice/Industry Training Systems Conference*, Washington, DC, 326-333.

Denson, R. W. (1981). *Team training: Literature review and annotated bibliography* (ARHRL-TR-80-40, A099994). Wright-Patterson AFB, OH: Logistic and Technical Training Division, Air Force Human Resources Laboratory.

Dieterly, D. L. (1978). Team performance: A model for research. In E. J. Baise & J. M. Miller (Eds.), *Proceedings of the Human Factors Society 22nd Annual Meeting*. Santa Monica, CA: Human Factors Society.

Driskell, J. E., & Salas, E. (1992). Collective behavior and team performance. *Human Factors*, 34, 277-288.

Driskell, J. E., & Salas, E. (Eds.). (1997). *Stress and human performance*. Mahwah, NJ: LEA.

Duncan, P. C., Rouse, W. B., Johnston, J. H., Cannon-Bowers, J. A., Salas, E., & Burns, J. J. (1996). Training teams working in complex systems: A mental model-based approach. In W. B. Rouse (Ed.), *Human/technology interaction in complex systems* (Vol. 8, pp. 173-231). Greenwich, CT: JAI Press.

Dwyer, D. J., Hall, J. K., Volpe, C. E., Cannon-Bowers, J. A., & Salas, E. (1992). *A performance assessment task for examining tactical decision making under stress* (Special Report No. 92-002). Orlando, FL: Naval Training Systems Center.

Dyer, J. L. (1984). Team research and team training: State-of-the-art review. In F. A. Muckler (Ed.), *Human Factors Review* (pp. 285-323). Santa Monica, CA: Human Factors Society, Inc.

Eaton, N. K., & Neff, J. F. (1978). *The effects of tank crew turbulence on tank gunner performance* (ARI Technical Paper 350). Alexandria, VA: U. S. Army Research Institute for the Behavioral and Social Sciences.

Eimer, E. O. (1987). *Team problem solving: Effects of communication and function overlap* (Technical Report No. AAMRL-TR-87-037). Wright-Patterson AFB, Ohio: Harry G. Armstrong Aerospace Medical Research Laboratory.

Fieldler, F. E., & Meuwese, W. A. T. (1962). *The leader's contribution to performance in cohesive and uncohesive task groups.* (NR 177-472, DTIC No. AD 729 420). Urbana, IL: University of Illinois, Department of Psychology.

Forgays, D. G., & Levy, B. I. (1957). *Combat performance characteristics associated with changes in the membership of medium-bomber crews* (AFPTRC-TN-57-120, DTIC No. AD 146414). San Antonio, TX: Lackland Air Force Base, Air Force Personnel and Training Research Center.

George, C. E., Hoak, G., & Boutwell, J. (1963). *Pilot studies of team effectiveness* (Research Memorandum No. 28, AD-627 217). Ft. Benning, GA: US Army Infantry Human Research Unit, Human Resources Research Office.

Gersick, C. J. G. (1988). Time and transition in work teams: Towards a new model of group development. *Academy of Management Review*, 31, 9-41.

Gill, D. L. (1977). Prediction of group motor performance from individual member abilities. *Journal of Motor Behavior*, 11, 113-122.

Gladstein, D. L. (1984). Groups in context: A model of task group effectiveness. Administrative Science Quarterly, 29, 499-517.

Glanzer, M., & Glaser, R. (1955). *A review of team training problems* (Prepared for the Office of Naval Research, DTIC No. AD 078 434). Pittsburgh, PA: American Institutes for Research.

Glanzer, M., & Glaser, R. (1959). Techniques for the study of group structure and behavior: Analysis of structure. *Psychological Bulletin*, 56, 317-322.

Glaser, R., Glanzer, M., & Morten, A. W., Jr. (1955). *A study of some dimensions of team performance* (NR-154-079, DTIC No. AD 078 433). Pittsburgh, PA: American Institute for Research.

Glickman, A. S., Zimmer, S., Montero, R. C., Guerette, P. J., Campbell, W. J., Morgan, B. B., Jr., & Salas, E. (1987). *The evolution of teamwork skills: An empirical assessment with implications for training* (NTSC Technical Report No. 87-016). Orlando, FL: Naval Training Systems Center.

Guerette, P. J., Miller, D. L., Glickman, A. S., Morgan, B. B., Jr., & Salas, E. (1987). *Instructional processes and strategies in team training* (NTSC Technical Report No. 87-016). Orlando, FL: Naval Training Systems Center,

Hackman, J. R. (1983). *A normative model of work team effectiveness* (Tech. Rep. No. 2). New Haven, CT: Yale University.

Hackman, J. R. (Ed.). (1990). *Groups that work (and those that don't): Creating conditions for effective teamwork.* San Francisco, CA: Jossey-Bass.

Hall, E. R., & Rizzo, W. A. (1975). *An assessment of U.S. Navy tactical team training* (TAEG Report No. 18). Orlando, FL: Training Analysis and Evaluation Group.

Hansen, R. A., & Wulff, R. A. (1985). The next training challenge for simulation: Team training. *Proceedings of the Seventh Annual Interservice/Industry Training Equipment Conference*, Orlando, FL, 395-399.

Henriksen, K. F., Jones, D. R., Hannaman, D. L., Wylie, P. B., Shriver, E. L., Hamill, B. W., & Sulzen, R. H. (1980). *Identification of combat unit leader skills and leader-group interaction processes* (ARI Technical Report 440). Alexandria, VA: U. S. Army Research Institute for the Behavioral and Social Sciences.

Hollenbeck, J. R., Sego, D. J., Ilgen, D. R., & Major, D. A. (1991). *Team interactive decision exercise for incorporating distributed expertise (TIDE ^{2}): A program and paradigm for team research* (Tech. Rep. No. 91-1). East Lansing: Michigan State University.

Johnston, W. A. (1966). Transfer of team skills as a function of type of training. *Journal of Applied Psychology*, 52, 102-108.

Johnston, W. A., & Briggs, G. (1968). Team performance as a function of team arrangement and work load. *Journal of Applied Psychology*, 50, 89-94.

Johnston, D. L., & Obermayer, R. W. (1984). An expert system as a replacement for a team member in an ASW simulation. *Proceedings of the Sixth Interservice/Industry Training Systems Conference,* Washington, DC, 35-44.

Jordan, N., Jensen, B. T., & Terebinsky, S. J. (1963). The development of cooperation among three-man crews in a simulated man-machine information processing system. *Journal of Social Psychology*, 59, 175-184.

Kabanoff, B., & O'Brien, G. E. (1979). The effects of task type and cooperation upon group products and performance. *Organizational Behavior and Human Performance*, 23, 163-181.

Kahan, J. P. (1989). *Corps and division command staff turnover in the 1980s* (Technical Report No. RAND/N-2994-A). Santa Monica, CA: RAND Corporation.

Kanki, B. G., & Foushee, H. C. (1988). Communication as group process mediator of aircrew performance. *Aviation, Space, and Environmental Medicine*, 60, 402-410.

Kidd, J. S. (1961). A comparison of one-, two-, and three-man work units under various conditions of workload. *Journal of Applied Psychology*, 45, 195-200.

Kinkade, R. G., & Kidd, J. S. (1959). *The effect of team size and intermember communication on decision making performance* (WADC Technical Report 58-474, DTIC No. AD 215 621). Wright-Patterson Airforce Base, OH: AERO Medical Laboratory.

Klaus, R. G., & Glaser, R. (1965). *Increasing team proficiency through training: Team learning as a function of member learning characteristics and practice conditions* (AIR-E1-4/65-TR, DTIC No. AD 471 469). Pittsburgh, PA: American Institutes for Research.

Klaus, D. J., & Glaser, R. (1970). Reinforcement determinants of team proficiency. *Organizational Behavior and Human Performance*, 5, 33-67.

Kleinman, D. L., & Serfaty, D. (1989). Team performance assessment in distributed decision making. *Proceedings of the Symposium on Interactive Networked Simulation for Training*, Orlando, FL, 22-27.

Klimoski, R., & Mohammed, S. (1994). Team mental model: Construct or metaphor? *Journal of Management*, 20, 403-437.

Kubala, A. L. (1978). *Problems in measuring team effectiveness* (Hum RRO Professional Paper 2-73, DTIC No. AD A049 560). Alexandria, VA: Human Resources Research Organization.

Leedom, D. K. (1990). *Aircrew coordination training and evaluation for Army rotary wing aircrews: Summary of research for fiscal year 1990.* Fort Rucker, AL: U.S. Army research Institute Aviation Research and Development Activity.

Leedom, D. K., & Simon, R. (1995). Improving team coordination: A case for behavioral-based training. *Military Psychology*, 7, 109-122.

Lorge, I., Fox, D., Davitz, J., & Brenner, M. (1958). A survey of studies contrasting the quality of group performance and individual performance, 1920-1957. *Psychological Bulletin*, 55, 337-372.

McCallum, G. A., Oser, R., Morgan, B. B., Jr., & Salas, E. (1989). *An investigation of the behavioral components of teamwork.* Paper presented at the 97th annual meeting of the American Psychological Association, New Orleans, LA.

McIntyre, R. M., Morgan, B. B., Jr., Salas, E., & Glickman, A. S. (1988). Teamwork from team training: New evidence for the development of teamwork skills during operational training. *Proceedings of the 10th Annual Interservice/Industry Training Systems Conference*, Washington, DC, 21-27.

McIntyre, R. M., & Salas, E. (1995). Measuring and managing for team performance : Emerging principles from complex environments. In R. Guzzo & E. Salas (Eds.), *Team effectiveness and decision making in organizations* (pp. 149-203). San Francisco, CA: Jossey-Bass.

Minionis, D. P., Zaccaro, S. J., & Perez, R. (1995). *Shared mental models, team coordination, and team performance.* Paper presented at the 10th annual meeting of the Society for Industrial and Organizational Psychology, Orlando, FL.

Modrick, J. A. (1986). Team performance and training. In J. Zeidner (Ed.), *Human productivity enhancement: Training and human factors in systems design* (Vol. 1, pp. 130-166). New York, NY: Praeger.

Morgan, B. B., Coates, G. D., Alluisi, E. A., & Kirby, R. H. (1978). *The team-training load as a parameter of effectiveness for collective training in units* (ITR-78-14, DTIC No. AD A063 135). Norfolk, VA: Old Dominion University.

Morgan, B. B., Jr., Glickman, A. S., Woodard, E. A., Blaiwes, A. S., & Salas, E. (1986). *Measurement of team behaviors in a Navy environment* (NTSC Technical report No. 86-014). Orlando, FL: Naval Training Systems Center.

Moses, F. M. (1996). The challenge of distributed training. *International Training Equipment Conference Proceedings* (pp. 358-364). Arlington, VA: ITEC Ltd.

Naylor, J.C., & Dickinson, T. L. (1969). Task structure, work structure, and team performance. *Journal of Applied Psychology*, 53, 167-177.

Nieva, V. F., Fleishman, E. A., & Reick, A. (1978). *Team dimensions: Their identity, their measurement, and their relationships* (Report No. DAHC 19-78-C-0001). Alexandria, VA: US Army Research Institute for the Behavioral and Social Sciences.

Obermayer, R. W., Vreuls, D., Muckler, F. A., Conway, E. J., & Fitzgerald, J. A. (1974). *Combat-ready crew performance measurement system: Final report* (AFHRL-TR-74-108(I), DTIC No. AD B005 517). Brooks Air Force Base, TX: Air Force Systems Command.

O'Brien, G. (1968). The measurement of cooperation. *Organizational Behavior and Human Performance*, 3, 427-439.

Orasanu, J. (1990). *Shared mental models and crew performance*. Paper presented at the 34th annual meeting of the Human Factors Society, Orlando, FL.

Oser, R. L., Dwyer, D. J., & Fowlkes, J. E. (1995). Team performance in multi-service distributed interactive simulation exercises: Initial results. *Proceedings of the 17th Interservice/Industry Training Systems and Education Conference*, Arlington, VA, 163-171.

Oser, R. L., McCallum, G. A., Salas, E., & Morgan, B. B., Jr. (1989). *Toward a definition of teamwork: An analysis of critical team behavior* (NTSC Technical Report No. 89-004). Orlando, FL: Naval Training Systems Center.

Prince, C., Chidester, T. R., Bowers, C. A., & Cannon-Bowers, J. A. (1992). Aircrew coordination: Achieving teamwork in the cockpit. In R. W. Swezey & E. Salas (Eds.), *Teams: Their training and performance* (pp. 329-353). Norwood, NJ: Ablex.

Prince, C., & Salas, E. (1993). Training and research for teamwork in the military aircrew. In E. L. Wiener, B. G. Kanki, & R. L. Helmreich (Eds.), *Cockpit resource management* (pp. 337-366). Orlando, FL: Academic Press.

Pritchard, R. D., & Montagno, R. V. (1978). *Effects of specific vs. nonspecific and absolute vs. comparative feedback on performance and satisfaction* (AFHRL-TR-78-12, DTIC No. AD A005 693). West Lafayette, IN: Purdue Research Foundation.

Roby, T. B., & Lanzetta, J. T. (1957a). *A replication study of work group structure and task performance* (DTIC No. AD 134 205). Lackland Air Force Base, TX: Air Force Personnel and Training Research Center.

Roby, T. B., & Lanzetta, J. T. (1957b). Conflicting principles in man-machine system design. *Journal of Applied Psychology*, 41(3), 170-178.

Root, R. T., Hayes, J. F., Word, L. E., Shriver, E. L., & Griffin, G. R. (1979). *Field test of techniques for tactical training of junior leaders in infantry units* (Project EFFTRAIN, ARI Technical Report TR-79-A21). Alexandria, VA: U. S. Army Research Institute for the Behavioral and Social Sciences.

Salas, E., Bowers, C. A., & Cannon-Bowers, J. A. (1995). Military team research: Ten years of progress. *Military Psychology*, 7, 55-75.

Salas, E., & Cannon-Bowers, J. A. (in press). The anatomy of team training. To appear in L. Tobias & D. Fletcher (Eds.), *Handbook of research on training*.

Salas, E., Cannon-Bowers, J. A., & Blickensderfer, E. L. (1993). Team performance and training research: Emerging Principles. *Journal of the Washington Academy of Sciences*, 83(2), 81-106.

Salas, E., Cannon-Bowers, J. A., & Blickensderfer, E. L. (1997). Enhancing reciprocity between training theory and practice: Principles, guidelines, and specifications. In J. K. Ford & Associates (Eds.), *Improving training effectiveness in work organizations* (pp. 291-322). Hillsdale, NJ: LEA.

Salas, E., Cannon-Bowers, J. A., & Johnston, J. H. (1997). How can you turn a team of experts into an expert team?: Emerging training strategies. In C. Zsambok & G. Klein (Eds.), *Naturalistic decision making* (pp. 359-370). Hillsdale, NJ: LEA.

Salas, E., Dickinson, T. L., Converse, S. A., & Tannenbaum, S. I. (1992). Toward an understanding of team performance and training. In R. W. Swezey & E. Salas (Eds.), *Teams: Their training and performance* (pp. 3-29). Norwood, NJ: Ablex.

Shaw, M. E. (1976). *Group dynamics: The psychology of small group behavior*. New York: McGraw-Hill.

Siegel, A. I., & Federman, P. J. (1973). Communications content training as an ingredient in effective team performance. *Ergonomics*, 16, 403-416.

Siegel, A. I., Wolf, J. J., & Fischl, M. A. (1969). *Digital simulation of the performance of intermediate size crews: Logic of a model for simulating crew psychosocial and performance variables* (prepared for the Office of Naval Research, DTIC No. AD 695 839). Wayne, PA: Applied Psychological Services.

Simon, R., & Grubb, G. (1993). *Development of crew coordination and evaluation methods and materials (E-21444U)*. Wilmington, MA: Dynamics Research Corp.

Simon, R., & Pawlik, E. A. (1993). *Development of candidate crew coordination training methods and materials (E-21983U)*. Wilmington, MA: Dynamics Research Corp.

Siskel, M., Lane, F. D., Powe, W. E., & Flexman, R. E. (1965). *Intra-crew communication of B-52 and KC-135 student and combat crews during selected mission segments* (AMRL-TR-65-18, DTIC No. AD617 598). Wright-Patterson Air Force Base, OH: Air Force Systems Command, Aerospace Medical Research Laboratory.

Smith-Jentsch, K. A., Salas, E., & Baker, D. (1996). Training team performance-related assertiveness. *Personnel Psychology*, 49, 909-936.

Smith-Jentsch, K. A., Zeisig, R. L., Acton, B., McPherson, J. A. (1998). Team dimensional training. To appear in J. A. Cannon-Bowers & E. Salas (Eds.), *Making decisions under stress: Implications for individual and team training*. Washington, DC: American Psychological Association.

Spiker, A., Tourville, S. J., Silverman, D. R., & Nullmeyer, R. T. (1996). *Team performance during combat mission training: A conceptual model and measurement framework* (AL/HR-TR-1996-0092). Mesa, AZ: United States Air Force Armstrong Laboratory.

Steiner, I. D. (Ed.) (1972). *Group process and productivity*. Orlando, FL: Academic Press.

Stout, R. J. (1995). Planning effects on communication strategies: A shared mental model perspective. *Proceedings of the Human Factors and Ergonomics Society* 39th annual meeting, Santa Monica, CA, 1278-1282.

Stout, R. J., Cannon-Bowers, J. A., Morgan, B. B., Jr., & Salas, E. (1990). Does crew coordination behavior impact performance? *Proceedings of the Human Factors Society 33rd annual meeting*, Santa Monica, CA, 1382-1386.

Stout, R. J., Salas, E., & Carson, R. (1994). Individual task proficiency and team process: What's important for team functioning. *Military Psychology*, 7, 123-139.

Stout, R. J., Salas, E. & Fowlkes, J. E. (1997). Enhancing teamwork in complex environments through team training. *Group Dynamics: Theory, Research, & Practice*, 1, 169-182.

Tannenbaum, S. I., Beard, R. L., & Salas, E. (1992). Team building and its influence on team effectiveness: An examination of conceptual and empirical developments. In K. Kelley (Ed.), *Issue, theory, and research in industrial/organizational psychology* (pp. 117-153). Amsterdam: Elsevier.

Tannenbaum, S. I., Jentsch, K. S., & Behson, S. (1998). Training team leaders to facilitate team learning and performance. To appear in J. A. Cannon-Bowers & E. Salas (Eds.), *Making decisions under stress: Implications for individual and team training.* Washington, DC: American Psychological Association Press.

Terborg, J. R., Castore, C. H., & DeNinno, J. A. (1976). *A longitudinal field investigation of the impact of group composition on group performance and cohesion.* Paper presented at the annual meeting of the Midwestern Psychological Association, Chicago.

Thurmond, P. & Kribs, H. D. (1978). *Computerized collective training for teams: (Final Report TR-78-A1)*. Alexandria, VA: US Army Research Institute for the Behavior and Social Sciences.

Trow, D. B. (1964). *Teamwork under turnover and succession* (Technical Report No. 2, DTIC No. AD 601 816). Endicott, NY: Harpur College.

Tuckman, B. W. (1965). Developmental sequences in small groups. *Psychological Bulletin*, 63, 384-399.

Turnage, J. T., Houser, T. L., & Hoffman, D. A. (1990). *Assessment of performance measurement methodologies for collective military training* (Contract No. N61339-85-D-0024). Orlando, FL: University of Central Florida.

Tziner, A., & Eden, D. (1985). Effects of crew composition on crew performance: Does the whole equal the sum of the parts? *Journal of Applied Psychology*, 70, 85-93.

Urban, J. M., Bowers, C. A., Monday, S. D., & Morgan, B. B., Jr. (1995). Workload, team structure, and communication in team performance. *Military Psychology*, 7, 123-139.

Volpe, C. E., Cannon-Bowers, J. A., Salas, E., & Spector, P. (1996). The impact of cross training on team functioning. *Human Factors*, 38, 87-100.

Weaver, J. L., Bowers, C. A., Salas, E. & Cannon-Bowers, J. A. (1995). Networked simulations: New paradigms for team performance research. *Behavior Research Methods, Instruments, & Computers*, 27(1), 12-24.

Wellens, A. R., & Ergener, D. (1988). The C.I.T.I.E.S. game: A computer-based situation assessment task for studying distributed decision making. *Simulation & Games*, 19, 304-327.

Wiener, E. L., Kanki, B. G., & Helmreich, R. L. (1993). *Cockpit resource management.* San Diego, CA: Academic Press.

Ziller, R. C. (1963). *The effects of changes in group composition of group performance* (DTIC No. AD 413 965). Newark, DE: University of Delaware.

Chapter 18

A History of Teams

The Case of Sweden and Volvo

Tommy Nilsson

Swedish National Institute for Working Life, Arbetslivsinstitutet, Solna, Sweden

Abstract

In this chapter I shall describe some aspects of the history of teams in Sweden with the focus on the Volvo car industry, especially its assembly plants in Gothenburg, Kalmar and Uddevalla. The question is: when did teams appear in a modern fashion at Volvo and in what way have they developed up till this day? Concerning the later I shall focus on work organization and how the work content in the teams has developed; which are the significant differences between teams of the 1970s and teams of today?

Introduction

What is the meaning of the team concept? The phenomena that occurred on the shop floor in most of the industrialized countries in the 1960s, and which Cole termed "small group activities" (Cole, 1989), have been given many names. Terms like "work groups", "self managing groups", "self regulating groups", "autonomous work groups", "semi-autonomous work groups", "production groups", "integrated teams" and "teams" are common. However, what we call these phenomena is maybe not so important; the most important thing is how we define the concept. I have chosen to use the term of "team" and the concept of a team is defined as follows: A team consists of a number of workers (in practice at least 4-5 workers) who work together at a common workplace in a systemized way. They have a common goal and they interact with each other in relation to the common goal. The team has at least some degree of responsibility for the production (for example the quality of the products). If workers are put into a "work group" without any responsibility what so ever, it is meaningless to talk about teams. The members of a team are and should be socially knitted together in one way or another.

When investigating teams and the development of teams, it is important to focus on what degree of responsibility and authority they have, how manual and intellectual work tasks are separated or integrated in the teams. Therefore I will try to describe the history of teams in terms of integration of work tasks, both the lateral and the vertical aspect of it.

The history of modern teams at the shop floor starts with the principles of scientific management - Taylorism or Fordism. It is a story about the path from specialized and simple work tasks, from non-qualified blue-collar jobs with very little responsibility to work with generalized qualifications, where the individual

M.M. Beyerlein (ed.), Work Teams: Past, Present and Future, 275–288.

worker performs several work tasks with a high degree of responsibility and authority.

Differences Between Countries

There is no doubt that the phenomenon of teams is increasing in the industrialized countries (Stymne, 1996). It is also true that there are differences between countries in terms of diffusion, degree of development of the teams and type of teams. In some northern European countries like Sweden the diffusion of teams is high, while this is not the case in the Mediterranean countries. In the former the teams are generally more developed if compared to many other countries, including Japan. As Kochan, MacDuffie and Lansbury (1997) have pointed out "lean production" is introduced in the car industry in different ways. This also concerns how teams are constituted. In the Mediterranean countries for example the companies rely more on the role of supervisors compared with the situation in companies in the northern parts of Europe (Kochan et al, 1997).

Some of the conditions that can probably explain these differences are the strength of the union and how the unions handle the issue of work organisation, the skill level of the (blue collar) work force and management culture and strategies. If comparing Sweden and France for instance, in Sweden the unions are stronger and have argued in favor of work development and "enriching jobs" which is not the case in France. The skill level of the blue collar workers is also higher in Sweden. A high skill level makes it easier for the workers to adopt new and qualified work tasks. In Sweden there is relatively little stress on hierarchy, and the demarcation line between blue and white collar workers is not as sharp as in France.

Teams Are Not New

Modern teams started to develop in the 1960s as a response to scientific management. But teams are not new. They have existed long before Taylor and Ford and were rooted in craft production. In some areas scientific management did not succeed in destroying the organization of teamwork. In Sweden for example teams have existed intact up till now within the process industry. In the steel industry and the chemical industry there has been "scope for fairly autonomous arrangements" for the teams (Bergman, 1995: 412). This is also true of the construction industry. As late as in the 1950s the teams of dock workers in the harbors were strong (Björklund, 1984). But in the engineering industry, food industry and other industries teams were abolished because of scientific management (Stymne, 1996).

The Way To Modern Teams

The academic criticism of scientific management started in the USA already in the 1930s. Kurt Lewin was one of those academics that during the 1940s and 1950s started group experiments based on theories of group processes. He could show that if the workers cooperated within a group they became more motivated and were more able to perform their duties. He stressed the importance of *human relation* within the work process.

Later on Lewin established contacts with the Tavistock Institute for Human Relations in London, where the ideas about team work organization was developed by Emery and Trist (Gustavsen, 1990). They founded the principles of socio-technical design: autonomous teams and rotation between various tasks within the team. The main point was to make "the best possible use of the intellectual and learning capability of operators" (Stymne, 1996:37). The advocates of socio-technical design had an impact not only on the work organization debate in Great Britain, but also in Norway in the mid 1960s. With the help of the Tavistock Institute, the main organizations on the Norwegian labor market jointly started work on organizational experiments in a couple of industries (Engelstad, 1970).

After a while these experiments also inspired the main organizations in Sweden. But not least the Swedish employers´ top organization, SAF (Swedish Employers´ Confederation), at that time had itself come to the conclusion that scientific management produced not only high productivity, but also problems, "something had to be done about them". In 1966, SAF established the so called Technical Department. The aim was to try to handle two problems, wage drift and the negative consequences of scientific management: a high turn over rate and a high degree of absenteeism (Cole, 1989). When employers at that time discussed a reorganization of work, they stressed the human aspect, in order to get a more motivated work force. It was not until the 1980s that they stressed efficiency. Then they realized that team organization and work development were directly connected to productivity and customer satisfaction. They turned the team to a "narrower business tool" (Cole, 1989: 252).

Around 1970, the unions started to show a new interest in improving the working conditions of their members. In the name of "humanization" and "industrial democracy" they started to cooperate with the employers. One expression of this interest was the establishment of the Development Council for Cooperation Questions and its research subgroup URAF (Development Council Working Group for Research). Together organized labor and capital started to build up an organisational infrastructure, which later on made it relatively easy to establish teams in the companies. The Co-Determination Act, that came into operation in 1976 and gave the right for the local unions to negotiate about organizational matters, probably played an important role for this development.

But in Sweden, like in other industrialized countries, except Japan, it was not until after the mid 1980s, that the diffusion of team organization really went ahead (Berggren, 1992). Talking about teams and setting up more or less isolated team experiments is one thing, establishing them profoundly and diffusing them is quite another. According to Cole there was a vivid discussion about job enrichment in the US during the 1970s and several team experiments were started. But lots of them died out in the 1980s. Very often it was a question of form rather than substance, and the degree of job enrichment and self-managing was often very low (Cole, 1989). Stymne is probably right when he asserts that the decline was due to the difficulties to show any significant rise in productivity in teams compared with traditional work organization (Stymne, 1996). As already mentioned, the only country in the industrialized world, in which team organization continuously grew was Japan. The team concept was established in the beginning of the 1960s, and in the mid 1980s almost all big industry companies were organizing their work force at the shop floor in teams (Cole, 1989).

Integrated Production Systems

Modern teams are related to integrated production systems (Brulin & Nilsson, 1995; Nilsson, 1996). This concept is close to the concept of lean production (Womack et al., 1991) and the concept of lean enterprise (Womack & Jones, 1994). The hypothesis is that integrated production systems and their preconditions must be established on a broad scale before a profound diffusion of teams can be realised.

The preconditions for integrated production systems are quite different compared to those of the Tayloristic and bureaucratic production systems. The old market conditions were characterized by a constantly increasing demand on markets which seemed to be almost insatiable, and there was almost no adaptation to single customer´s demands; it was a mass market. Production volumes were fixed on the basis of forecasts and large stocks of finished goods, raw materials and semi-finished products were kept.

The prerequisites for integrated production systems are saturated markets and customers with specific requirements in terms of choice and rapid redesign of products. There is talk about "fragmented markets and sophisticated customers" (Clark and Fujimoto, 1991). Strong cards for companies in the face of competition are therefore being fast and flexible, giving good customer service and adopting rapid manufacture of new products at low cost.

The very core of the ideal type of lean production is that, compared to mass production, it uses fewer resources in every respect, while at the same time increasing the production volume. This applies for manpower, premises, time and investments in tools and machines, etc. The goal of avoiding tying up capital plays an important role. If rationalisation of work is an important principle in the mass production system, then capital and time rationalisation is an important principle in integrated production systems. Integrated production systems also mean a closer relationship with subcontractors and retailers. In the case of subcontractors, the main manufacturer wants to involve them in the production process, i.e. wants them to be involved at the ideas stage and when new products are being developed. The aim is to shorten lead times and to improve quality.

In the context of the actual work process integrated production systems are very much about tearing down barriers and shortening lines of communication. The barriers to be torn down are those between different departments such as design, production and marketing, between different categories of employees, i.e. blue-collar and white-collar workers, between different blue-collar and white-collar groups and between sub-contractors and main manufacturers. The essential thing is to create continuous flows without having stocks, interim stocks or goods in storage.

Integrated production systems make special demands on the workforce. In the mass production system it was rational to have specialised manpower; in an integrated production system it seems to be rational to have a versatile and flexible workforce. In the next chapter I shall describe what has happened in Sweden concerning this proposition; how teams have been constituted?

Work Development within Teams: Sweden

During the 1990s there have been a significant diffusion of teams in Sweden. According to a representative of the Metal workers union, around 80% of its member worked in teams in 1996. (It is worth mentioning that about 90% of the blue collar workers in the engineering industry are unionized). The work development within the teams during the 1990s is also evident (*Towards Flexible Organisations*, 1996; Nilsson, 1996). In more and more companies team operators have a large number of duties in addition to their actual work with the machines or at the assembly line. The integration is both lateral and vertical. Lateral integration means that duties such as product control, maintenance and testing are integrated into the teams. Vertical integration means that duties of supervisors and white collar employees close to production are decentralised to the shop floor. In the most developed teams the following tasks are delegated from the supervisory level (Nilsson, 1996): Detailed planning of the work, personnel matters, instructors' work, problem solving, and ordering of materials/tools/measuring equipment/repairs. The following duties are delegated to the teams by production engineers, planners and other white-collar categories: Work on continuous improvements, production engineering, programming, contacts with customers, contacts with sub-contractors/dispatch, work on improvement of products and equipment (in project groups together with technicians and engineers), and follow-up of production objectives.

Complete Teams

In some of the most advanced companies there is a process of total integration of white-collar staff close to the production process into the work teams; there is talk about complete teams. These teams are supposed to handle duties such as manufacturing, production engineering, quality control, purchasing, planning, design (adaptation of standard products), and to manage contacts with customers and subcontractors. A further aim is to increase flexibility by allowing technicians to do some of the work involved in the ongoing production. At the same time, operators are supposed to acquire production engineering skills from the technicians and engineers. Another aim is that the dialogue and teamwork expected to be generated between operators and technical staff should help produce better solutions to problems and a more effective process of change. So far, complete teams are established only in a small number of companies, for example in some plants within the ABB group.

The Degree of Development is Dependent on the Type of Product and Work Activity

Far from all companies have the type of advanced team organization that is showed above. Sometimes it is found that team members are performing simple work tasks with responsibility only for the quality of the product. It seems as if the degree of work development within the teams is dependent on the type of product and on the type of work activity.

It seems as if jobs are most developed in the area of metal cutting activities (CNC-machines, FMS) of single customer adapted products. This also goes for assembling of big customer adapted products that are stationary assembled. Examples are drilling machines (Atlas Copco), road graders (Matsson Corporation) and dairy equipment (Alfa Laval). Jobs are less developed at assembly lines, final assembly of mass products. This can be found in the home electronic industry and also in the automotive industry. In between those two extremes one finds store activities and work in the process industry (Nilsson, 1996).

The Case of Volvo

In this report on Volvo I have chosen to describe Kalmar, Uddevalla and Torslanda/Gothenburg (Torslanda from 1991), but this trajectory mirrors most of the plants within the Volvo Company: It concerns the production of engines, gear boxes, trucks, etc. Uddevalla is special however, because of the stress on the principle of team-based whole saloon car building.

During the 1960s the degree of employment was very high, unemployment varied around 2%. This made it difficult for the companies to keep the workers, and this problem also concerned Volvo. But the ford-type production system did not make the workplaces attractive. In spite of improvements in work environment conditions - less of heavy lifting, better air quality and light conditions - satisfaction among blue collar workers was low. In the end of the 1960s absenteeism reached very high levels and the turnover rate now and then reached 100% at several Volvo plants (Auer & Riegler, 1990, Berggren, 1992). Like in the society as a whole, at Volvo both workers and the union expressed strong criticism of the working conditions.

The assembly plant in Gothenburg/Torslanda, producing saloon cars, had been established in the mid 1950s. It was built according to traditional ford-like principles. Productivity was raised by scientific methods of work rationalization and mechanization. Most workers on the shop floor were paid according to a piece rate system. Due to huge improvements in productivity and continuous wage increases, this production system worked well for many years. But in the end of the 1960s the excellence of this production system was questioned. Even management became sceptical of the traditional type of work organization.

Already in 1969 there were some local experiments at the Volvo company on new forms of work organization inspired by socio-technical design ideas. At Torslanda they were nothing more than small isolated attempts. But the experiences from these attempts were used when Volvo started to plan for the Kalmar plant (*Volvo Kalmarverken*, 1976).

Kalmar

The Volvo Kalmar plant was the first auto assembly factory that produced cars in large series without a mechanically driven assembly line (Berggren, 1992). It was also one of the first plants that introduced team organization in the plant as a whole (*Volvo Kalmarverken*, 1976). The plant opened in 1974, and was closed down in 1994, because of over-capacity in the Volvo production system. The aim of introducing a team organization at Kalmar, according to Gyllenhammar, the head of Volvo at that time, was to engage the workers more, decrease turnover and absenteeism, and get a higher product quality. The introduction of teams did not only concern work organization, but also influenced the design of the whole factory. For example, each team could work close to outer windows and had its own lounge. The idea was that each team should constitute "a little factory within the factory". It is worth mentioning that the standard of the physical environment was high; the noise level was low and the rooms were bright and airy.

Instead of the traditional assembly line, the not completed cars were transported through a system of battery-powered carriers. These carriers were arranged in a series-connected main flow through the factory. The flow was divided into several work areas, with between fifteen and twenty assemblers, constituting a team, in each area. Another innovation was that between each area/team there was a buffer. This made it possible for the teams to enjoy a bit of autonomy from each other. However, the speed of the carriers was controlled by a computer that automatically transferred the carriers from one area to the next. The computer was controlled by management, not by the teams. Changes in pace of the carriers were decided by the supervisor in consultation with the control center.

Ergonomics at the plant had a high standard for that time. The team members could perform the assembly on stationary carriers, in so called docks. The work postures were relatively favorable because of the possibility of tilting the carriers; they could be rotated 90 degrees.

If considering only the degree of team autonomy, work organization at the Kalmar plant was not so innovative. The factory was divided into a number of sections, each headed by a supervisor. Every section was in turn divided into two or three team areas. At each team area assembly, inspection, adjustment and materials handling were performed. There was no rotation between these work tasks, they were strictly divided. But there existed some rotation between the different manual tasks within the team area. The cycle times were relatively long, often up to 16 minutes. In traditional line assembling the cycle times were between one and two minutes. Every team also had a team leader, appointed by the supervisor.

The supervisor exerted a high degree of control. The distribution of work tasks, leaves, vacation and transfers were decided by the supervisor. He was also responsible for production engineering matters as work arrangements, methods and times. Sometimes he could consult the team leader. But the most important role for the team leader was to introduce newcomers. (*Förändrad arbetsorganisation*, 1987). Thus, the autonomy of the teams was low and the scope for reflection was more or less nonexistent. There were no common meetings for the team members to discuss production problems. The possibility for work development for the assembly worker at the shop floor was very low.

A while after the opening of the plant, critical comments started to show up: what is really new at Kalmar? Has work satisfaction increased? At times the turnover rate was as high as in the old plant in Gothenburg. According to a report from the Metal Workers Union in 1987, after more than ten years of experiences, "all criticism of the Kalmar plant was correct" (*Förändrad arbetsorganisation*, 1987: 115). The workers were highly controlled both by the technical system and by management.

In the beginning, work organization at the Kalmar plant was inspired by the socio-technical experiments in Norway and Sweden (Agurén & Edgren, 1979). But strictly speaking management failed to reach that aim. It succeeded in establishing two principles, team organization and rotation. But, as said, the autonomy of the teams was very weak and the rotation was very restricted. Maybe it is more correct to label the Kalmar concept as human relation-oriented. In spite of its limitation, the Kalmar plant was something new, and as Berggren wrote, it "has a place of honor in the development of new production systems. It showed, as the first factory of its kind in the world, that there were feasible alternatives to the traditional rigid assembly line" (Berggren, 1992: 129).

Uddevalla[1]

When the Volvo Uddevalla plant was established in 1989, the 350 invited journalists could witness more or less a revolution. For the first time serial produced saloon cars were assembled stationary. At Uddevalla one could also find all the ingredients from the socio-technical concept: team organization, rotation, long cycle times and a high degree of autonomy for the teams. But the most spectacular innovation was that the teams were to build a whole car on their own. Another aspect of the production was that it was customer ordered. No cars were stored, and the customers had the opportunity to visit the factory, meet the workers, and follow the production of the car they had bought.

Because the factory was closed down in 1993, the objective of establishing whole-car teams in the whole factory did not have time to develop fully. Some of the teams reached the objective, while others did not. In the "old" product shops (from 1989) cars were assembled on two different work stations. But generally speaking the skill level of the workers was high in 1993. All workers were able to assemble at least one quarter of a car, which corresponds to a cycle time of two hours. Only a small minority of the workers were able to assemble a whole car by themselves. In most cases the workers had a level of competence that made it possible for two individuals to assemble a whole car.

The main task of the teams was the assembly of cars. The team members put together a large number of preassembled kits, placed close to the local workplace. Most of these components were delivered by subcontractors. The teams were responsible for the pre-assembling of the engine dress up, the doors and the instrument panel. The teams also handled matters like maintenance, personal issues (information, recruitment and planned payoffs) and introduction. They were also responsible for the correction after testing of the cars. There were no repair people employed at the testing shop. If any defects were discovered, a representative from the team was sent to correct the problems. There existed no traditional supervisor at the Uddevalla plant. Instead a production leader was introduced responsible for two shops consisting of six teams. Each team had a team leader who was appointed by the team members together with the production leader.

The goal was to rotate most of the functions mentioned between the team members, but when the plant was closed down only a few teams had succeed to do this. These tasks were divided between specialists and the team leader. In Uddevalla there was a sort of work development ladder for the team members, with a horizontal and a vertical aspect (the first aspect was stressed). A team member could develop at work by building an ever larger part of a car, finally a whole car. He or she could also develop by performing more and more work tasks, except assembling. The team leader was the most qualified worker. In spite of efforts at minimizing the hierarchical levels, there was still a demarcation line between blue and white-collar workers.

Some of the white-collar employees were the production technicians. They supported six or eight teams each. These technical specialists were responsible for diffusing technical as well as organizational improvements into the teams. To keep up their car building competence the technicians worked in the teams for a portion of every week.

Since there existed no assembly line at Uddevalla, the workers could to some extent control the work pace. But how many cars they should assemble was decided by management. In an interview with one former Uddevalla worker I was told that the work intensity was at least as high as in Gothenburg, with a traditional line system, and most workers used at least 95% of their working time for assemblying.

The most interesting thing with the Uddevalla plant was that it had a capacity of developing assembly work, both laterally and vertically. In spite of the existing demarcation line between blue and white collar workers, the concept had a potential of a more developed integration; maybe there could have been established a type of complete teams at Uddevalla.

The Uddevalla plant was closed down in 1993. Like the Kalmar plant this was not due to the lack of quality or productivity. The main reason was the rapidly decreasing capacity utilization caused by the crisis in the motor industries that forced these plants to close. But the experiences gained from Uddevalla were not wasted. They were used when Volvo started to develop the assembly line in Gothenburg in 1991. Furthermore, Volvo has now re-opened the Uddevalla plant together with a British partner TWR, and the actual work organization is based on the former principles, albeit for such special products as exclusive convertibles.

QPE at Torslanda/Gothenburg

In 1991 Volvo at Torslanda in Gothenburg, Sweden launched a so-called KLE-program, the Swedish acronym for Quality, Precise Delivery and Economy - QPE. Torslanda is where Volvo's 800 models are manufactured. The change that has been taking place at Torslanda since 1991 relates to Volvo's efforts to create an integrated production system. The characteristics of such a system are, as said before, an orientation towards customer orders and short delivery times and an integration of production development and production departments to speed up model renewal as well as reducing the amount of tied capital, this also including the rationalization of time. Furthermore, as an obvious part of the assumption, the product must be of high quality and the production system must live up to a high deliverance security.

The New Work Organization[2]

In introducing the QPE Organization, Volvo management decided to produce cars on the assembly line principle. The socio-technical experiments in Kalmar and Uddevalla for the serial production of cars have been abandoned. However, the ambition is to create the prerequisites for job development within the framework of an assembly line-based work organization. Accordingly, in response to pressure from the Swedish Metalworkers' local union, conditions were created for workers on the line to develop themselves in their jobs and improve their earnings. According to the management of the assembly shop, if the conditions for genuine job development are to be created, the teams on the line must be provided with increasingly difficult work tasks, and the short balance times must be abandoned. Long balances also create improvements from the ergonomic viewpoint and make a contribution to quality assurance.

The QPE team organization has been agreed on by both management and the Metalworker's union. The Metalworkers' local union at Torslanda has accepted the phasing-out of the alternative production systems and the adoption of the line system, and the focus is now on creating the conditions for job development for the union's members within the framework of the line system.

The QPE-teams should be self-regulating, participate in change and development and carry out their own follow-up of the production result. Teams have been introduced in assembly, the paint-shop and the body-shop. Self-regulation means that in addition to its pure production work, the teams carry out maintenance, solve every-day problems, plan their activities and keep in touch with subcontractors. The teams identify the necessary skills needed to solve problems in everyday production. Furthermore, self-regulation means that the teams are responsible for material supply, which affects both the sub-orders from subcontractors and internal workshop transports. Participation in change and development work means that team members cooperate with other supportive teams that integrate several functions, for example at the Pilot plant (see below). The vision includes the possibility for the team members to analyze the problems, suggest solutions and participate in the realization of those solutions, a sort of participative continuous improvement activities (Lillrank & Kano, 1989). As part of the QPE-strategy, the teams themselves are responsible for the results of their work. They can focus on ratios such as the number of flaws per body and the scrap degree. The idea is to make the QPE-teams skillful both as "customers" and "suppliers" in the company's internal customer-supplier relations. The teams, which are goal-oriented, will also handle the recruitment of new team members themselves.

The QPE team concept means that the teams get involved in assignments that used to be outside the limits of current manufacturing. The objective is to break down the barriers between operators and officials close to the production. A new profession may result: a kind of technical QPE-generalist with certain basic specialities, who performs both manual and intellectual work. Every member of the team is supposed to grow in a car-assembly position; to gradually get involved in more and more difficult assignments.

QPE-Teams in Practice

QPE-teams have been spreading since 1991. The amount of progress made varies. In some places they have come a long way, in others progress is slower. The most developed areas are the body shop and the painting shop. The most advanced teams, some of these are to be found in the final assembly shop, are responsible for quality, production engineering, and the recruitment of new personnel and training. Furthermore, they keep in touch with some subcontractors and take part in development work on the process and the working environment (ergonomics). In several QPE-teams there is someone in charge of the purchase of articles of consumption and safety equipment. This person also keeps a record of any possible "waste" of resources.

Some of the most advanced teams also have their own follow-up systems. Guided by overall goals of quality and amount produced per unit of time, they do their own planning to improve ratios such as the number of flaws per auto body, the scrap level and their own work-hours and materials consumption results.

In addition to the introduction of QPE teams, there have been substantial changes in technical equipment and production technology. Firstly, a high degree of automation has been achieved with the latest models, not least in the body shop and the painting shop. In the final assembly shop the assembly line has been modified, with more carriers and a substantial reduction of work "from underneath". Assembly work now involves less walking alongside the line. Instead, the operator rides with the car on the line. The amount of lateral assembly off-line has largely remained constant. There has been a sharp increase in automation, particularly in the body shop, and this has resulted in an increase in the volume of process work.

The new team work organization involves the exclusion of traditional supervisors. They are replaced by so-called production leaders, a new type of supervisor with a broader area of responsibility who has overall responsibility for the manufacture and who handles financial follow-up, the presentation of resource and skills development of the personnel. The former supervisors mainly gave orders, made detail decisions and solved everyday problems. In order to co-ordinate the team, the function of team leader has been introduced. But he or she, appointed by the team members, is also supposed to do ordinary work tasks in the teams. Furthermore, in several teams this assignment rotates between at least two members of the team.

The question is what potential there is for developing work at the assembly plant, and especially the final assembly. Still most of the workers in the final assembly utilize at least around 90% of their working time on manual assembly work tasks, the rest is used for planning, quality control, pre-production activities, and continuous improvements. For there to be real work development these proportions have to be changed. Some projections give a proportion of 80% and 20%.

Problems

There are a number of reasons why development in the QPE teams has been slow. Some reasons have to do with inertia in the social system; another reason is the scheduling of work. An expression of social inertia is that maintenance staff is reluctant to become integrated into the teams. Integrating maintenance work into the team organization, into the workflow, would probably be the most efficient solution. Another problem is that some production leaders and product workshop managers find it difficult to delegate responsibility and authority to the teams. They still seem to harbor a traditional Taylorist view of assembly work.

Some of management's goals are related to developing the workforce, maintaining a high quality of production, maintaining lead times and constantly improving the work process. At the same time the goal is to reduce the number of man-hours in production, that is, increase productivity. This means that some production leaders and team representatives give priority to a low level of manning. They consider that they have no time to "experiment" on work organization along the line or to upgrade the qualification levels of the team members. There is a risk that the man-hours objective will become dominant, reducing the operators' motivation and having an adverse effect on quality, lead times and the reliability of deliveries.

It appears that it is less of a problem to make team members willing to develop themselves in their work, only a small minority of workers are unwilling. A larger problem is the fact that many workers, particularly in the final assembly shop, lack the training needed to take on QPE tasks. Another problem is that no new form of "metalworker identity" has as yet emerged. If the workers in the QPE teams actually manage to be self-reliant, united in their demands for development, and to take on new work tasks - for which there is scope - they would make a traditional work management hierarchy superfluous. A related problem is that the status of work in assembly line manufacture has yet to be upgraded to a satisfactory level, even though this work for some years has been given priority in terms of wages.

The Pilot Plant

At the Pilot Plant, located in Torslanda, the teams are more developed compared to the workers at the assembly plant. Especially the vertical integration of work tasks is more thoroughly worked out. Two reasons for this are that work is performed stationary and that the workers are highly skilled. The Pilot Plant is Volvo´s experimental shop, where most of the designing is tested. In the 1980s, work organization was traditional. Specialized and isolated operators working at the shop floor were controlled by supervisors. The shop floor was also subordinated to several staff levels of technicians and other white-collar employees.

The QPE-concept that was introduced at Volvo in 1991 was named NWW (New Way of Working) at Pilot Plant. The main principle in the NWW-concept is customer-ordering. In the machinery shop, the main shop consisting of workers doing metal-cutting with CNC-machines, the production works like this: Around 100 workers are divided into ten teams. They have a high degree of autonomy; no traditional supervisors are present. Every team has a function of a team leader, appointed by the team members, which normally rotates between at least some team members. Instead of being controlled by a supervisor, the workers (team members) are controlled by the customers, consisting of designers from Volvo´s design department. (The commissions that teams perform last from some days to six months.) Concerning economy and equipment, the teams are also responsible to the machinery shop manager. The amount of staff functions is strongly reduced. The teams are supported by a few white-collar employees close to production concerned with advanced programming and solving technical problems. Thus, the organizational structure is flat and non-bureaucratic.

Every team member is a "customer-order receiver", and the teams submit tenders on their own. They also handle the delivery of the invoices to the customers. The teams are confronted with competition from other producers outside Volvo. The designers can chose other firms to get their orders done. In this way the teams at Pilot Plant are forced to keep up product quality, short delivery time and "adequate" prices. The teams at Pilot Plant can themselves order help from firms outside Volvo, if they should find that they are not able to cope with the agreed delivery time.

The teams are involved in a "customers" and "suppliers" relationship, and in the contacts with the customers the teams get feedback that enables them to improve quality in work and lead time. It also makes them interested in improving work organization and working methods, which are means of reaching these goals. To be effective in improving their activities, the teams themselves are in control of the follow-up of the work results.

Thus, the teams of the Pilot Plant have a high degree of autonomy and perform lots of duties. Their main task is to do machinery work, but they are also responsible for duties like contacts with customers and subcontractors, the team area economy, pre-planning, material ordering and personnel matters. Furthermore, they are engaged in process development in cooperation with engineers.

Conclusion

In general there has been a steady work development in the teams at the shop floor at Volvo during the last 20 years. The scope of authority of teams and the degree of skill among the team members has improved. This development is mainly due to new market conditions. There has been a change from mass consumption to individual "sophisticated customers" and an increased international competition. As Charles Taylor said: "In the new world of open global markets and technological innovation...the employers need the commitment of their workforce to meet the challenges ahead" (Taylor, 1994: 197-98). But increased demands for enriching jobs from the workers and their union has also played an important role.

The history of teams at Volvo shows two important things. It seems to be more easy to develop work in teams if the assembling of cars or the work (at the Pilot Plant) is stationary, but it is possible to develop work also on the basis of a traditional assembly line. In Uddevalla there were two ways of development at the shop floor, to learn to build a whole car and to perform duties outside the manual work area. At the assembly plant in Torslanda there are no possibilities to build other than small parts of a car for the single team member. However, by integrating the short balances the cycle times can become longer. (A "balance" is equal to the time it takes for a worker to perform a specific work moment.) Work development at Torslanda means that the teams are taking on more and more assignments outside the manual work: quality control, maintenance, planning, production engineering, contacts with sub-contractor, etc. Thus, it is possible to create job development for operators on the line, at least in the upper market segment occupied by Volvo. At this level it seems to be more productive to break away from the Taylorist heritage than to continue to divide work into planning and performing work.

As questioned above, how can the teamwork, especially at the final assembly be further developed? The time for non-manual work at the final assembly must probably increase, from 10% to maybe 20-25%. More intellectual work tasks must be integrated. There are possibilities for a development in that direction. During the last year the local union has redefined the area of the QPE concept. Before it was restricted to the shop floor and white-collar areas close to production. Now the union defines the whole plant as the QPE area. This means that lots of duties can, potentially, be integrated into the teams. Parts of management are supporting these ideas. It is worth mentioning that there are intense discussions going on between management and the various unions about a so called co-workers agreement. Management takes the most active part in these discussions. This means that the traditional demarcation line between blue and white-collar workers will be abolished. If a co-worker agreement will be established this will pave the way for more integration and a building up of complete teams.

Notes

1. This paragraph is mainly based on Berggren, 1992; Ellegård, 1995 and some interviews with workers and union representatives that worked at Uddevalla. The interviews were made by the author, spring 1997.)

2. This paragraph, except the part on the Pilot Plant, is based on Brulin and Nilsson 1997. The part on the Pilot Plant is based on interviews with workers and management representatives working there, made in 1996.)

References

Agurén, S., & Edgren, J. (1979). *Annorlunda fabriker - Mot en ny produktion-steknisk teori*, SAF:s förlagssektion, Stockholm.

Auer, P., & Riegler, C. (1990). *Post-Taylorism: The enterprise as a place of learning organizational change*. Arbetsmiljöfonden and WZB.

Berggren, C. (1992). *Alternatives to lean production*. Ithaca: ILR Press.

Bergman, P. (1995). *Moderna arbetslag*. Arkiv förlag, Lund.

Björklund, A. (1984). *Hamnes arbetare*, Nordiska Museet.

Brulin, G. & Nilsson, T. (1995). *Läran om arbetets ekonomi*, Tiden: Stockholm.

Brulin, G., & Nilsson, T. (1997). The Volvo and Saab road to lean production. In A. T. Kochan, J.P. MacDuffie, and R. D. Landsbury (Eds.). *Evolving employment practices in the world auto industry*.

Clark, B. & Fujimoto, T. (1991). Product development performance strategy. *Organization and management in the world auto industry*. Boston MA: Harvard Business School Press.

Cole, R. E. (989). *Strategies for learning*, University of California Press.

Ellegård, K. (1996). The creation of a new production system at the Volvo Automobile assembly plant in Uddevalla, Sweden. In Å. Sandberg (Ed.), *Enriching production*, Avebury: Aldershot.

Engelstad, P. H. (1970). *Teknologi og sosial forandring på arbeidsplassen: et eksperiment i industrielt demokrati*. Oslo: Tanum.

Förändrad arbetsorganisation (1987). Svenska Metallindustriarbetareförbundet, Stockholm.

Gustavsen, B. (1990). *Vägen till ett bättre arbetsliv*, Arbetslivscentrum:Falköping.

Kochan, T. A., MacDuffie, J. P. & Lansbury, R. D. (1997). *Evolving employment practices in the world auto industry*. Cornell University Press.

Lillrank, P., & Kano, N. (1989). *Continous improvement: Quality control circles in Japanese industry*. Ann Arbor: University of Michigan.

Nilsson, T. (1996). Lean production and white collar work. *In Economic and Industrial Democracy*, Vol. 17, Sage Publication.

Stymne, B. (1996). *International transfer of organizational innovation*, IMIT, Stockholm, Manuscript, Forthcomming.

Taylor, R. (1994). *The future of trade unions*. London: André Deutsch Limitid.

Towards Flexible Organizations 1996: NUTEC, B 1996:6, Stockholm.

Volvo Kalmarverken 1976: SAF/LO.

Womack, J. P., & Jones, D. T. (1994, March-April). From lean production to the lean enterprise. *Harvard Business Review*.

Chapter 19

Functions and Emergence of New Work Organizations at Toyota

A Case of Emergent Socio-Technical Designs on the Assembly Line

Takahiro Fujimoto
University of Tokyo, Tokyo, Japan

Abstract

This chapter[1] examines Toyota's new assembly work organization that emerged from the late 1980s to early 1990s. The chapter describes and analyzes the structures, functions, and patterns of its emergence. Through this analysis, the chapter argues that the new system, when realized, significantly resembled so called "socio-technical" work organizations in terms of its structural and functional characteristics, but that Toyota did not intend the former to be a direct application of the socio-technical theory. The new system, instead, resulted from a complex emergent process that consisted of both intended and unintended actions by the company and the union in response to the changes in the product-labor markets. In this sense, Toyota's new assembly system may be regarded as an emergent (i.e., unintended but realized) socio-technical system in a broad sense, if not a deliberately planned one (Minzberg & Waters, 1985). The chapter explores this evolutionary logic behind the recent trend of work organizations at the Japanese automaker.

Introduction

Socio-technical theory has been known to the Japanese academics in social science for many years. Most of the Japanese text books in organization theory, for example, referred to the original socio-technical literature (e.g., Emery &Trist, 1960; Trist & Bamforth, 1951) as a micro-level technological contingency theory. Its impact on practitioners in the Japanese business firms was limited, though. Thus, the socio-technical theory tended to be regarded as a rather utopian, as opposed to practical, concept for work organizational designs.

Quite intriguingly, although the influence of the socio-technical theory on Japanese shop floor practitioners was limited, some of work organizations that emerged at Japanese manufacturing firms (e.g., Toyota and other automobile firms) by the beginning of the 1980s turned out to resemble the prescriptions proposed by the socio-technical theory, to a certain extent: broader task assignment and job rotation (i.e., job enlargement), higher involvement of workers in indirect and judgmental tasks such as inspection, process improvements, maintenance and

M.M. Beyerlein (ed.), Work Teams: Past, Present and Future, 289–307.

education (i.e., job enrichment), and so on, compared with traditional American mass production system. Teamwork was emphasized in various off-line jobs, if not in the direct work on the production line. Some advocates of lean production system (Womack, Jones & Roos, 1990), for example, emphasized team concepts of Toyota-style production system. Other advocates argued that Toyota System was human-oriented in a sense that the firms tended to treat workers as human resources rather than production inputs. This did not necessarily mean their emphasis on humanization of direct work on production lines, however.

Such a production system that emphasized broader task assignments and more involvement of workers in judgmental tasks resulted from the companies' post-war struggles to improve productivity and increase outputs with chronic shortage of labor supply and rapid product proliferation, rather than explicit emphasis on employee satisfaction (Fujimoto, 1994). In any case, the socio-technical theory did not play a major role in the process of building such work organizations. After all, the resemblance between the socio-technical concept and lean production system was at most partial (Benders, 1996). Toyota-style assembly system relied on Fordist moving assembly lines, relatively short cycle times, highly standardized job designs, hierarchical structures of teams and groups with appointed leaders, and so on.

The system, however, demonstrated international competitiveness in terms of assembly productivity and manufacturing quality (Womack, et al., 1990). Job satisfaction in this system was estimated to be reasonably high, judging from low ratios of turn-over, absenteeism, and so on, although no systematic international comparison was made on job satisfaction directly.

In the late 1980s to early 1990s, the Japanese auto firms faced a fundamental environmental change: increased difficulty in recruiting and keeping domestic work force in the labor market, and the end of the continuous growth era (1950 - 1990) in product markets. In this situation, Toyota's assembly operation was one of the most effective examples in which firms responded to the change with apparently coherent solutions.

Toyota's new work organization concept preserved its basic features of the traditional Toyota Production System: a hierarchy of groups and teams, multi-skilling and job rotation, Ford-style moving assembly lines, relatively short cycle times, etc. However, the relationships between the work organization and related task assignments, physical process designs, and plant infrastructures changed significantly.

In many senses, the system was changed as if Toyota had followed the socio-technical principles at least partially. The new system may be characterized as better alignment between work organization and physical assembly line designs, assignment of more meaningfully related set of tasks and jobs for each work group, decentralizing and integrating more indirect tasks and facilities at the work group level, empowering group/team members and leaders, and so on. Yet there is no evidence that Toyota directly applied socio-technical theory to the case in question. They did not imitate Volvo (i.e., its Uddevalla plant) system and other cases of more explicit socio-technical applications, either.

Instead, it was rather an adaptation of the firm to the new environments, which might have been somewhat similar to the ones in Europe from which socio-technical theories emerged. This may be one of the reasons why the new assembly system turned out to resemble socio-technical ones to a certain extent.

To sum up, Toyota's new assembly work organization, the subject of this chapter, may be regarded as an "emergent" socio-technical organization in a broad sense, although it was not so in a narrow sense (i.e. a socio-technical system as a deliberately planned one). In order to explore this intriguing dynamic of organizational adaptation, the present chapter analyzes structures, functions, and evolution of the new Toyota assembly system.

Conventional Toyota System of Production

Overall Patterns in Manufacturing

Let us start with the Toyota's conventional system of production as an ideal type. The typical volume production system of effective Japanese makers of the 1980s, particularly at Toyota, consists of various intertwined elements that might lead to competitive advantages. Just in Time (JIT), Jidoka (automatic defect detection and machine stop), Total Quality Control (TQC), and continuous improvement (Kaizen) are often pointed out as its core subsystems.[2] The elements of such a system include inventory reduction mechanisms by Kanban system; levelization of production volume and product mix (heijunka); Reduction of "muda" (non-value-adding activities), "mura" (uneven pace of production) and muri (excessive workload); production plans based on dealers' order volume (genryo seisan); reduction of die set-up time and lot size in stamping operation; mixed model assembly; piece-by-piece transfer of parts between machines (ikko-nagashi); flexible task assignment for volume changes and productivity improvement (shojinka); multi-task job assignment along the process flow (takotei-mochi); U-shape machine layout that facilitates flexible and multiple task assignment, on-the-spot inspection by direct workers (tsukurikomi); fool-proof prevention of defects (poka-yoke); real-time feedback of production troubles (andon); assembly line stop cord; emphasis on cleanliness, order, and discipline on the shop floor (5-S); frequent revision of standard operating procedures by supervisors; quality control circles; standardized tools for quality improvement (e.g., 7 tools for QC, QC story); worker involvement in preventive maintenance (Total Productive Maintenance); low cost automation or semi-automation with "just-enough" functions); reduction of process steps for saving of tools and dies, and so on.[3]

The human-resource management factors that back up the above elements include stable employment of core workers (with temporary workers in the periphery); long-term training of multi-skilled (multi-task) workers; wage system based in part on skill accumulation; internal promotion to shop floor supervisors; cooperative relationships with labor unions; inclusion of production supervisors in union members; generally egalitarian policies for corporate welfare, communication and worker motivation.[4]

It is important to note that this system was not established by a one-shot rational decision, but evolved gradually through a cumulative process of capability building (Fujimoto, 1994b). It is largely a product of the post-war history of the Japanese auto industry.

Toyota's Assembly Process

Let us now focus on the final assembly process at Toyota's conventional factories. We can characterize it as follows.

1. Toyota's volume factories adopt Ford-style moving assembly lines (typically chain conveyers). Thus there is nothing unique in body transfer mechanisms and basic layouts of Toyota's conventional assembly lines, except that Toyota's main assembly lines (typically about 1 km) tend to be shorter than those of US makers.
2. The conveyer lines tended to be separated into three line segments: trim, chassis, and final. Different conveyer systems tended to be used among them. However, no buffer body was allowed between the line segments, so the assembly process was operated as if there were one long and continuous line.
3. Unlike machining or welding, there have been few robots and automated equipment in traditional final assembly lines at Toyota. In fact, Toyota's assembly automation ratio tended to be lower than some European makers that adopted advanced assembly automation systems (VW, FIAT, etc.). In other words, Toyota has achieved the world class productivity in final assembly without relying on high-tech automation (Fujimoto, 1997).
4. In order to achieve a high level of line-balancing, Toyota's assembly lines trained multi-skilled workers who could handle multiple tasks, assigned a set of multiple work elements to each individual worker, and thereby reduced "muda" due to line imbalance. While such multiple work assignments raised productivity without increasing work speed, meaningfulness of the assembly jobs tended to be sacrificed: a mutually unrelated set of tasks tended to be assigned to each worker.
5. One of unique mechanisms at Toyota's assembly line is so called "andon cord" (or switch), which assembly workers activate when troubles happen on the assembly line. If the worker and/or team leader cannot fix the problem within the cycle time, the entire assembly line stops. This is said to be an example of Toyota's Kaizen mechanisms, which reveal and dramatize the manufacturing problems and thereby facilitate the shop floor problem solving activities.
6. Performances of Toyota's assembly lines have been traditionally evaluated internally in terms of efficiency and product quality, as well as safety. Quality of work environments had not been equally emphasized, though. There was an evaluation system that identified tasks that are potentially harmful to workers' health, but evaluation criteria for measuring work fatigue had not been developed in the past.

Changes in Product and Labor Environments in the 1990s

It is widely known that the basic system of Toyota's manufacturing capabilities had been established by the early 1980s. However, the environments had been changed significantly since then. Toyota's assembly system (as well as others) had to adjust itself to the new environments.

Labor Market

By a combination of structural and cyclical changes in Japan's labor market, it became increasingly difficult to hire and keep sufficient work force for automobile production. As population structure changed, average age of automobile workers increased. It was expected that the population of 18-year -old youth would shrink by about 40% from the mid 1990s to 2010. Young people became less willing to work in certain manufacturing factories which they recognized as "3-D" (dirty, demanding and dangerous), including final assembly. One measure to alleviate this problem was to reduce work hours per year, but this meant further decrease in labor supply. On the demand side, expansion of domestic automobile production peaked in 1990 (13.5 million units), and created additional labor demands for the automobile industry. As a result, the Japanese auto industry suffered from severe labor shortage problems in 1990 and 91, which forced the auto makers to emphasize employee satisfaction aspects of automobile manufacturing (assembly in particular). Although the subsequent recession and loss of competitiveness due to high yen wiped out the labor shortage problem, and labor surplus problems surfaced instead, companies like Toyota still regard the lack of job attractiveness as their long term problem to be solved.

Product Market

The so called "bubble economy" era in the late 1980s was the final stage of the 40 years of continuous growth in Japan's domestic automobile production. In the early 1990s, domestic production started to decline from 13.5 million units (1990) to about 10 million (1995), which created financial burdens of high depreciation costs for those companies that had built new and highly automated assembly factories during the bubble era. Although this period of production shrinkage was expected to be eventually replaced by that of fluctuation, a typical pattern in matured auto markets, it is clear that the era of continuous growth, which the traditional Toyota system enjoyed, is over.

Financial Situations

The Japanese automakers enjoyed relatively abundant cash flow in the late 1980s thanks to the bubble era. The companies also had expectation that, by issuing convertible bonds when stock prices were soaring, the companies could finance capital investments with negligible capital cost. Such atmosphere led the auto manufacturers to make capital spending decisions without deliberate assessments. The situation changed completely in the early 1990s: the stock market collapsed; the problem of cash flow shortage surfaced; and companies were forced to evaluate capital spending much more conservatively.

International Competition and Conflicts

Appreciation of yen and reverse catch-up of Western auto makers since mid-1980s have virtually eliminated cost competitive advantages of the automobiles built in Japan, if not overall advantages. Besides, trade friction against the US and Europe virtually restricted exports of completely built vehicles to such countries. The Japanese makers, in response to these problems, made adjustments in two main areas. First, the Japanese makers expanded local assembly and manufacturing of cars and components in the US, Europe, and Asia since the 1980s. Toyota, for example, now assembles cars at NUMMI (joint venture with GM), TMM I and II (Kentucky), and TMMC (Canada) in North America alone. Second, they made major cost cutting efforts for the products made in Japan. While a big jump in manufacturing productivity has become increasingly difficult since the 1980s (Fujimoto & Takeishi, 1995), the main contributor of the cost cutting in the 1990s has been simplification of product design itself, including product variety reduction, parts commonality, value engineering, and so on (Fujimoto, 1994c)

Toyota's New Assembly Concept: Structure and Function

In response to the new challenge from the environments, Toyota has modified its production system since the late 1980s. Final assembly has been the area where the change was most visible and significant. Reflecting the environments of the early 1990s mentioned above, the new assembly concepts aimed at improvements in employee satisfaction, as well as elimination of physically demanding jobs, with minimum capital expenditure. The new process also continued to focus on continuous company-wide improvements (Kaizen) in quality and productivity. To sum up, the new system attempts to preserve the strength of the conventional Toyota system in QCD (quality, cost, and delivery), while improving attractiveness of the assembly work, both physically and psychologically.

TABLE 1. Conventional versus new assembly system at Toyota.
(The case of autonomous-complete assembly process)

Conventional	New
Continuously moving conveyer line; about 1000m.	Unchanged.
Short cycle time (1-3 minutes).	Unchanged.
Decomposed into three line segments (trim, chassis, final).	Decomposed into 5 to 12 line segments (trim, chassis, final).
No buffer zones between segments.	Buffer zones between segments.
A few work groups per segment.	One work group per one segment.
Functionally unrelated tasks may be Packed into jobs for a worker or a group.	Functionally related tasks are combined for a worker or a group.
Group leaders play key roles in Kaizen and line management.	Group leaders function was strengthened.

The new system, as Toyota itself recognizes, consists of several subsystems, as summarized in Table 1: (1) Functionally autonomous and complete process; (2) In-line mechanical assembly automation concept; (3) Ergonomics evaluation system called TVAL (Toyota Verification of Assembly Line); (4) Low cost equipment for better work environment and work posture; (5) Supporting HRM (human resource management) policies (Kawamura, et al., 1993; Kojima, 1994; Kojo Kanri, 1994; Ogawa, 1994; Shimizu, 1995; Toyota Motor Corporation, 1994, etc.). Among these elements of the new assembly system, the focus of this chapter is the first one.

Structure

The autonomous and complete line has been implemented at Toyota Kyushu plant (1992), as well as Toyota's subsequent plant constructions and renovations. It consists of various elements, both physical and organizational, including the following. (see Figure 1)

1. The main assembly line is decomposed into 5 to 12 line segments, each of which is typically 100 meters or 20 work stations (process layout).
2. The shape of the assembly area is roughly square, so that the building can accommodate many short lines running back and forth (facility design).
3. Line segments are linked by buffer zones, where up to about five bodies can be temporarily stored (process layout).[5]
4. A group of functionally related assembly tasks (e.g., piping) are assigned to one segment (job design). Toyota defined 108 sub-categories of assembly tasks, and changed the task assignment so that each sub-category is completed within a group of workers. Also, assembly of a given component is completed as one person's job.[6]
5. A quality check station is located at the end of each line segment (process design). Criteria for quality assurance were defined for each of the 108 task sub-categories.
6. Each line segment corresponds to a group (kumi) of about twenty workers, within which job rotation and training are conducted (organizational design).
7. The function and responsibility of group leader are strengthened (organizational design). Each group leader, now in charge of a semi-independent line segment, enjoy more discretion in managing the group's operations. For example, each segment can fine-tune its line speed within a certain limit.
8. Other supporting equipment for line control (line speed controllers, switches for planned line stops), information sharing (monitoring displays, Andon boards), and self actualization (Kaizen shops, training centers, rest areas) is set up for each line segment.

Overall, the autonomous and complete line differs from Toyota's conventional assembly line in that the main line (typically about 1000 meters) consists of semi-independent segments, each of which is functionally, physically and organizationally de-coupled from the others. Each line segment is a short version of a Fordist assembly line equipped with continuously moving conveyers.

Functions

Both quantitative and qualitative results have been reported in terms of initial performance of autonomous complete lines, which are generally consistent with what the process designers aimed at (Niimi, et al., 1994).

Quality and Productivity

As each set of assembly jobs assigned to a work group became more meaningful and easy to understand, and as each group can self-inspect quality more effectively, productivity and quality of the autonomous -

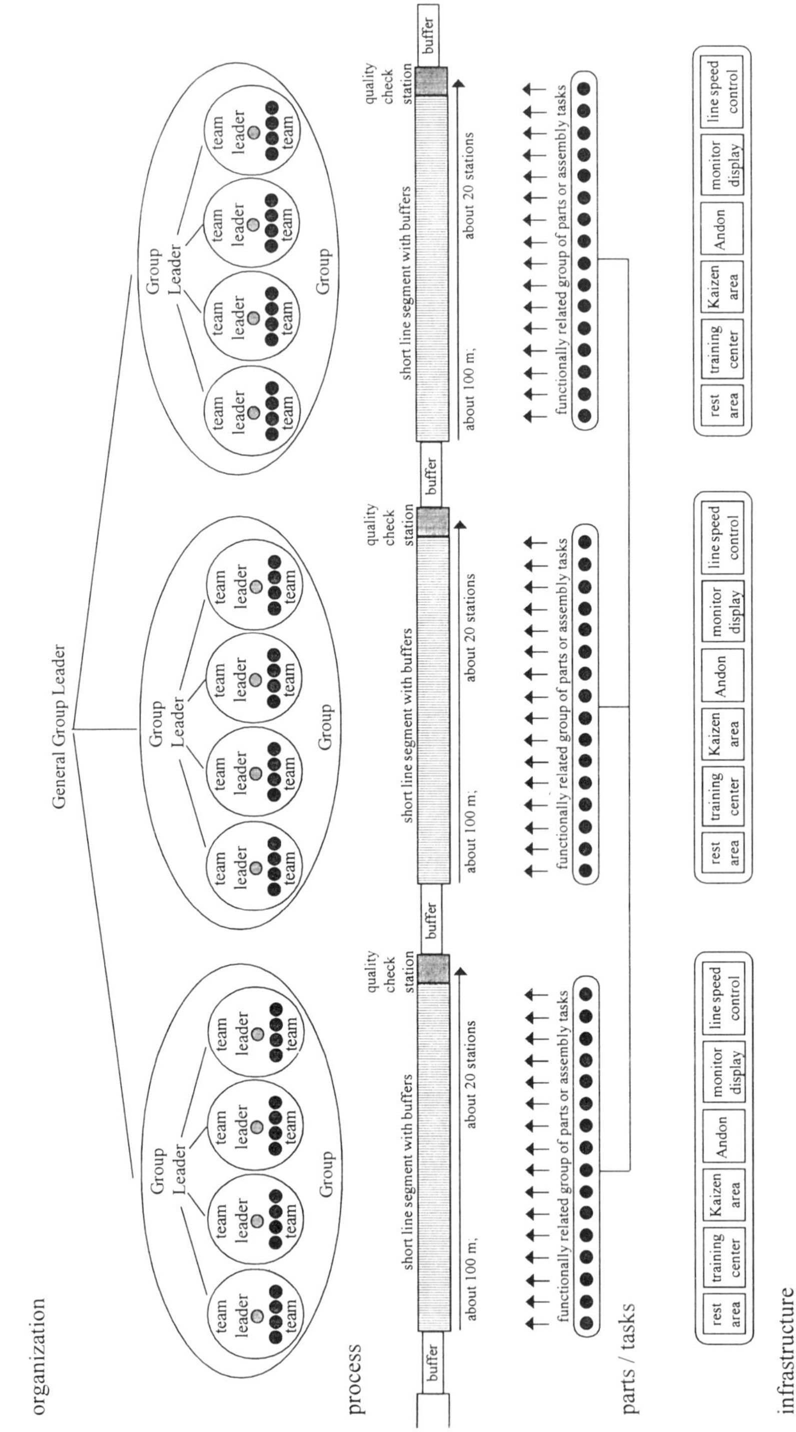

Figure 1. Autonmous & Complete Assembly Line Concept

complete line was generally higher than conventional assembly lines, particularly at the start-up period (Niimi, et al., 1994; Okochi Memorial Foundation, 1994). The period for mastering a job was shortened to about a half. According to a survey of Toyota Kyushu assembly workers, over 70% of the respondents said they became more quality conscious, and that their jobs became easier to understand, compared with pervious assembly lines. Also, because the body buffer areas absorb the impact of line stops at other segments, overall down time decreased (Kawamura, et al., 1993).[7]

Morale

Also, as the assembly job became more meaningful, morale of the assembly workers increased. In the survey mentioned above, about 70% of the respondents found their job more worth doing than before. According to our interview with group leaders and team leaders, they tended to become more proud of their job as instructor and Kaizen leader, as their tasks shifted from day-to-day trouble-shooting to Kaizen, supervising, and training. In the past, they tended to be swamped by the complexity and confusion on the line. Some first-line supervisors were feeling psychological pressures due to their increased responsibility, though.

To sum up, the autonomous and complete assembly line concept aimed at balancing customer satisfaction (quality, cost and delivery) and employee satisfaction (job meaningfulness, self-esteem, sense of growth) on the assembly lines, which has been generally achieved so far.

It should be noted, however, the autonomous-complete lines have to carry over both strength and weaknesses of Fordist conveyer lines with short cycle times. Also, its work organizational structure (i.e., a hierarchy of groups and teams) did not change much from that of the traditional Toyota Production System.

Nevertheless, the structures and functions of the new Toyota assembly system described above appear to share certain characteristics with the socio-technical concept. It aims at better alignment between work organizations and physical process designs. It emphasizes meaningfulness of the task sets assigned to each group or team. And, it enhances functional autonomy of basic work groups. Although Toyota's new system was still different from an ideal type derived from the socio-technical theory, the direction of the overall system change was in line with typical socio-technical prescriptions, even though the firm may not have intended to directly apply this theory.

Emergence of the Autonomous-Complete Work System

Having analyzed structures and functions of the new system, let us move on to the question as to how the system evolved over time.[8] As mentioned earlier, Toyota's managers and engineers apparently had virtually no intention to apply the socio-technical theory to their case. There is little evidence that the company borrowed ideas from some European plants that deliberately adopted socio-technical ideas when it came up with the autonomous-complete assembly process concept. It was rather a result of an emergent process in which the company struggles to adapt themselves to the changing environments by using and modifying existing resources and concepts.

Following the standard framework of problem solving, we will first examine the process of problem recognition about the labor issue, then move on to generation and evaluation of alternative plans in the case of the autonomous-complete concept.

Problem Recognition

While the changes in the product market (the end of the growth era) and financial performance after 1990 was obvious to Toyota's organizational members, the changes in labor market were much more subtle and equivocal. We will therefore focus on organizational problem recognition of the labor issues.

The problem related to attractiveness and employee satisfaction in manufacturing, particularly on the assembly lines, seems to have been recognized first by labor union in the late 1980s.[9] When Toyota Motor Worker's Union (Toyota Roso) announced its mid-long term action plans (Chu-choki Katsudo Hoshin) in October 1988, reduction of labor hours, new policies for aging workers, and absorption of excess labor demand were clearly depicted, but "attractiveness of work" was not explicitly pointed out.[10] While the quantitative aspect of labor shortage was much emphasized, the concept of assembly automation for better quality of work environment had not been articulated.

Attractiveness of the company and its shop floor, particularly in assembly process, was chosen as an agenda at the Union-Management Meeting (Roshi Kondan-kai) on Manufacturing Issues in April 1989, which was presumably the first official meeting where the "assembly line problem" (its attractiveness, work posture, and work load) was explicitly addressed. In the subsequent meetings on "Assembly Work Improvement" between union and management, the main issue was still quantitative labor shortage, but qualitative aspects of job attractiveness became an increasingly important agenda.

As mentioned before, Toyota's management became actively involved in the "job attractiveness" issue by spring of 1990, when it took initiative in creating the joint Committee for Improving Attractiveness of Production Work in May 1990. The Committee was coordinated by the Human Resource Division, whereas the Assembly Process Engineering Division, was not included in the main Committee.[11] Improvement of production work environment, as well as desirable assembly process design, was discussed.

Toyota's management side keenly recognized the assembly problem in 1990 to 1991 partly as a result of the alarming result of the opinion surveys that Human Resource Division had conducted bi-annually since the 1970s, as well as the turn-over record.[12] That is, turn-over ratio jumped up (particularly at the final assembly lines), and workers' subjective evaluation of job satisfaction and self-esteem dropped sharply. Thus, the early and qualitative information from the union, as well as subsequent quantitative data that the Human Resource Division collected that were reconfirming the problem, triggered a consensus-building process on the work attractiveness issue.

Also, the Project for Future Assembly Plants, which involved Assembly Process Engineering Division, Operations Management Consulting Office, Product Control Division, and Human Resource Division, may have functioned as the mechanism through which the awareness of the assembly problem was diffused among different divisions. Assembly-related Division Head Meeting was another means for coordinating an information exchange among different divisions.[13]

The communication between the shop floor organization and assembly process engineers were also strengthened in the early 1990s, facilitating diffusion of the knowledge from the shop floor to engineering departments. In 1992, for example, core members (section head level) of the Assembly Process Engineering Division were dispatched to work in the real assembly lines to gain direct experiences about the work load and fatigue on the assembly line. This helped the process engineers acquire tacit knowledge on the nature of the assembly work, which was used subsequently for development of a quantitative measurement system for assembly work load called TVAL.

To sum up, the problem in assembly lines, which existed at least potentially on the shop floor for a long time, was recognized as a main issue for the company first by the labor union in the late 1980s, while the management side, interfaced by the Human Resource Division, became increasingly concerned about the problem around 1990. This problem awareness was subsequently diffused to other sections through the Project for Future Assembly Plants, Assembly Head Meetings, participation of process engineers in direct assembly work, and so on. Also, it should be noted that the focus of the issue shifted from the quantitative aspect of labor shortage to the qualitative (and more profound) aspects of the problem. Thus, organizational problem awareness itself evolved over time in terms of both width and depth.

Evolution of Autonomous Complete Process: Ex-Post Synthesis

The evolution of the autonomous system may be summarized as a complex emergent process that may be called "ex-post synthesis." (Figure 2) That is, the system concept emerged as a result of synthesis of various elements, each of which were developed for a variety of reasons that may or may not be related to the ultimate objectives of the system in question. Some of the elements were not developed as components of the autonomous system, but were reinterpreted and adopted after they were developed.

For example, TMM, Toyota's transplant in Kentucky, already had multi-segment and buffered assembly lines, but it was developed apparently for logistics reasons, not as an element of the autonomous process. Tahara assembly plant #4 line was also multi-segment with buffer areas, but the concept of autonomous and complete assembly process was not linked to this layout (see Figure 3).

In the Project for Future Assembly Plants, "short assembly line" concept had already been discussed and reported in the summer of 1990. The discussion was headed by Mr. Shiramizu, head of Assembly Engineering Division Head then. By the end of 1991, the "Vision" Project was completed. "Complete Assembly Process" had already examined by then, but it was not the main concept yet at this point. Simplification of the assembly jobs to absorb variation proliferation seems to have been more emphasized.

As a part of the Project for Future Assembly Plants, a model line at plant A highlighted simple job designs to cope with increasing product variety and complexity, and it addressed the issue of group leaders and team leaders, but they

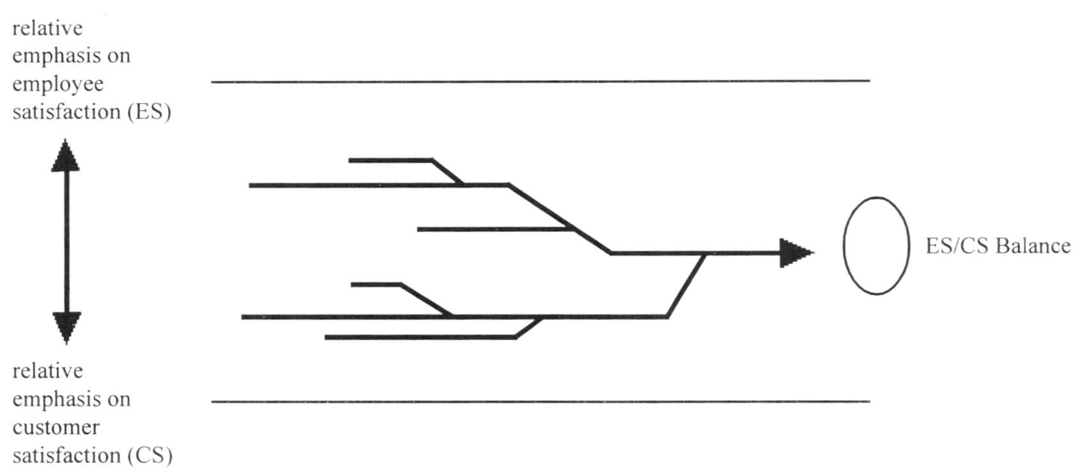

Note: Horizontal axis stands for time
Vertical axis stands for relative emphasis of a given system element between ES and CS. Note that this does not show ES and CS in absolute terms. For example, deviation from CS in this diagram does not mean decrease in absolute level of CS.

Figure 2. Ex Post Synthesis toward ES/CS Balance

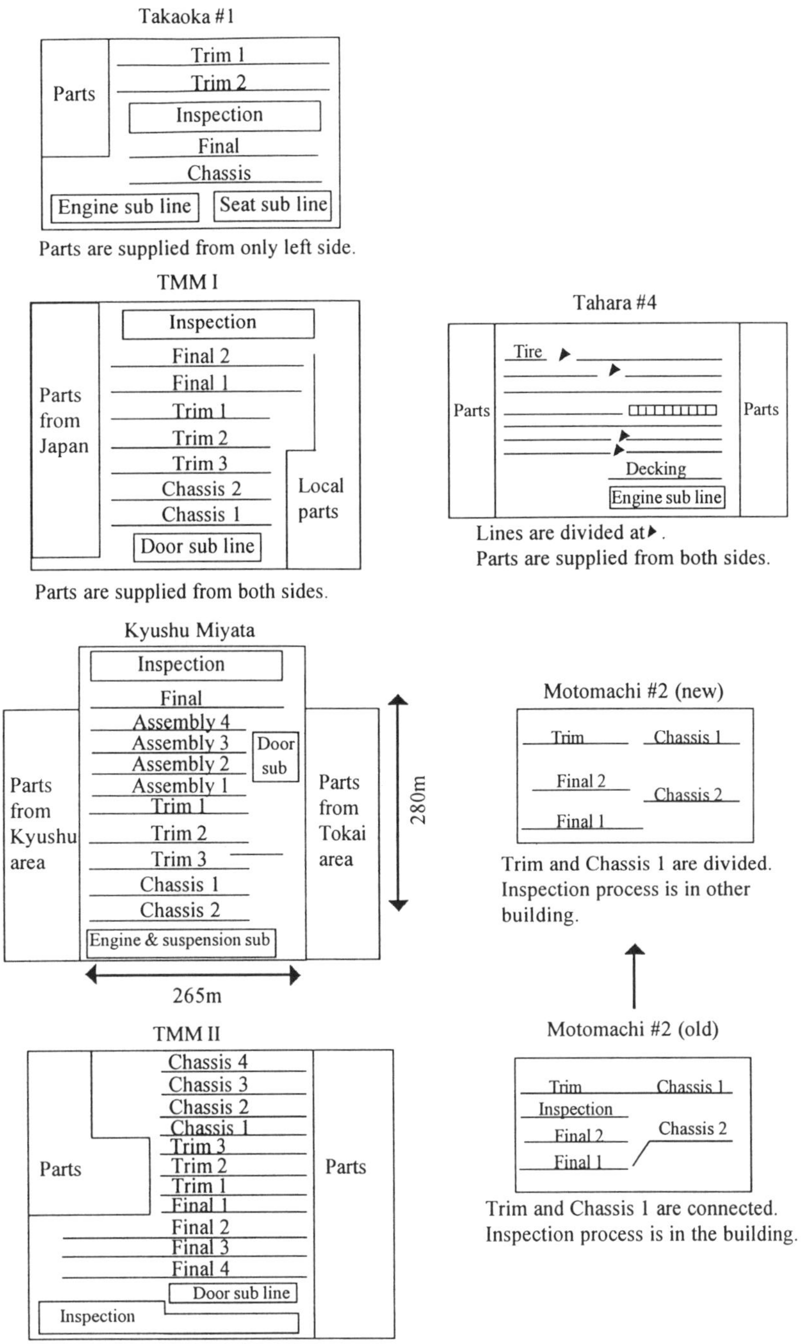

Source: Interviews and internal documents at Toyota

Figure 3. Evolution of Toyota's Factory Layout's

did not articulate the autonomy-complete concept. Another experiment at the Motomachi assembly plant in the late 1980s did address the issue of "complete" job for each component at the level of individual workers, but it did not articulate the "autonomous" assembly line concept at the work group level.[14] The Motomachi trial was made on conventional assembly lines.

By summer of 1992, the concept of "complete assembly process", as well as its main functions (morale, self-actualization, quality improvement) was articulated in the Assembly-related Division Head Meetings, as well as the plant design process for Toyota Kyushu by the Assembly Process Engineering Division For example, the word "complete assembly line" appeared for the first time in a union document in August 1992, where management responded that "complete line" had been discussed at the Assembly-related Division Head Meetings.[15]

After all, it was Toyota Kyushu plant (December 1992) that finally combined physical, functional and organizational elements of the new system and crystallized them as autonomous-complete assembly process. But there were many predecessors before the final synthesis occurred.

Conclusion

The foregoing analyses on structures, functions and historical evolution of Toyota's new assembly system in the 1990s may be summarized as follows.

1. Toyota's new assembly work organization, in many senses, turned out to be strikingly similar to an important part of socio-technical ideas in that:
   a. Employee satisfaction problem was explicitly addressed as a main goal, together with its continued pursuit of customer satisfaction.
   b. Meaningfulness of the work is emphasized in its job design
   c. Width and depth of task assignments (job enrichment and job enlargement) continued to be emphasized at the level of individuals, teams and groups.
   d. Alignment of work organizations (groups as elementary units) and physical process designs (short and buffered line segments) was emphasized

2. The system also maintained many of the traditional Fordist-Toyotist characteristics such as:
   a. The moving assembly line configuration.
   b. Relatively short cycle time (1 ~ 2 minutes).
   c. Standardized work designs (revised frequently by leaders)
   d. The Hierarchical group-team organization with appointed leaders

Thus, it did not follow radical versions of socio-technical assembly process designs that eliminate moving assembly lines (e.g., Volvo's Uddevalla concept), make cycle times significantly longer, or democratize work organizations with elected leaders. The new system was still a version of so called lean production or Toyota production system, in that it preserved much of the core competence of the past system. This author calls it "lean-on-balance" system in that the new system explicitly seeks for a balance between customer satisfaction and employee satisfaction (Fujimoto, 1994a).

3. The system change process was not intended to be an application of the socio-technical theory to Toyota's assembly plants, however. It was rather a result of its adaptation efforts to the emerging market-labor environments in the 1990s. It might have been the case, however, that the environment from which the new assembly system emerged and that from which socio-technical concepts were developed were somewhat similar in that both faced labor shortage and changes in attitudes of the workers. To the extent that the environments were similar, it may be reasonable to infer that Toyota's solution and prescriptions by the socio-technical school turned out to be similar to a certain degree.

4. The process of adaptation itself was not even a smooth and deliberate one, but the result of muddling through with many trials and errors, as well as refinements of existing resources and capabilities that the company acquired unintentionally. Such an emergent process may be called "ex-post synthesis."

5. The company's ability of managing to create effective organizational routines out of such emergent processes may be called *evolutionary learning capability*. This is a dynamic and non-routine organizational capability of handling non-repetitive and irregular system changes, which is distinguished from *static capability* (an ability of achieving high levels of competitive performance) and from *improvement capability* (an ability of making repetitive and deliberate changes of the systems). The latter two capabilities at Toyota are often emphasized in the existing literature, but the evolutionary learning capability of this company, which was not investigated in the past, seems to be the third and most important dimension of Toyota's organizational capability (Fujimoto, 1994b).

In conclusion, although Toyota's new assembly system was not intended to be socio-technical, and although it differed from the ideal socio-technical concepts in some important aspects, it may be still reasonable to regard Toyota's new assembly system as an emergent variant of the socio-technical system in a broad sense. Indeed, the new system is not a deliberately planned socio-technical system in a strict and narrow sense. It also remains to be essentially a variant of the lean production system (Womack et al., 1990) or Toyota Production System (Monden, 1983, 1993). We can nevertheless identify a clear trend of the Toyota system incorporating some part of socio-technical concepts regardless of its intention.

Thus, what we have observed in the 1990s is a clear trend of mutual learning: While virtually all the assembly plants in Europe and America are adopting some versions of Japanese lean production system, the very company which created the lean system concept, Toyota, is now adopting socio-technical components into its lean system, whether intentionally or unintentionally. To the extent that the global competition remains intense, and to the extent that the difficulty of recruiting and keeping work force at Japanese auto firms persists, we should continue to observe this intriguing dynamics of partial convergence.

Notes

1. This is an abridged and revised version of Fujimoto (1996). This research was assisted by a grant from the Abe Fellowship Program of the Social Science Research

Council and the American Council of Learned Societies with funds provided by the Japan Foundation Center for Global Partnership.

2. TQC emphasized clarification of quality goals, communication of the goals to the shop floor, involvement of all the employees, education of shop floor supervisors, diffusion of quality and cost consciousness, making good product the first time (tsukurikomi), cross-functional coordination, coordination with suppliers and dealers, smooth implementation of model changeover, and so on.

3. For standard explanations of the production system at Toyota and other effective Japanese auto makers of the 1970s and 1980s, see, for example, Imai (1986), Monden (1983, 1993), Nihon, Noritsu, & Kyokai (1978), Ohno (1978), Schonberger (1982), Shingo (1980), Toyota Motor Corporation (1987), and Womack et al. (1990).

4. For human resource management and labor relations of the post-war Japanese auto makers, see, for example, Cusumano (1985), Koike (1977), Nomura (1993), Totsuka & Hyodo (1990), Yamamoto (1981), etc.

5. Note that such body buffers between the line segments are essentially different from component inventories at the line side. That is, the existence of the body buffers does not necessarily mean relaxation of Just-in-Time principle.

6. This is called "parts-complete" (buhin-kanketsu) assembly line. At Toyota, different assembly tasks for a given component (e.g., setting, bolting, etc.) were often assigned to different workers as a result of efforts to maximize productivity by eliminating non-value time (muda) since the 1970s. Toyota's assembly line was originally following the parts-complete principle until 1960s. Thus, the re-establishment of parts-complete principle means a "back to the basics" effort for Toyota.

7. Another impact of the body buffers, according to a Toyota executive, is that the buffers lower psychological pressures for the workers to stop the line, as they do not have to stop the entire line (typically one kilometer) but stop their line segment only (typically twenty stations, one hundred meters). A plant engineer at TMCA (Toyota's Australian subsidiary) witnesses that the number of line stops actually increased after the buffered sassily line was introduced there in 1994, apparently because of the reduction of the psychological pressure. This means revealing more problems and facilitating more Kaizen.

8. For details of historical descriptions, see Fujimoto (1996).

9. The pressure of labor shortage itself had been recognized as a chronic problem for Toyota during the high growth era. Also, criticism against Toyota's assembly job is not new (See, for example, Kamata, 1973). Thus, it is likely that the problem was recognized by certain organizational members for a long time. This paper will,

however, focus only on the process that such problems became issues to be discussed at the company-wide basis.

10. The plan was prepared between 1986 and 1988.

11. Production Engineering Administration Dept. was included, instead.

12. Some plant managers were apparently recognizing the problem earlier, though. A former assembly dept. head, for example, says he recognized the problem when the number of temporary workers increased in the late 1980s. Relatively low morale of the young temporary workers at that time made him realize that the mind set of the young generation is changing, and that assembly process has to be changed accordingly.

13. Assembly Dept. Heads of seven factories, as well as heads of Human Resource Dept. Assembly Process Engineering Dept., Safety and Health Management Dept., Production Control Dept., and Operations Management Consulting Office were the members of the Assembly-related Division Head Meeting as of 1990.

14. The origin of the "parts-complete" concept and the "autonomous" concept are different.

15. Motomachi plant took initiative in this theme.

References

Benders, J. (1996). Leaving lean? Recent changes in the production organizations of some Japanese car plants. *Economic and Industrial Democracy*, 17(1), 9-38.

Chandler A. D. (1990). *Scale and scope*. Cambridge: Harvard University Press.

Chandler A. D. (1992). What is a firm? *European Economic Review* 36, 483 - 492.

Cusumano, M. A. (1985). *The Japanese automobile industry*. Cambridge: Harvard University Press.

Dosi, G. (1982). Technological paradigms and technological trajectories. *Research Policy* 11, 147-162.

Emery, F. E., & Trist, E. E. (1960). Socio-technical systems. In C. W. Churchman & M. Verhulst (Eds.), *Management science: Models and techniques* (pp. 83-97). New York: Pergamon.

Fujimoto, T. (1994a, January). The limits of lean production. *Politik und Gesellschaft, Friedrich-Ebert-Stiftung*, 40-46.

Fujimoto, T. (1994b, June). *Reinterpreting the resource capability view of the firm: A case of the development production systems of the Japanese automakers*. Discussion paper, Tokyo University Faculty of Economics 94-F-20. (Presented at Prince Bertil Symposium, Stockholm School of Economics).

Fujimoto, T. (1994c). *The dynamic aspect of product development capabilities: An international comparison in the automobile industry*. Discussion paper, Tokyo University Faculty of Economics. 94-F-29.

Fujimoto, T. (1996). *An evolutionary process of Toyota's final assembly operations: The role of ex-post dynamic capabilities*. Tokyo University Discussion Paper.

Fujimoto, T. (1997). Strategies for assembly automation in the automobile industry. In K. Shimokawa, U. Juergens, & T. Fujimoto, (Eds.), *Transforming automobile assembly*. Berlin: Spronger Verlag.

Fujimoto, T., & Takeishi, A. (1994). *Jidosha sangyo 21 seiki he no shinario [The automobile industry: A scenario toward the 21-st century]*. Toyko: Seisansei Shuppan.

Fujimoto, T., & Takeishi, A. (1995). An international comparison of productivity and product development performance in the automobile industry. In R. Minami, K. S. Kim, F. Makino, & J. Seo, (Eds.), *Acquiring, adapting and developing technologies: Lesson from the Japanese experience*. St. Martin's Press.

Grant, R. (1991, June). The resource-based theory of competitive advantage: Implications for strategy formulation. *California Management Review*, 114-135.

Imai, M. (1986). *Kaizen*. New York: Random House.

Kagono, T. (1988). *Soshiki ninshiki-ron [The theory of organizational perception]*. Chikura Shobo.

Kamata, S. (1973). *Jidoha zetsubo kojo. [The automobile plant of desperation]*. Gendaishi Shuppankai.

Kawamura, T., Niimi, A., Hisada, N., & Kuzuhara, T. (1993). Korekara no hito ga shuyaku no kumitate rain zukuri [Becoming worker friendly factory]. *Toyota Technical Review*, 43(2), 86-91.

Koike, K. (1977). Shokuba no rodo kumiai to sanka [Shop union and participation]. *Toyo Keizai Shinposha [Tokyo]*.

Kojima T. (1994). *Cho lean kakumei [The ultra-lean revolution]*. Toyko: Nohon Keizai Shinbun-sha.

Kojo Kanri (1996). *Plant Management*, 40(11).

Leonard-Barton, D. (1992). Core capabilities and core rigidities: A paradox in managing new product development, *Strategic Management Journal*, 13, 111-25.

Mintzberg, H. (1987, July/August). Crafting strategy. *Harvard Business Review*.

Mintzberg, H., & Waters, J.A. (1985). Of Strategies, deliberate and emergent. *Strategic Management Journal*, 6(3), 257-272.

Monden, Y. (1983, 1993). *Toyota production system*. Norcross, GA.

Nelson, R.R., & Winter, S.G. (1982). *An evolutionary theory of economic change*. Cambridge, MA: Belknap.

Nihon, Noritsu Kyokai (Ed.) (1978). *Toyota no genba kanri [Shop floor management at Toyota]*. Toyko: Nihon Noritsu Kyokai.

Niimi, A., Miyoshi, K., Ishii, T., Araki, T., Uchida, K., & Ota, I. (1994). Jidoka kumitate rain ni okeru jiritsu kanketsu kotei no kakuritsu [Establishment of autonomous complete process planning for automobile assembly line]. *Toyota Technical Review*, 44(2), 86-91.

Nomura, M. (1993). *Toyotism minelva*. Tokyo.

Nonaka, I. (1985) *Kigyo shinkaron [The theory of corporate evolution]*. Tokyo: Nihon Keizai Shinbunsha.

Ogawa, E. (1994). *Toyota seisan hoshiki no kenkyu [A study on Toyota production system]*. Tokyo: Nihon Keizai Shinbun-sha.

Ohno, T. (1978). *Toyota seisan hoshiki [Toyota production system]*. Toyko: Diamond.

Penrose, E. T. (1959). *The theory of the growth of the firm*. Oxford: Basil Blackwell.

Prahalad, C.K., & Hamel, G. (1990). *The core competence of the corporation*. Harvard Business

Schonberger, R.J. (1982). *Japanese manufacturing techniques*. New York: Free Press.

Shibata, F., Imayoshi, K., Eri, Y., & Ogata, S. (1993). Kumitate sagyo futan no teiryo hyokaho (TVAL) no kaihatsu [Development of assembly load verification]. *Toyota Technical Review*, 43(1) 84-89.

Shimizu, K. (1995, June). La trajectoire de Toyota de 1974 a 1994: Du Toyotisme au nouveau Toyotisme Automobile firms tajectories [The new industrial models: The new industrial models]. *GERPISA*, 15-17.

Shingo, S. (1980). *Toyota seisan hoshiki no ie-teki kosatsu [An industrial engineering analysis of Toyota production system]*. Toyko: Nikkan Kogyo Shinbunsha.

Teece, D. J., Pisano, G. & Shuen, A. (1992). *Dynamic capabilities and strategic management*. University of California at Berkeley Working Paper.

Teece, D. J., Rumelt, R., Dosi, G., & Winter, S. (1994). Understanding corporate coherence: Theory and evidence. *Journal of Economic Behavior and Organization* 23, 1-30.

Totsuka, H., & Hyodo, (1990). Roshi kankei no tenkan to sentaku [Changes and choices in industrial relation]. Toyko: Nihon Hyoronsha.

Toyota Motor Corporation (1987). *An Introduction to the Toyota production system.*

Toyota Motor Corporation (1994). Atarashii jidosha kumitate rain no kaihatsu [Development of new vehicle assembly system]. Dai 40-kai okochi-sho jusho gyoseki hokoku-sho (Reports of achievements in industrialization awarded the Okochi Memorial Prize 1994). Okochi Memorial Foundation. 99-109.

Trist, E. L., & K.W. Bamforth (1951). Some social and psychological consequences of Longwall method of coal-getting. *Human Relations* 4, 3-38.

Womack, J. P., Jones, D. T., & Roos. D. (1990). *The machine that changed the world*. New York: Rawson Associates.

Yamamoto, K. (1981). *Jidosha sangyo no roshi kankei [Industrial relations in the automobile industry]*. Tokyo: University Press.

SECTION IV.

FOUNDATION FOR 21ST CENTURY TEAMS

Chapter 20

Self-Managing Teams in a Crystal Ball

Future Directions for Research and Practice

Christopher Neck
Virginia Tech, Blacksburg, Virginia, United States

Charles Manz
University of Massachuetts, Amherst, Massachuetts, United States

Vikas Anand
Arizona State University, Tempe, Arizona, United States

Abstract

A plethora of benefits has been attributed to the implementation of self-managing teams including increased productivity, quality, employee satisfaction, and quality of work life for employees and decreased absenteeism and turnover. While additional research is needed to further validate and clarify the benefits of adopting a team-based organizational structure, the general conclusion is that empowered teams enhance organizational effectiveness. Given the growth of this self-managing team focus in both research and practice, the next logical question to ask is "What is the future of self-managing team research and practice?" This chapter will take the initial step toward answering this question.

Introduction

The topic of self-managing teams (SMTs) is receiving increased emphasis in both academic realms and practitioner outlets (e.g., Cohen & Ledford, 1994; Hackman, 1986; Katzenbach & Smith, 1993; Lawler, 1986; Manz & Sims, 1987, 1993; Orsburn, Moran, Musselwhite, & Zenger, 1990; Walton, 1985). In what has been described as a management transformation (Walton, 1985), paradigm shift (Ketchum, 1984), and corporate renaissance (Kanter, 1983), work teams now occupy a pivotal role in how work is organized and performed (Sundstrom, Meuse, & Futrell, 1990). SMTs typically consist of groups of 4 to 12 individuals who share responsibility for completing relatively whole tasks (Cohen, Ledford, & Spreitzer, 1996; Cummings & Griggs, 1977; Goodman, Devadas, & Hughson, 1988; Hackman, 1986; Manz, 1992).

M.M. Beyerlein (ed.), Work Teams: Past, Present and Future, 311–322.

The theoretical basis for SMTs derives primarily from socio-technical systems (STS) theory. STS theory prescribes joint optimization of the social and technical aspects of work (Cummings, 1978; Emery & Trist, 1969; Susman, 1976). This optimization frequently results in the adoption of self-managing teams because "a group can more effectively allocate its resources when and where required to deal with its total variance in work conditions than can an aggregate of individuals each of whom is assigned a portion of the variance (Susman, 1976, p. 183). Self-managing teams are typically introduced with the objective of simultaneously improving productivity for the organization and the quality of work life for employees (Manz, 1992). A primary goal of SMTs is to integrate the workers' social needs and the technological needs of the organization (Cummings, 1978).

Applications of self-managing teams have covered both the manufacturing and the service sectors. Many specific case studies have been reported, including a dog-food plant (Walton, 1977), coal mines (Trist, Susman, & Brown, 1977), a financial investment firm (Sims, Manz, & Bateman, 1993), a paint manufacturing plant (Poza & Markus, 1980), small parts manufacturing (Manz & Sims, 1987), an airline (Cohen & Denison, 1990), an independent insurance firm (Manz & Angle, 1986), a mental health hospital (Shaw, 1990), a warehouse (Manz, Keating, & Donnellon, 1990), a paper mill (Manz & Newstrom, 1990), and a telecommunications company (Cohen & Ledford, 1994).

Various benefits have been attributed to the implementation of self-managing teams including increased productivity, quality, employee satisfaction, and quality of work life for employees and decreased absenteeism and turnover (Cohen & Ledford, 1994; Corderey, Mueller, & Smith, 1991; Herbst, 1962; Lawler, 1986; Manz & Sims, 1987; Saporito, 1986; Verespej, 1990). SMTs have also been advocated as a means for improving organizational flexibility, thereby promoting adaptability to a rapidly changing business environment (Manz & Stewart, 1997). While additional research is needed to further validate and clarify the benefits of adopting a team-based organizational structure, the general conclusion is that empowered teams improve organizational effectiveness (U.S. Department of Labor, 1993). Given the proliferation of this self-managing team focus in both research and practice, the next logical question to ask is "Where do we go from here?" Or to phrase it another way, "What is the future of self-managing team research and practice"?

Self-Managing Teams: The Future

> "Most important, though, we have become increasingly mindful of one undeniable fact, the average human body requires at least 64 ounces of liquid every day just to survive, and our beverages currently account for not even 2 of those ounces."[1]
>
> Roberto C. Goizueta
> Coca-Cola Company

The above quotation was used by Coca-Cola's former CEO to illustrate a possible future direction of his company. Chiefly, these words reflect the enormous growth potential for Coca-Cola, that is -- where the company is now and where it has the ability to go in the next decade and beyond. In a similar light, the symbolism in these words closely parallel the current status of self-managing work teams in that there is much growth potential for the body of knowledge surrounding SMTs. In short, predictions proclaim that over 40% of U.S. employees may be working in self-managing work teams by the year 2000 (Manz & Sims, 1993; Verespej, 1990). The continued spread of teams (specifically self-managing teams) suggests they are beyond the "fad" stage. However, despite the proliferation of team implementations by organizations, research that examines the benefits of teams and the processes that result in team effectiveness is still in its early stages. To use the terminology in the quote above, we argue that there is a plethora of ounces available in terms of the total volume of SMT research left to be explored. This leaves us with at least one relative certainty within the work teams domain--that is, there is enormous growth potential for research that focuses on self-managing teams in practice.

Building upon the current body of knowledge, a look into the future of self-managing work teams reveals a number of emerging issues that need to be explored including: (a) The role of the individual within the team; (b) Looking beyond self-managing myths; (c) Self-managing team developmental processes; (d) An exploration of the concept of the team mind; and (e) The nature of team knowledge structures.

Balancing the Me with the We: The Role of the Individual

First, the study of SMTs needs to place greater emphasis on individual team members. In much of the writings on teams, the individual (or the me) has been heavily overshadowed by the heavy focus on the team (or we) concept (e.g., Herman, 1994). This overshadowing is important given the contention that an emphasis on both the team *and* the individual can serve as a competitive advantage for corporations (Herman, 1994; Klein and Miller, 1993). Since the effectiveness of SMTs are dependent on the capability of unique interdependent individuals, the role of the individual on team success deserves significant attention. One initial step in this direction is the teamthink concept (Neck & Manz, 1994; Manz & Neck, 1995; Neck, Stewart, & Manz, 1996). Janis (1982) introduced the concept of groupthink to describe a condition where individual viewpoints are suppressed within a team decision-making situation. Teamthink, on the otherhand, describes a condition where a more optimal balance between team coordination and individual participation is achieved (Neck, Stewart, & Manz, 1996). Neck and Manz argue for a greater focus on preserving the uniqueness of each individual team member:

> By maintaining their separate belief systems, members are able to critically examine the decision-making process without being influenced to conform to a group view that overwhelms individual viewpoints...the group reaches a decision of the quality that could not have been reached by adding the efforts of each separate member (1994, p. 941).

Thus Teamthink poses an important avenue for future research that examines the factors that enable the uniqueness of each individual member to be enjoyed by SMTs. Significant implications for team effectiveness are involved, because each team member is enabled to bring to the forefront his/her different viewpoints that in combination can possibly enhance SMT decisions. As we look into the future of

SMT research and practice, this issue becomes even more relevant given the vast demographic changes forecast for the 21st Century workforce (Carr-Ruffino, 1996). Specifically, more potentially unique viewpoints will be present in SMTs of the future which raises additional interesting questions for research and practice. For example, do teams that encourage individuals to speak out (that is, display symptoms of teamthink) perform better than those who don't encourage individual participation (display symptoms of groupthink)? Another interesting practical question is "How can SMTs manifest a teamthink process?"

Self-Leading Teams: Looking Beyond Self-Management Myths

It has been argued that in practice work teams take several different forms along a continuum depending on the amount of self-influence (or decision-making authority) possessed by the team (Manz, 1992, 1990). From the least amount of decision-making authority to the maximum self-influence, teams can be classified as (1) externally managed teams, (2) participative teams (e.g., quality circles), (3) self-managed teams, (4) self-leading teams (Manz, 1990; 1992). Several perspectives suggest that attempts at establishing employee self-management often fall short of providing employees with significant self-influence in their work and can even result in loss of autonomy for professional workers (Manz, 1992; Barker, 1993; Mills 1983). In short, it is suggested that participative work systems (especially self-managing teams) may sometimes provide primarily an illusion of self-influence and/or an opportunity for management to exercise even greater control over the workforce by acting as a control mechanism.

The concept of self-leading teams was introduced as a way to identify teams that are furthest beyond this "illusion of worker participation" in practice. They represent a more advanced employee self-influence alternative on a continuum away from external management and towards empowerment (Manz, 1992). Self-leading teams differ from SMTs in that self-leading teams influence the more strategic issues of what the team does and why, in addition to how it does the work. Another important distinguishing feature of self-leading teams is that workers' motivation to perform is increasingly founded on the natural (intrinsic) rewards that are built into the task as opposed to externally administered rewards. Under conditions of a self-leading team, workers' performance is driven more because they "want" to rather than because they "should" perform (Manz, 1992).

Highly dynamic and complex contemporary organizational environments seem to be especially suited for this self-leading team concept. Many organizations today are being forced to accomplish more with less personnel. Accordingly, teams that are truly self-leading perform many functions (including taking responsibility for higher level management tasks) that allow managers increased time to address other issues and tasks (e.g., long term planning, environmental scanning, scouting out new business opportunities, facilitating between team communication, identifying new training and development opportunities) needed to enhance the success of the organization. In addition, it has been increasingly recognized that contemporary workers are searching for greater meaning and purpose in their work (Neck & Milliman, 1994). Self-leading teams provide a significant step toward fulfilling this need in workers, since they place greater focus on intrinsic as opposed to extrinsic rewards.

What is the actual nature of self-managing teams in practice? Is the concept of self-leading teams a useful distinction from self-managing teams? If so, how can organizations truly move beyond self-managing myths to self-leading teams? Are self-leading teams in the long run more effective than self-managing teams? These are some of the more interesting questions that could be investigated as team research progresses into the future.

Self-Managing Team Developmental Processes

Another significant, yet related challenge regarding future exploration of SMTs centers on the paucity of research that examines SMT development. This limited body of SMT developmental knowledge suggests that as teams move toward increasing effectiveness, they tend to evolve from an initial beginning phase to a mature, seasoned phase (e.g., Hackman, 1986; Lawler, 1986, 1988; Manz & Sims, 1993). Probably, the most recognized model of group development includes the following specific stages: forming (orientation), storming (conflict), norming (cohesion) and performing (performance) (Tuckman, 1965; Tuckman & Jensen, 1977). Recently, researchers have attempted to build upon the existing research to broaden and deepen our understanding of SMT developmental processes (e.g, Neck, Connerley, & Manz, 1997; Gersick, 1988). For example, Gersick (1988) proposed a model of team development that encompassed the timing and mechanisms of change as well as the teams' dynamic relations with their contexts. Her team development model suggests that teams progress not gradually through a universal series of stages, but rather in a pattern of punctuated equilibrium--that is, through alternating inertia and revolution in the behaviors and themes through which they approach their work. Additionally, Neck, Connerley, & Manz (1997) proposed a five-stage continuum of SMT development based on a widely accepted clinical model of family development, the Beavers Systems Model (e.g., Beavers, 1977; 1989; Scarf, 1995). Their team development model consisted of the following stages (from least effective to most effective): chaotic teams (level 5), traditional or dictatorial teams (level 4), imprisoned or groupthink teams (level 3), ascending or emerging teams (level 2), and teamthink teams (level 1). It is argued that both within-group processes (e.g., personality of team members) and organizational factors (e.g., organizational culture) can influence a SMT's progression along this continuum (Neck, Connerley, Manz, 1997).

Further research is needed to enhance our understanding of these and other factors (organizational and/or individual) that influence a teams' developmental processes. Studies reveal that the successful implementation of SMTs in the workforce does not "just happen" (Manz & Sims, 1993) and thus knowledge of the factors that influence team maturation would certainly provide tangible benefits to practicing teams.

The Team Mind

An underlying assumption of recent SMT perspectives is the emergence of a group pattern of thinking that is more than the existence of a simple collection of separate individual minds (Neck & Manz, 1994; Neck, Stewart & Manz, 1996). This notion of a "group mind" has been further asserted by various researchers including LeBon (1985), Bion (1961), Freud (1922), McDougall (1921), and Weick & Roberts

(1993). For example, Freud (1922) observed that individuals in groups tend to subjugate their individuality and act as if they were of one mind. Similarly, Bion (1961) asserted that a group's mentality exists beyond that of the individual group members in that the group's mentality connects group members by an unconscious implied agreement.

Recently scholars and practitioners have suggested that work teams can enhance their performance through the collective application of various cognitive-related strategies (e.g., Hambrick & Mason, 1984; Sims & Gioia, 1986; Nonaka, 1994; Neck & Manz, 1994; Manz & Neck, 1995; Fisher, Rayner, Belgard, 1995; Neck, Stewart, & Manz, 1996; Losoncy, 1997). Some of these collective cognitive strategies include beliefs and assumptions (the elimination or alteration of distorted team beliefs that form the basis of dysfunctional thought processes), self-talk (what the team covertly tells itself), and mental imagery (the creation and, in essence, symbolic experience of imagined results of the team's behavior before it is actually performed) (Neck, Stewart, & Manz, 1996). While a plethora of research has examined the benefits of these cognitive strategies at the individual level, further empirical research is needed to examine the utilization of these cognitive concepts within a group at both the individual member and team level.

For example, the relationship between these team cognitive elements and individual physiology would be a beneficial area to study. In other words, a comprehensive view concerning the potential of teams to truly self-lead themselves certainly must be impacted by the members' fitness level and/or nutritional habits (Neck & Manz, 1996). Indeed, research provides support for the relationship between diet, fitness level, and employee performance. Several studies suggest that workers who eat balanced diets and who exercise regularly experience enhanced performance and reduced absenteeism over those not practicing these diet and exercise patterns (Cooper, 1982). As Cooper (1982) states: "The fit people [workers]...maintain a much higher level of energy and hence interest in what they're doing throughout the day. They tend to be more alert and more outgoing..."(p. 210). Consequently, building upon this literature, it would seem that teams who lead themselves, not only via behavioral and mental strategies, but also by the members engaging in sound physical exercise and nutritional practices, can achieve a more optimal level of SMT effectiveness techniques and nutritional and fitness-related components. For example, addressing questions such as "Does what team members eat impact the SMTs ability to effectively utilize mental imagery" is a step in this direction.

Team Knowledge

A related concept to team mind is that of team knowledge. An organization's knowledge has emerged as a critical determinant of its success (Grant, 1996; Quinn, 1992; Spender, 1992). An organization attains superior performance when its members are able to use adequate and accurate knowledge in critical activities (Anand, Manz, & Glick, 1998; March & Simon, 1984). Indeed the growing importance of knowledge as a critical firm resource has provided a rationale supporting the use of work teams. Specifically, teams benefit organizations, because they bring a larger amount of knowledge (due to the different knowledge possessed by team members) to a given work context. However, researchers examining knowledge creation and utilization within firms (Anand, et al., 1998; Anand, Skilton & Keats, 1996; Nonaka, 1990; 1994) have recently proposed theories with interesting implications for knowledge management within teams. Some of these implications are discussed below.

First, integration of knowledge held by diverse organization members can be achieved through the use of cross-functional teams (Anand, et al., 1996). Such integration serves as a building block for an organization's competitive advantage (Grant, 1996; Quinn, 1992). However, organizational learning theorists have argued that innovative solutions are generated when team members possess redundant knowledge -- that is, hold substantial knowledge in common (Nonaka, 1990,1994). Redundancy in knowledge leads to greater trust among team members and also allows them to more effectively combine knowledge with each other to generate innovative ideas (Nonaka, 1990). If this reasoning is correct, it would appear that there is a limit to the advantages of diversity of team member knowledge. Important research questions could address identification of specific work contexts in which such limits vary --for example, are there specific tasks that tolerate higher knowledge diversity? Also, investigating the relationship between knowledge diversity of team members and team performance would be important.

Second, the amount of knowledge that a team can bring to a given work situation is a function of the prior knowledge and interactions between team members and also of organizational support systems (Anand, et al., 1998). While the former have been the subject of intense research, the role of organizational support systems has largely been ignored (Anand, et al., 1998). For instance, the amount of knowledge available to a team can be enhanced if team members can tap the knowledge of organization members that are not part of the team. This requires team members to know the knowledge domains of individuals inside/outside the team and the existence of widespread communication networks between the team and other organization members (Anand, Manz, & Glick, 1997; Anand et al, 1996; Nonaka, 1994; Wegner, 1986). Additionally, March & Simon (1984) have suggested that knowledge transfer is facilitated when common labels and language exist within an organization. This is often achieved through the use of a variety of organizational activities such as socialization processes (Van Maanen & Schein, 1979), the use of in-house publications and electronic bulletin boards, and through job rotation. It would appear, therefore, that a variety of organizational processes are required to ensure that adequate knowledge is available to teams. Identifying such processes, and their impact on team performance, is likely to emerge as an important research area.

A de-emphasis and reduction of mid-managerial positions can promote the emergence of a team culture within organizations (Manz & Sims, 1993). This will increase the interaction between teams and organizational environments (Thompson, 1967). Since organizational environments of the 21st century are going to be marked by rapid and unpredictable change (D'Aveni, 1993; Grant, 1996; Volberda, 1996), teams will need to develop mechanisms which keep them informed of such changes (Anand, et al., 1998). Such mechanisms could include the networking of team members with key organizational boundary spanners (Anand, Skilton & Keats, 1996; Macdonald, 1995, Tushman & Scanlon, 1981a, 1981b). Alternately, necessary access to information and knowledge could be achieved by including non-organizational members such as suppliers and distributors, in teams or by empowering team members to actively seek information from individuals outside the organization (Anand, et al., 1998; Macdonald, 1995). The processes by which teams keep themselves abreast of environmental change are likely to become increasingly crucial factors in determining team success. Investigating such processes will augment our understanding of how to use the team approach in modern organizations.

Conclusion

It is important to note that while laboratory studies might be the best way to address some of these issues, the full spectrum of behavioral research methods, including comparative case studies and field experiments in natural settings, could be used to further refine and test the theoretical positions advanced here. Overall, we have briefly offered some issues that we believe will be interesting and fruitful for addressing the future of team practice and research. Our arguments represent a crystal ball view that we find particularly enticing. Indeed, team research and practice that focuses on the individual team member, the challenges of moving beyond self-management myths, the team developmental processes, the team mind, and the role of team knowledge, can serve as primary catalysts toward enhancing our understanding of teams and their effectiveness as we head into the 21st century.

Notes

1. Roberto C. Goizueta, Chairman, Board of Directors and Chief Executive Officer, Coca-Cola Company, Message to Share Owners February 26, 1996.

References

Anand, V., Manz, C. C, & Glick, W. H. (1998). An organizaitonal memeory apporach to information management. *Academy of Management Review,* 23(4): 796-809.

Anand, V., Skilton, P. F. & Keats, B., W. (Aug.,1996). *Reconceptualizing organizational memory.* Paper presented at the Academy of Management Annual Conference, Cincinnati, Ohio.

Barker, J. R. (1993). Tightening the iron cage: Concertive control in self-managing teams. *Administrative Science Quarterly*, 38, 408-437.

Beavers, W. R. (1977). *Psychotherapy and growth: A family systems perspective.* New York: Brunner/Mazel.

Beavers, W. R. (1989). Beavers systems model. In C. N. Ramsey, (Ed.), *Family systems in medicine* (pp. 62-74). New York: Guilford Press.

Bion, W. R. (1961). *Experiences in groups.* New York: Basic Books.

Carr-Ruffino, N. (1996). *Managing diversity: People skills for a multicultural workplace.* Cinncinati, Ohio: Thomson Executive Press.

Cohen, S. G., & Denison, D. R. (1990). Flight attendant teams. In J.R. Hackman (Ed.), *Groups that work and those that don't* (pp. 382-397). San Francisco: Jossey-Bass.

Cohen, S. G., & Ledford, G. E. (1994). The effectiveness of self-managing teams: A quasi-experiment. *Human Relations*, 47, 13-43.

Cohen, S. G., Ledford, G. E., & Spreitzer, G. M. (1996). A predictive model of self-managing team effectiveness. *Human Relations*, 49, 643-676.

Cooper, K. H.(1982).*The aerobics program for total well-being*. New York: Bantam.

Corderey, J. L., Mueller, W. S., & Smith, L. M. (1991). Attitudinal and behavioral effects of autonomous group working: A longitudinal field study. *Academy of Management Journal*, 34, 464-476.

Cummings, T. (1978). Self-regulation work group: A socio-technical synthesis. *Academy of Management Review*, 3, 625-634.

Cummings, T. G., & Griggs, W. H. (1977). Worker reactions to autonomous work groups: Conditions for functioning, differential effects and individual differences. *Organization and Administrative Sciences*, 7, 87-100.

D'Aveni, R. A. (1994). *Hypercompetition: Managing the dynamics of strategic maneuvering*. Free Press, New York: NY.

Emery, F. E., & Trist, E. L. (1969). Socio-technical systems. In F.E. Emery (Ed.), *Systems thinking* (pp. 281-296). London: Penguin Books.

Fisher, K., Rayner, S., & Belgard, W. (1995). *Tips for teams*. New York: McGraw-Hill.

Freud, S. (1922). *Group psychology and the awareness of the ego*. London: International Psycho-Analytical Press. (English version, translated by James Strachey).

Gersick, C. J. G. (1988). Time and transition in work teams: Toward a new model of group development. *Academy of Management Journal*, 31, 9-41.

Goodman, P. S., Devadas, R., & Hughson, T. L. G. (1988). Groups and productivity: An analysis of self-managing teams. In J. P. Campbell (Ed.), *Productivity in organizations* (pp. 295-327). San Francisco: Jossey-Bass.

Grant, R. M. (1996). Prospering in dynamically-competitive environments: Organizational capability as knowledge integration. *Organization Science*, 7: 375-387.

Hackman, J. R. (1986). The psychology of self-management in organizations. In M. S. Pollack & R. O. Perlogg (Eds.), *Psychology and work: Productivity change and employment* (pp. 85-136). Washington.

Hambrick, D. C., & Mason, P. (1984) . Upper Echelons: The organization as a reflection of its upper managers. *Academy of Management Review*, 9: 193- 206.

Herbst, P. G. (1962). *Autonomous group functioning and exploration in behavior theory and meas-urement*. London: Tavistock.

Herman, S. (1994). *A Force of ones: Reclaiming individual power in a time of teams*. San Franciso: Jossey-Bass.

Janis, I. L. (1982). *Groupthink*. Boston: Houghton Mifflin.

Kanter, R. M. (1983). *The change masters*. New York: Simon & Schuster.

Katzenbach, J. R., & Smith, D. K. (1993). *The wisdom of teams: Creating the high performance organization*. Boston: Harvard School Press.

Ketchum, L. (1984). How redesigned plants really work. *National Productivity Review*, 3, 246-254.

Klein, J. A., & Miller, J. G. (1993). *The American edge: Leveraging manufacturing's hidden assets*. New York: McGraw-Hill.

Lawler, E. E. (1986). *High involvement management*. Jossey-Bass: San Francisco.

Lawler, E. E. (1988). Choosing an involvement strategy. *Academy of Management Executive*, 11(3), 197-204.

LeBon, G. (1985). *The crowd: A study of the popular mind.* London: Ernest Ben.

Losoncy, L. E. (1997). *Best team skills*. Delray Beach, Florida: St. Lucie Press.

Macdonald, S. (1995). Learning to change: An information perspective on learning in the organization. *Organization Science*, 6: 357-368.

Manz, C. C. (1990). Beyond self-managing work teams: Toward self-leading teams in the workplace. In R. Woodman and W. Pasmore (Eds.), *Research in organizational change and development* (pp. 273-299). Greenwich, CT: JAI Press.

Manz, C. C. (1992). Self-leading work teams: Moving beyond self-management myths. *Human Relations*, 45, 1119-1140.

Manz, C. C., & Angle, H. (1986). Can group self-management mean a loss of personal control: Triangulating on a paradox. *Group and Organization Studies*, 11, 309-334.

Manz, C. C., Keating, D., & Donnellon, A. (1990). Preparing for an organizational change to employee self-management: The managerial transition. *Organizational Dynamics*, 19, 15-26.

Manz, C. C., & Neck, C. P. (1995). Teamthink: Beyond the groupthink syndrome in self- managing teams. *Journal of Managerial Psychology*, 10, 7-15.

Manz, C. C., & Newstrom, J. (1990). Self-managing teams in a paper mill: Success factors, problems, and lessons learned. *International Human Resource Management Review*, 1, 43-60.

Manz, C. C., & Sims, H. P., Jr. (1987). Leading workers to lead themselves: The external leadership of self-managed work teams. *Administrative Science Quarterly*, 32, 106-128.

Manz, C. C., & Sims, H. P., Jr. (1993). *Business without bosses: How self-managing teams are building high performance companies*. New York: Wiley.

Manz, C. C., & Stewart, G. L. (1997). Attaining flexible stability by integrating total quality management and socio-technical systems theory. *Organizational Science*, 8,59-70.

March, J. G., & Simon, H. (1984), *Organizations*. Cambridge, MA., Blackwell.

McDougall, W. (1921). *The group mind.* Cambridge: Cambridge University Press.

Mills, P. K. (1983). Self-management: Its control and relationship to other organizational properties. *Academy of Managment Review*, 8, 445-453.

Neck, C. P., Connerley, M, & Manz, C. C. (1997). Family therapy meets self-managing teams: Toward a continuum of self-managing team development. In M. Beyerlein, D. Johnson, and S. Beyerlein (Eds.), *Advances in interdisciplinary studies of work teams: Vol. 4. Team implementation issues* (pp. 193-216). Greenwich, CT: JAI Press.

Neck, C. P., & Manz, C. C. (1994). From groupthink to teamthink: Toward the creation of constructive thought patterns in self-managing work teams. *Human Relations*, 47, 929-952.

Neck, C. P., & Manz, C. C. (1996). Total leadership quality: Integrating employee self-leadership and total quality management. In S. Ghosh and D. Fedor (Eds.), *Advances in the management of organization quality (Vol. 1)* (pp. 39-77). Greenwich, CT: JAI Press.

Neck, C. P., & Milliman, J. F. (1994). Thought self-leadership: Finding spiritual fulfillment in organizational life. *Journal of Managerial Psychology*, 9, 9-16.

Neck, C. P., Stewart, G., & Manz, C. C. (1996). Self-leaders within self-leading teams: Toward an optimal equilibrium. In M. Beyerlein, D. Johnson, & S. Beyerlein (Eds.), *Advances in interdisciplinary studies of work teams: Vol. 3. Team leadership* (pp. 43-65). Greenwich, CT: JAI Press.

Nonaka, I. (1990). Redundant, overlapping organization: The Japanese approach to managing the innovation process. *California Management Review*, 32: 27-38.

Nonaka, I. (1994). A dynamic theory of knowledge creation. *Organization Science*, 5: 14-37.

Orsburn, J., Moran, L., Musselwhite, E., Zenger, J., & Perrin, C. (1990). *Self-directed work teams: The new American challenge*. Homewood, IL: Business One Irwin.

Poza, E. J., & Markus, M. L. (1980, Winter). Success story: The team approach to work restructuring. *Organizational Dynamics*, 3-27.

Quinn, J. B. (1992). *Intelligent enterprise*, New York: Free Press.

Saporito, B. (1986). The revolt against working smarter. *Fortune*, 114(2), 58-65.

Scarf, M. (1995). *Intimate worlds: Life inside the family*. New York: Random House.

Shaw, B. (1990). Mental health treatment teams. In J. R. Hackman (Ed.), *Groups that work and those that don't* (pp. 330-348). San Francisco: Jossey-Bass.

Sims, H. P., Jr. & Gioia, D. A. (1986). *The thinking organization: Dynamics of organizational social cognition*. San Francisco: Jossey-Bass.

Sims, H. P., Jr., Manz, C. C., & Bateman, B. (1993). The early implementation phase: Getting teams started in the office. In C.C. Manz & H.P. Sims, Jr., *Business without bosses* (pp. 85-114). New York: Wiley.

Spender, J. C. (1992). Limits to learning from the West. How western management advice may prove limited in East Europe. *International Executive*, 34(5): 389-410.

Sundstrom, E., De Meuse, K. P., & Futrell, D. (1990). Work teams: Applications and effectiveness. *American Psychologist*, 45(2), 120-133.

Susman, G. I. (1976). *Autonomy at work: A socio-technical analysis of participative management*. New York: Praeger.

Thompson, J. D. (1967). *Organizations in action*. New York: McGraw Hill.

Trist, E., Susman, G. I., & Brown, G. R. (1977). An experiment in autonomous working in an American underground coal mine. *Human Relations*, 30, 201-236.

Tuckman, B. W. (1965). Developmental sequences in small groups. *Psychological Bulletin*, 63, 384-399.

Tuckman, B. W., & Jensen, M. A. C. (1977). Stages of small group development revisited. *Group and Organization Studies*, 2, 419-427.

Tushman, M.L. & Scanlon, T. J. (1981a). Boundary spanning individuals: Their role in information transfer and their antecedents. *Academy of Management Journal*, 24: 83-98.

Tushman, M.L., & Scanlon, T. J. (1981b). Characteristics and external orientations of boundary spanning individuals. *Academy of Management Journal*, 24: 289-305.

U. S. Department of Labor (1993). *High performance work practices and firm performance*. Washington, DC: Office of the American Workplace.

Van Maanen, J., & Schein, E. H. (1979). Toward a theory of organizational socialization. In B. Staw (Ed.), *Research in organizational behavior*, 209-264. Greenwich, CT: JAI press.

Verespej, M. A. (1990). Self-directed work teams yield long-term benefits. *Journal of Business Strategy*, 11(6), 9-12.

Volberda, H. W. (1996). Toward the flexible form: How to remain vital in hypercompetitive environments. *Organization Science*. 7(4): 359-374.

Walton, R.E. (1977). Work innovations at Topeka: After six years. *Journal of Applied Behavioral Science*, 13, 422-433.

Walton, R.E. (1985). From control to commitment in the workplace. *Harvard Business Review*, 63(2), 76-84. Transactive memory: A contemporary analysis of the group mind." In B. Mullen and G.R. Goethals, (Eds.), *Theories of Group Behavior*, 185-208. New York: Springer Verlag.

Weick, K. E., & Roberts, K. H. (1993). Collective mind in organizations: Heedful interrlelating on flight decks. *Administrative Science Quarterly*, 38, 357-381.

Chapter 21

Teams in Organizations

Lessons from History

Eduardo Salas
University of Central Florida, Orlando, Florida, United States

Janis Cannon-Bowers
Naval Air Warfare Center, Orlando, Florida, United States

Abstract

This chapter reviews the preceding chapters of this text by drawing 10 principles from them to represent key lessons learned from the past. The lessons indicate the foundation we have to build upon for the future. The future of work teams look bright. However, it will require continued dialogue between researchers and practitioners.

Introduction

It is quite clear from the chapters in this volume that work teams have been a way of life in organizations for centuries. Work teams have been used to perform complex, difficult, important and dynamic tasks in almost all facets of work life. Few organizations have survived throughout history without employing some form of collective to manage their challenges and resources. Today, this trend continues at an increasingly accelerated pace. Organizations across the world rely on work teams more than ever to accomplish many objectives. In fact, it is a common assumption that groups, crews, teams and collectives have become the cornerstone of contemporary organizations in industry, government and the military (e.g., Bass, 1982; Salas, Cannon-Bowers, Church-Payne & Smith-Jentsch, 1998; Hackman, 1990). Work teams seem to be the human resource development tool du jour and there is no end in sight to this trend.

This reliance on work teams by industry and the military coupled with significant (and sometimes tragic) world events (e.g., WWI, WWII, Persian Gulf incidents, airline accidents) across the decades has created the need to understand how to design, compose and manage work teams. In fact, in recent years, we have seen a considerable investment—both in the public and private sectors—in research aimed

M.M. Beyerlein (ed.), Work Teams: Past, Present and Future, 323–331.

at uncovering the factors that facilitate and hinder team effectiveness (Salas & Cannon-Bowers, 1997). We now have, we believe, a wealth of information about the nature of work teams. The 20 chapters in this volume along with recent publications on the topic (e.g., Beyerlein & Johnson, 1994; Beyerlein, Johnson, & Beyerlein, 1995-1998; Guzzo & Salas, 1995; Guzzo & Dickson, 1996; Hackman, 1990; Salas, Bowers, Cannon-Bowers, 1995; West, 1996; Weiner, Kanki & Helmreich, 1993) provide the evidence that we do know a lot about work teams and their functioning. However, these historical chapters offer us an opportunity to reflect. What have we learned from history about work teams? What are these historical perspectives conveying to us about the nature of team performance? What do these essays and reviews tell us about the future? In this chapter, we offer our reflections and thoughts after reading this collection of enriching historical chapters about work teams.

Therefore, our purpose in this chapter is two-fold. First, to try to capture a few of the lessons that have been learned over time as scientists have observed, studied, and analyzed teams. We accomplish this by extracting from the collection of preceding chapters (and other sources as well) important and representative key lessons about what history has taught us to date about the nature of teams in organizations. Our second purpose is to provide the scientific community interested in team functioning, with a "spring-board" for the future. That is, we believe that these lessons could be used to shape present and future research agendas.

Emerging Lessons from History

Lesson 1: Teams have stood the test of time!

From the dawn of humanity, work teams have been in use as a management tool. Why? Teams are an intuitive work unit. Moreover, some tasks demand it. Therefore, as stated earlier, teams have become the basic form of organization. Now scholars and practitioners say it's an optimal way to organize (Tjosvold & Johnson, this volume; Hackman, 1990).

Lesson 2: We know a lot about work teams.

If history is telling us anything, it is that there is a wealth of knowledge about how work teams function. There is more information about team effectiveness than we can possibly acknowledge (or use). This does not mean that we should stop conducting research. Quite the opposite, some areas are in their infancy. But in areas where information exists, we still do not see much applied in practice. This may be due to poor translation mechanisms between science and practice. We have argued elsewhere (Salas, Cannon-Bowers, & Blickensderfer, 1997) that many areas of applied psychology suffer from a translation problem. That is, we seldom translate our research findings into a forum that can be used by those who seek to improve or manage team effectiveness.

Despite this shortcoming (to be dealt with in a different forum), there is a myriad of knowledge about work teams. For example, there is evidence that teams can be effective at their task, when certain conditions exist (Hackman, 1990). Teams are complex social systems that require care and feeding to work effectively. This is an ongoing process that as illustrated by Cordery (this volume), and Tjosvold and Johnson (this volume), is often overlooked. In fact, we know with assurance that in order for teams to succeed at their task they must be given the appropriate resources (e.g., Gully, this volume). For example, we know that:

1. Teams must have appropriate leadership and direction (Blickensderfer, Salas, & Cannon-Bowers, this volume).
2. Team members must have a shared common objective (Tjosvold & Johnson, this volume; Salas, Dickinson, Converse, & Tannenbaum, 1992).
3. Teams must have members trained on their individual tasks (Blickensderfer et al., this volume; Salas & Cannon-Bowers, 1997).
4. Team members must have clear responsibilities and roles (Neck, Manz, & Anand, this volume; Orasanu & Salas, 1993).
5. Teams adapt their strategies (Gersick, 1985, 1988).
6. Teams "do, think and feel," i.e., they possess behavioral, cognitive, and affective competencies (Blickensderfer et al., this volume; Salas & Cannon-Bowers, 1997).
7. Members of effective teams anticipate each other (Neck et al., this volume; Salas & Cannon-Bowers, 1997).
8. Cohesive teams, in general, perform better than non-cohesive teams (Bass, 1995).
9. Teamwork is comprised of performance monitoring, feedback, closed-loop communication and back-up behaviors (Gully, this volume; McIntyre & Salas, 1995).
10. Team decision-making under stress can be enhanced by a number of training interventions (Cannon-Bowers & Salas, 1998).

The bottomline is these chapters and the vast literature on work teams over the centuries has shown us that we have learned a lot about work teams. We must use and apply this knowledge.

Lesson 3: Not all work teams are created equal.

For a number of years, we have struggled with definitions and setting boundaries on the kinds of teams we observe and study (Antoni, this volume; Gully, this volume; Salas et al., 1992). This is still on going, but we believe that we have begun to accept that not all work teams are equal. There are important differences among them as illustrated in Cordery (this volume), Alexandrov, Karyakin, and Ceshinsky (this volume), Gulowsen (this volume) and others. Self-managed work teams are neither the same as command and control teams in the military, nor are they the same as surgical teams or aircrews. These work teams have different task interdependencies, synchronization, and communication requirements. They have different tempo and stakes. These teams employ different strategies and tools to accomplish their missions. Therefore, they require different interventions and must be managed differently. Hence, from a research point of view, we need to be careful. Additionally, our theories, paradigms and methodologies need to reflect the different kind (or continuum) of teams that exist. "One size fits all" is not an appropriate philosophy to adopt and, in fact, may be misleading (see Cannon-Bowers, Tannenbaum, Salas, & Volpe, 1995). Work teams must be studied using the right and relevant research paradigm as well as the appropriate boundaries as to avoid unwarranted generalizations. Knowing and acknowledging that all teams are not created equal is one thing, acting on this fact (i.e., focusing our theories, research paradigms and findings to avoid confusions and misrepresentations) is another. In the next lesson, we explore one of the problems created by a lack of focus in studying work teams in organizations.

Lesson 4: Accumulation of knowledge (and lack of coordination) may be a problem.

The convergence of findings in any field is difficult. Work team research suffers from the same problem as other disciplines. We have many diverse ways of communicating what our research has shown and in describing the phenomena in which we are interested. All scientists bring their own theoretical perspective to explain how teams perform and to describe what influences team effectiveness. Therefore, there are too many labels for explaining the same constructs (Gully, this volume; Bass, this volume). For example, a recent review of the team competencies literature by Cannon-Bowers and colleagues uncovered over 130 labels being used to describe the knowledges, skills and attitudes that teams must posses to function effectively. There are also too many models to explain the dynamics of teams (Neck et al., this volume; Guzzo, 1995). All of these, of course, are grounded in some truth and do aid in our understanding of the nature of work teams. But, are all of these necessary? Only history will tell...one explanation is in the next lesson.

Lesson 5: The study of work teams is a multidisciplinary activity and therefore, no one owns it.

As illustrated by numerous chapters in this volume, work teams are studied by many related (and unrelated) disciplines. Works teams are not only researched by social psychologists. Work teams are now researched by industrial/organizational, mathematical, human factors, cognitive, military, and engineering psychologists, as well as sociologists, (e.g., Guzzo & Salas, 1995; Salas et al., 1995; Kleinman & Serfaty, 1992; Campion et al., 1993) management scholars, and anthropologists (this volume).

There is good news and bad news about this lesson. The good news is that we can gain a deeper and richer understanding of work teams by studies from multiple perspectives, views, methods, and approaches. We get a better picture of how work teams function and what makes them effective. The bad news is that it generates a number of problems that begin with many labels and definitions for the same constructs across disciplines. We end up with piecemeal, unorganized, and redundant knowledge about work teams. This is certainly one of the most pressing problems within the work teams field.

Lesson 6: The study of work teams is a cross-cultural and international activity and, therefore, there are many interpretations about team functions.

This volume has chapters from Russia, Germany, Sweden, Yugoslavia, U. S. A., Norway, and Australia. Each of the authors from these chapters draws on their theoretical perceptions and research to draw different conclusions about work teams. Some of this can be explained, of course, by the cultural and environmental context under which these work teams function. This, in some ways, calls for carefully managing and understanding the diverse points of view about work teams functioning across the world.

Lesson 7: Teamwork is comprised of a set of knowledges, skills and attitudes.

As we mentioned earlier, we have learned a great deal about teams. More specifically (and maybe more importantly for work organizations), we now know what comprises teamwork. All of the chapters in this volume, whether explicitly or implicitly, touch on this topic -- teamwork. Teamwork is at the heart of how work teams accomplish their objectives. It is through the processes of teamwork that teams become successful. Good teamwork equals good team performance. Moreover, we know that teamwork leads to better productivity. Therefore, it is not surprising that we have tried to uncover, over the centuries, what teamwork is, and how it can best be facilitated.

The chapters in this volume, drawing upon recent literature, begin to piece together what comprises teamwork. Teamwork seems to be more than the task accomplishments of the individuals comprising the team. Teamwork seems to be more than just cohesion and communication. Teamwork **is** a dynamic process that comes to light when the task demands are such that no one individual can successfully perform the task without some form of coordination. This coordination is explicit or implicit and requires that team members possess certain knowledges, skills and attitudes (KSAs) to facilitate teamwork. Fortunately, research has begun to uncover these KSAs (see Cannon-Bowers et al., 1995; Salas & Cannon-Bowers, 1997; in press).

Lesson 8: Teams work!

This volume clearly illustrates that, under the right circumstances, teams work. There is also a body of scientific evidence that has begun to shed light on when and how teams work (see Blickensderfer et al., this volume; Guzzo & Salas, 1995), as well as how to enhance their effectiveness (see for example, Cannon-Bowers & Salas, 1998; Salas & Cannon-Bowers, 1997; Tannenbaum, Salas, & Cannon-Bowers, 1996); that evidence is getting stronger. As we learn more from the situations discussed by Gully, Antoni, Cordery, and others chapters in this volume more information (hopefully) will be available to scientists and practitioners about work teams effectiveness. So, we know through history that if one composes, manages, and trains teams..."dream teams" can happen.

Lesson 9: Even high performance work teams derail.

Just as we have seen "dream" teams, we have seen "nightmare" teams as well. The discussion by Blickensderfer et al. (this volume), Purser (this volume) bolster this conclusion. In fact, the resurgence of team research in the late 80's was precipitated, in part, by a number of unfortunate world events. For example, the shoot down of an Iraqi airbus by the USS Vincennes where over two hundred people died is an example of poor teamwork (Cannon-Bowers & Salas, 1998). In the aviation world, it has been noted that 60-80% of accidents and mishaps are attributable to human error and lack of teamwork in the cockpit (Foushee, 1984; Wiener et al., 1993). There are many other examples that can be drawn from sports, management, and industrial teams.

Lesson 10: The future of the science and practice of work teams is as bright, exciting, and rich as its history!

So, what does the history of work teams tell us about the future? It tells us, at least, that the future of the study of work teams is promising and bright. The science of work teams is now poised to design and develop management tools for enhancing teamwork. Results will benefit industrial and governmental organizations as well as those in charge of implementing human resource interventions.

In the future, further research on teamwork will be needed to realize this goal. Our assessment of the current state-of-the-field leads us to recommend the following research areas as good candidates for further study. Understanding the mechanisms of team cognition; that is, what do team members need to know in order to perform successfully and what knowledge must they share. Development of team modeling tools including how we can capture what we know about team performance and cast it into a format (tool) that can aid in designing teams and team tasks. Studying teams in their natural environments. As noted, we believe that team effectiveness is contextual; that is, it depends on the environment in which it occurs. Hence, future work aimed at understanding better how task demands and the team's context affect performance is needed.

Concluding Remarks

Teams are alive and well in organizations. They have been for a long time; and history tells us that they will be around for some time to come. Much has been learned about their functioning and effectiveness but much more remains to be learned as we move to the next millennium. It is only through consistent dialogue, reciprocity, and debate between scholars and practitioners that work teams will produce the expected payoffs in organizations. Only time will tell...

References

Alexandrov, Y., Karyakin, A., & Ceshinsky, A. (in press). The formation of work teams in Russia: Commanding methods of labor organizations in the Czarist Russia. In M. Beyerlein (Ed.), *Work teams, past, present, and future.* Norwell, MA: Kluwer Academic Publishers.

Antoni, C. H. (in press). From group fabrication to self-designing work teams: The development of work teams in Germany. In M. Beyerlein (Ed.), *Work teams, past, present, and future.* Norwell, MA: Kluwer Academic Publishers.

Bass, B. M. (1996). Early history of work teams. *Comportamento Organizacional E Gestao 2(1)*, pp 25-32.

Bass, B. M. (1982). Individual capability, team performance, and team productivity. In E. A. Fleishman & M. D. Dunette (Eds.), *Human performance and capability: Human capability assessment.* Hillsdale, NJ: LEA.

Beyerlein, M. M., & Johnson, D. A. (Eds.). (1994). *Advances in interdisciplinary studies of work teams* (Vol. 1). Greenwich, CT: JAI Press, Inc.

Beyerlein, M. M., Johnson, D. A., & Beyerlein, S. T. (Eds.). (1995-1998). *Advances in interdisciplinary studies of work teams* (Vol. 2-5). Greenwich, CT: JAI Press, Inc.

Blickensderfer, E., Salas, E., & Cannon-Bowers, J. A. (in press). When the teams came marching home: U. S. military team research since World War II. In M. Beyerlein (Ed.), *Work teams, past, present, and future.* Norwell, MA: Kluwer Academic Publishers.

Campion, M. A., Medsker, G. J., & Higgs, A. C. (1993). Relationships between work group characteristics and effectiveness: Implications for designing effective work groups. *Personnel Psychology, 46,* 823-850.

Cannon-Bowers, J. A., Tannenbaum, S. I., Salas, E., & Volpe, C. E. (1995). Defining team competencies and establishing team training requirements. In R. Guzzo & E. Salas (Eds.), *Team effectiveness and decision making in organizations* (pp. 333-380). San Francisco: Jossey Bass.

Cannon-Bowers, J. A., & Salas, E. (1998). *Making decisions under stress: Implications for individual and team training.* Washington, DC: APA.

Cordery, J. L. (in press). Work teams in Australia. In M. Beyerlein (Ed.), *Work teams, past, present, and future.* Norwell, MA: Kluwer Academic Publishers.

Gersick, C. G. (1985). The life cycles of ad hoc task groups: Time, transitions, and learning in teams. *Dissertation Abstracts International, 46 (5-B)*, 1742.

Gersick, C. J. (1988). Time and transition in work teams: Toward a new model of group development. *Academy of management journal, 31(1)*, 9-41.

Gully, S. M. (in press). Work teams research since 1985: Recent findings and future trends. In M. Beyerlein (Ed.), *Work teams, past, present, and future.* Norwell, MA: Kluwer Academic Publishers.

Gulowsen, J. (in press). Three kinds of autonomy at work in Norway. In M. Beyerlein (Ed.), *Work teams, past, present, and future*. Norwell, MA: Kluwer Academic Publishers.

Guzzo, R. A. (1995). Introduction: At the intersection of team effectiveness and decision making. In R. A. Guzzo & E. Salas (Eds.), Team effectiveness & decision making in organizations. San Francisco, CA: Jossey-Bass.

Guzzo, R. A., & Dickson, M. W. (1996). Teams and organizations: Recent research on performance and effectiveness. *Annual Review of Psychology*, *47*, 307-338.

Guzzo, R. A. & Salas, E. (Eds.). (1995). *Team effectiveness & decision making in organizations*. San Francisco, CA: Jossey-Bass.

Hackman, J. R. (Ed.). (1990). *Groups that work (and those that don't): Creating conditions for effective team work*. San Francisco: Jossey-Bass.

Kleinman, D. L., & Serfaty, D. (1989). *Team performance assessment in distributed decision making*. Paper presented at the Simulation and Training Research Symposium on Interactive Networked Simulation for Training, University of Central Florida.

McIntyre, R. M., & Salas, E. (1995). Measuring and managing for team performance: Emerging principles from complex environments. In R. Guzzo & E. Salas (Eds.), *Team effectiveness and decision making in organizations* (pp. 149-203). San Francisco: Jossey-Bass.

Neck, C. P., Manz, C. C., & Anand, V. (in press). Self-managing teams in a crystal ball: Future directions for research and practice. In M. Beyerlein (Ed.), *Work teams, past, present, and future*. Norwell, MA: Kluwer Academic Publishers.

Orasanu, J., & Salas, E. (1993). Team decision making in complex environments. In G. Klein, J. Orasanu, R. Calderwood, & C. E. Zsambok (Eds.), *Decision making in action: Models and methods* (pp. 327-345). Norwood, NJ: Ablex.

Purser, R. E. (in press). The human relations myth unveiled: Deconstructing the history and origins of work teams. In M. Beyerlein (Ed.), *Work teams, past, present, and future*. Norwell, MA: Kluwer Academic Publishers.

Salas, E., & Cannon-Bowers, J. A. (1997). Methods, tools, and strategies for team training. In M. A. Quiñones & A. Ehrenstein (Eds.), *Training for a rapidly changing workplace: Applications of psychological research* (pp. 249-279). Washington, DC: APA Press.

Salas, E., & Cannon-Bowers, J. A. (in press). The anatomy of team training. To appear in L. Tobias & D. Fletcher (Eds.), *Handbook on research in training*. New York: MacMillan.

Salas, E., Bowers, C. A., & Cannon-Bowers J. A. (1995). Military team research: Ten years of progress. *Military Psychology*, *7*, 55-75.

Salas, E., Cannon-Bowers, J. A., & Blickensderfer, E. L. (1997). Enhancing reciprocity between training theory and practice: Principles, guidelines, and specifications. In J. K. Ford & Associates (Eds.), *Improving training effectiveness in work organizations* (pp. 291-322). Hillsdale, NJ: LEA.

Salas, E., Cannon-Bowers, J. A., Church-Payne, S., Smith-Jentsch, K. A. (1998). Teams and teamwork in the military. In C. Cronin (Ed.), *Military psychology: An introduction* (pp. 71-88). Needham Heights, MA: Simon & Schuster.

Salas, E., Dickinson, T. L., Converse, S. A., & Tannenbaum, S. I. (1992). Toward an understanding of team performance and training. In R. W. Swezey & E. Salas (Eds.), *Teams: Their training and performance* (pp. 3-29). Norwood, NJ: Ablex.

Tannenbaum, S. I., Salas, E., & Cannon-Bowers, J. A. (1996). Promoting team effectiveness. In M. A. West (Ed.), *Handbook of work group psychology* (pp. 503-529). Sussex, England: John Wiley & Sons.

Tjosvold, D., & Johnson, D. W. (in press). Deutsch's theory of cooperation and competition: An enduring contribution to teams. In M. Beyerlein (Ed.), *Work teams, past, present, and future.* Norwell, MA: Kluwer Academic Publishers.

Weiner, E. L., Kanki, B. G., & Helmreich, R. L. (1993). *Cockpit resource management.* San Diego, CA: Academic Press.

West, M. A. (Ed.). (1996). *Handbook of work group psychology.* New York: John

INDEX